Why So Slow?

Fritz von Uhde, *Kinderstube*. © Elke Walford, Hamburger Kunsthalle, Hamburg, Germany.

Why So Slow?
The Advancement of Women

Virginia Valian

The MIT Press
Cambridge, Massachusetts
London, England

This book was set in Sabon on the Miles 33 typesetting system by Graphic Composition, Inc. and was printed and bound in the United States of America.

Library of Congress Cataloging-in-Publication Data

Valian, Virginia.
  Why so slow? : the advancement of women / Virginia Valian
        p.   cm.
  Includes bibliographical references and index.
  ISBN 0-262-22054-7 (hardcover : alk paper)
  1. Sex discrimination against women—Psychological aspects.
2. Sexism. 3. Women in the professions. 4. Sex differences
(Psychology)   I. Title.
HQ1237.V35   1997
305.42—dc21   96-37029
                                                              CIP

To the memory of Rose KorKoian Valian

To Jack Valian

To Virginia Brostron

Contents

Preface

One of the first things I knew about myself was that I was going to college. At age 5 I knew my name, my address, my telephone number, and that I was college-bound. I had no idea what college was, but I knew I was going. My parents had not gone to college. My father had had neither the interest nor the means. But he wanted a college education for his children. My mother had had the interest, but not the psychological means. She had won a one-year scholarship but her father would not allow her to accept it—it would have meant living away from home in another state. My mother saw a college education for me as essential.

I resented on my mother's behalf the injustice that she had suffered. I resented, though she did not seem to, her subservient role in the household: it was inexcusable that she was at the beck and call of my grandfather, my father, my brother, and me. But I never failed to avail myself of her services. The only expression of my solidarity with her was my vow that my life would be different. I would get the college education she did not have. In my household I would not live a life of servitude; I would do my share of the work and no more.

My parents recognized my abilities, though they seldom praised me. They expected me to perform well in school, and I did. When I brought my report cards home they catechized me about the rare grade below "Excellent." Yet my own notion of my abilities came not from report cards, but from discussions and arguments with my parents and other adults. I felt that, if one went strictly by the merits of each case, I won. I was clearly right. The fact that the adults did not acknowledge my superiority did not cause me to doubt it. On my analysis, the adults won only because they were adults. I could hardly wait to be an adult myself, when nobody could pull rank, and my arguments would prevail. When I was an adult everyone would have to agree that I was right if I was.

One way my parents expressed their aspirations for me was through the books they bought me. I remember a series on the childhoods of famous Americans, a number of whom were women: Jane Addams, Harriet Beecher Stowe, Louisa May Alcott.[1] My mother's suggestion for my professional future was a job as librarian or schoolteacher. My father rejected those occupations as too low-paying. When I was a child he thought I should be an actress; when I was older he thought I should go into business.

At age 12 I acquired my own professional ambition. I saw the film *The Snake Pit,* and decided immediately that I would become a psychologist. I wanted to understand mental illness and help people get better. I wanted to understand how the mind worked. That general rubric—how the mind works—has covered my interests my entire life, although my research specialization became cognitive psychology, especially language acquisition, and not mental illness.

Throughout my teens I felt destined to accomplish something significant. I had no idea what that achievement might be. I just knew that I would contribute something important to the world.

In my teens I also thought about marriage. I wasn't sure if I would get married. If I did, it would be to the perfect man: someone who would be smarter than I and better than I at all the things I was good at. My perfect husband would be interested in and understand everything I had to say. He would love me completely. He would be handsome. He would be Armenian so that our children, if we had any, would be Armenian. His last name would begin with V, so that my initials (VVV) wouldn't change when I got married.

I had never met such a person (nor even read *Gaudy Night*). I would have agreed that the total package was highly unlikely. But I couldn't imagine marriage unless I admired and respected my husband, and could only imagine doing that if he were more intelligent than I. I also wanted *him* to admire, respect, and love *me,* and could only imagine him doing so if he were very intelligent.

In adolescence, then, I had a clear picture of my ideal future. It would consist of two things—the important psychological something I would do with my life, plus the perfect man. And, no matter what, I would not be a servant at home, and I would not lose any arguments unless I was actually wrong. Although I was clear about the endpoint, I gave no thought to how I would get there. Other than doing well in school and going to college, I had no plans. It would all just happen.

Putting myself back into the mind of that child, I know how she would evaluate the adult me. She would judge my work as worthwhile but note severely that her aspirations have yet to be fulfilled. She would agree that J, the man I live with, meets the spirit if not the letter of all her serious requirements. She would approve of the household arrangements, but be astonished and dismayed to learn that the backing of an entire women's movement had been required to achieve that most basic form of fairness.

She would be furious about continuing to lose arguments even when she's right. She would be furious about not being listened to.

And that is the real reason I wrote this book.

From the beginning of my professional life in academia, I was aware of certain problems that seemed too petty to bother with, gnatlike. They detracted from my enjoyment but had, I thought, no major negative effect on my, or any other woman's, professional development. One common scenario went like this. I made a comment during a group discussion. The comment was ignored. A little later someone else made the same comment as if it were being made for the first time. The comment was discussed by the group.

What made it hard to get a handle on this problem was its variability. It didn't happen *every* time I or another woman made a comment. It didn't happen *only* to women. It wasn't *always* a man who restated the comment. Perhaps I simply wasn't making my points as well as I might have. The most reasonable generalization seemed to be that low-status people weren't listened to as much as high-status people, and that women tended to have lower status than men. The same thing happened to low-status men. End of story.

Until—in the early 1980s—I read a monograph called "Seeing and Evaluating People" by Geis, Carter, and Butler (1982). (That monograph was never published, but Haslett, Geis, & Carter 1992, published a book covering much of the same material.) The monograph suggested that women were systematically evaluated less favorably than men were in achievement-related contexts and provided evidence from experiments in social psychology. What happened in professional discussions happened generally in professional life.

I read the monograph with a certain amazement. It seemed that my childhood anticipation of adulthood had failed to take gender into account. It had never occurred to me that the same argument would be received differently if made by a man than if made by a woman. It certainly had never occurred to me that the same resumé would be rated more highly if a man's name rather than a woman's were at the top of the page (Fidell 1975). The monograph suggested that the two phenomena were related, that the same undervaluation of women was at work in both. The monograph inspired me to begin reading widely in social cognition, sex differences, economics, sociology, and organizational management.

I gradually began to develop my own understanding of how and why women were evaluated negatively relative to men. The analysis I formulated to explain the data I discovered affected me personally. It clarified events that formerly seemed mysterious or particular to the individuals involved. It increased my awareness of the importance of apparently trivial events. In addition to making me more observant, it helped me become more detached, more amused, and more tolerant. That is not to say that my capacity for outrage has died. There is a graph in chapter 11 that never fails to make my blood boil. But I don't take it personally.

On to the merits of the case.

Acknowledgments

Amazingly, I have never discussed gender and work with someone without learning something of value. The talks I have given and classes I have taught provided many such cases. I happily thank the audiences at Barnard College, Duke University, the University of Rochester, Cornell University, the University of Texas at Austin, the University of Pennsylvania, the University of Massachusetts at Amherst, Hunter College, the Cognitive Development Unit of the Medical Research Council in London, and the New School. Jane Bennett, Alice Kaplan, Thomas Bever, Amy Sheldon, Carlota Smith, Justine Cassell, and Judith Kroll, as hosts at those institutions and as individuals, gave me many useful comments and criticisms.

Thanks to a grant from the Russell Sage Foundation, I had the time to write the first draft of this book. I am especially grateful to Eric Wanner, President of the Foundation, for his backing and for his insightful and trenchant comments.

For years, I have had the good fortune to be surrounded by people who constructively challenge my every claim and argument, the contents of this book being no exception. With great pleasure, I thank Jerrold J. Katz, Mary C. Potter, Judith Kroll, Gail Hornstein, Susan Carey, and Anne Cutler.

Many readers provided expertise and critical commentary, either of single chapters or the entire book. Some of those readers were anonymous; I appreciate the thoughtfulness of their comments.

Readers whom I can thank by name include Carole Beal, Ned Block, Amy Pierce Brand, Roberta Clark, Arthur Collins, Linda Collins, Michele

Crow, Catherine Cullen, Bénédicte de Boysson-Bardies, Zena Eisenberg, Uta Frith, Rebecca Huselid, Andrea Levitt, Maureen Linker, Victoria Luine, Michele Paludi, Sara Ruddick, Ivy Sichel, Janet Swim, and Julia Wrigley.

Donna Foster-Paley and Helen Whatford contributed substantially to this book by helping with the research, critically reading the text, and offering numerous examples. Daniel Pasquini of the National Research Council provided unpublished data for analyses of academics' careers. Daniel Byrnes provided the graphs. Lauren Schlesinger, Ivy Sichel, and Mihai Vinereanu tracked down and organized references. The Hunter College Library staff, especially Suzanne Siegel and Norman Clarius, made heroic efforts to sate my greed for books and articles. Ivy Sichel and Donna Foster-Paley created the index.

Finally, I thank my colleagues in the Psychology Department at Hunter College for maintaining an atmosphere in which work is possible.

A Note on Method and Scope

The spine of *Why So Slow?* is data from statistical studies of women and men in the professions and from psychological studies conducted in the laboratory and in the field. I have focused on recent studies and studies that report the combined results of many different experiments (meta-analyses). I have selected experiments and data that are both representative of the literature as a whole and interesting in and of themselves.

Most of the concepts I discuss come from social, cognitive, and developmental psychology, but I also include work in sociology and economics to indicate how psychological processes interact with sociological and economic ones. The parenthetical references in each chapter will allow interested readers to delve further into specific issues. Issues that are primarily of concern to the specialist, from data complexities to conflicting interpretations, are discussed in chapter notes.

Throughout the book, my arguments and conclusions rely on statistical and experimental data, not on anecdotes. I only use anecdotes if I think they are faithful to the main body of empirical data. But examples can effectively highlight or encapsulate particular social processes or illustrate research findings. They can give emotional life to discussion of a phenomenon, spark memories of similar examples, and condense a lot of information into one packet. So I do use examples, but only to illustrate a point, not to make one.

A major limitation of the research included in this book is its restricted basis. To date, there has been little research on the interaction of sex, ethnicity, class, and culture. Thus, although I use the terms *women* and *men* throughout, the researchers I cite have overwhelmingly studied white, middle-class, college-educated American women and men. Moreover, most of the laboratory-based research is with college students.

We do not know, therefore, how generally the findings apply across different social groups. For the subtle processes described in this book, people's interpretation of an event, and their reactions based on that interpretation, are at least as important as the event itself. For example, awareness and expectation of discrimination are part of the conscious lives of African Americans from childhood on. No American of African descent doubts the existence of discrimination. One consequence of knowing you belong to a stigmatized group is that you interpret negative reactions from others less personally than when you are oblivious of their cause (Crocker & Major 1989). Do African-American women therefore interpret their professional success or failure differently from women who do not experience race-based discrimination? We can ask similar questions about Hispanic-American, Asian-American, and Native-American men and women. What about women and men in different regions of the country? Or people in other countries? Do homosexuals and heterosexuals interpret and react differently to expectations about their professional potential? At present we cannot provide firm answers to any of these questions or evaluate the important role of culture and subculture.

Research on sex differences within different cultures has begun, however, and will do much to deepen our understanding of gender and clarify those situations in which people's attitudes are similar and those in which they are different (Landrine 1995). For example, there is research suggesting that both black and white college-educated women see women as having little influence in American political life (E. R. Cole & Stewart 1996). On the other hand, there is also research showing that interactions between African-American adolescent girls and boys are more nearly equal than those between white adolescent girls and boys. The greater equality is largely due to the assertiveness of African-American girls (Filardo 1996).

Most of the research discussed in this book has been conducted by white women in the United States within the last twenty years. We owe most of our current knowledge about gender to the influx of women into psychology and sociology during that time. A similar expansion of our knowledge will take place when research is performed with, and by, people of different ethnic, class, and cultural backgrounds. We will then obtain a genuine understanding of what leads to achievement differences, and we will have a psychology that has earned a claim to universality.

Despite the restrictions in our knowledge, throughout the book I use terms like *male* and *female* without the modifiers *white, middle-class, young, heterosexual,* and *American.* I made that decision on the grounds that it would be better to err in the direction of generality than in the direction of specificity, a decision others may take issue with (e.g., Malveaux 1990).

Why So Slow?

1

Gender Schemas at Work

The term *glass ceiling* has become a popular way of referring to the scarcity of women at the top levels of organizations. The phrase suggests that invisible factors—as much as, or more than, overt discrimination—keep women from rising to the top. It also assumes that those hidden influences are unlikely simply to disappear over time; a ceiling is not a structure that evanesces. Finally, the term suggests that women's job performance is at least the equal of their male peers'; a ceiling is something that keeps people down despite their competence. All three assumptions, I will argue, are correct. There *are* invisible barriers; they will not go away on their own; any objective differences in performance are insufficient to explain existing sex differences in salary, rank, and rates of promotion.

There are also, of course, visible problems for women in the workplace, of which sexual assault and harassment are the most obvious examples. I do not discuss those abuses, despite their importance, because I want to explain women's lack of achievement in situations where nothing seems to be wrong. Even in apparently egalitarian environments, women do not advance as far or as rapidly as men. Something invisible limits their progress.

But if there are invisible factors at work, what are they, and how do they operate? My goal in this book is to make the invisible visible: to show what retards women's progress, so that fair and accurate evaluations of men and women will become possible. To do so, I draw on concepts and data from psychology, sociology, economics, and biology.

What Holds Up the Glass Ceiling?

Gender Schemas

The central thesis of this book is that a set of implicit, or nonconscious, hypotheses about sex differences plays a central role in shaping men's and women's professional lives. These hypotheses, which I call *gender schemas,* affect our expectations of men and women, our evaluations of their work, and their performance as professionals.[1] Both men and women hold the same gender schemas and begin acquiring them in early childhood. Their most important consequence for professional life is that men are consistently overrated, while women are underrated. Whatever emphasizes a man's gender gives him a small advantage, a plus mark. Whatever accentuates a woman's gender results in a small loss for her, a minus mark.

We are accustomed to calling our conceptions of certain groups *stereotypes.* The word is misleading, for it implies that something is fundamentally wrong with having such concepts. But hypothesis formation is a natural and essential human activity; it is the way we make sense of the world. We all form hypotheses about social groups. Such hypotheses may contain primarily positive characteristics, mostly negative ones, only neutral ones, or some combination of all three. The word *stereotype* refers to one kind of hypothesis, but *schema* is a better, more inclusive, term. It is not the attempt to develop schemas that is wrong, but the errors that can inadvertently creep into the formation, maintenance, and application of schemas.

Gender schemas are usually unarticulated. Their content may even be disavowed. Most men and women in the professions and academia explicitly, and sincerely, profess egalitarian beliefs. Conscious beliefs and values do not, however, fully control the operation of nonconscious schemas. Egalitarian beliefs help, but they do not guarantee accurate, objective, and impartial evaluation and treatment of others. Our interpretations of others' performance are influenced by the unacknowledged beliefs we all—male and female alike—have about gender differences.

Although most people want to judge fairly, genuine fairness demands that we understand that our reactions to an individual are, inevitably, affected by the group the person belongs to. Our implicit ideas about men and women as a whole condition our reactions to men and women as individuals. Only by recognizing how our perceptions are skewed by non-conscious beliefs can we learn to see others, and ourselves, accurately. Fairness requires a more sophisticated understanding of social perception than most of us acquire in the ordinary course of life. To be really fair, we need to know what perceptual distortions are likely and what steps we can take to perceive others more accurately.

Thus, although this book is about a particular set of schemas, it can also be seen as a case study of the more general problem of ensuring fair evaluations for members of any group. Schemas based on sex, age, race, class, or sexual orientation have different contents, but all schemas influence how we perceive and treat group members. Only by discovering a schema's content and mode of operation can we make our evaluations of individuals fairer.

Accumulation of Advantage

The long-term consequences of small differences in the evaluation and treatment of men and women also hold up the glass ceiling. A useful concept in sociology is the accumulation of advantage and disadvantage (J. Cole & Singer 1991; Fox 1981, 1985; Long 1990; Merton 1968).[2] It suggests that, like interest on capital, advantages accrue, and that, like interest on debt, disadvantages also accumulate. Very small differences in treatment can, as they pile up, result in large disparities in salary, promotion, and prestige. It is unfair to neglect even minor instances of group-based bias, because they add up to major inequalities.

A computer model of promotion practices at a hypothetical corporation convincingly demonstrates the cumulative effects of small-scale bias (Martell, Lane, & Emrich 1996). The simulation created an organization with an eight-level hierarchy staffed at the bottom level by equal numbers of men and women. The model assumed that over time a certain percentage of incumbents would be promoted from one level to the next. It also assumed a tiny bias in favor of promoting men, a bias accounting for only 1 percent of the variability in promotion. The researchers ran the simulation through a series of promotions. After many series, the highest level in the hierarchy was 65 percent male. The model shows clearly that even minute disadvantages can have substantial long-term effects.

In fact, the simulation *under*estimates the problem women have in rising to the top, for it reflects only what occurs at the stage of promotion. At every point along the path to the first promotion possibility, however, advantages or disadvantages can accumulate. If conditions for women are only very slightly unfavorable along the way, they are less likely even to be considered for promotion.

One example of how advantage and disadvantage can accrue occurs in a common professional setting—the meeting. Let's say I am attending a meeting with a group of people who know each other but whom I have never met. I notice that some people's comments are taken seriously by the group, while other people's are ignored. Although my assessment of individual participants is formed in part by my own evaluation of the content of their remarks, I cannot always independently evaluate that content. Further, I am likely to be influenced by the reactions of others in the group. Through observing the group dynamics, I learn who has high status and who does not. By the time the meeting ends, people who were equal in my eyes when it began are unequal.

Those whose remarks were ignored have suffered a small loss in prestige, and their contributions have been labeled, implicitly, as low in value. Because they now have less prestige, they will be listened to less in the future; they will carry their previously earned labels into the next professional encounter, losing a little more standing with each negative experience. The gap between them and people who are gaining attention for their remarks will widen as their small initial failures accrue and make future failures more likely.

Successful people seem to recognize that one component of professional advancement is the ability to parlay small gains into bigger ones. Ambitious people worry if their comments are ignored and are pleased if they are taken seriously. A series of disregarded comments can signal failure, while remarks discussed by superiors and coworkers contribute to success. If everyone understood explicitly what some people understand implicitly—that success comes from creating and consolidating small gains—no one would counsel women to ignore being ignored. The concept of the accumulation of advantage lets us see that the well-meaning advice often given to women—not to make a mountain out of a molehill—is mistaken. That advice fails to recognize that mountains *are* molehills, piled one on top of the other. Fairness requires appreciating the importance of each molehill of advantage and disadvantage and taking steps to ensure that molehills do not accrue to individuals on the basis of their group membership.

But even that is not enough. Everyone must also understand that in most organizations women begin at a slight disadvantage. A woman does not walk into the room with the same status as an equivalent man, because she is less likely than a man to be viewed as a serious professional. Moreover, since her ideas are less likely to be attended to than a male peer's, she is correspondingly less likely to accumulate advantage the way he might. A woman who aspires to success *needs* to worry about being ignored; each time it happens she loses prestige and the people around her become less inclined to take her seriously.

The concept of the accumulation of advantage explains another, otherwise puzzling, difference between men and women: women talk less in public and professional settings than men do (see discussion in Haslett, Geis, & Carter 1992).[3] Let us assume that women know—through experience—that their remarks are likely to be ignored. They may then correctly infer that they are better off not speaking and staying at their current level than making a comment and accruing a disadvantage. Saying nothing exacts its own toll, for no one acquires prestige through silence. Still, the tacit loss brought about by saying nothing is smaller than the explicit loss of prestige incurred by speaking and being ignored. A slower accumulation of disadvantage is, on a rational analysis, preferable to a faster accumulation of disadvantage. I am not suggesting that women explicitly or consciously formulate such a policy, only that it *is* rational: women risk less disadvantage overall by remaining silent. (We can also interpret women's behavior more simply: being ignored is painful and humiliating, and people seek to avoid pain.)

This may be a good time to emphasize that, although I speak of *women,* I am not claiming that what is true of women in general is true of every woman on every occasion. Nor do I argue that men are never ignored in favor of women. At a recent faculty meeting, in fact, I observed a reversal of the usual effect. The chair of my department gave me the credit for an excellent comment that a junior male colleague had made earlier in the meeting. (I was so bemused and amused by the reversal that

I failed to correct him.) The exceptions should not, however, obscure the rule. The existence of an exceptional woman who frequently speaks out in public settings and whose contributions are acknowledged and valued does not invalidate the rule that women in general have lower professional status than men and are less likely than men to profit from their positive contributions.

Schemas, Exceptions, and Fairness

Several problems are encountered in efforts to ensure fairness. One of them is convincing ourselves that our judgments really are prone to error. We all want to believe we are unbiased and unaffected by stereotypes we have consciously rejected. We are convinced that we know quality when we see it. Even people who are overtly prejudiced think they can judge others impartially; the facts, they believe, speak for themselves.

A compelling laboratory experiment, however, demonstrates that people are unable to evaluate others accurately, even when a completely straightforward quality like height is involved (Biernat, Manis, & Nelson 1991). In this experiment, college students were shown photographs of various people and asked to guess their heights in feet and inches (including shoes). The photos always contained a reference item, such as a desk or a doorway, to help students with their estimates.

Without telling the students, the experimenters chose the test items so that every photograph of a male student of a given height was matched by a picture of a female student of the same height. Here, then, was an easily visible characteristic that could be measured in objective units—feet and inches—rather than in subjective terms like *short* and *tall*. The students' judgments should have been accurate. They were not. They were affected by one component of gender schemas—the knowledge that men are, on average, taller than women. When exposed to a sample contrary to the general rule, the students saw the women as shorter and the men as taller than they actually were.

Using a scale marked in objective units does not, therefore, prevent error. (Of course, if the students had had an actual ruler they could have estimated the heights more accurately.) If people have a schema about gender differences, that schema spills over into their judgments. The problem is exacerbated when the schema is accurate—as it is in the case of height differences—because erroneous judgments of individuals are supported by real overall differences between groups. Individuals who diverge from the schema are perceived in the light of the observers' schemas. The implications for judgments of professional competence are clear. Employers faced with a man and a woman matched on the qualities relevant to success in a particular field may believe they are judging the candidates objectively. Yet, if their schemas represent men as more capable than women, they are likely to overestimate the male's qualifications and underestimate the female's.

A second problem in the attempt to ensure fair evaluations is that people find creative ways to justify their perceptions. To take one example, to reassure themselves—and others—that they have rejected stereotypical attitudes or can judge fairly in spite of them, people point to professional women they admire and respect. For another example, people point to women who are successful as evidence that hiring and promotion practices are based on merit. Finally, people use examples of incompetent women to explain women's overall lack of success.

Such examples, however, are irrelevant if they are not representative of the general population. My claim is that they are not. They are atypical—exceptions to a general rule confirmed by the preponderance of the evidence. Examples that represent exceptions do not refute general findings. For instance, on Wall Street in 1996 only 8 percent of the managing directors were women (Truell 1996). Each of the women in that 8 percent is an exception someone might cite as evidence that women can succeed in the investment business. Invalidation of a general rule, however, requires proof that the rule typically does not hold; it is not good enough to show that it occasionally fails to apply. The existence of successful women shows that *some* women are evaluated positively *some* of the time. Fairness demands much more: the guarantee that there is no consistent advantage for members of one group relative to another.

Gender Schemas at Work

Keeping in mind the obstacles to ensuring fairness, we can consider the story of a university department. During the past ten years fifteen men and three women were added to the faculty. When he is queried about the ratio, the chair of the department explains that his only interest is to hire the best, most able, people in order to build the strongest possible department. He makes it clear to search committees that quality is the only issue, and informs them of his views of the candidates. He is sincere in his belief that he is gender-blind and confident of his ability to judge others' competence. And, since the people he chooses *are* able, he has no reason to doubt his judgment or leadership. Even if he were to track the careers of the women he failed to hire, he would probably not question his decisions. Those women are likely to have been undervalued by other prospective and actual department chairs and to have, as a result, careers that are on average less stellar than those of the men he hired.

For the chair to see that the facts call for more self-doubt, he needs an education in social cognition and gender. He needs, first, to learn that people are likely to misperceive men and women in professional settings, to overrate the former and underrate the latter. Clear marks of prestige, ranging from having a degree from an elite institution to sitting at the head of a table, are interpreted differently, depending on whether the person is a man or a woman (see chapters 7, 10, and 11). Even judgments of height, as described earlier, are affected by the person's gender.

Second, the chair needs to understand how errors of evaluation mount up over time and affect the career trajectories of young professionals and Ph.D.s. Data suggesting that women must meet higher standards than men to gain promotion, partnership, or tenure (see chapters 10 to 12) demonstrate the detrimental consequences of the accumulation of disadvantage, showing for example, that only a few years after earning their degrees, young men and women with the same on-paper qualifications have different professional lives. Finally, the chair needs to learn how expectations of men's and women's achievements can affect their actual performance, as well as their aspirations.

He needs, in short, to see that his confidence is misplaced, that it is the product of ignorance. (He needs this book!) He is unlikely to be exempt from the processes that affect everyone else, unlikely to have equally high expectations of men and women, and unlikely to know how to change his perceptions and decisions to adjust for the advantages men have incorrectly received. He believes he is different, but that is what everyone thinks—just as we all think we are above average. Even those who are actively concerned about gender equality are affected by gender schemas;

the odds are that he is, too. As a good scholar, he should entertain the possibility that his judgments are skewed and consider what steps he can take to make them more accurate. He needs, in sum, a better theory and better data. Then he can be more alert to the pitfalls inherent in making judgments about ability.

Not long ago, a new grandfather happened to read a draft of chapter 2, "Gender Begins—and Continues—at Home" just before meeting his infant granddaughter for the first time. As he held her in his arms he said automatically, "You're so soft"—which of course she was. As the words reverberated in his ear, they reminded him of the data he had just read about fathers' misperceptions of infants' characteristics. He paused, squeezed the baby gently, and added, "and firm"—which of course she also was. There is nothing like observing yourself in the act of an inaccurate or partial perception to engender humility about your freedom from gender schemas and to help you change your perceptions.

In the remainder of this introduction, I touch on some of the issues related to the origins of gender schemas and their role in the professional lives of women. In the ensuing chapters I supply the experimental and observational data that support my claims, develop my argument that common cognitive processes are at the heart of gender schemas, trace the effects of schemas on men's and women's professional lives, and suggest remedies for breaking through the glass ceiling.

The Origins and Effects of Gender Schemas

Childhood Learning
Where do ideas about sex differences come from? Expectations about gender differences, and plans to inculcate them, occur even before children are born. Here's a conversation between a man and a woman who are thinking of having a baby:

She: If we have a girl, I'll get her a truck.
He: Of course.
She: If we have a boy, I'll get him a doll.
He: Well, . . . if he *asks* for one.

Infancy and childhood are a critical period for the development of implicit hypotheses and expectations about the self and others. Small children observe unequal divisions of labor between men and women—both in the home and in the wider world—and notice that adults treat girls and boys differently. Like adults, children search for explanations of the differences they observe, aided by what they are implicitly—and sometimes explicitly—taught. As the conversation quoted above suggests, children are provided with data that require an explanation, such as paternal readiness to give a girl a truck and paternal reluctance to give a boy a doll. The explanation suggested to children, and the one they arrive at themselves, is that there is a causal link between their biology (about which they understand very little) and their talents, interests, preferences, attitudes, and behaviors. Children learn very early that they are not simply children, they are boys and girls. Chapters 2 and 3 focus on how adults treat children and what children learn.

Saying that children *learn* to be boys and girls does not deny the possibility that there are biologically based differences above and beyond reproductive capacity and the organs that mediate reproductive behavior. In some domains, such as rough-and-tumble play and skill at mentally rotating three-dimensional figures, there is good evidence that hormonal differences are important. But in every domain—including those with a clear hormonal influence—there is good evidence for social and cultural influences. Neither biology nor society act alone, nor could they. Chapters 4 and 5 summarize important findings on the role of hormones in behavior and cognition, and explain how to understand those findings.

Sex, Gender, and Schemas

The terms *male/female, man/woman,* and *boy/girl* distinguish people on the basis of their reproductive role, but do not imply that the characteristics of those groups are due to that role. If, for example, I refer to the superior spelling skills of females, I am not implying a link between the female reproductive role and spelling, though there may conceivably be one. Rather, I am saying that the people we single out on the basis of their having XX chromosomes are superior at spelling to those we single out on the basis of their having XY chromosomes. The difference in spelling skill may be partly influenced by chromosomal status, or it may be solely influenced by differences in how we treat people with XX status versus XY status; females may be especially good at spelling for reasons that have no direct link to their chromosomes. The term *sex difference,* then, refers to a difference between males and females, with no implication that the difference noted is directly linked to chromosomal or reproductive status.

When I speak of *gender,* on the other hand, I am highlighting our psychological and social conceptions of what it means to be a man or a woman. Thus, the term *gender schemas* refers to our intuitive hypotheses about the behaviors, traits, and preferences of men and women, boys and girls. Correspondingly, the term *gender roles* refers to our ideas about how men and women are expected to behave. In sum, *sex* is used to categorize people into two groups, and *gender* is used to describe our beliefs about sex-based categories.[4]

In discussing the contents of gender schemas I sometimes use the adjectives masculine and feminine. When I mention *masculine* characteristics, I refer to the characteristics we traditionally associate with men. I do not mean to suggest that only men have those characteristics. Similarly, if I talk about *feminine* toys, I am referring to toys seen as appropriate for girls to play with. I do not intend to suggest that there is anything inherently suitable for girls or unsuitable for boys about feminine toys. I am indicating only that those toys are seen as the "right" toys for girls. Although I am sometimes tempted to put quotation marks around the words feminine and masculine—to indicate that I do not believe such traits are inherently more natural for women or men—I do not do so. In my terminology, the words are part of gender schemas, part of our belief systems, not a description of the way things are.

Expressions in popular culture, such as "Real men don't eat quiche," are not intended as biological claims. Instead, they are comments about our notions of masculinity and femininity. The idea of a really good example of something—a "real" man or "real" woman—occurs with other concepts as well. For example, people judge the number 2 as a "better" even number than the number 736. At the same time, people agree that both numbers are even numbers and that it is ridiculous to talk of one even number being better than another (Armstrong, Gleitman, & Gleitman 1983). But 2 is psychologically a better example of evenness than

736 is; it is closer to our prototype of what even numbers are. Similarly, at least in North America, men who don't eat quiche are closer to our prototype of what men are than men who do.

The Cognition of Gender

Reproductive status is one way of distinguishing people. It is a distinction most cultures find psychologically compelling, and around which they form the implicit hypotheses I call gender schemas. As I mentioned earlier, all humans form implicit hypotheses to explain their social world.[5] Whenever there is an observable difference between social groups, people develop hypotheses to explain the difference and look for data to support their hypotheses. Hypothesis-formation and hypothesis-testing are natural and valuable human activities. Human cognition seeks explanations of physical and social phenomena. Schemas and their impact on perception and evaluation are discussed in chapters 6 and 7.

The sexual division of labor is one example of a social phenomenon. One way to explain and justify it is to appeal to differences in men's and women's natures (Eagly 1987; Hoffman & Hurst 1990). To explain and justify the fact, for example, that almost all engineers are men and almost all homemakers are women, people may say that men have traits and abilities that fit them to be engineers and cause them to choose engineering over homemaking, and women have traits and abilities that fit them to be homemakers and cause them to choose homemaking over engineering.

Such an explanation is an implicit appeal to the deterministic power of built-in, essential differences. As I will show in the following chapters, there is no evidence in favor of such a picture and considerable evidence against it. There are built-in differences, but biology is not destiny. Biology is one factor in a multifactor equation. In considering the role of hormones in physical and cognitive differences between males and females in chapters 4 and 5, I try to avoid both extremes of an increasingly polarized discussion. Biology is not destiny, but neither is the social environment. Neither determines behavior; both influence it.

Our cognitions—how we interpret information, store it in memory, reason with it, draw inferences from it—are yet another important factor.

The role of cognition in our everyday understanding of sex differences has not, I think, been adequately examined. In this book I am proposing that cognitive processes are at the heart of our conception of sex differences and help to create and maintain the inequalities among us.

Expectations and Gender Traits
Having attributed different traits and behaviors to men and women to explain the sexual division of labor, people then treat men and women in accordance with their expectations about those characteristics, setting in motion a self-fulfilling prophecy (Merton 1948; Rosenthal & Jacobson 1968). All of us—boys and girls, men and women—become in part what others expect us to become, thereby confirming hypotheses about the different natures of males and females. While no one is infinitely malleable, no one is completely indifferent to others. One way we learn who we are is through others' responses to us. As men and women, we also develop expectations for our own behavior, based on characteristics we believe we possess. We then explain our successes and failures in terms of those abilities and traits. Chapters 8 and 9 review the findings on the impact of schemas on people's behavior.

In white, western, middle-class society, the gender schema for men includes being capable of independent, autonomous action (agentic, in short), assertive, instrumental, and task-oriented. Men act. The gender schema for women is different; it includes being nurturant, expressive, communal, and concerned about others (Bakan 1966; Spence & Helmreich, 1978; Spence & Sawin 1985). Women nurture others and express their feelings. Men who are nurturant and emotionally expressive are perceived as feminine; women who are agentic and assertive are seen as masculine. Schemas are not wholly inaccurate: on the whole, men have more masculine traits than feminine ones; women have more feminine traits than masculine ones.

But gender schemas oversimplify. Masculine and feminine traits are not opposites of each other; they are not contradictory. Everyone has both to some degree and expresses different traits in different situations. Differences exist, but the sexes are more alike than they are different. It is easy to lose sight of that reality, even though most differences between the sexes are small.

In college I took a vocational-interests test in a psychology course. This test supposedly matched people's dominant interests and traits with different occupations. At the time, I was planning to become a clinical psychologist—not that I knew exactly what that meant—and I had a male friend, Richard, who wanted to be a psychoanalyst. I had learned that women tended to score higher on social and aesthetic traits and that men tended to score higher on, as I recall, scientific and analytic traits. Because the test items pitted the traits against each other, I had to express preferences I often didn't have. I found myself splitting the difference from answer to answer. Richard, half teasing and half taunting, said he could guess what my profile looked like. When I showed it to him, he pounced on how high my social traits were compared to his. "But look at my analytic traits," I insisted.

I now look at the test and my reactions rather differently. First, I should have said, "Richard, you're a jerk. You want to be a psychoanalyst and your social traits are low?" Second, I see that the test is based on misguided assumptions: it portrays occupations as unidimensional, and it forces people to be one thing *or* another. I now know that being a scientist is a social activity, as well as a solitary activity, as well as an analytic activity, as well as an aesthetic activity. Indeed, what I find wonderful about science is how many different parts of myself are satisfied in the doing of it. Third, I see that I accepted the assumptions of the test and felt correspondingly trapped by my feminine traits: I felt that if I acknowledged them, I would be condemned to a feminine future, always acting in the service of others, never acting for myself. I did not see a way to be nurturant *and* agentic. The either-or implication of gender schemas ruled out the self I wanted to be.

Schemas and Professional Evaluations
People and occupations are multidimensional, but our schemas simplify both. They portray the professions as suitable for men, and men as suitable for the professions. Without exception, every prestigious or high-paying profession in the United States is dominated by men, dominated numerically and in terms of who wields power (Gutek 1993).[6] A man or woman who goes into law or business or academia is entering a field in which positions at the highest levels are disproportionately occupied by

men and those at the lowest levels are disproportionately occupied by women. All prestigious professions are professions for men, not simply professions.

The immediate consequence for a woman entering a profession is that those around her, both men and other women, perceive her as at least slightly unsuited to that profession, because her gender doesn't fit in. The schema for women is incompatible with the schema for a successful professional, resulting in lower expectations of a woman's potential achievement. Those low expectations will, in turn, affect evaluations of her work. There is usually room for disagreement about the quality of someone's work. Observers of women will lean in a negative direction, in line with their low expectations. If she performs badly, that will confirm their expectations. If she performs well, she may still fail to receive her due, because her achievement runs counter to expectation. Or, she may be appropriately rewarded, but be seen as an exception to the general rule that women do not make good professionals.

There are a number of potential pitfalls for women professionals that originate in the perceived discordance between the two schemas. Women must appear neither too feminine nor too masculine (see chapter 7). At either extreme they make others uncomfortable. A woman who is very feminine runs the risk of seeming less competent; the more she typifies the schema for a woman, the less she matches the schema for the successful professional. On the other hand, a woman with masculine traits runs the risk of appearing unnatural and deviant. The more she typifies the schema for the successful professional, the less she matches the schema for a woman.

Some women—such as the subject of the following admiring description—manage to appear both competent and feminine: "She is a tough, tough lady. She has a soft, genteel way about her, but she is an adversary of steel." That characterization of Janet Reno was offered shortly after her 1993 nomination for U.S. Attorney General (Rohter 1993, quoting a former judge and prosecutor who had hired Reno as state attorney in Florida). Former British Prime Minister Margaret Thatcher, with her sobriquet "The Iron Lady," has been described in similar terms. It is possible, then, to be perceived simultaneously as "tough" (masculine) and a "lady" (feminine), as having a "soft" and "genteel" manner while being "an adversary of steel." Although such a blending of opposites may appear almost impossible, observation suggests that it is reasonably common among successful women.

Less common is the woman who concentrates on competence and ignores femininity. It is the rare woman who is completely unconcerned about whether she is perceived as feminine, and the rare environment that is similarly unconcerned. Women who do not have a "soft, genteel way" about them may be told—despite their manifest competence—that they should wear more make-up and go to charm school. That was what Ann Hopkins's evaluators wrote about her when, despite her outstanding record, they rejected her bid for a partnership at Price Waterhouse, an accounting firm (see chapter 13; Fiske, Bersoff, Borgida, Deaux & Heilman 1991).

The partners were openly critical of a woman who didn't act like a prototypical woman. Other people's overt beliefs in equality may cause them to avoid making such stereotypic statements, but their nonconscious schemas may not prevent them from making stereotypic judgments. People who eschew statements such as, "Women do not command respect from their subordinates," may nevertheless feel comfortable saying, "Lee does not command respect from her subordinates." The latter comment is just a "fact" about Lee, arrived at through impartial and fair observation. In their laudable resolutions to judge fairly, people may be unaware that their perceptions are guided not only by someone's objective performance, but in addition by their nonconscious expectations of the person's performance.

Lee, then, may be misperceived due to the influence of gender schemas. She might genuinely have her subordinates' respect but be perceived otherwise because of a gender schema that says women do not command respect. Or, her subordinates might express their respect for her somewhat differently than they would for a man. Onlookers, failing to see traditional marks of deference and tacitly believing that women are poor authority figures, might conclude that respect is absent. Finally, Lee might lack her subordinates' respect, not because of her behavior but because her subordinates resent having a woman superior and therefore refuse to grant her the respect they would give a man exhibiting the same behavior. Observers, because of their expectations about women, could mistakenly locate the problem in Lee's performance, rather than in her subordinates' schemas.

A story about a science department at a prestigious university, circa 1990, illustrates how expectations stemming from gender schemas can affect a woman's career. A young Ph.D. who has just been hired has a conference with her department chair about what courses she will teach. She is eager to teach a large introductory lecture course. The chair refuses, saying that students won't accept a woman instructor in that format. The woman presses a bit, saying she thinks she can do it and would like to try. The chair doesn't want to take a chance and instead assigns her to a laboratory course. The woman is not happy with the substitution, because laboratory courses are extremely time-consuming. As a young faculty member, she needs to spend as much time as she can developing her research and getting it published, in order to earn promotion and tenure. She will now have less time for research than will her male peer who is assigned to the lecture course.

The example nicely captures the many different factors—especially gender expectations—that intersect to place a woman in a poor position. The chair believes he is being objective about the students' preferences and is minimizing any risk to an important course. Nothing about the conference causes him to consider the possibility that his decision is guided by gender schemas or might be unfair. The conference has also set a bad precedent. In the conference, the chair activated his nonconscious views of women and attached them to the new faculty member. He explicitly articulated the view that, as a woman, she would not do a good job as a lecturer. In the future, he is likely to reactivate his views about women when he is evaluating her. In a way, she has already failed, because he has already labeled her to himself as an unacceptable lecturer.

What might the chair have done if he had been aware of gender schemas and committed to gender equality? He would still have been concerned about the students' reception of a woman lecturer, but he could have tried to work out with her some techniques to ease her acceptance. He could have recommended that the woman speak to experienced colleagues to learn what has worked well in the past and to plan her response to the authority-challenging events that large lecture classes are prone to no matter who is teaching—newspaper reading, whispered conversations, snoring, and so on. He could have suggested that, to solidify her authority, she schedule several moderately rigorous quizzes early in the semester. Finally, he could have been prepared with statements of full support for her, were students to bring complaints to him. As things stand, however, the chair has put the woman at an objective disadvantage: he has taken time away from her on the basis of her gender.

Statistics on women's progress in the professions (reviewed in chapters 10 through 12) back up the idea that a succession of small events, such as not getting a good assignment, results in large discrepancies in advancement and achievement. They also suggest that gender schemas work to women's disadvantage in other ways. Women generally benefit less from their positive achievements than men do. In their first academic appointment, for example, men benefit more than women do from the prestige of the institution where they received their training. Men get better jobs. Men are promoted more quickly. Men are tenured more quickly. Men make more money. Men are overrepresented at senior levels. As the discussions in chapters 11 and 12 make clear, the differences hold even when men and women are equated on performance (to the extent that they can be).

What is true for academia holds even more strongly in the corporate world. A 1990 *Fortune* magazine survey of 799 of the largest U.S. industrial and service companies found that only nineteen women—less than one-half of 1 percent—were listed among the more than four thousand highest-paid officers and directors (Fierman 1990). In business, as in academia, women earn less than men (two of those nineteen women had cash compensation under $85,000 per year), are promoted more slowly, and work in less prestigious firms. Women's salaries have improved. In a 1996 survey of the twenty most highly paid women, the lowest salary was $152,977 (Greene & Greene 1996). But 615 men earned more than the twentieth woman on the list. Again, as in academia, to the extent that performance can be accurately measured, men and women appear to perform equally well.

Independent of all other factors, gender appears to play a major role in people's ability to get ahead. Gender schemas are objectively costly for women. Relative to women, men have a leg up. Men look right for the job.

Qualifications and Responsibilities

In the same way that some theorists have suggested a deterministic role for biology, others have suggested a deterministic role for educational and professional qualifications. In both cases, women's lower professional status is attributed to something they lack. There often are sex differences in qualifications (as chapters 10 to 12 review). But, like biology, qualifications are not destiny. They too are but one factor in a multifactor equation, as is evident from the fact that men and women with equal qualifications do not advance at the same rate. In evaluating the role of qualifications in chapters 10 through 12, I have tried to avoid both extremes of a polarized discussion. I conclude that qualifications influence people's ability to advance but do not fully determine advancement. Gender schemas play an important role in disadvantaging women.

Men's lack of responsibilities outside of work may also contribute to their faster professional advancement. Men accept less responsibility than women do for the day-to-day operation of their households, as documented in chapter 2. Men are less likely than women to work part-time in order to raise their children. Inequities at home reverberate in the work place. But men's advantages and women's disadvantages on the job are not solely a function of their differing participation in family life. Men receive a greater reward for their performance than do women, independent of all other factors.

Self-Perception

Subjective costs add to the objective costs of gender schemas. Consider again the young professor who has not been permitted to teach a large lecture course. If she is rational, she must now wonder what other jobs she will be perceived as unable to fill. She may reaffirm to herself that she is competent and willing to work hard. Or she may begin to question her competence and motivation. Either way, she has borne and continues to bear an emotional cost that a comparable man will not have had.

Everyone experiences successes and failures and must then explain to themselves just why they succeeded or failed (as discussed in chapter 9). A somewhat oversimplified description of men's reactions to success and failure is that they take the credit for their successes but do not accept the blame for their failures. A similarly oversimplified description of women's reactions is that women take the blame for their failures but do not take the credit for their successes.

Because the professions are perceived as requiring masculine abilities and traits, a successful man can reasonably credit himself with the abilities and traits that are necessary for success—and feel masculine into the bargain. A man's success and his masculinity reinforce each other. A man's failure is incompatible with his masculinity. Since people want to feel compatible with their gender—and to perceive others the same way—a man will attempt to interpret his failures in terms that leave his masculinity intact (and others will attempt to do the same for him). One response is to try to escape the blame. Paradoxically, another response is "the-buck-stops-here": the man shoulders the responsibility. Tone seems to be everything here. By taking responsibility in the right way, a man can actually seem more masculine and more in control. Although he acknowledges his failure, he also manages to reduce its overall importance.

For a woman, success and failure work differently. If a woman is professionally successful, she must either see herself as having masculine traits—and thereby run the risk of seeming unfeminine to herself and others—or as having compensated in some way—through luck or extraordinary effort—for a lack of masculine characteristics. Unlike a successful man, a woman has something to lose from success: her gender identity or belief in her ability. Conversely, failure and femininity reinforce each other. Women are expected to fail and potentially have something to salvage from failure, namely, reinforcement of their femininity. A woman who fails is more of a woman than one who succeeds.

For men, then, there is complete congruence between professional goals and the need to feel like a good example of their gender. For women there is a potential conflict. Naturally, not every woman, on every occasion, will perceive herself or be perceived in terms of a conflict between competence and femininity. But even a small dilemma of that sort, occasionally experienced, will accrue disadvantage for a woman relative to a man, who never has to choose between competence and masculinity.

In experimental investigations, people are asked to apportion the reasons for their success or failure at a task among four different factors: ability, effort, luck, and easiness or difficulty of the task. The results are reviewed in chapter 9. Women and men contrast most in how they view the role of luck. Women see luck as more important for both their successes and their failures than men do.

"Luck" may be a grab-bag category in such experiments—a reason people use when they don't know exactly why something happened, when they cannot establish a clear cause-and-effect relation. Because luck is by its nature unstable and uncontrollable, attributing outcomes to it is deleterious. If you see a success or failure as due to luck, you cannot learn anything from it. There is no point in trying to figure out what went wrong or right, no point in developing a plan for the future based on the past, no point in putting forth a lot of effort the next time. Chance undoubtedly enters into every result, but consistent success demands competence, strategic analysis, and effort.

Although an emphasis on luck is detrimental to achievement, it is also a rational response for women. Luck, in the guise of an unstable and uncontrollable set of external circumstances, plays an unwarranted role in women's professional lives. Women do not reliably profit from their competence, strategic analysis, and effort to the same extent men do, as the research reviewed in chapters 10 through 12 demonstrates. Yet no professional woman can succeed without those qualities. One might even argue that they are more important for women than for men, because women's objective circumstances are more difficult than men's. But individual effort is insufficient. Trailing behind every successful woman are the unsuccessful women—who knows how many?—who were equally competent, strategic, and hardworking, but not lucky.

Women would have to close their eyes to the facts to deny the role of factors outside their control and to insist on the potential efficacy of their own actions. Yet how effective can women be unless they act as if luck were irrelevant? Here is another small dilemma women face that men do not—one that, over time, takes its toll.

I remember a heated discussion with my mother when I was a young teenager. I showed her a poem I had read about being the captain of one's ship. To me the poem was a validation of what I most deeply believed: that my longing and determination to achieve something significant would make reality conform to my will. Here was a poem—a voice from the outside world I planned to succeed in—to lend authority to my certainty that I could control my future. I wanted my mother to have the same opinion, not just about me, but about herself. I wanted her to have high aspirations as well.

But she argued with me. "No," she said, "it isn't so." One wasn't the captain of one's ship, one couldn't do exactly what one wanted.

I was upset and angry. Of course you couldn't be the captain of your ship if you didn't *believe* you could be, if you didn't *try* to be. I rejected my mother's defeatism and took comfort from the poem.

It is of course true that the race is not always to the swift. But women, as a group, do not experience as tight a fit between cause and effect as men do. Women enjoy fewer successes and suffer more failures than comparable men. Men and women live in different environments, environments that are the same only on the surface. Women have puzzles to solve that men do not. Some women decide that they are exceptional and will succeed where others have failed. Others ignore the unstable relationship between cause and effect, action and result. Still others forgo professional ambition, perhaps without realizing why.

Remedies

What can we do to foster equality? In chapters 13 and 14, I propose remedies. Affirmative action policies, legislation, and recourse to the courts remain important avenues to change in the workplace. The courts make it harder for employers to use gender schemas to justify denying women advancement in the form of salary, promotion, partnership, and tenure.

But the unexpressed and nonconscious nature of gender schemas and their subterranean mode of action require more subtle remedies as well. The first, and most important, remedy is learning about gender schemas: how they develop, how they work, how they are maintained, and how they influence aspirations and expectations. Using this knowledge, organizations and individuals can devise procedures and programs to neutralize gender schemas, as I recommend in chapter 14.

I hope that this book will itself serve as a remedy. Fairness is the leitmotif of this chapter and this book. I trust that understanding what is required for fairness will help to bring it about.

2

Gender Begins—and Continues—at Home

At a restaurant in Manhattan near the end of the lunch hour I sit watching the manager's child, not quite two, toddling among the mostly empty tables. The child is wearing a brightly colored and stylishly patterned jacket and pants. A baseball cap worn back to front partially covers the child's ear-length curly blond hair. Is the child a girl or a boy? The baseball cap and pants suggest a boy, but the hair length and clothing suggest a girl. The toddler's adventurousness might signal a boy, but its looks are androgynous and I can't make up my mind. As the child wanders too far out of his reach, the father calls, "Come back, honey." O.K., I say to myself, it's a girl; he wouldn't have said "honey" if it were a boy. By now, the child has reached an occupied table at the front of the restaurant, and the father goes to retrieve it. The customers there, having arrived at a different conclusion, ask the father how old "he" is.

Turning Babies into Girls and Boys

The first fact adults want to establish about a child is its sex, even if the child is a neonate, a being whose behavior is largely independent of its sex. Unless a baby is naked, though, it's usually impossible to tell what sex it is, so people snatch at cues like type of clothing and hair length. Even so, they frequently guess wrong. To avoid this mistake, I've developed a stratagem: "How old is your baby?" I ask. The parent's response uses the appropriate pronoun, and I'm home free. But why do adults need to know a baby's sex? What does it tell them about the child?

Not Just a Baby

Adults need to know a child's sex because the label tells them how to interpret the child's behavior, even its physical features. The label allows the adult to categorize an attractive baby as "pretty," if it is a girl, or handsome, if it is a boy. The label brings into play the adult's pre-existing beliefs about differences between the sexes. Those beliefs—some conscious and some unconscious—constitute an intuitive conception, or schema, of gender.

We can see adults' conventional perceptions of infants in the greeting cards sent to congratulate parents on their new baby (Bridges 1993). Such cards reflect a social consensus about what boys and girls are like. A researcher who looked at them found, as expected, no pink greeting cards for boys and no blue ones for girls. Pictures of birds and rabbits appear much more often on girls' cards, while bears and dogs are more frequent on boys' cards. When toys are shown, rattles and mobiles are pictured more often on girls' cards than on boys', and balls, sports equipment, and vehicles show up more often on boys' cards. Girl babies are pictured as sleeping or immobile more often than boys are, whereas boys are shown in active play more often.

Decorative elements show gender differences, too. Frills, lace, ribbons, flowers, and hearts are all used more for girls than for boys. Verbal descriptions of infants also differ; the term *sweet,* for example, is applied far more often to girls than to boys. The most striking difference is that expressions of happiness or joy are found more often on cards for boys— 64 percent of cards—than for girls—49 percent of cards. People expect parents to be happier about the birth of a boy than the birth of a girl.

Greeting cards thus project babies as already embodying gender schemas. One class of human infants is pink, decorative, sweet, and passive— like birds or rabbits—and the other is sports oriented and physically active—like bears or puppies—and brings happiness and joy.

Similar indications of the influence of gender schemas on adult perceptions of babies come from studies of adults' descriptions of infants. In one study, researchers asked college students to rate the behavior of a baby who was videotaped crying. Some students were told the baby was a boy and others that it was a girl. They described the baby labeled as male as angrier than the same infant labeled as female (Condry & Condry

1976). In another study, parents were asked to rate their newborns on a number of different dimensions when the babies were no more than twenty-four hours old. According to objective measures, there were no differences in weight, height, color, muscle tone, reflex irritability, heart rate, and respiratory rate between the girls and boys. Yet the parents of baby boys perceived their sons as bigger than the parents of daughters perceived their baby girls—even though the babies were all the same weight and height (Rubin, Provenzano, & Luria 1974). Knowing a child's sex influences perceptions, even in a domain like size, which we think of as unambiguous and impervious to bias.[1] The inaccuracies of height judgments of adults described in chapter 1 have their corollary in perceptions of infants.

The fathers' perceptions of their infants were more extreme—hence less accurate—than the mothers' were. For example, although both parents saw daughters as having finer features than sons, fathers saw them as much finer featured than mothers did; similarly, fathers saw sons as much larger featured than mothers did. On the dimension of firmness–softness, mothers correctly rated sons and daughters as equal, but fathers erred in rating sons as much firmer and daughters as much softer than mothers did. Fathers of sons also judged their babies as better-coordinated, more alert, stronger, and hardier than did fathers of daughters. Fathers, then, are especially susceptible to the influence of gender schemas; they tend to see their infants as the adults they will become, rather than as the infants they are. Fathers' perceptions of their offspring's physical characteristics are inaccurate and objectively unwarranted.

Even when infants are simply infants—that is, before they show any signs of behaving like a "boy" or a "girl"—adults view them as distinctively male or female. One woman told me that her cousin gaily refers to her one-year-old as "Joshua, the macho baby." If infants really do not show any differences other than genitalia, how can adults project nonexistent masculine and feminine qualities onto them? How can they see a baby as "macho"? One reason is that they are largely unaware of what they are doing. Although parents are not immune to the reality of their children's characteristics, their perceptions of and reactions to their babies are affected by their own beliefs, attitudes, and expectations. Yet parents believe that their perceptions are accurate.

Moreover, adults can project gender onto infants precisely because much infant behavior is ambiguous. Parents can interpret an infant's cry in a variety of ways. Even if they correctly identify it as a plea for nourishment, they may hear it as an angry demand—"Feed me now!"—or as a piteous wail—"Please feed me." Gender schemas provide the interpretation. To his mother, Joshua, the macho baby, cries "Feed me now!" Because behavior is ambiguous, parents have little chance to correct their errors.

Thus guided—or misguided—by their gender schemas, parents unintentionally and unwittingly misperceive reality. One aim of this book is to replace people's false subjective impressions with objective information, to replace incorrect intuitive conceptions about gender with a picture that is scientifically more accurate. To consider the possible consequences of adults' inaccurate perceptions, we can ask which baby seems better suited to an active and successful professional life: the baby who is better coordinated, more alert, hardier, and stronger, or the one who is less coordinated, less alert, less hardy, and weaker? Which baby is better suited for doing more housework and child care? Just as it is unfair to picture one child as less capable than she is, it is also unfair to see the other as more capable than he is. From the first child too little will be expected, and from the second too much.

The baby is only a few hours old. It lies in its crib, blissfully unaware that its parents are planning its future, based, in part, on qualities it does not possess. In the following sections of this chapter, we look at differences in parents' treatment of the baby as it grows into childhood and examine the consequences of that treatment for division of labor at home.

Not Just a Child

Any adult who spends time with young children is at first stunned by the prevalence of sex differences. My own research group on language acquisition in two-year-olds typically finds no sex differences in the development of syntax. When we play and talk with the children, however, we see many other differences. We usually begin a session with a child by looking at a particular picture book. One student commented that when she gets to the page picturing different kinds of vehicles, the boys focus on the vehicles but the girls talk about the people and animals *in* the vehicles. We also notice that the boys do more running around during the session and that the girls seem to have a longer attention span. The children are only two years old, but they are already clearly different.

A tape-recording of one little boy talking to himself just before his second birthday revealed that he knew cars were guided by steering wheels, but airplanes by sticks. Since I didn't know what kind of steering mechanism airplanes have, I had some difficulty transcribing his tape. What he seemed to be saying—that planes had sticks instead of wheels—made no sense to me. At age two he also knew the difference by name between a front-end loader, a back-end loader, a dump truck, a cement mixer, and other kinds of trucks. I was astonished, not just by this child's expertise but by the depth of his passion for vehicles. His parents said that when he was eight months old they couldn't figure out why he periodically got very excited. They finally connected his excitement with the sound of a neighbor's Volkswagen driving down the street. This child was unusual in the extent of his fascination with vehicles, but even very young children show gender differences in their toy preferences, with boys preferring vehicles to dolls and girls preferring dolls to vehicles.

Early sex differences convince most casual observers that girls and boys differ intrinsically on a broad range of characteristics, from physical appearance, to toy preferences, to play style. What most people are not able to see, however, is how differently they treat boys and girls, from the first moment of babies' lives.

Many parents believe that they treat all their children the same, whether they are girls or boys. Nor are they completely wrong. A review of 172 studies of parental behavior suggests that in many areas parents *do* treat daughters and sons similarly. They have the same amount of general and verbal interaction with girls and boys, encourage achievement to the same extent, use material rewards to the same degree, and discourage aggression equally (Lytton & Romney 1991).[2] Thus, parents' views of their behavior are partly correct.

Yet parents also treat boys and girls differently. Often without realizing it, they react to children in terms of who the children will become as well as who they are at present. Because children will become gendered beings, parents project gender onto them at an early age, thereby encouraging sex differences. They tend to stimulate boys' motor behavior more than girls'.

They encourage dependency in girls more often than in boys and adminis-ter physical punishment to boys more frequently than to girls. Since par-ents see men as physically tougher than women, they extend that view to their children, perceiving boys as better able than girls to absorb rough physical treatment. Joshua the macho baby can be handled roughly, but his sister cannot. Such differential treatment encourages boys to be tougher than girls. Boys and girls cry equally often during infancy (Mac-coby & Jacklin 1974), but as development proceeds, boys cry less and less.

Parents are especially likely to encourage activities they consider appro-priate to a child's gender (Lytton & Romney, 1991) and to guide the child toward activities, preferences, and dress that are stereotypically masculine or feminine. Parents are more rigid in their treatment of boys, encourag-ing masculine activities for boys more strongly than they encourage femi-nine activities for girls. Finally, in line with the fact that they are more likely than mothers to misperceive infants, fathers emphasize gender ap-propriateness more than mothers do and tend to be particularly extreme in this respect with boys (Lytton & Romney 1991).

The toddler in the restaurant at the beginning of this chapter was, as I thought, a girl. I had based my surmise on a study that looked at differ-ences in the ways fathers and mothers talk to their young children (Glea-son & Greif 1983). Fathers with traditional attitudes about gender use imperatives and threats more often than mothers do and in talking to sons are more prone to use jocular names and names with a slight pejorative undertone (such as *buster*). Fathers also interrupt their children more of-ten than mothers do, use rare words more often in speaking to their chil-dren, and demand more challenging responses from them. Fathers are tougher on children than mothers are and are especially tough on boys. From my knowledge of that evidence, I predicted that even a father who dressed his child androgynously would be unlikely to call a boy "honey" in public.

Before looking in detail at differences in treatment of boys and girls, we can reconsider why parents are unaware of the extent to which they encourage gender-appropriate behavior. In part it is because they are not conscious of the extent to which they themselves are affected by gender schemas. It is unlikely, for example, that most parents notice that they speak differently to their sons and daughters. Most parents also neither realize how extensive their beliefs about gender differences are, nor know that many of their beliefs have no basis in fact.

Another factor that blinds some parents to the gender-stereotyped ways they treat their sons and daughters is their conviction that, in behaving differently toward their children, they are guided by the children's individual personalities. Thus the child who is gentler and more vulnerable gets gentler treatment than one who is perceived as self-assertive. Parents see themselves as responding sensitively to already-existing differences in their children. Their beliefs are, of course, not delusional. Children are not blank slates. Each child does have its own temperament and traits. The reality of the child's particular personality only makes it harder for parents to see which aspects of their own behavior are *not* guided by who the children are, but by who the parents think the children will become.

Even parents who deliberately try to rear their children nonstereotypically are subject to the influence of gender schemas. A study of six-year-olds, for example, compared children whose mothers explicitly tried to bring them up in gender-neutral ways with children whose mothers had conventional attitudes about gender roles. When independent observers who were unaware of the parents' beliefs rated the children's clothes as masculine or feminine, the ratings showed that the boys and girls in both types of families were dressed according to gender norms (Weiner & Wilson-Mitchell 1990). The mothers who were committed to gender equality, however, saw their children's clothes as less gender-stereotypical, even though they were not.

The effects of differences in dress and manner may be very subtle and may affect how others perceive a child more than how the child sees herself or himself. Girls are encouraged to dress in stereotypically feminine ways (wearing ornaments for the hair and body, skirts, and somewhat constrictive clothing); to walk and sit in stereotypically feminine ways (using a short stride, swaying the hips, and sitting with knees together and arms close to the body); and to talk in stereotypically feminine ways (higher voice pitch, greater use of "please"). There is evidence that both males and females see feminine women in general as less likely to be competent (see chapter 7). There is, however, no evidence that girls interpret their own stereotypically feminine dress or manner as incompatible with traditionally masculine achievements. For a variety of reasons, a woman may exempt herself from an assessment of lesser competence. Thus, how we dress children may not affect their own aspirations, but it does—at least in U.S. culture—affect how others perceive them.[3]

Everyone, it appears, is likely to be affected—deeply and nonconsciously—by their culture's view of what it means to be male and female. Even people who consciously espouse egalitarian beliefs do not realize how profoundly they have internalized the culture's norms and applied them to their children. There is wide implicit consensus—across income level, education, and sex—about the core features of gender schemas. For those features, parents are much more alike than they are different. Regardless of demographic variables, most subscribe to basic gender norms, dress gender-stereotypically themselves, and unwittingly treat their children gender-stereotypically.

Parents who actively endorse gender schemas, or are unaware of the impact of gender schemas on their perceptions and interpretations, perceive children as gendered from birth and treat them accordingly. For parents who recognize and actively oppose the limitations of gender schemas, matters are more complex (Weiner and Wilson-Mitchell 1990). Such egalitarian parents have, on the one hand, explicit beliefs that affect some of their child-rearing practices. They encourage their children, especially girls, to consider a wide range of possible occupations, and that encouragement influences the children's aspirations. Without realizing it, on the other hand, they are affected by gender schemas, dressing children in ways appropriate to their gender. Their egalitarian beliefs prevent such parents from perceiving that they do encourage gender-specific patterns and from seeing how closely their children conform to the norm. Gender schemas are powerful cultural forces. Adults cannot simply abandon them, especially when they are unaware that they hold them and that they conform to them in such matters as dress.

Children's dress is one example of the way egalitarian parents are unwittingly affected by gender schemas, but there are others. For example, even parents who each retain their own name after marriage typically give their children the father's name as a last name, perhaps with the mother's last name as a middle name. Though the child is the mother's to take care of, it is the father's in name. Egalitarian parents also make gender distinctions about playthings. Many strongly discourage gun play for both sexes but discourage it more strongly for girls (Weiner & Wilson-Mitchell 1990). That is because it is culturally deviant for girls to play with guns and culturally normal for boys to do so. A parent who disapproves of gun play will project that disapproval to boys, but will project both that disapproval and an attitude of deviance to girls.

Similarly, parents are likely to encourage doll play for girls but, at most, permit it for boys (Weiner & Wilson-Mitchell 1990). A boy who plays with dolls is culturally deviant. Thus an egalitarian parent's belief that boys should learn to be nurturant conflicts with the gender schema that labels nurturance as a violation of masculine norms. The result is that even egalitarian parents at best allow their sons to play with dolls, as the conversation quoted in chapter 1 exemplifies. Since nurturance is at the core of the female gender schema, parents will experience no conflict when their daughters play with dolls and may actively encourage doll play.

Adults know that infants will become gendered adults and they see that endpoint as inevitable. As parents, they are cognitively primed to look for the seeds of sex differences and, therefore, to interpret ambiguous data in that light. Boys will grow up to become men who wash the family car and do not cry. Girls will grow up to become women who wash the dishes and cry at sad movies. In short, adults perceive children as apprentice adults.

Turning Play into Work

In the Hamburg Art Museum hangs a painting entitled *Der Kinders-tube—The Nursery—*by Fritz von Uhde. The scene—a pleasant room with blue wallpaper, a parquet floor, and pink curtains at a window opening onto a small balcony beyond—seduces the viewer. A large iron crib stands along the left wall, and a round wooden table is in the right foreground. In the room are three girls and a woman.

At the center a small child—she looks about four years old—holds a doll by the hands, as if dancing with it. On the floor in front of her are another doll and some toy trees. She is the only person in the picture whose entire face is visible. She gazes directly ahead, as if looking at the viewer, who has just entered the room. To her left is a somewhat older child, perhaps six years old. She sprawls somewhat awkwardly on a child's chair with her legs slightly apart. Looking toward her left, she smiles at the doll perched on her left leg. Nearby is a doll's carriage with another doll inside.

In the background, an older girl, perhaps nine years old, sits composedly and neatly at a window, her head bent over her sewing. Her right leg is crossed over her left, which does not quite reach the floor, because she is sitting on a chair intended for adults. As our eyes follow the scene around to the right, we see a woman in bare quarter-profile with her back toward the table and her face toward the window. Her head is also bent, and she is knitting something with several needles, perhaps a sock. She sits on the same kind of chair as the nine-year-old. On the table are knitting and sewing baskets and an assortment of dolls.

The painting takes us through female development, from play with dolls and doll carriages to sewing and knitting, from facing the viewer head on to being almost invisible. Though painted in 1899, *Der Kinderstube* remains an accurate portrayal of little girls' progress from toys to chores, as the data reviewed in the next section show.

Children's Chores

Parents not only look for the seeds of sex difference early on, they cultivate them. The data on children's chores show that girls over five years old not only spend more time at household tasks than boys do, they also begin their tasks at an earlier age (see Goodnow 1988 for a review). Children's work is divided along the same gender lines as parents' work. That is, girls "specialize" in cooking and cleaning—jobs that need to be performed frequently—while boys are assigned chores that need to be performed less often—such as garbage removal and outdoor work (White & Brinkerhoff 1981).

Because parents see infrequent tasks as ones that call for payment, they are not likely to pay a daughter, for example, for washing the dishes, but they will pay a son for washing the family car. Except for babysitting and restaurant work, girls are less likely to market their skills outside the family than boys are. Girls do not earn money by cleaning bathrooms, vacuuming, dusting, cooking, or washing dishes at other people's homes—perhaps because those jobs are already performed by the woman of the house. Paying jobs like mowing neighbors' lawns, shoveling snow, and washing windows are, in contrast, often performed by boys, perhaps because, even though the jobs are defined as masculine, the man of the house isn't getting them done.

Children do not passively float through their environment. They try to make sense of it. They form generalizations. The sexual division of their own household labor provides children with data about the implications of sex differences (see Eagly 1987, and Hoffman & Hurst 1990, on the sexual division of labor). Children can rightly conclude that females do the jobs that have to be done daily or more frequently, while males' jobs are occasional. That situation implies that females are more closely connected to and defined by household work than males are. In fact, it even sounds odd to call masculine tasks like emptying the garbage housework.

From the data they gather on chore allocation, children have reason to conclude that the tasks males perform have monetary value but the tasks females perform do not. Children have reason to think that boys labor for payment, while girls labor "for love" (Goodnow 1988).[4]

A story a woman's in-laws told her about her husband Joe's childhood illustrates how early boys learn to expect payment. When only three years old, Joe proposed to his grandmother, who lived with the family, that he would empty her bedroom wastebasket for a quarter. He had learned—precociously—that some tasks are worth money and that if you are a boy it is acceptable to try to bargain for compensation, even from your grandmother.

The early division of household chores along gender lines accustoms boys and girls to seeing their contributions to the household differently. Yet, it should be noted, there is little direct evidence of cause-and-effect relationships. There are no data, for example, to demonstrate that boys who take out the garbage are more likely to take it out as adults than boys who do not—even though it sounds reasonable. Here, as in many areas, while we know there are sex differences among adults and apparently corresponding differences in the way adults treat children, we do not know which, if any, of the early experiences are causally related to adult behavior (Eccles & Blumenfeld 1985).

Some data, however, do suggest that performing household chores is related to showing concern for others in the family. One study queried mothers, and children between twelve and fourteen, about the children's performance of household chores (Grusec, Goodnow, & Cohen 1996). The investigators looked particularly at chores that benefited the household (such as cleaning up after dinner) and compared children who performed the chores on a regular basis with those who were requested to perform them. The children, especially girls, who regularly did chores without being asked were more likely to show spontaneous concern for others in the household than those who carried out such tasks only when specifically requested to do so. One reason the effects were limited to girls may be that girls perform many more chores on a regular basis than boys do. Girls are led to take more moment-to-moment responsibility for what goes on in the home than boys are.

Gender and Play

Children's play becomes gender-differentiated even earlier than their household chores. Little girls and boys have many playthings in common, such as clay, puzzles, small blocks, records, and books (Fagot 1985). In addition to such gender-neutral play, many boys and girls engage in both masculine and feminine play. Many little girls like trucks, as well as dolls, and at least some little boys play with both dolls and fire engines. Even children who play with both, however, are likely to spend more of their time playing with the toys that "match" their sex—a pattern that emerges as early as one year of age (see below). Girls play with dolls more than they do with vehicles, and the converse is true for boys.

We do not know exactly how children's toy preferences develop. One study of how fathers react to their one-year-olds does suggest how parents may affect children's preferences, and also illustrates the consistent finding that fathers are more concerned that their sons behave like boys than that their daughters act like girls (Snow, Jacklin, & Maccoby 1983). Fathers were observed playing in a room with their twelve-month-old sons or daughters. On a shelf within the babies' sight but out of reach were two dolls, two trucks, a toy vacuum cleaner, and a shovel. The question of interest was which toys the fathers would give to their children.

Fathers of sons gave the boys a truck about twice as often as they gave them a doll. Fathers of daughters gave the girls a doll about as often as they gave them a truck. Compared to fathers of daughters, fathers of sons gave the boys a doll only half as often. The fathers in both groups gave trucks equally often. Thus, fathers were much more concerned about the gender identification of the toys their sons played with than they were about the gender of the toys their daughters played with. Girls were given greater flexibility in their choices.

I repeat the conversation quoted in chapter 1 here because it summarizes the data just reviewed perfectly:

She:　If we have a girl, I'll get her a truck.
He:　Of course.
She:　If we have a boy, I'll get him a doll.
He:　Well . . . If he *asks* for one.

Although the baby has yet to be conceived, this father-to-be, like the fathers in the study, wants his son to be masculine more than he wants his daughter to be feminine. (An alternative interpretation is that he sees dolls as feminine and trucks as neutral.) Also like the fathers in the study, this future father seems determined not to offer his son a doll unless the child specifically requests it.

In the same study (Snow et al. 1983), boys who were given dolls played with them for a shorter time than did girls who were given dolls. Girls and boys given trucks, however, played with them for the same amount of time, although there was a slight tendency for boys to play with them longer. The children's toy preferences along traditional gender lines had thus begun by the age of twelve months, to be completed as infant girls' interest in masculine toys wanes—or is suppressed—in the course of development.

There are two possible explanations of children's early toy preferences. The first is that children develop their preferences independently of parents' attitudes. The second is that parents influence their children's choices at an early age. A study of parents of three- to five-year-olds suggests that the second explanation is more likely. It examined how parents respond to children's selection of toys (Langlois & Downs 1980).[5] Mothers reacted favorably when either boys or girls chose feminine toys but were especially likely to praise or show affection to girls when they made feminine choices. Mothers tended to reward their children's choices (by praising, helping, or showing affection) instead of punishing them (by, for example, interfering with children's play or ridiculing the children) for nontraditional choices. Thus, mothers were relatively permissive, but looked especially favorably on the "girllike" actions of their daughters.

Fathers reacted somewhat differently. They rewarded boys for masculine choices and punished them for feminine choices. Similarly, they rewarded girls for feminine choices and punished them for masculine ones. Thus, fathers made clear, in a way that mothers did not, what toys their children should prefer. They were particularly likely to reward boys for masculine choices (Langlois & Downs 1980).

It appears, then, that both mothers and fathers want their children of the same sex to conform to gender norms. It may instead be, however, that each parent is simply most knowledgeable about how their own gender is expected to behave: mothers know more about feminine norms, and fathers know more about masculine norms.

It is worth emphasizing the important differences in the way mothers and fathers in this study used rewards and punishments. Regardless of the child's sex, mothers tended to use reward more often than punishment. With girls, fathers too used reward more often than punishment, but with boys they were more likely to use punishment. Fathers thus enforce gender norms more vigorously than mothers do—not only by approving of "appropriate" choices but by disapproving of "inappropriate" choices, particularly boys' feminine choices.

How, then, do the research findings about children's early play and chores fit together? Little girls play with dolls, feeding them, changing their diapers, dressing them in different outfits, and putting them to bed. Doll play is direct practice for the child care they will perform if they become mothers. Middle-class girls also decorate dollhouses, move the furniture around, and play with miniature tea sets. They play "house" and "dress-up." On television, they see cunning miniature refrigerators with tiny plastic ice-cube dispensers and a light that goes on when you open the door. Here, too, girls' play is practice for the kitchen work and home decoration they are likely to be in charge of as adults. A great deal of girls' play imitates what they will do in earnest as women: take responsibility for the well-being of others, decorate their houses, decorate themselves. Were boys to spend time playing with dolls, they would learn the same skills; but boys spend little time with dolls.

Although play is intrinsically enjoyable, adults help children learn what to enjoy. Adults portray little girls' play—mock housework and child care—as fun for girls, and most girls seem to agree. With that background of enjoyment, it would be surprising if the pleasure did not linger when play was transformed into work. Instead of a doll to care for, a real baby; instead of playing house, real tea sets to buy, real tabletops to dust, real dishes to wash, real refrigerators to open, real food to prepare. Little girls' play with dolls and dollhouses evolves into older girls' and women's work.

Adults thus prepare girls for their grown-up role in two ways. First, they give little girls dolls to play with; as play is fun—by definition— and is performed purely for pleasure, pleasure becomes associated with housework and child care. Moreover, in playing "mother" the child experiences, momentarily, the mother's role and the power associated with it. Second, adults assign girls chores that duplicate those they will perform as adults. In this way, girls' childhood play and household chores provide a solid foundation for women's household responsibilities, fostering the familiar picture of women as nurturers and caretakers. The painter von Uhde intuitively understood this evolution: he shows play becoming housework within the frame of a single painting portraying female development from age four to adulthood.

Adults prepare boys differently. Fathers in particular encourage play that rarely involves being responsible for another's welfare and is seldom direct practice for adult work. Boys do not, in their play, pretend to be taking out the garbage or washing the car. If their play does involve responsibility, as in playing a firefighter, the role is one for which adults are paid. Most of boys' play, however, has no adult counterpart as work; it remains play.

Boys are, for example, encouraged to engage in rough-and-tumble games with other boys, to play cops-and-robbers and cowboys, to build and ride vehicles of all sorts, and to participate in sports. Most boys do not, however, become professional boxers, cops, robbers, cowboys, truck drivers, or athletes. Boys' play turns not into work, but into men's play. Older boys and men play or watch sports, hunt, practice target shooting, and pursue hobbies. They watch films whose main protagonists are cowboys, male athletes, or male criminals and law enforcers (whose vehicles careen and crash as toys do).

Girls' play shades imperceptibly into housework; boys' play remains play.

Boys and girls thus receive long apprenticeships in their respective activities. That is not to say that children are unformed lumps of clay being sculpted by their environment. Children come equipped with certain mental structures and predispositions—the most important of which, perhaps, is the capacity to form explanatory theories and hypotheses. (I discuss how that capacity mediates children's developing understanding of gender in chapter 3.) Nor do I argue that the gender-differentiated activities children engage in have no inherent appeal; the play of both girls and boys is intrinsically satisfying.

Yet each kind of play also seems to be something of an acquired taste. Some girls never acquire a taste for dolls, and some boys never learn to like sports. At the same time, some children glory in their gender roles from an early age. By the age of two some boys are daredevils and some girls are coquettes. Most children, however, take longer to learn what they like. Both nurturant play and physical play may require years of nourishing by adults.

At present our culture divides the nourishing along gender lines. It is as if we took half the children and encouraged an interest in writing, and took the other half and supported only an interest in drawing. Some children might well be naturally drawn to one or the other activity without adult intervention, because they are both inherently gratifying. Without instruction, though, most children would not discover the pleasures of either. Since drawing is not taught in contemporary U.S. culture, most children and adults do not draw. Yet in the nineteenth century, skill in drawing was common among the English middle classes.

What would happen if children were not given years of practice in either nurturant or physical play? We don't know. As things stand, children learn to enjoy only half of what is potentially open to them, the half adults give them access to. Girls learn to take pleasure in being nurturant, and boys learn to take pleasure in physical skills. Girls' increasing interest in sports shows how quickly some of them acquire a taste for physical activity. We have yet to provide boys with a parallel opportunity for nurturance.

Injustice at Home

The gender differences evident in children's work and play come to fruition when adults form partnerships and establish homes. Almost all employed women in heterosexual relationships live in households where the division of labor is grossly and visibly inequitable. Studies of housework show that women perform far more than their fair share (e.g., Robinson 1988; Biernat & Wortman 1991). The imbalance exists among all groups of women who live with men, including professional women. Married women who work for pay average about thirty-three hours of housework per week—about two-thirds of the total household work. Married men who are employed do fourteen to eighteen hours of housework a week (e.g., Lennon & Rosenfield 1994, from 1987–88 data; Blair & Lichter 1991, from 1988 data).[6] These figures do not distinguish between housework and child care because of the difficulty of apportioning tasks. When a man makes dinner for his children, for example, is that housework or child care? To solve that problem, many studies query people about specific tasks, such as making dinner.

One study queried both women who primarily work in corporations and academia and their husbands (Biernat & Wortman 1991). Overall, the partners had roughly equal professional commitments and responsibilities. The women, who were slightly better educated than their husbands and a few years younger, earned somewhat less money and were more intensely involved in their jobs. Despite their rough equality in the workplace, the men and women were not equal at home.

Questioned independently, the wives and husbands agreed that the wives carried out more of all child care tasks but one—playing with the children. In that one area, the partners were equally involved. Yet when they rated themselves as parents, the women expressed more guilt than men about not being a better parent. Moreover, the women gave their husbands higher marks as parents than the men gave themselves. Many professional women apparently believe they should bear the major responsibility for children and rate their husbands as good parents even though they do less than their share of child care.

Survey data show that most married men and women who work see nothing wrong with an unequal division of labor at home (Lennon & Rosenfield 1994; Sanchez 1994; for qualitative analyses, see Hochschild 1989). In one study of couples employed outside the home, about 67 percent of men and 60 percent of women said that the unequal division of labor in their households was fair (Lennon & Rosenfield 1994). In another study, 72 percent of husbands and 66 percent of wives saw the unequal division as fair (Sanchez 1994).

Men and women also agree about the cut-off points in perceptions of fairness. Men perceive doing an almost equal amount of household labor—48 percent—as unfair to themselves; they see the division as fair to both parties when they are doing just 36 percent of the work. Only when their wives average just over 70 percent of the work do husbands see the inequality as unfair (Lennon & Rosenfield 1994).

Married women who work have similar cut-off points. They do not find the division of labor unfair to themselves until they are doing about 75 percent of the household work. When they are doing 66 percent of the work they judge the division as fair to both parties. Women even see the division as unfair to their husbands when they, the wives, are doing close to 60 percent of the work. These perceptions held even when the investigators corrected for factors that should be important in determining fairness—such as differences in education, age, ethnic group, or hours spent working outside the home (Lennon & Rosenfield 1994). Men and women are in basic agreement: women should do most of the household work.

Economic factors account for some of the differences in time spent working at home, but less than one might expect. One hypothesis based on economics is that men do less work than women at home because they do more work than women outside the home. An arrangement whereby men spend more time working outside the home than women do might itself have an economic basis—men can earn more money than women—or it might be due to gender schemas that portray men as naturally belonging outside the house and women as naturally belonging inside it. Whatever the source, once an unequal arrangement is in place, couples may act to equalize the division of their total labor.

A different economic hypothesis suggests that the partner who makes more money has more power and, therefore, does less work at home. The more powerful partner can buy his or her way out of housework. Here, too, the situation in which male and female partners are unequally compensated may originate in gender schemas that measure a male's worth according to his professional status but apply a different standard to a woman. Once an external inequality is in place, it can generate further internal inequalities.

There are two different ways to test such economic hypotheses. The first method looks at households in terms of differences between partners' earnings, time spent working outside the home, and amount of housework performed. Economic hypotheses would predict that as the husbands and wives approach equality outside the home they will also approach equality in household labor. (The increase in equality could result from hiring outside help, the man's undertaking more household tasks, the woman's performing fewer tasks, or a combination of all three.)

The second method of testing would select households in which both partners have full-time jobs to which they are equally committed and from which they earn approximately equal salaries. Economic hypotheses would predict that housework would be equally divided among such couples.

Studies that examine the relation between outside income and housework do not, however, support the predictions. They find only a limited correlation between salary and the number of hours men spend at housework. In dual-earner couples, men do not do more housework as women make more money (Blair & Lichter 1991, from 1988 survey data). Nor does the size of the disparity in salary affect how much housework men do. In fact, the absolute number of hours males contribute to household work is affected by relatively few variables. Men do little housework, period.

Among the variables that do influence the amount of housework males carry out is the number of hours they or their partners work outside the home. As men work longer hours away from home, they perform somewhat less housework; and as their partners work longer hours, the men perform somewhat more housework (Blair & Lichter 1991; Ferree 1991). Time availability is, therefore, a modest factor in determining how much work men do. Another factor with a modest effect on the division of labor is beliefs about sharing household tasks. In households where people express the belief that housework should be shared equally, men perform somewhat more work (Blair & Lichter 1991; Ferree 1991; Starrels 1994, from 1981 survey data).

The *proportion* of housework males perform is larger among those with female partners who earn higher salaries and have more education. Coupled with the finding that such female characteristics do not affect the *absolute* amount of work men do, the men's higher proportion appears to be due primarily to women's spending less time on housework. A woman's earning power and high education results in her doing less housework but does not necessarily result in her male partner's doing more. Instead, since she does less, his constant contribution becomes a larger percentage of the whole.

Men and women who want an equitable relationship could take the following message from the data reviewed thus far. Equality in housework is approached—but not reached—when the partners work equal hours outside the home and have equal incomes and education. Yet even the combination of those economic factors is not sufficient to guarantee equality. Household labor is disproportionately done by women, even when they have professional full-time jobs to which they are deeply committed (Biernat & Wortman, 1991). Earnings and hours spent outside the home have some effect on housework time but fail to account for all the sex differences (South & Spitze 1994).

One of the most puzzling aspects of the research findings is women's own view that the markedly unequal division of labor is fair. Could economic factors explain their perception? Here, too, economics seems to play only a modest role. The percentage of a couple's income earned by the woman does not affect perceptions of fairness (Lennon & Rosenfield 1994). Nor do the number of hours either partner works outside the home account for women's perceptions of fairness (Lennon & Rosenfield 1994).

The partner's sex always influences the household division of labor more than economic differences. Economic equality helps, but it does not guarantee an equitable division. Explicit beliefs about equality at home also help, but—even when combined with equal work commitment, equal salary, and equal education—do not guarantee a fifty-fifty split of household work.

Explaining Inequity at Home

On the face of it, the inequity between men and women in their work at home is mysterious. Why doesn't the man *want* to do his share? In the workplace slackers exist, but they are looked down on by others. On the job, most people are willing to do their share and feel some shame if they do not. Why doesn't the man want to take care of his children? And, even if he doesn't want to do his share, why doesn't the woman insist on it? In a two-person relationship in which both partners work outside the home, a woman should be in a good position to demand and receive equity. The facts are simple: housework and child care have to be done; there are two people to do it.

There are, then, two things to be explained: why men behave at home in a way they would find unacceptable at work; and why women accept an inequitable division of labor. One part of the explanation is that both men and women see equity as a relevant concept in the workplace, but neither sees the home as a workplace (see Prentice & Crosby 1987 for a related point). The sexual division of children's play and labor induces both boys and girls to see housework and child care as women's responsibility, a responsibility that, ideally, is performed with love and pleasure. If housework, especially child care, is a woman's labor of love, equity does not come into the picture.

Because child care is a labor of love, a woman who insists on equity seems heartless. She appears—even to herself—to be someone who does not love her children. If she lies in bed while the baby cries, telling her husband that it is his turn to get up, she is perceived as cold and unfeeling. Even though it *is* his turn and he should know that without being told, even though he should be subliminally listening for the baby's cry and leap out of bed the moment he hears it, he is not a monster—either to himself or to the baby's mother—if he does none of those things but mumbles that he is too tired. From the perspective of fairness, none of this makes sense. Yet boys and girls spend years learning that fairness is irrelevant at home.

Women are educated to specialize in love, and for many of them love yields real rewards. It is a pleasure to soothe and kiss a baby, to be the recipient of a baby's smile. The father who does not leap up at the baby's

cry misses those pleasures. What finally enmeshes women in their inequitable situation is the real joy to be gained from exercising their duty, a
pleasure most men have not developed a taste for.

The result is that men do not perceive themselves as getting a free ride,
anymore than women see themselves as giving one. Women have learned
to help others directly, by caring for them, even if that help comes at their
own expense. Men, on the other hand, have learned to help others indirectly, by earning money to provide material well-being and educational
opportunities.

Another part of the explanation is that, because of their years of training in nonoverlapping roles, both men and women define certain jobs as
feminine and others as masculine. A woman is less of a woman if she
does not make a house a home, and a man is less of a man if he does.
Both sexes feel that way. The cartoon character Dagwood, who came to
the door in an apron, was a figure of fun because he donned a feminine
role. Since the cultural definition of a man—as the research on parental
responses to toy choices indicates—is less flexible than that of a woman,
a man finds it particularly difficult to retain his identity as a man if he
performs feminine jobs.

A third part of the explanation is that men tend to compare themselves
to other men and that women compare themselves to other women (Major 1993). Because most men do little housework or child care, an individual man comparing himself to other men (e.g., his father; see Hochschild
1989) can easily feel that he is behaving appropriately when he follows
their example. Similarly, the role of other women (e.g., her mother) as
homemaker and child-rearer can easily convince an individual woman
that her burden is normal (Thompson 1991).

By the same token, when partners compare their spouses to others, they
are likely to do so along gender lines. So, if a husband thinks about how
much housework and child care his wife does, he will compare her with
what he knows of other women and conclude that she is only doing what
is normal; if a wife compares the amount of housework her husband does
with what she knows of other men, she will see her husband as normal—
or even a bit better than average.

An additional measure of household power is related to women's perceptions of fairness. Women who believe that their standard of living,

social life, and career opportunities would be diminished by separating from their partners are somewhat more likely than others to see an unequal division of housework as fair. Similarly, women who think their standard of living would drop below the poverty line if they left their partners are somewhat more likely than other women to judge an unfair division of labor as fair (Lennon & Rosenfield, 1994). Overall, however, how much a woman has to lose by ending her marriage makes a relatively modest contribution to her perceptions of fairness.

Although both sexes misperceive their living situation, women are more likely than men to perceive the unfairness accurately (Lennon & Rosenfield 1994; Sanchez 1994). Why, then, do women who see the injustice allow it to continue? One reason is that there are costs—not all of them monetary—to perceiving injustice. Women who acknowledge the unfairness of their living situation are more depressed than those who deny it (Lennon & Rosenfield 1994). Another reason is that many women do not know how to rectify the problem. They do not see the home as an arena in which negotiation and bargaining are appropriate, even though calm negotiation might benefit both parties (Mahony 1995; Carter, with Peters 1996).

Newspaper and magazine articles about heterosexual women who work outside the home typically pose the question of how *women* can handle both their household and job responsibilities. It is young *women* who are especially concerned about how they will combine a professional life with having a family. From an Olympian perspective, there is an inexplicable lacuna. Why are there so few articles posing the question of how *men* can handle both their household and job responsibilities? What about the problem of "working fathers," of men who work "outside the home"? What about the problem of educating men so that their lack of training in child care and household work can be remedied? What about children's need for *two* nurturing and involved parents?

Instead, the usual solutions proffered to solve "women's" problem are higher-quality, more affordable, more widely available child care; flexible work hours; and family-leave policies. All those improvements are needed, but they fail to question the way the problem is framed. They do not ask why combining work and family is a female problem rather than a human problem, and thus do not address it as a human problem.

Childhood training in the sexual division of household labor is so powerful that few males or females ask who will bring up the children, let alone question who will *want* to bring them up. So strong is the perception of household inequity as normal that people see no need to explain it, do not perceive it as an injustice, do not see that men are missing a valuable experience, and do not plan realistically how to avoid inequity. People realize there is something wrong with an intimate relationship in which one person physically abuses the other but fail to see that something is wrong when one person bears more than half the burden of work.

As I mentioned above, neither men nor women think of their home as a negotiation site. That reluctance makes it difficult for couples to plan how to avoid work–home conflicts or to negotiate such conflicts when they arise. Yet, unless both parties are willing to resolve conflicts so that sometimes the male's and sometimes the female's work life suffers, there will be no change. Change will occur only when each partner believes that the other should have an equal chance for professional and domestic fulfillment and works to make fairness a daily reality. Change will occur only when both partners agree that their household arrangements should pass on the message of fairness to their children. Finally, long-term gender equality can only originate in homes that give children two functioning parents, not one who functions and another who earns money.

In the following words from 1958, Eleanor Roosevelt was not specifically addressing gender equality in the home, but her eloquent statement is a fitting end to this chapter. "Where, after all, do universal human rights begin? . . . In small places, close to home. . . . Such are the places where every man, woman and child seeks equal justice, equal opportunity, equal dignity."

3

Learning About Gender

Children "master" their culture's gender divisions at a relatively young age, a fact that testifies both to the ubiquity of gender cues in the culture and to children's ability to develop gender schemas. Gender schemas are in place before the child begins the first grade. Children perceive social behavior through gender schemas, just as adults do. Although there is still much to understand about *how* children learn about gender, we know a great deal about *what* they learn.

In talking about the development of knowledge about gender, a variety of partially-linked concepts is relevant. One concept, *gender discrimination,* refers to the child's ability to perceptually distinguish between human males and females. That ability is usually tested by showing children photographs or drawings of people's heads and shoulders. A little after the age of two, children can label adults by sex, although they are closer to three years old before they can reliably label children (Fagot & Leinbach 1993). The secondary male and female characteristics we rely on to make sex discriminations are better developed in adults' faces than in children's. Yet even some five-month-old infants can use such tertiary characteristics as hair length and clothing to distinguish between the sexes. The child in the restaurant in chapter 2 was hard to categorize precisely because its primary sex characteristics were hidden by clothing, its secondary characteristics had not yet developed, and the parents had left tertiary characteristics ambiguous. To make my judgment, I therefore had to rely on a characteristic of the parent—how he spoke to the child— rather than a characteristic of the child.

Another concept, *gender stability,* refers to the child's understanding that one's sex is fixed for life. This concept develops after children can label correctly, but it is mastered by many children by the age of four (Fagot 1985; Slaby & Frey 1975). *Gender constancy*—the knowledge that someone's sex is not altered by adopting behaviors more characteristic of the other sex—varies much more. But most children know by age eight that a girl with short hair is still a girl and a boy who wears a skirt is still a boy (Frey & Ruble 1992). Even adults, though, sometimes say things like So-and-so is not a man, or a woman, because of his or her dress or manner. The book title *Real Men Don't Eat Quiche,* for example, alludes to how well an individual conforms to gender norms, not to the person's biological classification.

Yet another concept, *gender schema knowledge,* refers to the child's knowledge that certain objects—such as a hammer or an iron—are associated with different sexes, that girls and boys tend to play in different ways and with different toys, that males and females tend to display different psychological traits, and that men and women are likely to have different occupations. Children demonstrate their awareness of gender schemas before they are three years old by categorizing toys, games, clothing, and household objects by gender (Huston 1983). They become progressively more aware of the range of characteristics and behaviors embraced by gender schemas as they develop; by the age of six, children are experts at gender schemas.

Cognitive Components of Gender Knowledge

Gender labeling, gender constancy, and gender schema knowledge all reflect children's knowledge of the characteristics that are culturally associated with each sex, whether the characteristics are physical, psychological, occupational, or attitudinal. Those abilities appear, then, to be cognitive achievements on the child's part. If so, they should be related to children's other cognitive achievements—unrelated to gender—and they are. Schema knowledge, for example, is significantly related to purely cognitive measures of development, such as the child's ability to judge that the weight of a substance stays the same even if its shape is changed (Serbin, Powlishta, & Gulka 1993).

Childrens' developing knowledge of gender schemas is also related to the development of their preferences and behaviors. One example of the association between gender labeling and behavior comes from a cross-sectional study that observed a group of children between the ages of one year and nine months and three years and six months (Fagot, Leinbach & Hagan 1986). Children who could respond accurately to the labels *boy* and *girl* spent more time playing with peers of their own sex than did children who could not reliably distinguish between drawings of boys and girls. Further, girls who had mastered the labels were significantly less aggressive than girls who had not, as well as less aggressive than boys, whether or not the boys had mastered the labels. The results for girls are particularly interesting, since they suggest that girls' early aggression diminishes as they learn to apply the label *girl* to themselves. Not all behaviors, however, were related to gender labeling: preferences for sex-typical masculine or feminine toys, for example, were marked even in children who could not supply gender labels reliably.

Another study, which observed children first at the age of one year and six months and again at two years and three months, also found links between gender labeling and behavior (Fagot & Leinbach 1989). At the first observation, none of the children could apply gender labels, and girls and boys were equal on a wide variety of measures, including what kinds of toys they played with and how much aggression they showed. At two and a quarter years old, half of the children could apply gender labels; those who could spent more time playing with sex-typical toys than those who could not apply gender labels. And, as in the cross-sectional study, girls who could apply gender labels showed less aggression than girls who could not as well as less than either group of boys.

Although a developmental association between gender labeling and behavior is apparent, the underlying reason for it is not. One possibility is that children's developing gender knowledge influences their behavior. Say, for example, that girls learn to apply gender labels and also learn that aggression is associated with the label for boys but not the label for girls. Once girls label themselves as girls, they realize that any aggressive behavior they might be tempted to engage in is inappropriate. Like adults, children tend to compare themselves with similar others. To be consistent with other members of the group they now see themselves as part of, they alter their behaviors. The timing between gender labeling and aggression reduction in girls is some evidence for this possibility.

A second possibility is essentially the opposite—that children's developing behavior contributes to their knowledge of gender labels. Parental admonitions in response to a behavior could cause a girl to reduce her aggression or a boy to reduce his crying. Especially if accompanied by statements that "girls don't hit" or "boys don't cry," the admonitions could encourage the child to develop knowledge of gender differences.

Yet a third possibility is that knowledge of labels and gender-appropriate behavior develop in tandem, each resulting from inferences the child draws from adults' behavior and expectations. The child receives encouragement to behave in one way or another and simultaneously attempts to understand the gender divisions it observes. The fact that children show gender-stereotyped toy preferences (i.e., behavior) before they can accurately apply gender labels supports the hypothesis of separate but parallel lines of development.

On balance, the evidence favors no single possibility to the exclusion of the others and is most compatible with the conclusion that all three processes occur simultaneously. Children's knowledge of gender schemas affects their behaviors; their behaviors influence their schemas; environmental influences affect both schemas and behaviors. (Chapter 4 considers the role of hormones in the development of sex differences.)

Influences of Adults and Peers

As the studies cited earlier suggest, children's aggression appears to be learned, at least in part. An observational study of infants thirteen months old found that the boys and girls made the same kinds of attempts to communicate with their day care teachers (Fagot, Hagan, Leinbach, & Kronsberg 1985). The teachers, however, responded to them differentially. When the babies gestured, babbled, or talked, the teachers paid more attention to girls. When they demanded physical attention, whined, cried, or screamed, the teachers responded more to boys.

The children were observed again nine to eleven months later. By then, the children's attempts to communicate had diverged. The girls talked to the teacher more frequently than the boys did, and the boys whined, cried, and screamed more often than the girls did.

Thus, when the children were young and behaving similarly, teachers geared their reactions to a combination of the child's gender and behavior. "Girllike" behavior from girls and "boylike" behavior from boys got reactions from teachers. The reasonable conclusion for a baby girl to draw in that situation is that talking is the best way to get results. The reasonable conclusion for a baby boy to draw is that whining, crying, and screaming are the best ways to get results. Those appear, in fact, to be the conclusions that the children drew. When the children were older and differed in their efforts at communication, the teachers geared their reactions primarily to the children's behavior, not their sex. But by that time, the sex differences in the children were well established.

In the beginning, the children were also equally aggressive; boys and girls grabbed for objects, hit, pushed, or kicked with the same frequency. Here too the teachers geared their reactions to a combination of the child's gender and behavior. They ignored girls' aggression 80 percent of the time but disregarded boys' aggression only 34 percent of the time. Nine to eleven months later, the girls were less aggressive, and the boys were more aggressive than the girls. The girls had learned that aggression did not pay off in increased teacher attention, and the boys had learned the opposite lesson.

The teachers' behavior is understandable. They expected infant girls to become verbally sophisticated and therefore paid attention to the first seeds of emotionally neutral communication. Believing that girls' aggression would never become a problem, they assumed it could be safely ignored. With boys, the teachers probably had a different set of assumptions. Boys, they believed, can become behavior problems, so firmness is needed in dealing with any signs of negative behavior, especially aggression. The data suggest, however, that paying attention to a child's behavior increases it; even negative attention is somewhat gratifying. Teachers' responses may thus be counterproductive, increasing exactly what they want to decrease.

Such studies are suggestive but cannot be definitive, because they demonstrate only a temporal sequence, not a direct cause-and-effect link. They suggest that boys' and girls' behaviors are initially very similar but— as adults respond to children on the basis of their own beliefs about sex differences—their behavior acquires the characteristics that we associate with each sex. We know that expectation effects—in which people act as they are expected to—are common among adults. Children may well respond in a similar fashion (Fagot et al. 1985).

That possibility is consistent with the research reviewed in chapter 2, which shows that adults (especially fathers) perceive babies differentially at birth, that fathers treat boys and girls differently even before the age of one year, and that gender differences in babies' toy preferences are already apparent by the end of the first year. It is thus not surprising that gender differences become even more extensive as development proceeds.

Another study looked at young children's aggression and their teachers' and peers' reactions to it (Fagot & Hagan 1985). The researchers observed toddlers in three age groups: a year and a half to two years; two to two and a half; and two-and-a-half to just under three years old. In all age groups, boys were more physically aggressive than girls, which is consonant with the assumption that differences in aggression develop during the second year of life. The investigators looked both at how teachers and peers responded to a child's aggression, and at how the aggressive child reacted to others' responses.

As in the study of one-year-olds, teachers reacted differently to the aggressive behavior of boys and girls; so did other children. Both teachers and peers ignored girls' aggression half of the time but ignored boys' less than a third of the time. Teachers and peers were much more likely to respond negatively to boys—for example, by criticizing or physically restraining them—than to girls.[1] In the two older groups, both boys and girls were most likely to continue being aggressive if they received a *negative* reaction to their aggression. (In the youngest group, aggression was very brief, no matter how teachers and peers reacted.) A child's early aggression may simply be an uncontrolled response to frustration. A negative reaction from adults or peers may then exacerbate the frustration: the child not only fails to get what it wants, but is also being punished. Since boys get negative reactions more often than girls do, their aggression builds as a way to achieve their goal.

What was more effective in stopping children's aggression was ignoring the child or responding positively. Aggression was more likely to diminish, for example, if the adult gave the child physical affection, helped the child with a project, or talked to the child. Both boys and girls received some positive reactions; but, because boys received negative reactions more often and their aggression was ignored less often, boys overall received more feedback that increased their aggressiveness.

Aggression aside, teachers tend to react positively to all children when they engage in neutral play or play that is typical of girls (Fagot 1985). When children between one year and nine months and two years and one month were observed for several months, the investigator found that teachers reacted to the children's behavior rather than to their sex—perhaps the teachers saw neutral and feminine play as less disruptive and more easily managed or as good preparation for school (Brophy 1985).

The children's peers, however, responded differently. Girl peers reacted positively to other girls, whether the latter were engaged in feminine, masculine, or neutral play. In other words, girl peers responded on the basis of gender. Boy peers gave the most differentiated reactions: they behaved very positively toward boys who played in masculine ways and gave few positive reactions to boys who took part in feminine or neutral play. Boys seldom reacted favorably to girls, no matter what type of play the girls engaged in. Thus, boy peers restricted their positive responses to boys who played like boys.

In sum, teachers rewarded toddlers for feminine and neutral behavior, girls rewarded other girls regardless of their type of behavior, and boys rewarded boys who acted in a masculine way. From a cognitive point of view the study is very interesting. First, it shows that two-year-olds reliably distinguish girls from boys. Second, it shows that for girls, the kind of play other children engage in is less important than their playmates' sex. Girls of this age distinguish between the sexes but may not label different types of play as restricted to one sex or the other. Third, the study shows that boys make the finest distinctions: they distinguish other children on the basis of both sex and the gender style of play their peers engage in. Boys prefer boys who act like boys.

The same study also measured how likely children were to continue a particular form of play after receiving positive or negative reactions to it from a teacher, male peer, or female peer (Fagot 1985). The results provide an estimate of the relative importance of teachers and peers for children. Boys were primarily sensitive to male peers; if a male peer responded positively to a behavior, boys were more likely to continue it than if the peer responded negatively. The reactions of teachers and female peers were irrelevant; a boy was as likely to continue a behavior whether teachers or female peers responded positively or negatively. So, at the age of two, boys already control each others' behavior: they selectively reward stereotypically masculine behavior in other boys and continue activities boy peers reward. The girls were sensitive to teachers and other girls, but not to boys.

At least as early as two years old, then, girls and boys both have well-developed and different play preferences, respond differently to each other, are responded to differently by adults, and are differentially affected by others in their environment. Boys are particularly attuned to other boys and to stereotypically masculine behavior. Girls are affected by other girls and by teachers but do not differentiate between stereotypically masculine and feminine behavior as much as boys do. Girls' preferences appear to be more flexible. In this respect, two-year-olds are already like adults.

The data also point up a problem for teachers. Many studies have suggested that elementary and high school teachers give a disproportionate amount of their attention to boys (Brophy 1985; Eccles & Blumenfeld 1985; see also Sadker & Sadker, 1994). In part, that may be because boys demand more attention than girls do, but it may also be because boys are less susceptible to teachers' influence. To affect the behavior of boys—who are more tuned in to their male peers than to teachers—teachers must monitor them closely and make strong attempts to arouse their interest.

Both boys and girls, moreover, arrive at elementary school with fully developed beliefs about gender differences and with behaviors that are differentiated by gender. Even if teachers were to respond to children solely on the basis of children's behavior and not their sex, the teachers would inevitably respond in ways that reinforce gender differences—because the children's behaviors are already gendered. Teachers must work harder to engage boys in classroom activities and keep them focused on learning. On the other hand, teachers can safely "ignore" girls. Girls, even when they are inattentive, are quietly so, while inattentive boys are likely to be noisy and disruptive.[2]

Not only are boys more rigid in their toy preferences than girls are, but boys who enjoy feminine activities are seen as weaker and more deviant than girls who enjoy masculine activities (Archer 1992; Martin 1990; Smetana 1986). Masculine activities gradually acquire a superior status, initially through fathers' reactions to boys' choices of feminine activities and later through the disapproval of male peers. A study of three- and five-year-olds found that, while girls tended to be neutral about other girls' choices, boys were especially likely to punish their male peers for feminine choices by ridiculing them or interfering with their play physically or verbally (Langlois & Downs 1980).[3] Boys thus learn to devalue feminine activities and to shun them in order to avoid compromising their higher status. Boys cannot risk the stigma of being girllike.

Children's sensitivity to adults' and peers' reactions is apparent very early, at least as soon as the second year of life. After an apparent initial sensitivity to teachers, boys become particularly sensitive to other boys and relatively indifferent to teachers and girls. Fathers and male peers may have this disproportionate influence because they represent the wider—masculine—culture more completely than mothers, teachers, or girls do (see Lytton & Romney 1991, for father-mother comparisons). Girls, by contrast, are influenced both by teachers and other girls but are relatively indifferent to boys.

With each group tuned out to the other, the importance of same-sex groups increases. Boys are unlikely to discover the pleasures of stereotypically feminine activities if they are prevented by ridicule from engaging in them. Girls, similarly, will have little chance to explore the pleasures of stereotypically masculine activities if boys' opinions matter little to them or if they can't get positive recognition from boys during play with them.

"The Boys Don't Cheer": Children's Play in Middle Childhood

One of the most striking features of middle childhood is sex-segregated play. Although the segregation is not absolute, girls tend to play with girls and boys tend to play with boys. The reasons for this pattern are still obscure (see discussion in Maccoby & Jacklin 1987; Thorne 1993), but the segregation begins early and intensifies in the early school grades. Sex segregation appears to begin earlier for girls than for boys but is relatively well established for both sexes by the age of three. At four and a half, children spend three times as much time with children of the same sex as the other sex. At six and a half, they spend eleven times as much time with members of their own sex (see discussion and data in Maccoby 1988).[4]

Early training may account for some of the sex segregation in children's play. Boys, as we have seen, are urged to prefer masculine-typed toys and activities over feminine ones. Calling a boy a sissy, or even simply a girl, is an insult (Thorne 1993). The message is clear: it is degrading, demeaning, and weak for a boy to act like a girl. Girls are encouraged to choose feminine toys and activities, but they are freer than boys to engage in play primarily identified with the other sex. Girls may be told on occasion not to act like a boy, because it isn't "nice," but they are not ridiculed or demeaned in early childhood for having masculine interests.

By the time children enter elementary school, boys already see themselves as the sex with more power and the sex with something to lose by consorting with girls. Girls give boys "cooties," rather than the reverse; that is, girls contaminate boys. Girls designated as "cootie queens" are usually handicapped not only by sex but also by other characteristics, such as being overweight or poor (Thorne 1993). Boys go from being indifferent to girls in very early childhood, to actively avoiding them in public arenas like the playground by middle childhood.

Boys can display their superior power and influence when group decisions are being made. Males of all ages are more influential than females at such times; this is especially true when the task is seen as masculine (see the meta-analysis in Lockheed 1985). As children grow older, girls have increasing difficulty negotiating with boys, even though their style of verbal persuasion is effective with other girls (Powlishta & Maccoby 1990). Even among children under three years old, there are influence differences. Most girls, for example, withdraw when either boys or other girls tell them not to do something, but boys do not withdraw if girls express a prohibition (Jacklin & Maccoby 1978). Girls can't win in their interactions with boys.

Sex segregation thus appears to reflect two independent processes. Girls, for their part, avoid boys because they are often ineffective in their dealings with them (Maccoby & Jacklin 1987). In addition, some activities have become associated more with boys than with girls, as with certain toys and sports. Girls increasingly tend either to ignore those activities or to engage in them only with other girls.

Boys, on the other hand, shun girls to avoid the risk of being contaminated by girls' lower status and power. Boys' early indifference to girls becomes a necessity: if a boy were to be influenced by a girl that would demonstrate his own weakness. A boy cannot allow himself to be "henpecked." Activities that are associated more with girls than with boys must be devalued by boys.

A teacher asked his fourth-grade class why girls and boys didn't play soccer together at recess (Karkau 1976). The boys and many of the girls said that the girls could play but didn't want to. But one girl who did play occasionally said: "The boys never ask us to play. Then when we do play, only boys are chosen to be captains. And girls don't get the ball passed to them very often, and when a girl scores a goal, the boys don't cheer."

This quote, with terms suitably transposed, could describe adult professional life as well as fourth-grade recess. In the professions, men have the dominant positions and seldom choose women to be the equivalent of captain; nor do women get equal opportunities to perform. If you can't get your hands on the ball you can't show what you can do with it. Most evocative is the statement that "when a girl scores a goal, the boys don't cheer." A female's achievements are not recognized, and it's no fun playing when people don't acknowledge your contributions.

The girl's phrasing expresses her feelings of helplessness, her tacit acknowledgment that the boys run things, and her mystification about how it all came about. And there is something of a mystery here. Why don't the girls insist on playing, whether the boys ask them or not? Why don't the girls band together to elect other girls captain? Why don't the girls cheer each other and not worry about whether the boys cheer?

The mystery dissolves when we consider the children's history. By the fourth grade, sports have belonged to boys more than to girls for several years. Even at age six, boys rate themselves as better at sports than girls do (see summary in Jacobs & Eccles 1992). Because more boys are active in sports, they outnumber girls in team contexts. Further, boys have exercised more power and behaved more aggressively since toddlerhood. Finally, because of their longstanding beliefs about gender differences, boys frequently do not recognize girls' achievements.

If girls do not like competitive situations—and there is some evidence that girls enjoy competition less than boys do—the reason may lie not in an inherent dislike of competition but in girls' learned recognition that they can't win when they try to compete with boys.

Cultural Influences

The well-documented influence of adults and peers appears to owe some of its power to the surrounding culture. The culture's well-articulated norms about sex differences tend to overwhelm parental variables like education, income level, and occupation. Data from study to study show few clear effects of such variables (see review in Serbin et al. 1993 and Weiner & Wilson-Mitchell 1990). Children between kindergarten and the sixth grade whose mothers work outside the home, for example, appear no more likely to have gender-neutral preferences than children whose mothers do not. Nor does the mother's level of occupation or the father's educational attainments influence children's preferences. (Too few studies have examined ethnic differences for any conclusion to be drawn about subcultural differences.) In sum, parental education, parental income, and maternal employment outside the home have no substantial effects on children's preferences and behaviors. That is probably because most parents have similar gender schemas regardless of their economic and social status.

As chapter 2 detailed, in most households women do more than their fair share of the work. A study examining the effects on children of the type of housework parents do, asked parents who in their (heterosexual) family typically performed such tasks as cooking and taking out the garbage (Serbin et al. 1993). As expected, women were more likely to perform masculine tasks than men were to perform feminine tasks; that is, women were more likely to take out the garbage than men were to dust. The investigators looked separately at the effects of how many masculine tasks mothers performed and how many feminine tasks fathers performed. The results were limited and selective. Children had less-stereotyped occupational preferences if their mothers performed masculine as well as feminine tasks; but they were not affected by how many feminine tasks their fathers performed—probably because the fathers performed so few of them.

Other research supports a similar conclusion (Weiner & Wilson-Mitchell 1990). Children's occupational preferences are influenced by how egalitarian their parents are, but their clothing and hairstyle, type of play engaged in, and whether they play primarily with children of the same sex, are unaffected. That pattern is probably the joint effect of two influences. First, as discussed in chapter 2, even parents who are egalitarian conform to gender norms in many respects and treat their children in a sex-stereotyped fashion. Second, children may not perceive the parents' values if they conflict with dominant cultural values. At present, U.S. culture has fairly uniform norms about how children dress, what kind of play they engage in, and whom they play with. In the past decade or two, however, the culture has become more flexible concerning occupations. Thus, in the occupational arena, parents' differences in values have more of an opportunity to affect children's preferences than they do in areas like dress, where the culture is more restricted.

The major reason, then, that individual families have a limited impact on their children's development is that even families who believe in equality unwittingly treat their children differently on the basis of sex. Parents believe that they treat their sons and daughters identically, especially in the early years. And, as the meta-analysis mentioned in chapter 2 shows, parents do treat their children similarly in many domains. But in the area of gender, they do not. Parents' own gender schemas make them blind to the specific ways they perceive and treat their children differently.

Expectations and Children's School Performance

By the time they start school, children's gender schemas are almost fully formed and many gender differences in behavior are already in place. Children know which characteristics are associated with males and which with females. They know that males are "superior" to females in the eyes of the world. Boys already own most areas of achievement; girls' main dominion lies within the household.

Even if, from the time children started school, parents' and teachers' treatment of them was determined solely by children's actual behavior, children would continue to act in ways that are compatible with gender schemas and would continue to perceive more, and more extreme, gender differences than actually exist. Schools need do nothing to keep children's gender schemas securely in place. They would have to do a great deal to dislodge them.

Adults do not, in any event, respond to children solely in terms of their behavior. As I have shown, adults also respond to children in terms of gender schemas. In middle-class U.S. culture, parents emphasize doing well in school, and males and females achieve similar grades from grammar school through college. Parents do not, however, have the same hopes and aspirations for their sons and daughters. Parents' differing aspirations affect the courses their children take in school and the attitudes children bring to those courses.

For their son, parents want a professionally successful and financially secure future. A boy's life is influenced by his knowledge that he must make a living; he must be self-supporting. Parents hope, in addition, that their son will have a family, but they do not expect him to make sacrifices in his professional life for that family. Instead, parents see a son's professional success as a prerequisite for a family.

Such a perspective does not mean that parents view a son's future family as unimportant or as unlikely to require sacrifice. Parents can, and do, sincerely tell their son that the family comes first. To that end, they may urge him to go into a business rather than become an artist. Parents will not, however, advise a son to consider putting his professional life on hold for several years while he raises a family. Nor will they recommend part-time work until the children are in school or imply that he should assume the major day-to-day responsibility for childrearing and housekeeping. Nor will they suggest that he should follow his wife to her new job location.

Since sons are to serve their future families by being professionally successful, it is important for them to take courses that will maximize success. Sons need to take, and do well in, math and science courses—to insure that they will be qualified to pursue any high-prestige, high-income profession they may decide to enter. Parents, knowing that math and science skills make money, encourage boys to master those skills. In addition, because of active gender schemas, parents associate proficiency in math and science with males (Jacobs & Eccles 1992). Middle-class parents thus see taking a full complement of math and science courses as both natural and advantageous to their sons.

Parents have converse expectations for a daughter, whose service to her family they see as coming not through professional success but daily caretaking. Many parents hope their daughter will have meaningful work out-side the home or that she will be able to supplement her family's income. Nonetheless, for a daughter, the message that the family comes first means that professional achievement has to come second. Parents see their daughters' education as important in and of itself. But because pro-fessional life is not a necessity for a daughter, neither is achievement in math and science. A girl need not take or do well in math and science courses, because she is not preparing herself for a lifetime of supporting herself and her family. Moreover, parents do not have high expectations for their daughter in math and science because those areas are perceived as masculine (Jacobs & Eccles 1992).

Girls as a whole do not "turn off" math and science so much as fail ever to turn on to them. As the studies reviewed in chapter 5 show, girls are less successful than boys in applying their mathematical knowledge as early as the first grade (Lummis & Stevenson 1990). They score as well as boys do on tests of math achievement and get equally high math grades, but that is in part because of the content of the tests. Word problems—which require application of math concepts —are seldom included in ele-mentary school math tests.

At least as early as the third grade, girls in the United States rate math as more difficult than boys do and consider themselves worse math stu-dents than boys do (Stipek & Gralinski 1991).[5] Girls are also less likely than boys to attribute a good score on a math exam to their ability and, conversely, more likely than boys to see a poor score as a reflection of lack of ability (Stipek 1984; Stipek & Gralinski 1991). Further, girls see making an effort in math as less likely to lead to success than boys do. A cross-national study of students in twelve countries also found that thirteen-year-old boys consistently rate math more positively than girls do (Steinkamp, Harnisch, Walberg, & Tsai 1985).

In a study of children in the fourth through the twelfth grades, investi-gators found that boys and girls treated math and language arts dif-ferently (Ryckman & Peckham 1987). Boys tended not to distinguish be-tween the two content areas in explaining their own success or failure. Girls did. They attributed success to ability much more in language arts than in math and, conversely, saw failure as a sign of lack of ability much more in math than in language arts. Girls thus demonstrate a belief that they are inherently less able in math, so that making an effort will help them less in math than in language arts. Since making an effort often implies doing more of the same, girls may be partially correct in concluding that extra efforts will yield only minor results. What they need may not be simply greater effort but more effort plus a different approach.

The importance of girls' early math performance and attitudes becomes obvious in adolescence, when children have a choice about how much math or science to take. Girls take fewer high school math and science courses than boys do. That phenomenon appears to be simply the visible culmination of years of subtly, and not so subtly, conveyed expectations that children themselves have internalized at a young age. There is no crisis or dramatic turning point in adolescence. Rather, the fruits of childhood are harvested at this time.

Two studies of sixth graders illustrate the impact of adult expectations and gender schemas on children. In the first study, the researchers queried mothers about their children's abilities in math, in sports, and at making friends (Jacobs & Eccles 1992). They asked also the mothers to rate the skills of females and males in each area and to rate the importance of each area for males and females. The investigators thus measured the mothers' beliefs about their own particular child and the mothers' gender schemas.

To determine how well the children were actually performing, the investigators asked the children's teachers to evaluate the children's abilities in the three areas (Jacobs & Eccles 1992). (That measure of performance could itself have been influenced by gender schemas.) Finally, the children were asked to rate their own abilities in math, sports, and making friends.

The study raised two interesting issues. One was whether mothers' gender schemas affect their beliefs about their children's abilities. It could be that parents' views of their children are affected solely by the children's actual accomplishments, not by gender schemas. The better you know someone, according to this hypothesis, the less impact such schemas may have. If, on the other hand, gender schemas organize our perceptions of others—even of those with whom we have a great deal of contact—parents' beliefs about their children should be affected by the parents' gender schemas as well as by children's performance.

The second prediction was borne out. The mothers' perceptions were strongly influenced by their children's behavior, but they were also affected by the strength of their own gender schemas. Mothers who believed that girls were much poorer than boys in math tended to underestimate their daughters' math abilities and to overestimate their sons'. Similar effects were found for sports and social skills. The relative strength of the mothers' gender stereotypes directly influenced how accurately they perceived their children's actual abilities. Children cannot be guaranteed an accurate evaluation even by those who are closest to them.

The second issue the study raised was whether mothers' perceptions of their children influenced the children's own perceptions of their aptitudes. The researchers found that the children's views of themselves were more affected by their mothers' perceptions than by their own achievements. Although the children did not ignore their own performance, their parents' evaluations carried more weight.

Thus, children's beliefs about themselves are strongly affected by maternal perceptions, and those perceptions are influenced by mothers' own gender schemas. The study did not examine the consequences of children's beliefs about themselves for their performance. But it is likely that children's choices about what activities or courses to pursue are influenced by their self-evaluations.

The second study took up where the first left off. The investigators examined the effects of teachers' expectations on sixth graders' actual math accomplishments, as measured by a standardized achievement test (Jussim & Eccles 1992). Because, as discussed earlier in this chapter, teachers respond to children on the basis of their behavior rather than their sex (Brophy 1985; Eccles & Blumenfeld 1985), we might predict that teachers' expectations would have no effect on children. Children's behavior is already so gender-differentiated by the time they begin school that teachers would have to react to boys and girls differently in order to change those gender patterns (Brophy 1985); for example, they would have to ignore boys' questions and the answers they volunteer and call on girls more often.[6]

Despite teachers' lack of overt bias, their expectations do exert subtle influences on children's math achievement. Like parents, teachers are primarily affected by children's performance—their classroom and standardized test grades. But, also like parents, teachers are influenced by gender schemas as well. Teachers believe boys have more mathematical ability than girls and perceive girls as trying harder than boys, even though they are nut. Teachers therefore tend to explain girls' good performance as the outcome of effort, and to regard boys' accomplishments as the result of ability (Jussim & Eccles 1992).

When the investigators looked at the relations between teachers' perceptions and children's performance on the standardized test, they found that the children's test performance was affected both by their real ability (as measured by previous math performance) and by teachers' perceptions of that ability. Even though the influence of teachers' expectations on these sixth graders was small, it was measurable.

The notion of the accumulation of advantage and disadvantage reviewed in chapter 1 can help explain the implications of teachers' expectations. The sixth grade is but one slice in a child's twelve-year elementary and secondary education. The small but measurable effects of teachers' expectations are likely to occur in each of those twelve years. As with the computer simulation demonstrating that a minor bias in evaluation can have a major cumulative effect on gender balance at an organization's management level (Martell, Lane, & Emrich 1996), the small but consistent effect of teachers' expectations can have a major cumulative impact on children's performance. Expectation effects help elevate boys' beliefs about their math ability, thereby indirectly elevating their actual achievement. Expectations help depress girls' self-perceptions and thereby indirectly lower their level of performance.

In sum, parents and teachers perceive children in the light of their own gender schemas, which in turn affect boys' and girls' perceptions of themselves as more or less talented in math. Girls spend an educational lifetime in the company of adults who—often nonconsciously—underestimate the girls' math and science abilities and depress both their expectations of what they can achieve and their actual performance. Adult expectations are, of course, not the only influence on children's math performance, but they are important. Every biasing influence that can be eliminated should be, because math and science are important to success in a variety of professions, ranging from medicine to engineering to finance.

Several researchers have documented gender differences in classroom participation among students of all ages (see, e.g., Sadker & Sadker

1994). Boys participate more loudly and actively, speak out more often without waiting to be called on, and appear to thrive in classroom situations that demand fast responses. Not all boys fit that description, just as not all girls are quiet and well-behaved. Girls who adopt more "masculine" behaviors, however, are likely to be penalized by other girls, boys, and even teachers for violating gender norms.

The small, subtle, behaviors that convey different expectations for girls are difficult to measure and difficult to perceive, like the small, subtle signs of lower expectations for women that occur in professional settings. Nonetheless, even in the first grade, girls appear to begin accumulating disadvantage, if only through benign neglect.

An adult who is ignored has, at least potentially, the resources needed to insist on being heard. Even an adult, however, must determine the source of the problem. Was my contribution lacking? Was my presentation faulty? Was my timing bad? Or, is there something wrong with the world? A child who is ignored has the same need to understand what is happening but is far less likely than an adult to consider the last possibility.

In chapter 2 and this chapter, we have looked at the consequences of adults' treatment and expectations of children. Adult behavior provides children with data that they develop hypotheses to explain. Those hypotheses take the form of gender schemas. Adults do not write on the blank slate of the child's mind. Instead, they display patterns that children attempt to understand, not unlike adults' attempts to understand a culture different from their own. That does not mean that there are no intrinsic differences between males and females. In chapters 4 and 5 I review the findings on biological differences and explore their implications for fairness.

Why Do Girls and Women Do So Well?

It is not surprising that girls and boys are affected by the differential treatment they receive and the different expectations they experience. Adults too are affected by others' evaluations and expectations. Children, as they attempt to learn about their own abilities and develop realistic aspirations, are even more susceptible to others' expectations and even more dependent on others' evaluations. Both girls and boys learn that boys have a higher claim to professional success than girls and can expect to excel at the skills associated with eventual professional success.

The final question raised by the research on the effects of adult expectations is why do women do as well as they do in professional life? Why do any girls develop professional aspirations? Why do girls perform as well as they do in school, including in math courses? Why are girls and women evaluated as well as they are? If girls acquire a minus sign very early in life, and if that minus sign affects their own and others' evaluations, why are there *any* women with major achievements?

One answer is that the schema for females is more flexible than the male schema. Because masculine interests are highly valued by the culture as a whole (see chapter 10), girls and women can develop those interests more freely than boys and men can develop feminine interests. Although girls and women are not expected to perform at the same high levels as boys and men, they are not forbidden participation in masculine activities. Boys and men, in contrast, must regard feminine pursuits as out of bounds.

Another reason for some women's success in fields culturally defined as masculine is that people's perceptions can change if they adopt a new hypothesis: for example, that all people should have equal opportunities to pursue whatever professions they choose. The surge in middle-class white female applicants to law, medical, and graduate schools in the early 1970s testifies to the power that a new framework for understanding one's role in the world can have on both perceptions and behavior. Writers in the early 1970s explicitly questioned the notion that women's work should be restricted to household work and child care. By leaning heavily on the concept of equality, they effected a simple intellectual reorientation that had a major impact. Within the space of a few years—much too short a time for gender schemas to undergo a thorough change—white middle-class women flocked to the professions.

4

Biology and Behavior

The data on how parents treat boys and girls reviewed in chapter 2 and on how children learn about sex differences reviewed in chapter 3 raise the question of whether all the sex differences we see are differences that adults construct. What about built-in sex differences? In this chapter and the next I summarize what we know about intrinsic differences between males and females and consider the implications of those differences.

One of the problems involved in discussions of sex differences is that many people view biological influences as all-powerful and final. If a sex difference—such as mathematical ability—can be shown to have a biological component, it seems immutable and eternal. Our perception of immutability stems, I think, from an inaccurate understanding of what it means for a characteristic to have a biological basis. We interpret a biological sex difference as a difference that is a direct result of having a certain set of sex chromosomes. Since we cannot change the set we have, we are stuck with the differences that go along with being XX or XY. This everyday interpretation of biology, however, is radically uninformed. Although chromosomal differences may be qualitative, none of the ensuing differences are. Biology leaves us a lot of room to manoeuvre. Biology is not necessarily destiny.

In a way, it is odd that we should interpret sex differences as immutable, when we do not accept biology as destiny in other aspects of human existence. For example, biology sets limits on the human life span, but we need not and do not for that reason accept a short average life span as our fate. As a society, we put forth great efforts to understand the mechanisms of health and to cure disease and illness. We practice good hygiene, we investigate the roles of diet and exercise, we sterilize, we vaccinate, we inoculate, we medicate. Although we agree that no one can live forever, we successfully invest tremendous resources in trying to live longer. Our success is evidence of the lability and complexity of the processes that underlie life and death and of humans' ability to intervene in those processes.

I propose that we adopt the same attitude toward biological sex differences. Biological sex differences arise through the actions of sex hormones operating in our physical and social environments. Like the processes relevant to life and death, those relevant to sex differences are intricate and susceptible to change. Biology sets limits, but we need not for that reason accept the differences we see as immutable. We have good evidence from cultural, situational, and temporal differences that the differences are *not* immutable.

In this chapter and chapter 5, I have applied my own interpretation to the research findings on physical, behavioral, and cognitive differences, highlighting some findings the researchers themselves did not and deemphasizing others. Many different points of view on these data exist: while some people deny the existence or importance of a biological influence, others refer all differences to biology. My own position is that biological influences exist and are important, but are only part of the story.

Sex Hormones

When we talk about "biological" sex differences, we are talking about the influence of the hormones responsible for differentiation of the sexes. The sex chromosomes themselves (XX for females and XY for males) do not have an automatic and rigid set of consequences. They do not act like on–off switches. Nor are they, even, the immediate agents of sex differentiation. They exercise their influence through the differing hormonal developments they set into motion. Those developments, in turn, have their effects within one or another context and are inherently variable. The same thing is true of genetic effects in general (see discussion in Neisser et al. 1996). So, although we cannot change our chromosomes, they are, in a sense, irrelevant.

Mammals with XX chromosomes develop ovaries that secrete one set of hormones; mammals with XY chromosomes develop testes that secrete the same set of hormones but in different amounts. The action of those hormones underlies further physical sex differentiation. The three main types of sex hormones—androgens, estrogens, and progestins—occur in both sexes; the sexes differ, sometimes dramatically, in the amount of each hormone they produce. For example, testosterone levels in college-age males and females are very different. The male-to-female ratio has been reported to be as high as ten to one, with no overlap between the two groups (Udry & Talbert 1988). Average testosterone-concentration levels in saliva have been reported to be about three times as high in males as in females, again with no overlap between the two groups (Gouchie & Kimura 1991). Within each sex, however, there is a considerable range of secretions of each hormone.

Within-Sex Variability
It is in the realm of behavior that the variable effects of sex hormones within each sex are clearest. The effects vary depending on the social-psychological context they occur in, for nonhuman animals as well as humans (Buchanan et al. 1992; Collaer & Hines 1995). Hormonal effects, in other words, are context-dependent. Even in rats, the effects of sex hormones differ, depending on the sort of handling the animals receive, the type and amount of stimulation provided by their environment, and the kind of maternal care they receive. (See Collaer & Hines 1995, for a summary of these and other effects of gonadal steroids.)[1]

Although we commonly speak of the environment modifying or moderating or influencing hormonal effects on human behavior, I find that terminology misleading. It suggests a primacy and a univocality for the action of sex hormones that do not exist. It would be similarly inappropriate to label environmental effects on human behavior as primary, and speak of hormones as modifying or moderating those environmental effects. Rather, hormonal and environmental effects act together—they coact—to jointly influence people's and animals' traits and behaviors (Moore 1985). Within the realm of behavior, there is no such thing as a pure hormonal effect, because there is no such thing as a zero or neutral environment. Equally, there is no such thing as a pure environmental effect, because there is no such thing as zero or neutral hormones. To understand any behavior, it is necessary to understand the contribution of both hormones and the environment.

We can get a small idea of the complexity of the interactions between sex hormones and the environment in adult humans by looking at how time of year and level of circulating testosterone affects men's ability to rotate objects mentally (Kimura & Hampson 1994). In the fall, North American males have higher levels of testosterone than they have in the spring; they also have lower scores on spatial rotation tests than they do in the spring. As individuals, males who are below the average in circulating testosterone also score higher on spatial rotation tests than those whose levels are higher than average. Men's cycles occur on a daily basis as well. When testosterone levels are higher, in the morning, men perform more poorly on tests of spatial rotation. (See Kimura 1996 for a summary of this and other experiments involving hormonal effects.)

Males' spatial rotation scores are linked to testosterone level in ways that our gender schemas would not predict. Gender schemas represent testosterone as contributing to masculinity and label certain kinds of skills—like map reading and mental rotation—as masculine. But the data show that, for mental rotation, having less testosterone is better than having more—up to a point.

Being below the median is better than being above it, but for males being very far below it is worse than being somewhat below. There appears to be a curvilinear relationship between testosterone level and scores on mental rotation tests. Aging males, who have very low testosterone levels, have lower scores on tests of mental rotation than college-age males whose scores are below the median (Kimura 1996). Women's testosterone levels are very low.

The data on men's variability show that our notions of people's abilities are oversimplified. It is obvious that the component of spatial ability that is due to knowledge of spatial relations cannot fluctuate over a twenty-four-hour period. Still, spatial ability undoubtedly involves more than knowledge. It also requires registering the spatial properties of objects, storing that information, and then mentally rearranging the objects to see what they would look like from different angles. Those processes appear vulnerable to changes in testosterone level.[2] Researchers do not know whether male-female differences in spatial abilities are due to underlying differences in knowledge or to processing differences.

There are at least some spatial tasks where males perform better than females that seem unrelated to testosterone levels. For example, although male homosexuals and heterosexuals have comparable testosterone levels, homosexuals generally perform the task of throwing a ball at a target less well than heterosexuals do (Hall & Kimura 1995; Kimura 1996).[3]

Female scores on spatial-orientation tests fluctuate somewhat across the menstrual cycle and show some individual variability. When estrogen levels are very high, females score worse on some—but not all—tests of spatial ability than they do when estrogen levels are moderate or low (Hampson 1990a, 1990b). For women, there is also some indication of a curvilinear relation between estrogen and spatial skills, just as there is a curvilinear relation between men's testosterone levels and spatial performance (Hampson 1990b).

At the same time, female monthly fluctuations are considerably smaller than male seasonal variations. The hormonal effects in women are relatively small and do not show the other patterns we would expect to see if estrogen level alone controlled behavior. For example, undergraduate women who major in science score better on tests of spatial ability than do women who major in other fields. If estrogen level predicted spatial ability well, women in science would have estrogen levels different from other women, but they do not (Hampson 1990b).

Females' levels of testosterone, however, are related to scores on at least some tests of spatial ability, even though those levels are much lower than males' levels. Females with above-average testosterone levels for females score as well on spatial tests as males with below-average levels for males (Gouchie & Kimura 1991). That is so even though the testosterone levels of these women are only half as high as the male levels. A similarly low level in males would be associated with poor spatial performance. Perhaps because of differences in brain structure, a very low testosterone level in males—a level too low to mediate good spatial performance—is adequate for females to attain good spatial performance.

The research on hormonal influences on behavior thus contradicts any notion we might have that sex chromosomes determine our destiny, or that hormones act independently of the environment in which they are embedded. Hormones are relevant influences on our traits and behaviors, but their effects are labile. Evaluation of the effects of hormones on the specific physical and behavioral traits discussed in the remainder of the chapter confirms this general conclusion.

Variation in Trait Expression

We can illustrate the relations between biology and trait expression with an example unrelated to sex differences. Although some hearts are intrinsically less efficient pumps than others, diet and exercise can increase their efficiency, just as a poor diet and lack of exercise can decrease it. The environment influences how well a heart does its work. For most traits, biology establishes a continuum of values rather than a specific value. In the case of hearts, biology establishes the usual range within which they operate, rather than a specific efficiency value that holds for all hearts.

In the same way, some sex differences change in value from one situation to another, while others are relatively invariant over an individual's adult lifetime. Variability that occurs within an individual is variability that can be altered.

Reproduction

Most people's everyday experience is that there are two, clearly different sexes. Male and female genitalia differ markedly. (Ambiguous genitalia exist but are rare.) A concomitant functional difference is as marked as the anatomical difference: females are capable of birth and lactation and males are not.[5]

Unlike other sex differences that we pay attention to, anatomical differences hold to the same degree across all cultures, across all situations, and across time. Cognitive and behavioral sex differences, on the other hand, exist along a continuum, with a great deal of overlap between the sexes and a great deal of variability within each sex. Only in the reproductive area are the differences qualitative. All other differences between the sexes are quantitative and inherently variable, though the type and size of the variability differs from trait to trait. In all the physical and behavioral characteristics we consider here, the variability within each sex is greater than the (average) difference between the sexes.

Height

In all cultures, males are on average taller than females—a difference that has persisted for thousands of years. Nonetheless, even with height, some types of variability do exist. Within each sex, some people are taller than others. Some females are taller than others and are also taller than some males. The difference between the extreme heights within each sex is larger than the difference in the average height between the sexes.

Height also varies from individual to individual as a function of nutrition—which is environmentally determined—and development. Among children born in the same place at the same time, those who are well nourished grow taller than those who are poorly nourished. In old people, height decreases because of bone loss.

Changes in the social environment, however, do not affect adult height. People are not, for example, taller at work than they are at home. Even here, though, perceptions of height can be manipulated: people may wear shoes that increase their apparent height, or they may, by slouching, reduce it. Compared to other characteristics we consider later in the chapter, however, individual height has only limited variability.

Voice Pitch

Other physical sex differences show much more mutability within an individual. Consider voice pitch. Like height, it has a underlying biological basis: on average, males have larger and more muscular larynxes, and larger and more resonant throats. The result is that, within any culture, males' voices tend to be deeper in pitch than females'. Unlike height, however, an individual's adult voice pitch is not fixed. We all possess a fairly wide range of possible pitches. Pitch is responsive, for example, to emotional stress.

If the expression of a trait can vary within an individual from one moment to the next, it follows that all other types of variability can also exist. Again, voice pitch is a good example. The size of the sex difference varies from culture to culture. In Italy, for instance, the difference is less than it is in the United States (McConnell-Ginet 1983).

Unlike height, voice pitch could be, on average, almost the same in males and females, because of the variability within an individual, and because of the responsiveness of pitch to social and cultural factors. Females could speak nearer the lower end of their range and males nearer the upper end. (British Prime Minister Thatcher reportedly profited from lessons in lowering her voice pitch so that she would appear more authoritative.) By the same token, the average difference in pitch between the sexes would be extremely high if females spoke at the upper end of their range and males spoke at the lower end of theirs. Thus, even for traits with a clear underlying physiological connection, societies can "choose" how extreme the behavioral differences will be. Traits whose expression is inherently variable—like voice pitch—rather than more rigid—like height—allow for the largest cultural and gender differences.

In essence, what matters in evaluating sex differences is not the existence of a biological connection but the inherent variability in the expression of a trait. Height and voice pitch both have a clear biological connection, but adult height cannot be directly influenced by culture, whereas voice pitch can. If a trait is inherently variable, like voice pitch, the expression of it is malleable. The variability makes it correspondingly difficult to assess the influence of biology. For some sex differences, biology limits the range of a behavior; further, the midpoint of the range for one sex may be higher or lower than the midpoint for the other sex. The differences in the midpoints may or may not have practical significance, depending on how great the range is for each sex. To assess the sources of sex differences we need to know both whether a given behavior has a direct biological connection and, if it does, whether the proper analogy is to height or to voice pitch. Yet we often do not know. For the traits that could be relevant to professional achievement, voice pitch seems a better analogy, because those traits are responsive to cultural, social, and psychological influences.

When I speak of influences, I am not suggesting that the environment shapes or molds children or adults. Rather, people form nonconscious hypotheses based in part on the data they receive from the environment. Those hypotheses about sex differences—gender schemas—then guide people's behavior. When a trait is malleable, gender schemas can affect its expression.

Behavioral Traits and Professional Achievement

None of the traits discussed so far have any direct connection to people's intellectual or professional abilities. Height and voice pitch have nothing to do with competence, even though we tend to think of competent people as tall and having a low voice. Other differences, however, have more potential significance.

Activity Level

Males are more active than females, a difference that appears to increase throughout childhood and into early adolescence (Eaton & Enns 1986).[6] Since few studies have examined activity differences after the age of fifteen, we do not know whether the differences persist throughout the life span or begin to diminish at some point. Higher activity levels could indirectly cause more exploration and, even more indirectly, be related to achievement. But that is speculation.

The existence of infant sex differences in activity level has not gone unquestioned. Relatively few studies have looked at infant sex differences; those that have found no differences in global activity level, although there is some suggestion that infant boys' movements are more vigorous than girls'. One careful study comparing girl and boy babies at two and a half months and at five months found almost no differences either in activity level or in vigor of movement (Cossette, Malcuit, & Pomerleau 1991). The few differences observed were small and could have been due to chance.

Even fewer studies have looked at prenatal activity levels, but one or two have found differences. If the existence of *in utero* sex differences were confirmed, that would suggest very strongly that activity differences are indeed hormonally initiated, as male and female fetuses receive no differential social stimulation (Eaton & Enns 1986). The fact that sex differences in activity increase as development proceeds is compatible with two possibilities: (1) that high activity is encouraged in boys and discouraged in girls; or (2) that activity levels mature and follow different paths of biological development in boys and girls.

One indication that differences in activity level are initiated by hormonal differences comes from data on children who experienced overly high levels of androgens *in utero*. In a relatively rare genetic disorder (occurring approximately once in every ten thousand births), an enzyme deficiency leads to overproduction of androgens by the fetus's adrenal glands. The disorder, commonly called congenital adrenal hyperplasia (CAH), is usually visible in chromosomal females soon after birth, because the genitals are masculinized. As newborns, the girls typically receive genital surgery and hormonal treatment to counteract further effects of the androgens. Both boys and girls with CAH have very high levels of circulating androgens. Detection at birth is more difficult in boys, and solid data on the effects on boys are not available.

Most studies have found that girls with CAH have higher activity levels than normal girls, levels that are similar to those of normal boys (see discussion in Collaer & Hines 1995). Rough-and-tumble play, which is much more characteristic of boys than of girls, is also frequent in girls with CAH. A study comparing three- to eight-year-old girls with and without CAH found that the girls with CAH spent more time playing with toys associated with males, such as vehicles and construction toys, than the others did (Berenbaum & Hines 1992). A study of older children produced similar results (Berenbaum & Snyder 1995). The girls with CAH spent the same amount of time with masculine toys as boys without CAH did. Toys typically associated with boys may lend themselves to high-activity play more easily than do toys typically associated with girls.

To summarize, activity level seems like a good candidate for a hormonally influenced sex difference. Data both from boys and girls with normal prenatal hormonal development and from girls who experience excess androgens *in utero* suggest hormonal involvement. But interactions with social-psychological factors cannot be ignored. We know that parents treat boys and girls differently; parents of girls with CAH may be more tolerant of active play than the parents of girls with no history of atypical hormonal production (see also chapter 5, n. 8).

There is no evidence that a high activity level or rough-and-tumble play is either necessary or sufficient for later achievement. If either were important, changes in the child's social environment could increase girls' participation.

Aggression

Another candidate for an intrinsic sex difference in behavior is hostile physical aggression—defined as touching another person with the intention of inflicting harm, with or without the desire to obtain some goal. There is a higher incidence of such hostility in boys, although the sex differences appear to develop later—around the age of three—than differences in activity level (see review in Berk 1994).

Sex differences in aggression increase throughout adolescence, then diminish, apparently because society looks less and less favorably upon physical aggression as children become adults. Overall, studies reliably show males to be more physically aggressive than females, with little or no difference from one generation to the next (Eagly & Steffen 1986; Knight, Fabes, & Higgins 1996). Cultures vary in how often people express hostile physical aggression, but there is usually a sex difference, with males being more active and aggressive. Females of one culture may well be more physically active or aggressive than the males of another culture, but they are likely to be less physically aggressive than males of their own culture. Even that difference, however, is not universal, as Mead demonstrated (1935).

Although males are usually more aggressive than females, the actual level of individual aggression is inherently highly variable. As with other characteristics, the range of aggression within each sex is larger than the average difference between the sexes. Interestingly, boys seem less prone to aggression if they have had experience looking after younger children (see Maccoby & Jacklin 1980; Tieger 1980). Hostile behavior can apparently be reduced by practicing nurturant behavior.

Most girls in most cultures either have actual child care experience, or the surrogate experience of playing with dolls. Unlike boys, girls may thus be diverted from aggression throughout their childhood. If more boys were given the opportunity to take care of young children, reduced aggression might result.

Again, there is no evidence that a tendency to physical aggression is either necessary or sufficient for later achievement. I emphasize physical aggression because that is where sex differences are most marked. Aggressive thoughts and words, on the other hand, are more equally shared between the sexes.

Studies of white college-age males from the North or South of the United States demonstrate that a tendency to aggressive solutions is influenced by an individual's subculture. In a series of experiments, researchers arranged for the young men to be mildly insulted by a peer (Cohen, Nisbett, Bowdle, & Schwarz 1996). After the insult, the students participated in various tasks designed to measure their aggression. Northerners and southerners responded differently in those follow-up tasks. In one task, the students were asked to complete a story in which a male student's girlfriend complained to him that a male acquaintance had tried to kiss her. Southerners who had been insulted completed the story more aggressively than northerners who had been insulted, as well as more aggressively than southerners or northerners who had not been insulted.

The researchers concluded that, for southern males, aggression and notions of "honor" are interwoven: southerners may be easier to offend than northerners and may also respond more aggressively to a perceived offense (Cohen et al. 1996). (Naturalistic data also indicate that white southern males are more likely to be violent in certain settings than their northern counterparts (Cohen et al.)) For our purposes, the important aspect of the experiment is its evidence that aggression is not just culture-bound, but subculture-bound.

Aggression also varies from situation to situation (Eagly & Steffen 1986). A review of sixty-four experimental studies of aggression demonstrates that, depending on the type of provocation to aggression, men may be either more or less aggressive than women (Bettencourt & Miller 1996). Men, for example, react more aggressively than women do when their intelligence is insulted. Women, however, react somewhat more aggressively than men to other types of insults.

The wide variability in the expression of aggression in each sex, and the concomitant variability in the presence and extent of sex differences in aggression, indicate that cultures and subcultures play a major role in determining people's reactions to frustration or provocation. As it does with voice pitch, the variability suggests that there is great flexibility in the amount of aggression males and females express. No particular amount is natural or inevitable for either sex. Males may exhibit very little aggression or a great deal; females exhibit a similar range of behavior.

Given that inherent variability, I interpret the pervasiveness of a sex difference across cultures as an indication that the social arrangements of many cultures have something in common, something that is conducive to the development of similar gender schemas that set sex differences in place and maintain them. Such an interpretation does not rule out a contribution from sex hormones but, rather, suggests that the hormonal contribution neither dominates nor effaces the environmental influences.

Putting together the data on activity—especially rough-and-tumble play—and on aggression, we can see how they might be related. A high activity level may be suppressed or encouraged, directed toward objects or toward people, intended to help others or to hurt them (see discussion in Parsons 1982). Hostile aggression is not a necessary outcome of high activity. Girls with CAH are not more aggressive in their behavior than other girls, even though their activity levels and liking for rough-and-tumble play are greater. Although girls with CAH do score somewhat higher on questionnaires asking about aggressive tendencies, they do not act out those tendencies (see summary in Collaer & Hines 1995).

Nonetheless, high activity level may be a predisposing factor to aggression. If combined with anger and lack of cultural prohibitions against the expression of anger, high activity can result in hostile aggression. Anger may be a natural human emotion, but there is no natural way to handle it. As the North-South differences suggest, an individual's response is affected by beliefs about what is appropriate.

That hormones predispose but do not determine aggression is also apparent from changes that occur during puberty, when boys' testosterone levels increase greatly. Although the hormone increases in all boys, most boys in most situations do not become more aggressive (Buchanan et al. 1992). Boys with higher levels of testosterone do seem to display more physical aggression if they feel threatened or perceive a situation as unfair. And boys who had behavior problems before puberty may have those problems exacerbated by an increase in testosterone. Otherwise, however, most boys do not show more aggression as a consequence of higher levels of testosterone. To summarize, sex differences in aggression may be linked to hormonal differences, but even physical aggression is strongly influenced by social and psychological factors.

The Significance of Sex Differences

Physical and behavioral sex differences exist. Those differences include reproductive role, height, voice pitch, activity level, and aggression. All are affected to some degree by sex hormones, but in most cases we know neither the extent nor exact nature of the influence.

To some degree, however, the presence of a hormonal influence on behavior is irrelevant. Except for reproduction, sex differences are not qualitative but average, quantitative differences. The variability in the expression of a trait both within an individual and across individuals demonstrates the importance of the social environment. The variability tells us that hormones and the social environment act together to produce behavior. We need not change people's hormones to change their behavior; changing the social environment has clear effects.

5

Biology and Cognition

Difficult as it is to determine what behavioral sex differences are intrinsic, it is even harder to distinguish between innate and acquired cognitive differences. Certain differences, such as the ability to apply mathematical knowledge, are evident early in development and are seen across many cultures. We do not know to what extent those differences are mediated via hormones or social factors. My conclusion—not surprisingly—is that both are involved. Even though hormonal differences are clearly related to sex differences in some cognitive domains, they do not fully account for any cognitive difference.

The two strongest candidates for the mediation of hormones are perceptual speed, at which females excel, and mental rotation of three-dimensional figures, at which males excel. Unfortunately, few data are available to relate perceptual speed to other areas of cognitive ability. We have a great deal of data about mental rotation, but still lack a clear understanding of its connection with other cognitive skills, including mathematics.

No cognitive domain is homogenous. Verbal ability, for example, encompasses a range of skills and knowledge, from vocabulary to writing clear prose. Mathematical ability also has many subcomponents, ranging from skill in arithmetical operations like addition and subtraction to the ability to apply mathematical knowledge to solve new problems. It is important to keep the differences between males and females in perspective. The sexes overlap in all areas of all cognitive skills but show average differences in some. The differences within each sex are always greater than the average differences between the sexes. Here, as elsewhere, the sexes are more alike than they are different.

In addition, cognitive sex differences have not been constant over time; several differences have declined over the years. That diminution is good evidence that some portion of cognitive differences is socially constructed. Between 1947 and 1980, sex differences among children in grades eight through twelve declined in eight cognitive domains (Feingold 1988; see Halpern 1989 for a contrary view).[1] In 1947, for example, tests of verbal reasoning, abstract reasoning, and ability to deal with numbers showed higher performance by boys. Thirty-three years later, in 1980, those differences had been eliminated, and numerical ability showed, if anything, higher performance by girls. Mechanical reasoning showed extremely superior performance by boys in 1947, an advantage that was almost cut in half by 1980. Similarly, tests on which girls were superior to boys in 1947 showed declining sex differences by 1980. Other work has examined studies of sex differences in verbal ability and mathematics published before and after 1973 and compared their results. The later studies reported differences that were half the size of those found before 1973 (Hyde & Linn 1988; Hyde, Fennema, & Lamon 1990). Children's biology didn't differ before and after 1973, but what we expected of children did.

Verbal Ability

Despite the beliefs of many parents and children that girls are superior in verbal ability, it is now widely agreed that there are no intrinsic sex differences in reading comprehension or vocabulary (Feingold 1988; Hyde & Linn 1988; Lummis & Stevenson 1990; see Halpern 1989 for a contrary view). Most standardized tests of verbal ability show no sex differences overall, although girls are superior in fluent speech production and anagrams and boys are superior at analogies.

The writing of high school girls, however, is markedly superior to that of boys. In fact, writing differences are the largest cognitive sex differences found in national samples of high school students (Hedges & Nowell 1995). The success of male writers shows, however, that even a large disadvantage in average performance need not rule out equal or superior professional attainment.

Among very young children, girls do initially have a larger vocabulary than boys have; but boys catch up quickly (Fenson, Dale, Reznick,

Bates, Thal, & Pethick 1994). Among preschool and school-age children, girls seem to have more sophisticated conversational skills (Sheldon 1992, 1996). Those two differences may be responsible for parental beliefs.

In verbal ability as in many other cognitive areas, it is important to realize that an underlying intrinsic difference in favor of either girls or boys could actually exist but be behaviorally invisible and so of no importance. Because education and social practices may have eliminated the expression of a sex difference, failing to observe one is not the same thing as demonstrating the absence of intrinsic differences. Conversely, a pervasive sex difference in behavior can exist even if there are no intrinsic differences—again because of education and social practices.

Perceptual Speed

One area that reliably shows superior female performance is perceptual speed (see, e.g., Hedges & Nowell 1995). Females are generally faster than males at tasks such as finding all the examples of the letter *a* in a passage. Since almost no studies of the possible implications of this ability exist, we cannot currently evaluate either the importance of this ability or its origins.

For the subareas of verbal ability and perceptual speed, we currently have no good explanations of sex differences in either the domain of hormones or of gender schemas. It is possible, as has been suggested for mathematics (Geary 1996), that skills can be divided into primary and secondary ones. Primary skills are part of human endowment and do not differ by sex. Secondary skills may be affected both by hormones and by gender schemas to yield sex differences. At present we can only speculate.

Mathematical Ability

Samples of the U.S. population as a whole show no overall sex differences in mathematics test scores (Hyde, Fennema, & Lamon 1990). Data from tests given to teenagers by the National Assessment of Education Progress (NAEP) show only very small average differences between male and female students (Hedges & Nowell 1995). When mathematics and science

scores from 1978 are compared with scores from 1992, the small differences seen in the earlier scores are even slightly smaller in 1992. Data
from other large national samples comparing 1960 to 1988 scores in
math and science show a similar decline (Hedges & Nowell 1995). Moreover, the decline in average score differences is robust; that is, it shows up
consistently.[2] A reduction in sex differences over so short a period of time
indicates that social and psychological influences are responsible for both
the appearance and the diminution of sex differences.

In the following discussion, it is important to keep in mind the small
size of the overall differences in mathematical scores. My focus is not
on overall score differences but on certain subareas of mathematics that
reliably show male-female differences. Examples of subareas are word
problems, number concepts, mathematical operations, the reading of
graphs and tables, measurement, estimation, visualization, spatial relations, and speed of addition (Lummis & Stevenson 1990). The generalization I propose to cover the research findings is that girls and boys
understand mathematical concepts equally well but boys apply their
knowledge to new areas better than girls do. In particular, compared to
girls, boys are better at ignoring irrelevant information in word problems
and better at coming up with unconventional solutions.

Mathematical ability, like verbal ability, is heterogeneous. In some subareas of mathematics, there are no sex differences at all. In others, there
are reliable and continuing differences, some of which begin at an early
age. Males are typically better than females at word problems, graph interpretation, and estimation problems.

From the heterogeneous list of subcomponents, one can see that mathematics tests look both at knowledge of mathematical concepts and operations and at skills in applying mathematics. For example, a question on
mathematical operations may ask the student to divide 198 by 33. The
student will be successful if he or she knows how to carry out division
and makes no errors in the computation. On that sort of problem, there
are no sex differences.

In a word problem, the student may be told that a truck will hold 33
boxes of oranges and asked how many trips will be needed to carry 198
boxes of oranges to a store. Here the successful student must first understand that division is the operation to perform. Then she or he must per-

form the division accurately. To solve a word problem the student must represent the problem properly, determine what operations are needed and, finally, perform them. A word problem, in short, requires the solver to apply mathematical knowledge. On that sort of problem, males perform better than females. The male superiority is seen across cultures and appears as early as the first grade.

Cross-Cultural Differences
Mathematical achievement is usually distinguished from mathematical applications. Achievement tests, on which there are no sex differences, measure children's mastery of the concepts taught in school. In achievement tests, boys and girls show the same understanding and mastery of concepts. There are, however, cultural differences, with children in the United States performing worse than children in Asian countries.

Application tests measure children's ability to apply the concepts they have learned to new areas. Here, in a subset of areas, there are both sex and cultural differences.

Both achievement and application were studied in a comparison of children in kindergarten, grade one, and grade five in the United States, Taiwan, and Japan (Lummis & Stevenson 1990). The achievement tests examined the children's understanding of the same concepts, which were taught in the same grade in all three countries. The children from the United States were always in third place.[3] Other studies, using very large samples, have demonstrated that American thirteen-year-olds score much worse than Japanese thirteen-year-olds on tests of mathematical achievement (Steinkamp, Harnisch, Walberg, & Tsai 1985). In a comparison of twelve countries, American children scored lower than children from eight other countries.

In the comparison of children in the United States, Taiwan, and Japan, tests of the ability to apply mathematical knowledge in nine subareas also showed cross-cultural differences (Lummis & Stevenson 1990). Children in the United States were in third place on almost every subcomponent and were never in first place.

To summarize, American children performed badly on both achievement and application tests, compared to children of other nations. Their poor performance could, in theory, reflect an intrinsic inferiority in mathematics. Alternatively, and more likely, it reflects differences in schooling, motivation, and other environmental influences—differences that may apply equally to sex differences within a single culture. The United States does a poor job at educating children in mathematics.

Sex Differences

On achievement tests comparing children from the United States, Taiwan, and Japan, boys and girls performed equally well at each grade in each country (Lummis & Stevenson 1990). That finding confirms typical findings that there are no sex differences among American schoolchildren in the early grades and suggests that boys and girls have equal knowledge of mathematical concepts.

On application tests, girls and boys were also equal on most of the nine subcomponents, although boys scored higher than girls did on three of them in the first grade and on four of them in the fifth grade. Girls did not score higher than boys on any subcomponent. Interestingly, children in all three countries showed sex differences in the same set of components. As early as first grade, boys were better at solving word problems than girls were.

Although the sex differences were consistent across cultures, there was also a great deal of variation. For example, on every subcomponent at every grade, Japanese girls scored higher than U.S. boys did, showing that there is flexibility in potential mathematical skill in both sexes. No particular level of skill is natural or inevitable for either sex. The superiority of Japanese girls over U.S. boys was equally noticeable on the items that showed sex differences as on the other items. Consider word problems, where Japanese girls in first grade performed slightly worse than Japanese boys—6.4 compared to 6.7—but much better than American boys, who scored 3.9. Girls in the United States scored worst: 3.4. As is apparent, the difference between Japanese girls and U.S. boys was much larger than the difference between Japanese girls and boys or between American girls and boys. The sex differences within each culture were tiny compared to the cultural differences.

Like the differences in aggression reported in chapter 4, cross-cultural sex differences in subareas of mathematics are not convincing evidence of intrinsic sex differences. That is because the differences within each culture are smaller than those between cultures. The pervasiveness of small relative differences suggests, instead, that some factor common to all the cultures sets the sex differences in place and maintains them.

In the cross-cultural study of thirteen-year-olds' mathematical achievement referred to in the preceding subsection, researchers also found consistent, though typically very small, sex differences in favor of boys (Steinkamp et al. 1985). Out of the twelve countries studied, girls performed better only in Israel—where children's overall performance was high—and in Finland—where it was low. In all the countries, sex differences in word problems were larger than in several other subareas; intuitive geometry showed the greatest differences.

Early Childhood Differences

As the cross-cultural studies of children in grade one suggest, sex differences in the ability to apply mathematical knowledge appear in the early grades. A study of early differences that focused on academically talented students in the United States found that girls in grades two to six performed worse than boys on a mathematics test requiring application of conceptual knowledge (Mills, Ablard, & Stumpf 1993). The questions asked students to say which of two quantities was larger, if either, or if there was not enough information to tell which was larger.[4] For example,

Which quantity, if either, is larger?
(a) a number, if one-half of it is 4   (b) 5

The most important result from the study is that sex differences were apparent as early as the second grade and remained essentially the same size through the sixth grade.

To summarize, sex differences in mathematics are small and limited to particular subareas, such as word problems. In those subareas, there are very early differences in favor of boys. Differential mathematical performance does not suddenly materialize at adolescence; it is a problem from the beginning of school. Since girls and boys receive equivalent schooling in those early years, the differences cannot result from differential formal exposure to mathematics.

Nature of Difficulties with Word Problems

Studies that ask children to evaluate mathematical problems according to the amount and kind of information they contain may shed light on children's difficulties with word problems (Low & Over: 1989, 1990, 1993). In one study, students in the tenth grade were given three types of word problems. One type contained enough information for someone to solve them; another provided too little information; the third gave the needed information but also some irrelevant information (Low & Over 1989). The children were asked to classify each problem according to the type of information it contained.

All the children found problems with irrelevant information the hardest to classify, but girls found them even harder than boys did. Girls also found it harder to identify problems with too little information. The girls and boys in the study appeared to have different biases in the way they labeled problems. Girls were slightly more likely to label problems as having enough information, even when there was too little or not enough. In contrast, when boys were faced with problems containing too little information, they were slightly more likely to detect that than they were to correctly identify problems with sufficient information. Put in terms of bias, boys have a slight bias to say that a problem has too little information, and girls have a slight bias to label a problem as providing just enough information.

How can we explain such sex differences? My suggestion is that girls and boys have different assumptions about problems, based in part on the sex differences in attitudes toward mathematics and math ability reviewed in chapter 3. They are also based, I conjecture, on differential reliance on conversational principles.

Ordinary conversational principles require speakers to give as much information as is necessary, neither too little nor too much; that is, speakers must make their contributions relevant (Grice 1989; Wilson & Sperber 1986). If, for example, someone asks me, "Have you seen Anne?", I should not reply with a simple "Yes." Equally, I should not reply with "She's in the lab. I really like Anne." In the first case, I give too little information; in the second, too much.

The intricacies of social conversation are such that if I give a simple "yes" the questioner will wonder, depending on the nature of our relationship, if I am trying to be amusing, if there is some reason I do not want to reveal Anne's whereabouts, or if there is some other explanation for my cryptic answer. Similarly, in the second case, the questioner will wonder if the apparently irrelevant information I am including is actually somehow relevant. Am I, for example, indicating that I admire Anne's diligence in the lab and think my interlocutor should be similarly diligent?

Girls are more likely to be attuned to conversational principles than boys are. If girls try to bring such principles to bear on word problems—some of which violate those rules—girls will be less likely to detect the irrelevant information, compared to boys. Their superiority in decoding conversational subtleties will put them at a disadvantage in solving such word problems. Girls' first assumption, even when the problem requires a decision about how much information it contains, may be that it contains the right amount.

A greater sensitivity to conversational principles is only one reason that girls may not apply their mathematical knowledge to the same extent that boys do. As we saw in chapter 3, parents' and teachers' different expectations for girls and boys in math are subtly conveyed to children and influence children's actual performance.[5] Girls also rate their ability in math lower than boys do, have different attitudes toward math, and have different views about the relation between effort and math achievement.

Girls might thus be more likely than boys to interpret a difficulty in understanding a problem's structure as a deficiency on their part, rather than a deficiency in the problem. A problem with too little information could look like a problem with enough information that the solver is unable to detect. Similarly, a problem with too much information could be seen as a problem challenging the solver to make use of all the information given. Girls may be more likely to search for a hypothesis that is consistent with conversational principles, while boys may be more likely to restructure the problem.

When asked to solve problems, rather than simply identify how much information the problems contain, boys and girls also perform differently (Low & Over 1993). Another group of tenth graders was asked to solve problems that contained enough information or enough information plus irrelevant information but were not told that some of the problems included irrelevant information. All the children did worse on those problems, but girls had even more difficulty with them than boys did. The major error children made was to try to incorporate the irrelevant information into their solution, an error girls made more often than boys. That attempt is compatible with my hypothesis that girls are more likely to assume that problems conform to conversational principles.

From the first grade through, at least, the sophomore year in high school, then, girls both approach problems differently than boys do and expect to do less well on them. Whenever teachers and parents treat boys and girls differently, it is in the direction of expecting boys to be superior in working out the solution to a math problem. Adult expectations converge with boys' and girls' self-ratings in math, producing a difference in ability to apply mathematical knowledge.

The Mathematics Scholastic Assessment Test (SAT-M)

The SAT-M, typically taken in the last year of high school, is composed of arithmetic, algebra, and geometry problems. It highlights the ability to reason mathematically. In 1996, as in earlier years, males scored higher than females. According to some researchers, the major category favoring males is algebra (Becker 1983, cited in Feingold 1988); reviews of other tests, however, found no sex differences in algebra but instead showed differences in geometry (Hyde et al. 1990). To some extent, the SAT sex differences in math are due to the fact that a more selective sample of males than females takes the test (Feingold 1988; Hyde et al. 1990). The P-SAT, which is administered to a representative sample of high school juniors and seniors, has shown declining sex differences in math in recent years. A more selective male sample cannot, however, explain all of male superiority.

Another possible factor is math background. In their mid-teens, when children can choose some of their courses, girls enroll in fewer math courses than boys do. High school boys also receive more practice in math through their higher rates of enrollment in science courses, which require them to use mathematics (Hyde et al. 1988). Differences in students' preparation can explain some portion of the SAT-Math differences but, again, cannot explain all of the sex difference.

Cognitive analyses of young people's math performance indicate that the differences between girls' and boys' scores on problems that girls typically solve less well are largely a function of (1) how much prior knowledge students have and (2) how easily they can put together an effective solution strategy (Byrnes & Takahira 1993). In other words, sex does not account for the variability on the SAT problems as well as prior knowledge and, especially, effective strategies do.

Yet, even with sufficient prior knowledge and effective strategies in hand, girls are less successful at solving certain problems than boys are. Girls do not put their knowledge and strategies to use to the same degree that boys do. What is apparent as early as the first grade becomes even more apparent with more complex math problems. Girls and boys do not approach problems in the same way.

Unconventional Problem Solving

Even high-ability high school students show sex differences in their approaches to math problems. Female students seem more likely to use a conventional approach, while male students appear more likely to use an unconventional approach. The problems a group of high-ability students were presented with in one study could be solved by either conventional or unconventional approaches (Gallagher & De Lisi 1994). Since the conventional approaches involved much more time and calculation than unconventional approaches, they were harder to implement correctly. Male students' greater propensity to adopt unconventional approaches therefore resulted in their solving more problems than the female students did.

An example of a problem that can be solved in two ways is the following multiple-choice word problem from an actual SAT test (reprinted in Gallagher & De Lisi 1994): "A blend of coffee is made by mixing Colombian at $8 a pound with espresso coffee at $3 a pound. If the blend is worth $5 a pound, how many pounds of the Columbian coffee are needed to make 50 pounds of the blend?"

The difficulty involved in applying a conventional approach is that the blend costs $5 a pound rather than $5.50 a pound. Thus, the two coffee types cannot be used in equal amounts; the blend must contain more espresso than Columbian, and the proportion of each type must be calculated. A look at the answer choices, however, shows that it is not necessary to adopt the conventional approach. The choices are 20, 25, 30, 35, 40. An unconventional approach would exploit those answers to see almost at a glance that the answer must be 20. All the other choices require equal or larger amounts of Columbian than espresso; as there must be less Columbian than espresso, no calculation is needed at all.

Children appear to behave differently if their first strategy fails. Boys may be quicker to switch to another strategy, while girls may continue with the first, believing it to be the right way to proceed. I am not proposing that girls and boys think differently (but see Belenky, Clinchy, Goldberger, & Tarule 1986). What we know about the sexes is that they are mostly alike. Rather, I am suggesting that boys and girls adopt different strategies in approaching a problem.

When I began working through this example, I saw that unequal amounts of the two types of coffee were required; $8 + $3 \div 2 = 5.50. Oh no, I thought, I'll have to set up an equation to figure out the exact amount. Then I looked at the answers and saw that I could avoid any further calculations. But I felt vaguely as if I were cheating. I was getting the answer by an illicit shortcut.

I could remember other instances of "cheating." In grammar school, for example, I had figured out that I could do subtraction by adding. To subtract 14 from 21, I would ask what number plus 14 would add up to 21. I found that calculation easier than direct subtraction, but I also felt I was doing something not completely kosher, something I shouldn't let anyone know I was doing. It was too easy and I wasn't following the rules. I didn't see that I was exploiting the relationship between addition and subtraction. Later, as I thought about grammar school and high school mathematics, I remembered feeling that there was a single right way to obtain an answer. Because there was a single right answer, I thought—fallaciously—that there must be a single right way to get to the answer. In a sense, I felt that mathematics didn't "belong" to me.

There is a story about the mathematician Friedrich Gauss as a child. His teacher asked the class to add the numbers from 1 to 10. Gauss raised his hand quickly, too quickly for him to have added up the sum. When his teacher asked him how he had arrived at the answer he pointed out that $1+9=10$, $2+8=10$, and so on, and, with another 15 for 5 and 10, the answer was 55. That kind of freedom in thinking about the relations between numbers would have been impossible for me. If I *had* thought of it, I would have seen it as a cheat, since the teacher clearly wanted the students to add up all the numbers individually.

The sex differences in mathematical strategies, ranging from trying to incorporate all the information given in a problem to adopting unconventional strategies, seem amenable to experimental investigation and change. Although we do not yet know the reasons why girls and boys generally take different approaches to problems, we can find out.

Importance of Sex Differences

A final question about sex differences in mathematics—whether hormonal in origin or an effect of gender schemas—is how important are they? A robust and reliable difference is not necessarily an important difference. Overall math differences are small, considerably smaller than the range within each sex. We might argue that the areas in which boys are superior to girls are not that important. There is something to be said for that view. Two studies have shown that SAT-M scores falsely predict that females will receive lower grades than males in college math courses (Bridgeman & Wendler 1991; Wainer & Steinberg 1992). Although young women's scores on the SAT-M are reliably worse than young men's, they do not get lower grades than men, even in advanced math classes. In addition, the types of problems the SAT contains are diverse, and no one has yet examined the relationship between students' performance on particular problems and their grades to see whether the test would predict grades just as well if the problems on which women tend to do worse were eliminated.

On the other hand, taking each sex separately, SAT-M scores do a good job of predicting students' college math grades. In addition, even among the best students—the top-scoring 1 percent of those who take the SAT-M—very small differences in scores are related to achievement in college math courses (Benbow 1992). Thus the math SAT *is* predictive. Overall, however, it is presently impossible to be definitive about the value of the SAT-M.

Even if we put aside the questions raised by SAT-M test, it seems obvious that we want girls and boys to feel equally comfortable with mathematics, to be equally likely to explore unconventional solutions, and to be equally able to apply their knowledge. Mathematical skills are important in many professions—too important to be sacrificed. What we know of inherent differences between males and females does not suggest that achieving equality in mathematics is beyond our ability.

Spatial Visualization and Mental Rotation

The largest and most enduring sex difference is found in speed of solving mental-rotation problems, at which males are superior (Linn & Petersen 1985; Masters & Sanders 1993; Voyer, Voyer, & Bryden 1995). There are many tests that involve manipulating objects spatially. In the test that typically shows the largest sex differences, the person is presented with a drawing showing a three-dimensional target figure—often a figure composed of interlocking blocks—and several other three-dimensional block figures shown at different rotations (i.e., from different angles). The task is to indicate which rotated figure matches the target figure.

Of all the spatial tasks examined, the ability to mentally rotate three-dimensional figures is probably the best candidate for an intrinsic cognitive difference between males and females. Over the years other spatial tests have shown declining sex differences, but mental rotation has not (Voyer et al. 1995).

Mental Rotation and Math Performance
It seems intuitively reasonable to see mental rotation and mathematics as reflecting related abilities, at least for some classes of problems, such as geometry problems. Yet few data confirm such a relationship. When all the available studies are reviewed, they show at best inconsistent relations between mental rotation and mathematics performance (Friedman 1995). Skill at mental rotation may not be necessary, or even strongly helpful, for good mathematics performance. In fact, scores of verbal ability usually predict quantitative scores better than spatial scores do (see, e.g., Gallagher 1989).[6]

The problematic relations between mathematical and spatial performance are illustrated by a detailed study of children in the tenth and twelfth grades. It examined students' performance on a range of mathematical tests, spatial tests, and a language test (Pattison & Grieve 1984). As expected, the boys performed better than the girls on some of the mathematical tests and on the spatial tests. Yet there was no correlation between the boys' and girls' scores on any of the spatial tests and their scores on any of the math tests—even those mathematics tests that seemed intuitively to contain a spatial component.

Another study, however, found that mental-rotation ability predicted scores on the math portion of the SAT for a wide range of female groups: preadolescents, high- and low-ability teenagers, and college students (Casey, Nuttall, Pezaris, & Benbow 1995). For the comparable male samples, though, there was no consistent correlation.[7] Even for females, rotation ability accounted for only 6 to 12 percent of the variability in the scores once verbal ability had been taken into account. The lack of symmetry in the findings for each sex, and the large amount of unexplained variability, suggest that many factors other than rotation ability contribute to SAT math scores. They also suggest that girls and boys approach mathematical problems in different ways (see related data in Bat tista 1990; Fennema & Tartre 1985; Friedman 1995; Gallagher 1989).

Data on females with CAH—people with XX chromosomes who were exposed to atypically high levels of androgen *in utero*—suggest that spatial ability and quantitative ability are largely independent skills. One apparent consequence of the higher androgen is that females with CAH have higher scores on spatial tests than females with normal *in utero* hormonal development (Collaer & Hines 1995). That finding, along with data on the role of testosterone in spatial tasks reviewed in chapter 4, suggests that spatial performance is linked to hormones.

If ability in mental rotation were associated with math performance, then females with CAH would score higher on quantitative tests than females without CAH. They do not. If anything, females with CAH do somewhat worse on quantitative tests than females without CAH (see Collaer & Hines 1995), which supports the suggestion that spatial and mathematical performance are largely independent of each other.[8]

Problem-Solving Strategies

Earlier I suggested that there are many ways of arriving at the correct answer to a mathematical problem. Spatial visualization is but one way among many. It may not be the only way, even for geometry problems. If spatial visualization does not work, more abstract, logical, approaches might. Depending on the approach a teacher emphasizes, girls and boys might perform differently.

Some data suggest that teachers' methods do affect children's problem-solving strategies. One study looked at the role of spatial visualization in high school students' ability to solve geometry problems (Battista 1990). As it happened, the children were in two different geometry classes. One was taught by a female teacher who said she stressed the ability to visualize; in the other class, the male teacher used drawings but did not stress spatial visualization because, he said, he was not good at it. In the female teacher's class, the girls scored worse on a test of geometric problem solving than the boys did. In the male teacher's class, the girls and boys scored equally. There was no average difference in scores between the two classes.

Since the two teachers may have differed on a number of characteristics other than their use of visualization, those data cannot be taken as definitive, but they are intriguing. They suggest that girls do not use spatial visualization as effectively as boys do and, further, that girls can perform as well as boys do when allowed to develop alternative methods. So if teachers (falsely) believe that geometry requires spatial visualization, girls may be at an unnecessary disadvantage. Teachers will emphasize one solution technique, visualization, at the expense of another, logical reasoning, which girls might utilize more easily.

Of course, boys can reason logically and girls can use spatial visualization, and both sexes can learn to do better at both. It may be, however, that in their first experience with a particular problem boys tend to adopt one strategy and girls another. If instruction is geared to a single approach, and that approach is not the child's first choice, she or he will suffer. My speculation that girls believe that there is only one way to approach a problem implies that they may be particularly at risk when that first method doesn't work.

When I took high school geometry I was totally in a fog for the first marking period. We were supposed to keep a notebook of problems and hand it in for grading at the end of the first five weeks. I had no notebook to hand in because I couldn't solve a single problem. I was completely flummoxed. I was astonished that my peers, including my best friend, were treating the material like any other material. I thought there was too little information given in the problems to solve them. On the day that everyone else handed in their notebooks, my (female) teacher said, "Valian, you flunk." My report card bore its first F, circled in red to signify that I could do better.

The situation seemed impossible. I couldn't understand the material. I couldn't drop the course because geometry was a required course for students planning to go to college. Equally, I couldn't get an F.

When my best friend tried to help me I couldn't understand her explanations, and she couldn't understand my problem. Out of desperation, I consulted two boys in my homeroom who had already taken geometry. I don't remember what they said over the course of several days, but I finally had an aha! experience. I got it. Geometry became pure and beautiful. And easy. I could prove everything.

I don't remember what teaching method my teacher used. I am reluctant to blame her, for most of the other students had no special difficulty. Yet my example is a testament to how people can fail totally because they cannot find a problem-solving approach that works for them. I finally succeeded because success was a psychological imperative: I had to go to college; therefore, I had to do well in high school. Those two demands, which from the point of view of geometry were completely irrelevant, and which I never questioned, forced me to find a way to solve geometry problems. Without them I would have concluded that geometry was impossible for me.

Girls, I suggest, are particularly at risk for drawing such conclusions. I had no conscious notion that girls were bad at math, nor that I was bad at math. I never had been before. Nevertheless, my first hypothesis when I failed to understand how to perform well was that I *couldn't* succeed. I didn't attribute it to being a girl; I attributed it to being me. I not only thought there was a single right answer but assumed there was only one way to get to that answer, and I didn't know what it was.

My experience with geometry should have taught me that there are multiple routes to mathematical problem solving, but it did not. Instead, I thought I got lucky. I never explicitly formulated the idea that problems can be solved in a variety of ways or that an instructor's teaching methods are only one approach. If I had, I might have drawn different conclusions. I might have thought, when I had difficulties, not just that I needed to work harder but that I needed to find my own way of getting to the answer.

Practice

Experience positively affects how well both males and females perform on spatial tests, and boys may get more experience from an early age. They may be given more toys, such as blocks, that encourage visual spatialization and mental rotation (Block 1983). A training study of sixth, seventh, and eighth graders lends support to the idea that experience with blocks improves spatial skills (Ben-Chaim, Lappan, & Houang 1988). Children from three different schools took a standardized spatial visualization test just before they received three weeks of instruction in spatial visualization. In the training, the students used small cubes to make buildings and made drawings of cube structures from various angles, including corner views. At the end of the instruction they took the spatial test again. The results were clear. The instruction had dramatically improved the children's performance. Although differences between girls and boys remained, the amount of improvement was much greater than the differences between the sexes. In addition, both sexes showed the same degree of improvement.

College students also differ by sex in a similar ability, adeptness at judging the relative velocity of objects presented on a computer screen. When given feedback about the correctness of their estimates, however, both males and females improved within a single session (Law, Pellegrino, & Hunt 1993). Similar results were found in a study of video-game skills among undergraduates (Okagaki & Frensch 1994). At a minimum, the results show that females' lower performance on mental-rotation tasks can be modified by experience. Were girls to have more of such experiences early in life, sex differences in mental rotation might disappear.

Instructions

Other studies have indicated that, for some spatial tasks, the kinds of written instructions given to college students affect the size of sex differences in rotation ability. If instructions emphasize the spatial character of the task, males perform better than females do. If they do not, no differences between males and females are in evidence (Sharps, Price, & Williams 1994; Sharps, Welton, & Price 1993). Some portion of females' poorer performance appears to be due to the way they conceptualize the task. (See chapter 8 for an experiment in which college women solved fewer math problems when told that women tended to perform worse on them than men did.)

Time

Students' performance on tests of mental rotation is also affected by time pressures. In one study, high school students were allowed to go back to problems they had failed to solve during the timed portion of a test (Gallagher & Johnson 1992). Both males and females improved, but females improved dramatically. The difference between males and females still favored males but was reduced substantially. As practice of a skill generally improves speed of performance, the results of this study suggest that differences in experience with rotation tasks play an important role in the sex differences observed on tests.[9]

On balance, the data suggest that a sizable proportion of the sex difference in the ability to mentally rotate three-dimensional figures rapidly is related to hormonal differences between the sexes. At the same time, they show that performance is sensitive to practice and to the way students conceptualize a task. While hormones undoubtedly play a role, they neither guarantee that males will excel nor prevent females from excelling.

What is most important is the likelihood that strong spatial skills may be functionally independent of strong quantitative skills. Students can do well in math regardless of their spatial skills. From an educational policy point of view, the data on mathematics and spatial skills suggest that children should be taught a variety of approaches to problem solving.

Conclusion: The Significance of Cognitive Sex Differences

There is little evidence for intrinsic verbal cognitive differences. Differences in subareas of mathematics exist, but hormonal differences appear to play a relatively small role. Instead, the variability in performance—across cultures, across time, and across situations—indicates a prominent role for environmental factors.

Even with the cognitive difference most likely to have a biological connection—mental rotation of three-dimensional figures—it is difficult to estimate the relative contributions of hormonal and environmental effects. We know that practice, kind of instructions given, and changes in the time allowed to solve problems can affect the sex differences. Since skill in mental rotation does not seem necessary for most quantitative performance, its importance seems to have been overemphasized. The difference in perceptual speed that favors females, on the other hand, has been little studied. Hence, we do not know what the basis of those differences may be, nor how strongly they contribute to other cognitive skills. It is an area in need of investigation.

Where cross-cultural comparisons are available, they indicate that the expression of cognitive sex differences is extremely variable and subject to environmental influence. The decline of cognitive differences over short periods of time (e.g., decades) also suggests flexibility in the expression of cognitive abilities. The variability of trait expression across cultures and across time argues in favor of social influences, although the persistence of some sex differences across many different cultures may indeed reflect intrinsic differences. Because the absolute differences within each sex are usually much larger than the average differences between the sexes, however, it is difficult to ascertain the relative roles of biological and social influences.

In the chapters that follow, I review many other sex differences. For none of those is the evidence for a biological connection as clear as it is for the behavioral and cognitive differences discussed in this chapter and in chapter 4. Should further research demonstrate such connections, the point reiterated throughout would apply: the presence or absence of a biological connection is less important than a trait's inherent variability.

Given what we know about flexibility in the expression of a given ability or skill, the possible existence of intrinsic sex differences has little practical relevance. As intuitive scientists we tend to think that if a characteristic has a biological component it is immutable. But this idea is factually incorrect. No cognitive ability is solely a result of hormones; each is affected by a host of social and cultural factors.

We can acknowledge the existence of biologically connected sex differences without drawing incorrect inferences from them. Biology is one contributor to behavior; the social environment is another. Even differences which we think of as hallmarks of sex difference—voice pitch, aggressiveness, verbal ability, mathematic ability—seem to owe at least as much to environmental as to biological influences.

As intuitive scientists we may also tend to view roughly analogous sex differences in the animal world as models of human sex differences and conclude that differences in male and female behavior are inevitable. Here too our inference is unsupported. It is true that the animal world is a useful model for the human world in many ways, including the fact that the display and development of biologically mediated traits is influenced by the environment. But animal models are always only partial models. We do not copy an animal's behavior when we can improve upon it. We use our intelligence and imagination to understand the underlying mechanisms of our behaviors and traits so that we can live as fulfilling a life as possible. We can put that intelligence and imagination to use in eliminating sex differences in valued skills like mathematics.

6

Schemas That Explain Behavior

In chapters 2 and 3 we saw that adults—men and women alike—systematically misperceive and misevaluate children in terms of their expectations about sex differences. In chapters 4 and 5 we saw the limits of hormonal explanations of sex differences. As I will show in chapter 7, adults similarly misperceive and misevaluate each other, often underrating women and overrating men. Those misperceptions set up expectations that are at least partially fulfilled (as described in chapter 8). In this chapter I present a cognitive explanation of the distortions humans impose on reality. The notion of a schema introduced in chapter 1 plays a central role in the explanation.

Schemas are hypotheses that we use to interpret social events.[1] Because our implicit hypotheses about males and females include expectations about their professional competence, they bias our interpretation of people's performance. To oversimplify, we expect men to do well and see their behavior in the rosy light of our positive expectations. Conversely, we expect women to do less well and judge their actual performance in the darker light of our negative expectations.

How Schemas Affect Perceptions, Interpretations, and Expectations

A schema is a mental construct that, as the name suggests, contains in schematic or abbreviated form someone's concept about an individual or event, or a group of people or events. It includes the person's or group's main characteristics, from the perceiver's point of view, and the relationship among those features. (See Fiske & Taylor 1991, for a fuller explication of schemas.) The term *schema* is broader and more neutral than the term *stereotype,* which tends to connote an inaccurate and negative view of a social group. Schemas may be accurate or inaccurate, and they may be positive, negative, or neutral.

At the most basic level, our schemas of individuals allow us to recognize people at a glance—even when they change their clothing, facial expressions, or hairstyle. But schemas also play a more important role. They are cognitive frameworks that help us perceive and categorize new individuals and provide explanations of people's actions; they also give rise to expectations about others' future actions. Schemas are thus a form of hypothesis, a small-scale intuitive hypothesis. Without schemas, our world would consist of millions of unrelated individuals and events; we would be unable to form any generalizations. They are a cognitive necessity for making sense of the social world of everyday life. Schemas may contain errors, but they are indispensable.

The schemas most relevant to human perceptions of women's and men's professional competence are *role schemas,* such as those of lawyer, professor, father, woman (Fiske & Taylor 1991). As the mixed list suggests, some roles are professional (lawyer and professor), others refer to a person's family role (father), and yet others refer to the role someone plays in society as a whole (woman). It can be argued that a status—such as being a woman—should not be termed a role; but the exact classification is not important. What is important is that we not only have schemas or conceptions about people based on professional roles—including both what we think they should do to properly fill their roles and what we think they typically do—but we also have schemas based on people's place in society. (Sometimes, of course, people's different roles conflict.)

An example of a schema illustrating these is a college student's schema of a professor. All students have a conception of what professors are like, a conception that becomes more detailed through their undergraduate years. The schema gives rise to certain expectations: such as that the professor will have a solid understanding of his or her subject, will attend all class sessions, will be on time, will be prepared, will give homework assignments and examinations that reflect the course material, will grade fairly, will be in the office during posted office hours, and so on.

The student's schema of professor does not contain all the features of the professor's own schema of professor, which probably also includes conducting research and fulfilling various administrative functions. No matter how full the student's schema may be, the professor's is considerably fuller, due to his or her greater knowledge of the profession. Nevertheless, the student's schema does allow the student to predict the general outline of a professor's behavior. Even though some of the predictions may be inaccurate, the student is still farther ahead, with the schema, than she or he would be by treating each professor as a new individual unrelated to all other professors.

Schemas also allow observers to interpret behaviors. A student who hears a professor describe the spring day the clocks changed without her realizing it and the odd succession of events that ensued—from "early" closing of restaurants to movies starting off-schedule—will be amused by this evidence of an absent-minded professor who kept supplying increasingly elaborate explanations for a day gone haywire. The student is unlikely to conclude that the professor is an idiot. A schema rules out some interpretations and makes others more likely.

Finally, perhaps most important, schemas fill in gaps when evidence is lacking or ambiguous. Even a professor whose behavior is blatantly at variance with the schema may for some time be perceived as consistent with it. A professor who is not present during office hours, for example, may be seen as having an emergency that prevented him or her from meeting that obligation. The student's first thought is not that the professor is too lazy to come in. The schema has produced the expectation that the professor will meet his or her pedagogical obligations, and the professor is perceived in the light of the schema. The failure to show up will be attributed to external causes, especially if the professor is later apologetic and produces a plausible excuse.

On the other hand, if the professor continues to skip office hours and makes no or only the most casual apology, the student will have more solid evidence that that professor does not fit the schema: that professor is a bad professor. But the schema for professor does not change; instead, the professor is perceived as an exception to the schema, a "subtype," the irresponsible professor.

In general, when observers receive information about an individual that contradicts their schema, they handle the information in one of two ways. They can ignore it by supplying a different interpretation of it. For example, the professor is not irresponsible; the absence is due to reasons beyond his or her control. Or the contradictory information can be treated as exceptional; the professor then falls into the subtype of bad professor. Almost never is the schema itself changed. The student still expects other professors to behave responsibly, knowledgeably, and fairly.

If a schema is reasonably accurate and based on a large sample, it is completely appropriate to treat the exception as a special category, a subtype. People should not change their beliefs about an entire group because of the behavior of one individual. The exception *should* be treated as an exception. The problem with social schemas is that observers can receive a great deal of information that is discrepant with the schema without altering it.

Our schemas constitute informal hypotheses, and we ourselves are informal scientists doing informal experiments. Just as scientists sometimes make errors because they interpret their data in the light of their working hypothesis, we as informal scientists can make similar mistakes. Cognitive and social psychologists and sociologists who specialize in the study of science have explored a phenomenon called *confirmation bias* (see initial work by Wason 1960). The term refers to the human tendency to seek information that confirms a hypothesis and to discount information that does not. When the information is not clearly contradictory but is ambiguous, people see no compelling reason to discard a hypothesis.

Once a hypothesis is firmly in place—especially a social hypothesis—it is very difficult to dislodge, no matter how much disconfirming evidence comes in (see Ross, Lepper, & Hubbard 1975, on *belief perseverance* and discussion in Nisbett & Ross 1980). People hang onto a hypothesis until they have a new one to replace it, ignoring contradictory evidence, or labeling the evidence as an exception that the otherwise-good hypothesis does not seem to handle. This phenomenon is now almost a truism of the history of science (see Kuhn 1962, esp. pp. 77ff.). Often, the process of looking for confirming evidence is very helpful; it allows us to build up the hypotheses we need to make sense out of our world, and it lessens the likelihood that we will abandon a successful hypothesis too early.

Schemas thus serve a number of functions. They give rise to expectations. They interpret behavior in ways that are consistent with the schema rather than inconsistent with it. They supply explanations where data are missing or ambiguous. They direct the search for new information. They make subtyping a likely way of handling exceptions.

The student's schema for professor is relatively benign (if *my* schema of the student's schema is correct). Some role schemas, however, have a negative character. The schema for politician, for example, has a negative cast, as does the schema for used-car salesperson.

The schema for used-car salesperson includes being deceitful, manipulative, crafty, and untruthful. It provides a good example of how individuals who do not fit the schema can be misperceived. A used-car salesperson who is honest, truthful, helpful, and sincere may be perceived, instead, as particularly clever, devious, and wily. In fact, it is hard to imagine anything a used-car salesperson could do to be seen even as an exception to the schema. The nature of this schema is such that any action or demeanor can be perceived as consistent with it: any behavior, no matter how straightforward it appears to be on the surface, can be interpreted as manipulative and crafty.

Schemas are thus extremely powerful shapers of our interpretations—and misinterpretations—of others' behaviors and motives. Although the student's schema of a professor, as I outlined it, is reasonably accurate, role schemas can be inaccurate—even if they include accurate elements—in three different ways: they may portray characteristics as more extreme than they actually are; they can give more weight to positive characteristics than to negative ones (or the reverse); and they can fail to indicate how much variability there is in the possession of a characteristic (Judd & Park 1993). Our schema of used-car salespeople may be inaccurate in all three ways. First, we may exaggerate their untrustworthiness, perhaps because of a single bad experience in the past. Second, we may pay more attention to their negative characteristics, such as venality, than to their positive features, such as knowledge of cars. Third, we may think that all used-car salespeople are alike, perhaps because we have had relatively few experiences and base our opinion on a small sample.

Sex Differences

There are hundreds of observable sex differences that we, as intuitive scientists, try to explain. Our hypotheses are an attempt to make sense of the data the environment provides us with. As we form our conceptions of what it means to be male or female, we do not consider where the sex differences came from or the actual extent of those differences. Even if the differences arise from cultural conventions, and even if they mask underlying similarities, they become for us hallmarks of sex differences. When I was thirteen years old I was allowed to place a waxy, pinkish-red compound on my lips. If asked, I would have agreed that application of this compound was a cultural convention. Nonetheless, it would have seemed laughable and faintly repugnant to me to see my male classmates doing the same thing. The convention seemed right and fitting, despite the fact that male and female lips are by nature exactly the same range of colors.

The data on which we base our gender schemas come from numerous sources. First, men and women look different. Some of the differences we see are given by nature, some are determined by nature but manipulated by culture, and some are purely cultural in origin. Besides genital differences, some of the "natural" differences are size, body shape, and amount of body hair.

Body hair is an example of a natural trait affected by cultural norms. Women naturally have much less chest, back, and facial hair than men. The norm in U.S. culture diminishes the difference in facial hair: men shave. In two other regions—the legs and armpits—there is high overlap between the sexes in amount of hair, although women have less than men. Here, American culture exaggerates the difference: most women shave or otherwise remove the hair in these areas. Finally, women naturally have more hair on their heads than men do, another difference that the cultural norm exaggerates. In the area of body hair, then, there exist several basic differences between American males and females; the culture exaggerates some, thereby presenting observers with misleading data about the "typical" male and the "typical" female. The sexes are actually physically more similar than our culturally conditioned observations would suggest.

Other purely conventional sex differences in U.S. culture are visible in the realm of dress. Mature males and females dress very differently, in everything from height of shoe heels to amount and type of facial decoration. With an effort of will one can abstract away the superficially imposed differences and notice how much overlap there is, for example, in the facial structure of males and females, especially older people. But it takes an effort of will, precisely because our perceptions are mediated by our gender schemas. Our observations are responsive to apparel, the wearing of metal, stone, and glass ornaments, and facial decoration. That is the purpose of such cultural conventions; they add information that the raw material does not convey.

Men and women also sound different. As we noted in chapter 4, voice pitch is a natural difference that is culturally manipulated; differences in pitch are only partially accounted for by anatomical differences (Sachs, Lieberman, & Erikson 1973). Sex differences in voice pitch are greater in North America than they are in Europe (McConnell-Ginet 1983), and smaller in England than in Japan (Loveday 1981). Although pitch is a subtle difference, it is one people readily recognize. When asked about men's and women's voices, Americans estimated that 73 percent of men had deep voices but that only 30 percent of women did (Deaux & Lewis 1984).

In pitch as in other superficial traits, observers usually do not know what the underlying facts are. Such knowledge requires access to information about large numbers of people from a variety of cultures and to facts about anatomy that most observers do not have.

Men and women also act differently in a number of ways. Here are a few random examples of such differences. Men have a much higher threshold for crying than women do. Mixed-sex couples in restaurants tend to occupy different seats, with the woman sitting with her back against the wall and the man facing the wall. In automobiles, the woman rides in the passenger seat and the man sits in the driver's seat. Men take showers and women take baths. Such behavioral differences are strong and ubiquitous. Although the differences are purely cultural, they have powerful effects. When I take the "man's" seat in a restaurant I feel faintly uncomfortable if my companion is male. I am transgressing an unspoken code.

Finally, there are personality differences in the way men and women see themselves. Men portray themselves as acting as an independent, effective agent more than women do, and as more task-oriented, and instrumental (Spence & Helmreich 1978; Spence & Sawin 1985). Women see themselves as more expressive and communal and more interested in people than men do.[2] Most people of both sexes believe they have each attribute to some degree. That is quite reasonable, since the attributes are not mutually exclusive. One could have all of the traits, or none of them, and one could possess each of them to different degrees at different times. Men, however, do report one cluster of traits more often than women do; and women report a different cluster more often than men do. Those two clusters appear to form the core of our gender schemas; they capture the differences we see as essential to the natures of males and females.

A quantitative review of studies of personality characteristics conducted between 1940 and 1992 shows several enduring and sizable sex differences (Feingold 1994). It confirms that men consistently see themselves as an initiator of action more than women do, and that women see themselves as communal more than men do. Males also portray themselves as more assertive than females do. Females portray themselves as more anxious, more trusting, and more nurturant, than males do. Gender schemas are alive and well, and have moderated only slightly over the years. Sex differences in personality have changed less than sex differences in cognition.

Who's Normal? Who's Better?

Males tend to be perceived as the norm against which females are measured, not only in male-dominated areas like business but also in gender-neutral areas like citizenship. One study illustrates how pervasive this assumption is. When male and female college students were asked to imagine a typical American voter and were then asked questions about that person, about 75 percent of the students envisioned the voter as male (Miller, Taylor, & Buck 1991). As is usually the case, there were no differences between the male and female students; both tended to see the male as the norm. A man is a better example of a voter than a woman is.

In another question, the students were told of a fictitious difference in voting patterns between men and women and asked to account for it. For example, students were told that 8 percent more men than women had voted in the past several presidential elections. In the 1996 presidential elections there was a real gender gap: men showed less of a preference for Clinton than women did.

One possible way of explaining a difference would be to attribute characteristics to each sex that might affect their voting. For example, men are concerned about X and therefore vote for candidate Jones, who promises to do something about X; or women are concerned about Y and therefore vote for Smith, who promises to do something about Y. That form of explanation takes neither group as the norm. Each group's voting pattern gets attention and requires explanation. The students' explanations did not take that form.

A second possible way of explaining a difference is to take one group as the norm, the group whose behavior needs no explanation. When one group—say, in this case, men—is the norm, the other group's behavior—in this case, women's—needs explaining. If that is the case, then an explanation will refer to women's characteristics rather than men's. That is what the students did in this study (Miller et al. 1991). They saw the women's behavior as the deviant pattern that required explanation. They thus explained sex differences in voting in terms of how women are different from men, rather than in terms of how men are different from women, or in terms of how each group has particular characteristics that result in the observed differences.

Men exemplify the normal in other ways as well. It is more acceptable for a female to adopt masculine characteristics than for a male to adopt feminine ones. As in childhood, so in adulthood. A woman may wear pants but a man may not wear a skirt. A woman with a low-pitched voice is more acceptable than a man with a high-pitched one.

Such latitude for women is not, however, without its limits. When Ann Hopkins was being evaluated for partnership at the accounting firm Price Waterhouse, her evaluators criticized her for not wearing make-up and said she needed to go to charm school. Despite her outstanding performance, she was denied partnership. She clearly suffered because she had too few feminine characteristics and too many masculine ones. Of course, a man with too few masculine characteristics and too many feminine ones would probably not have been hired in the first place. The basis of the asymmetry appears to be the higher value placed by the culture as a whole on masculine traits compared to feminine ones.

I was reminded of this in class one day when I commented on a Halloween party I had attended. A couple had dressed their nine-month-old son in a dress and bonnet. I brought up the example in a discussion of the subtle differences in treatment of boys and girls that could affect later sex differences. The infant was very uncomfortable in the dress; its full skirt kept getting caught between his legs, and the snug fit of the bodice prevented him from moving his arms freely. His plight made me notice for the first time how constricting baby girls' clothing is. As one of the major differences observed between girls and boys is level of activity (as reviewed in chapter 4), I speculated in class that sex differences in infants' clothing could exaggerate that difference by restricting girls' freedom of movement.

The class, however, paid no attention to my speculation. They could not get beyond the idea of dressing a baby boy as a baby girl. One female student said, "When you described it, my first reaction was that it was cruel." Cruel not because the dress limited the child's movements, nor because he would suffer any lasting harm from spending a few hours in girls' clothing, but cruel because a boy was being made into a girl—and thus devalued. Dressing a girl as a boy, the same student said, would not have seemed cruel, just odd. The student's comment does not exhaust what the students found so shocking about the Halloween example, but it does illustrate the extent to which our culture values masculinity and how extreme reactions to dress violations can be.

Ten years later, in the late summer of 1995, I see a young man on the street in London wearing a slightly A-line skirt, which I later realize is the skirt of a dress. It comes down to just below his calves. He is wearing moccasins with no socks. I mentally salute him for his courage. As I discreetly watch him, I see him give a tug in an effort to align the skirt better. Like the baby boy, the young man finds the dress uncomfortable. I think of how often we see women tug, pull, align, and straighten their clothes. Women's garments demand that the wearer pay attention to them, whether the wearer is male or female.

What, in a situation like this, is the norm? Should we explain why men do not wear clothing that requires frequent attention, why women do, or both? Our everyday actions speak for us. Masculine clothing, except for the symbolic tie, defines the norm.

Origins of Gender Schemas

The hundreds of sex differences we observe every day could be the basis of our gender schemas; that is, our conceptions of the sexes might be the direct result of our observations. Or, alternatively, most of the sex differences we observe could be the result of gender schemas. That dichotomy, however, oversimplifies the possibilities. A more complex possibility is that a small number of intrinsic differences are the basis for gender schemas. The schemas, then, operate quasiindependently to elaborate and produce further differences between the sexes.

Yet another hypothesis is that gender schemas are based, not on intrinsic sex differences, but on the sexual division of labor. Eagly (1987) suggests that the typical social roles played by women and men call for the characteristics that we have come to associate with each sex. Because men have tended to occupy positions that, for competent performance, require characteristics like agency, independence, instrumentality, and task-orientation, we transfer the requirements of the roles to the personalities of the people who occupy them. We therefore see men as independent agents, task-oriented, and so on. Similarly, because women have tended to occupy positions that require nurturance and expressiveness, we have come to think of them as possessing the characteristics required to be a parent and homemaker.

There are at least two ways to interpret Eagly's hypothesis. The first one would argue that the cognitive and personality traits of the two sexes are identical but that we perceive males and females differently because they hold different jobs. A more plausible possibility, given the data, is that men and women develop the characteristics needed to fill certain roles at the expense of other characteristics, which are not needed. Although everyone might have the same intrinsic potential characteristics, some would predominate and others recede, depending on the role the person assumed. Thus, on Eagly's hypothesis, both actual sex differences and perceived sex differences could arise from the fact that men occupy certain roles and women others. The role differentiation could have originated in the absence of any intrinsic personality or cognitive differences between the sexes.

A weak spot of Eagly's (1987) intriguing hypothesis is the assumption that different roles genuinely require different personality characteristics along the divisions represented by gender schemas. Some roles, such as professor, therapist, minister, and doctor, could be seen as requiring nurturance, communality, and expressiveness as much as instrumentality and agency—and indeed the roles of professor and doctor are so perceived (Conway, Pizzamiglio, & Mount 1996). Yet those roles are primarily filled by men and were filled almost solely by men until the 1970s. Other roles, such as housekeeper, social worker, or nursery school teacher, could be seen as demanding instrumentality and the ability to act as an independent agent as much as nurturance and expressiveness. Yet those roles are still primarily filled by women. We might see still other roles, such as assembly-line worker, as calling for neither masculine nor feminine traits.

If, contrary to Eagly's assumption, most jobs require both masculine and feminine characteristics, the aspects of a job that are seen as primary should change over time, depending on the sex of the people occupying it (Reskin & Roos 1990). That prediction is borne out by the history of jobs ranging from bartending to bank work. For example, in 1917 there was a shortage of male bank workers. Low-level banking jobs were then described by banks as suitable for women because women were neat, tactful, and intuitive. During the Depression, a surplus of males led banks to redefine the same jobs as unsuitable for women, on the grounds that the banking public would not want women to handle their money. During World War II, jobs as tellers were again seen as suitable for women, on the grounds that women were good at dealing with the public (Reskin & Roos 1990). Jobs, it seems, can change their gender at employers' will.

World War II provides another example of how rapidly jobs can be redefined. In the United States and Britain, jobs previously held only by men, such as work in munitions plants, were increasingly held by women. Because only men were allowed to fill combat positions in the armed services, their departure left civilian jobs unoccupied. Suddenly, women found that they could rivet and solder and carry large pieces of metal. After the war, the jobs and the women who carried them out changed again, just as suddenly, so that returning male veterans could reoccupy the "masculine" positions they had left.

If many sex-segregated occupations do not genuinely require personality or cognitive traits that are differentially distributed between the sexes, our notions of masculinity and femininity cannot derive solely from the jobs males and females typically hold. The plasticity in how work is defined suggests instead that our conceptions of what characteristics different jobs require are shaped by our conceptions of the people who occupy them. If a job is predominantly held by women, we see it as a feminine job, emphasize the feminine characteristics it requires and, correspondingly, devalue the job. If a job is predominantly held by men, we see it as a masculine job, emphasize its masculine characteristics, and, correspondingly, value it more highly.

The occupation of physician is perhaps the best example of how people's conception of a profession is shaped by their conception of the people practicing it. In the United States, physicians have been largely male, and the occupation is both prestigious and lucrative. The average young male M.D. earned $155,000 a year in 1991 (Baker 1996). In Russia, where physicians are largely female, the occupation is neither prestigious nor lucrative. Eagly's assumption that most occupations require either "male" or "female" characteristics thus seems less than fully tenable.

A somewhat different hypothesis is Hoffman and Hurst's (1990) proposal that our gender schemas are an attempt to justify a pre-existing sexual division of labor. They argue that even if sex segregation was initially completely fortuitous, once it exists it requires rationalization. People expect jobs to be filled by different groups in proportion to their representation in the total population. If, instead, there is an imbalance in some occupations or roles, people will search for an explanation of the unequal division—in short, for a rationalization. Their explanation would attribute different internal characteristics to members of different groups: people from group X are highly represented in a particular position because they have a particular set of characteristics; group Y members are not highly represented because they lack those characteristics.

Hoffman and Hurst thus differ from Eagly in an important respect. Jobs do not create actual sex differences. Instead, jobs create gender schemas via the sexual division of labor. Still, they are similar to Eagly in taking job differentiation as the basis for gender schemas. They both hypothesize that the jobs men and women happen to fill at some point are seen, after the fact, as requiring certain traits, and that those traits are the foundation for gender schemas. Thus, Hoffman and Hurst's proposal has a weak spot similar to Eagly's. If the jobs occupied by men do not really require agency, aggressiveness, instrumentality, and task-orientation more than the jobs occupied by women, or if the jobs performed by women do not really require nurturance, communality, and expressiveness more than the jobs performed by men, something else must explain why we perceive men and women in those terms.

The discussion thus far has ignored what may be the most distinctive role occupied by women, motherhood. Although motherhood requires masculine as well as feminine traits, the trait most often associated with it is nurturance. That is probably because mothers physically nurture their children, and physical cues are disproportionately important in the formation of schemas. Motherhood may thus provide the missing link in the explanation of gender schemas. The cognitive analysis I propose combines Hoffman and Hurst's (1990) rationalization theory with the facts that only women can be mothers and that nurturance is a preeminent physical trait of mothers. *One* set of sexually differentiated activities, giving birth to and physically nursing infants, qualitatively separates the sexes; it lays the foundation for gender schemas and dominates conceptions of women among both men and women. The act of physical nurturance is extrapolated to the personality realm, so that we—both women and men—see women not only as literally nurturing but also as metaphorically nurturing.

My own hypothesis about the origin of gender schemas views the components of schema development as cognitively based: we apply the same reasoning to our social world as we do to our physical world, and we make mistakes in both. In the case of gender schemas, we make a mistake right at the beginning, by using physical nurturance as a metaphor for psychological nurturance. It is, I would argue, our beliefs in sex differences, based on our perception of a single difference, that create and amplify other sex differences.

Some evidence that people's thought processes fit my description comes from a passage in Parsons and Bales (1955). The authors are trying to explain the historical development of the sexual division of labor and sex differences. They express explicitly a line of reasoning that, I suggest, people implicitly adopt as intuitive social scientists. My concern here is not with the correctness of their account, which has been criticized from many points of view, but with its relevance to the way we form gender schemas.

The fundamental explanation of the allocation of the roles between the biological sexes lies in the fact that the bearing and early nursing of children establish a strong presumptive primacy of the relation of the mother to the small child and this in turn establishes a presumption that the man, who is exempted from these biological functions, should specialize in the alternative instrumental direction.[3]

The use of the terms *presumptive* and *presumption* shows that Parsons and Bales realize there is no logical connection between the premise that women give birth and nurse their infants and the conclusion that men and women have different societal roles. They suggest, as my proposal does, that people leap metaphorically over that logical chasm.

Parsons and Bales's use of the term *presumption* also makes it clear that no logic forces men into specializing in an "alternative instrumental direction." Being instrumental is not an alternative to being nurturant; nor do people have to specialize at all. Male and female schemas are not mutually contradictory, inconsistent, or incompatible. A single individual can possess all of the socially desirable masculine and feminine traits or none of them; data from rating scales show that some individuals do possess many traits of both types, while others possess only a few of each (Spence, Deaux, and Helmreich 1985).

Yet, as Parsons and Bales (1955) indicate, we do contrast instrumental to nurturant and often see so strong a contrast between them that we cannot see how one person could be both. As social beings, we tend to perceive the genders as alternatives to each other, as occupying opposite and contrasting ends of a continuum. The familiar term, the *opposite sex,* appears in scientific articles as well as in everyday speech, even though the sexes are not opposite but are much more alike than they are different.[4]

Parsons and Bales also describe men as "exempted from" childbirth and nursing, as if these functions were like military service—an activity most people would avoid if they could only get a deferment! Another reflection of our everyday thinking is implicit in their references to the two persons in the passage as "mother" and "man." The woman is defined by her role vis-à-vis another person, but the father is defined by his sex.

I have drawn on Eagly's (1987) and Hoffman and Hurst's (1990) theorizing to suggest that the sexual division of one particular labor—the bearing and nursing of infants—leads people to develop gender schemas, the core of which is women's metaphorical nurturance. I am proposing that nonconscious hypothesizing and reasoning about the sexes along the lines of the passage from Parsons and Bales cause us to jump to conclusions that do not follow from the premises.

Hypothesis-formation is a natural and desirable cognitive activity, whether the domain is the physical world or the social world. It helps explain our world and guide our behavior. But the naturalness of hypothesis-construction does not guarantee the truth of the hypotheses we construct. The notion of a flat earth is a notable example of a natural concept, a concept most people's experiences seem to verify. People need very special data or specific instruction to discover that the flat-world hypothesis is false. The naturalness of a concept and its apparent fit with everyday experience is independent of its truth. Gender schemas, I suggest, are similar to a belief that the earth is flat.

An important difference between the two beliefs, however, is that no matter how deeply we believe the earth to be flat we cannot make it so. But beliefs about human nature can create evidence that superficially appears to confirm false beliefs. The cultural elaboration of gender schemas can lead, in turn, to the creation of real sex differences. Cultural expectations and practices that amplify existing differences can create other differences out of whole cloth. Even though the social world is not infinitely malleable, it is much more malleable than the physical world, which makes detecting our errors more difficult.[5]

According to my analysis, even if we were to wipe the slate clean and start over today, we would recreate gender schemas and a sexual division of labor. The "presumptive primacy" of childbirth and nursing would be the grist for our cognitive mill. Without access to informative data or instruction to counter our natural logical leaps, we would form the same hypotheses about sex differences and recreate differences that would appear to confirm the hypotheses. Our uncorrected errors of reasoning would further entrench our false beliefs.

Entrenching Gender Schemas

There are three processes that work together to entrench gender schemas in our minds and social practices. The first, as the passage from Parsons and Bales illustrates, is the exceptional responsiveness of gender schemas to physical differences (Deaux 1987). If people look consistently different, we conclude that they are different. Males and females do look different, even though we have created many of those differences. We also want people to look different if our concept of them is that they are different. (The neighbors are always surprised to learn that the ordinary-looking person who lives next door is a murderer.) So males should look masculine and females should look feminine. We view people as odd if they fail to conform to gender norms. It is as if we need to be physically reassured about an individual's gender identity and can tolerate the crossing of gender lines in personality and intellect more easily if the person adheres to our physical gender conventions.

Another mechanism that entrenches gender schemas is our tendency to reason from extreme examples. We are prone to interpret extreme examples as an indication that a trait is more common than it actually is (Fiske & Taylor 1991). Some time ago, I taught a class in which one of the students was a recent immigrant from Israel. He was an exceptionally intelligent and diligent person who participated actively in class. I was impressed by the way he compensated for his unfamiliarity with English by looking up every unknown word in a dictionary. I soon found myself concluding that Israeli students in general were hard workers. The reasoning underlying my conclusion seems to be that if a behavior that extreme can occur in one person, it must be present to some degree in the group as a whole. An Israeli graduate student whom I later spoke to laughed at my schema. In Israel, she said, college students didn't work particularly hard. If there was any truth to my schema, it only applied to Israeli students who were studying in the United States.

In the domain of sex differences, we apply the same kind of reasoning. The existence of a few hyperfeminine-looking and hypermasculine-looking individuals contributes to our seeing the sexes as more different than they genuinely are. Moreover, because we tend to generalize from physical differences to differences in other domains, hyperstereotypic individuals help create a continuum, not just for physical differences, but for our conceptions of difference in general. The hyperstereotypic individuals at the poles act like metaphorical magnets, subjectively pulling males and females apart.

A third mechanism that entrenches gender schemas is our tendency to see the sexes as dichotomous and see gender traits as mutually exclusive. It is not just that we are primed to notice traits that are consistent with a male or female schema, but also that we tend *not* to see traits that are inconsistent—because they "belong" elsewhere. We tend not to perceive women's instrumentality, because it is already spoken for by men. We cannot simply add it to our conception of women, because it is already part of our conception of men.

The combination of these three processes thus results in a constant validation and reconfirmation of our gender schemas. The first process, the tendency to generalize from physical cues to cognitive and personality traits, leads us to see the innumerable small but consistent behavioral differences between men and women as confirmation that men and women are different. The second process is our tendency to translate extreme values into evidence of typicality. We see a few hyperstereotypic examples, and they lead us to distort the average tendency. The third process, our tendency to view the sexes dichotomously, makes us more sensitive to traits that are consistent with a given gender role and less sensitive to inconsistent traits.

Schema Interactions and Schema Clashes

Thus far we have looked at the role schemas for professions and gender schemas separately. To consider the issue of how women are evaluated, however, we need to know how schemas interact, since one or more schemas can be simultaneously active.

Consider, for example, a student encountering a female professor and a male professor. In addition to perceiving each person as a professor, the student will perceive them as female or male. As mentioned above, physical cues that signal age, ethnic group, and sex are among the first characteristics observers notice about a person and are the most likely to activate associated schemas (Fiske & Taylor 1991). Whether the student responds to each professor in terms of the professorial role, the gender role, or both, will vary, depending on what is at issue.

For certain expectations—for example, fair grading—the professor role, not the gender role, dictates behavior. Because gender schemas do not suggest greater fairness on the part of either sex, gender is irrelevant. In a situation where one schema gives rise to an expectation that is not relevant to the other, the first schema will completely determine expectations. The reverse situation can also arise; the gender schema is more important than the professor schema when the gender schema produces an expectation that the professor schema does not. The schema for professor, for example, includes nothing about receptivity to student requests for extensions on homework; some professors are receptive and others are not. In deciding whom to approach with a request to turn in a paper late, a student may rely on other schemas, such as gender. Since the gender schema for women presents them as nurturant, the student will, all other things being equal, prefer to approach a female professor than a male professor.

But what happens when schemas clash because they are associated with contradictory expectations? When this happens, interesting problems with highly emotionally charged overtones can arise. When schemas clash, something has to give. The more central a schema is to a person's beliefs, the more painful the clash will be.

Take, for example, the roles of executioner or military combatant. Each seems antithetical to the role of woman, whose schema has nurturance at its core. The debate over military women in combat is as intense as it is because the roles of killer and nurturer are in such apparent contradiction. When two schemas are in conflict, both cannot survive intact. Either the schema for women or the schema for military combatants must change fundamentally. Yet both schemas resist change. We see nurturance as an essential immutable trait of women. It would be difficult instead to see women as having no defining trait, but as sometimes nurturant and sometimes willing and able to kill. Similarly, we see military combatants as essentially masculine. It would be difficult to see the role as gender-neutral.

Discussions about women in the military first focused on their competence. That discussion too was a clash of schemas. Women could not be competent, even in noncombat roles, because the schema for military life demanded traits that were not only masculine but hypermasculine. There now appears to be general agreement at the high-command level that women are as capable as men, even though they have nothing like equal rank status. Apparently, some schema change—or at least the possibility of a subtype, military woman—is possible.

Military discussion then shifted to the "real" issue, the issue that underlay the doubts expressed about women's competence, namely that being physically aggressive to the point of killing another person is incompatible with being a woman. What is really at stake is our conceptions about what it means to be female or male. To preserve those false conceptions, women who want combat status are denied it.

The other contemporary debate about military life—the role of homosexuals—has focused on homosexual males.[6] It too is related to gender
schemas. There have been two principal negative reactions: the fear, expressed primarily by the military high command, that a lack of cohesion
would result if openly homosexual men served in the military; and a fear,
expressed primarily by the rank and file, of a predatory sexuality on the
part of homosexual men—with heterosexual men as the prey. From a
gender schema perspective, the two fears are related; both concern the
self-schema of heterosexual men in the military.

Cohesion, a psychological concept, refers to the ability of a group of
people to act as a unit because of their trust and confidence in one another. Why should the presence of people known to be homosexual
threaten the cohesion of a military unit? The frankness with which some
heterosexual men have expressed their fears of sexual victimization by
homosexual men suggests part of the answer.

Their fear reveals an implicit schema of heterosexual relationships in
which men are victimizers and women are victims (a schema that is veridi-
cal—in most abusive heterosexual relations the male is the predator). Sex
and victimization are inextricably entwined in this schema. When extended to include all sexual relationships, it suggests that to be the object
of another's sexual attention is to be that person's potential victim, a serious problem if one is not the physically stronger party. Another man's
sexual attention leads to that possibility and is thus tantamount to being
demasculinized (Kimmel 1995). The military reaction to the open inclusion of homosexual men reveals the strength of heterosexual men's fears
of demasculinization. Data on sexual predation, however, show that most
male-male sexual abuse is perpetrated by heterosexuals, not homosexuals
(Herek 1993). Heterosexual males use sexual assault—in prisons, for example—to assert power over other men.

There is another way in which open inclusion of homosexual men in
the military would challenge the male schema. Like giving combat status
to women, it would drive a wedge between military life and a culture of
hypermasculinity in which discipline, courage, camaraderie, maleness,
and heterosexuality are tightly interwoven. Detaching discipline, courage,
and camaraderie from sex or sexual orientation would simultaneously

undo both a long-standing gender schema and a long-standing military schema.

That the debate has involved heterosexual males' self-schemas rather than military competence is confirmed by the policy implemented in 1993 that homosexuals should neither be asked about their sexual orientation nor reveal it. "Don't ask, don't tell, don't pursue" would be an unthinkable policy if there were any actual performance issues at stake. The policy is a tacit acknowledgment that homosexuals and heterosexuals perform equally well. The problem the policy "solves" is the schema problem. It allows heterosexual males in the military brass and in Congress who cannot tolerate the breakdown of two particular schemas to retain them despite their inaccuracy.

In 1870 the University of Michigan allowed women to enter its medical school but deemed it necessary to erect walls in classrooms so that women would not hear certain lecture material in the presence of men (Bonner 1992). Whose embarrassment was being safeguarded against is not clear. In time, in certain classrooms, the walls were replaced by curtains. In other classrooms the "wall" was simply a red line on the floor, in symbolic obeisance to irrelevant differences. "Don't-ask-don't-tell-don't-pursue" is the late–twentieth-century's red line on the floor, a tribute to the power of gender schemas.

7

Evaluating Women and Men

It is the first day of my upper-level university seminar entitled Gender and Achievement. All the students, who range in age from 18 to 40, are women. They come from a variety of social and ethnic backgrounds and have, or intend to have, professional careers. If asked explicitly, they would all say that women are as professionally capable as men. To begin the course, we conduct an experiment that is a short variation of one the students will soon learn about. First, they are given a checklist of descriptive phrases, such as "has leadership ability," and are asked to rate the "typical woman" on those qualities. Then they rate the "typical man" and, finally, "the typical successful manager."

When I analyze the data afterward, I am not surprised to find that the students have rated women lower than men on many of the characteristics seen as typical of successful managers. That is why I performed the experiment. I wanted to show the women something they would have rejected and denied if I had told it to them directly: that they believe, implicitly, that women in general have fewer of the abilities needed to be successful professionals than men do. Our gender schemas for women do not include professional competence.

Perceptions of Leadership

In the study on which I based the in-class experiment, the investigators asked several groups of male managers ranging in age from 24 to 63 to rate different groups of people on a series of adjectives (Heilman, Block, Martell, & Simon 1989). The first group rated successful managers on ninety-two different characteristics according to how typical of the group they thought each quality was. The characteristics ranged from leadership ability to fearfulness. Most people, naturally, rated successful managers as typically high in leadership ability and low in fearfulness. A second group rated women in general on the same qualities, and a third group rated men in general. The managers' ratings of men in general and successful managers were very similar, much more similar than their ratings of women in general and successful managers.

The 1989 study was a replication of a 1973 study in which male managers also rated men as having many more of the characteristics typical of successful managers than women had (Schein 1973). Sixteen years later, male managers' attitudes had not changed.

In the 1989 study, however, several groups of male managers rated two additional categories, successful female and successful male managers. Once "successful manager" was explicitly part of the definition of women, most of the sex differences in the ratings disappeared. But an important difference, perhaps *the* most important difference, remained: even successful women managers were perceived as having less leadership ability than successful men managers. Furthermore, women managers were seen as possessing negative qualities that men managers did not have, such as being bitter, quarrelsome, and selfish.

The experiments did not address men's and women's actual qualities but only male managers' perceptions of them. Women might in fact have less leadership ability than men; they might in fact be more likely than men to be bitter, quarrelsome, and selfish. The experiments don't tell us. What they tell us is that a woman selected at random who aspires to a management position will initially be seen by her superiors as less likely to succeed than a comparable man. Even if she is as capable as a man, she will initially be regarded as less capable.

As the example about perceptions of height discussed in chapter 1 demonstrates, even an accurate schema—such as that women are on the average shorter than men—can yield inaccurate perceptions and judgments. People will mistakenly see women who are as tall as men as shorter than men. In the case of leadership, the schema may or may not be accurate; we have no ruler for measuring leadership. But even if the schema is accurate, it will yield inaccurate perceptions and judgments of individuals. People will misjudge women who do possess leadership ability, perceiving them as less capable than they really are.

Even when a woman bears the traditional emblems of leadership, she will not necessarily be perceived as a leader. In another study of leadership perception, college students were shown slides of five people sitting around a table (Porter & Geis 1981). The group was described as working together on a project. Two people sat at each side and one person sat at the head of the table. Sometimes all the people were male, sometimes they were all female, and sometimes the group included both males and females.

When asked to identify the leader of same-sex groups, the students always identified the man or woman sitting at the head of the table. In mixed-sex groups, the students identified a man at the head of the table as the leader. But when a woman was at the head, the students did not reliably label her the leader; instead, they labeled a man seated elsewhere as the leader about equally often.

Several points about this experiment are worth noting. First, failing to perceive a woman at the head of a table as the leader may have no discriminatory impetus behind it. On average, a woman is less likely to be a leader of a group than a man is—perhaps even when she is sitting at the head of the table. Observers may be responding to the situation only on the basis of what is most likely, and men are more often leaders, wherever they sit.

It is also important to notice, though, that regardless of the reason, a female leader sitting at the head of a table loses out compared to a male leader. The symbolic position of leadership carries less symbolic weight for her. She is less likely to obtain the automatic deference that marks of leadership confer upon men. Her position will be weakened—even if observers do not intend to undermine her authority. Finally, it is important to notice that male and female observers see the situation in the same way: they are both less likely to perceive women as leaders. Gender schemas affect us all.

Perceptions of Competence

Other studies look at how a woman fares when her qualifications are identical to a man's. In one study, fictitious résumé summaries of ten psychologists with Ph.D.s were sent to 147 heads of psychology departments (Fidell 1975). The chairs were asked to rank the psychologists according to the professorial rank they should be hired at. The summaries contained information about productivity, teaching, administrative work, and sociability. Four of the fictitious names were female, and six were male. The names were rotated in such a way that the same résumé sometimes carried a male name and sometimes a female name. The résumés with male names were assigned the middle rank of associate professor. When the same résumés carried female names, however, they were assigned the entry-level rank of assistant professor. The identical qualifications bought a man a higher rank than a woman. This occurred even though the men and women were rated as equally desirable appointments.

In an actual situation, it is hard to know the reasons for a woman's lack of success relative to a man's. An individual may be properly judged as performing below the standard of her profession. Alternatively, her evaluators might be unable to judge her accurately. In an experiment, the researcher can tease apart the contributions of the judge and the person being judged. In the résumé experiment, the department chairs were affected by their preconceptions about which gender has more professional ability and perceived candidates' qualifications for a given rank in those terms. Other studies report similar findings. A review of several studies on the relationship between gender and the likelihood that a candidate will be recommended for hiring found an overall advantage in favor of men (Olian, Schwab, & Haberfeld 1988). The phenomenon of overrating men and underrating women job candidates appears to be widespread.

Once women achieve positions of authority, however, subordinates appear to evaluate them as positively as they do men. When asked to evaluate managers in equivalent positions in a research and development organization, the people who worked under them rated male and female managers equally positively (Ragins 1991). It may be more difficult for a woman to achieve a position of power, but once she attains it she appears to receive equal recognition and respect from subordinates. That holds whether the subordinates are male or female.

Subordinates' evaluations, however, are not necessarily shared by other people in the organization or by outsiders. Managers wield power over the people below them, but not over peers, their own supervisors, or outsiders. Another study examined supervisors' ratings of the low- and mid-level managers who worked directly under them in three different companies (Greenhaus & Parasuraman 1993). The data, collected in the 1980s, showed that female managers were just as likely as males to receive highly successful job-performance ratings from their supervisors. Yet, in evaluating the extent to which highly successful managers' achievements were due to ability (as opposed, for example, to hard work), the supervisors rated the male managers as having more ability.[1] For managers who were rated as only moderately successful, there were no sex differences in their supervisors' ability ratings.

The results suggest that moderate success in low- or mid-level positions does not violate gender schemas. Supervisors do not see moderate success as unusual for women (Greenhaus & Parasuraman 1993). High success, however, is less compatible with the female gender schema; one way of retaining the schema is to attribute women's high success not to their ability but to other factors, like hard work.

In sum, studies of managers suggest that both subordinates and supervisors can recognize the high achievements of women managers. In the eyes of their supervisors, however, women's success may be attributed to factors other than ability.

Perceptions of Assertiveness

When women actively adopt an assertive leadership style, they are perceived more negatively than men. The focus of one laboratory study was people's facial reactions to men and women trained to act as leaders, co-leaders, or nonleaders (Butler & Geis 1990). The study demonstrates that both women and men—nonconsciously but visibly—react negatively to women who take a leadership role in a group trying to solve a problem. People respond especially negatively to women's attempts to be assertive.

The experiment is worth describing in detail. The researchers created a common everyday situation, a meeting of four people who had ten minutes to reach a decision. Their task was to rank the usefulness of nine items (such as a first-aid kit and a map) to a person who had crash-landed on the moon. Two members of each group—one male and one female—were naive participants, undergraduate college students. The other two members—also one male and one female—were upper-level undergraduates trained to play three different roles. In one role the student acted as a leader, using a friendly, cooperative, and pleasantly assertive style. In another role, she or he acted as a nonleader. In a third role the student acted as coleader with the other trained student. The trained students rotated their roles from one group to another so that they each performed each role an equal number of times.

During the group meeting, one trained student proposed four items as very important and four as less important. The other trained student proposed a list that reversed the importance of the items. That scenario corresponds to common work situations in which different people have different goals that they want to persuade others to implement. The trained students followed well-practiced scripts in which they presented their reasons for preferring some items over others. In that way, regardless of whether a female or male student was proposing an item, the suggestions, proposals, and reasons given were identical, and the styles were as similar as possible.

The experimenters' main interest was the subtle reactions of the naive participants to the females and males who were making the same suggestions in the same way. The researchers observed the groups to measure the naive participants' negative and positive facial reactions to the proposals. Facial reactions, because they are under less direct control than verbal comments, are a good, subtle measure of a person's response to another person.

As expected on the basis of gender schemas, no matter which role they played, the trained females received a greater number of negative facial reactions than positive ones. The trained males, by contrast, always received more positive reactions than negative ones. Overall, the females also received more negative reactions than the males did. Those data show that women in general are perceived less positively than men in problem-solving situations, even when they adopt the role of a nonleader.

The particular role adopted, however, also made a difference in the number of reactions the trained students received. When the students played the role of nonleader, they received, as might be expected, the fewest reactions of any sort. When they played the role of leader, both men and women received more negative reactions as well as more positive reactions. An assertive leader appears to arouse a certain amount of resentment in other group members, even when the leader is male. For male leaders, though, the negative reactions they receive are more than offset by positive reactions. Men end up with a net gain. For female leaders, on the other hand, the negative reactions outnumber the positive ones. Women end up with a net loss.[2]

When the naive participants were queried afterward about the personalities of the trained students, they rated the trained males in each leadership condition as having more ability, skill, and intelligence than the corresponding females. The females were rated as too emotional, relative to the males. When the females served as leaders or coleaders, they were perceived as bossy and dominating relative to the males. Yet, in answering questions designed to measure any explicit bias against women, the naive participants expressed none. They may have been sincerely egalitarian in their overt beliefs, but their facial reactions and personal evaluations revealed their underlying beliefs.

To be sure that the trained students' performances were equal, the experimenters videotaped some sessions and asked a separate group of people to rate the students' performances on a variety of measures. The experimenters found no differences between male and female students on most measures, including aggressiveness; the male and female confederates used exactly the same content and the same cooperative and pleasantly assertive style.

The one difference that independent coders observed between the trained males and females was that women talked more than the men did when they were leaders or coleaders. The reason for that difference was that the naive participants paid less attention to the women than to the men; for example, they made fewer facial reactions to the women per minute of talking time than they did to the men. Since the trained students' job, as leader or coleader, was to influence the naive participants to accept their suggestions, the women had to speak more in order to obtain equal attention for their ideas. This finding coincides with the experience of professional women, who frequently get the impression that they receive less attention than men and that their suggestions are more likely to be ignored than the same suggestions coming from men. Those perceptions are likely to be accurate. Objectively, women are attended to less, even when they say the same things in the same way as men do.

When women attempt to be leaders they lose, relative to men, in three steps. First, they are attended to less; they have more difficulty than men do in gaining and keeping the floor. Second, when women do speak and behave like leaders, they receive negative reactions from their cohorts, even when the content and manner of their presentations are identical to men's. Men are encouraged to be leaders by the reactions of those around them, and women are discouraged from being leaders by the reactions of those same people. Third, even observers with no overt bias are affected by negative reactions to women leaders and tend to go along with the group judgment.

An incident illustrating the problems women encounter in getting and keeping the floor occurred at a professional conference I attended in 1994. Immediately after the first talk of a session held in a large auditorium I raised my hand to ask a question of the male speaker, whom I had never met. I was seated in the middle of the fourth row, directly in his line of vision. He saw my raised hand but called on a man two rows behind me. The man asked his question and then a lengthy follow-up question.

When the speaker finished answering I immediately raised my hand again. The speaker looked at me for a second time and then called on a man in the last row of the auditorium. The second man asked his question and a follow-up question.

When the speaker finished answering I immediately raised my hand a third time. The speaker looked at me for the third time and began to call on yet a third man. Perhaps my face showed astonishment. Perhaps the speaker realized on his own that he was about to pass me by for the third time. For whatever reason, he stopped and said, "I guess you were next." I asked my question, which the speaker answered. I opened my mouth to ask my follow-up question, but the speaker was already calling on the third man.

The studies reviewed thus far suggest that the event was a net loss for me. To the extent that my difficulty in getting the floor was noticed, it was likely to be perceived by those who did not know me as a difficulty that would be encountered by someone with nothing worthwhile to say. Similarly, to the extent that my being prevented from asking a follow-up question was noticed it was likely to be perceived as due to the lack of interest of my question.

Another laboratory study has shown that evaluators rate an individual's comments positively if the people around the individual respond to them positively and negatively if the surrounding people respond negatively (Brown & Geis 1984). Thus, it is likely that the speaker's lack of interest in what I had to say negatively influenced other people in the auditorium—again to the extent that they registered the incident.

During a break at the same conference I overheard a conversation about the morning session. One man asked a woman what she thought of a talk that had criticized her theory. She said she thought the speaker had misrepresented her theory. The man said, "Oh, why didn't you say something?" She replied, "I tried. I had my hand raised the whole time, but he called on five other people."

The combined results of the studies reviewed in this section indicate that women face a very difficult situation. In trying to assume leadership, a woman will have to work overtime to get people's attention and, when she does, is likely to evoke disproportionately negative facial reactions from those she is trying to influence. Those reactions, in turn, will have a negative effect on other observers who might originally have been neutral or undecided. Because all concerned are unaware of the extent to which they are affected by the woman's gender, they will attribute their reaction to the woman's lesser ability, or to her bossiness. Thus, even a woman who is herself completely unaffected by and indifferent to the reactions of those around her will have a tough time being a successful leader.

The extent to which we perceive men and women as leaders is relevant to women's chances of professional achievement. It is harder to be a leader if the people around you do not perceive or accept you as a leader. The studies reviewed thus far—whether the evaluators are business managers, heads of academic departments, or college students—converge.[3] Evaluators see leadership and professional ability as masculine traits that are valued more positively when displayed by men than when displayed by women.[4]

The Cost for a Woman of Being Masculine

A meta-analysis of studies concentrating on evaluations of women as leaders suggests that women are at a particular disadvantage when their leadership style is perceived as masculine (Eagly, Makhijani, & Klonsky 1992). Having a style that is assertive to the point of appearing autocratic, rather than cooperative and participative, is especially costly for a woman. In experiments investigating the effects of autocratic leaders—

bosses who tell their subordinates what to do without consulting them—women received especially negative evaluations. The reviewers hypothesize that a highly assertive style is incongruent with our conception of women and that women are penalized if they adopt such a style. Ann Hopkins, the woman who failed to make partner at Price Waterhouse despite her outstanding achievements (see chapters 6 and 13), is a vivid example of the consequences for women of behaving in a masculine manner (Fiske, Bersoff, Borgida, Deaux, & Heilman 1991). Her evaluators advised her to wear make-up and go to charm school.

The meta-analysis also concludes that women whose styles are identical to men's are seen as more task-oriented than men (Eagly et al. 1992). A focused woman appears more focused on business than an equally focused man, because being oriented to the demands of the job is seen as a masculine characteristic. Being masculine is not noteworthy for men, but it is for women.

Yet another, later, meta-analysis notes that leaders are likely to be judged in terms of the fit between their sex and the conception of the job (Eagly, Karau, & Makhijani 1995). If the job is seen as masculine, men will be considered more effective leaders, but if the job is characterized as feminine, women will be perceived as better leaders. Whether a job is seen as masculine or feminine depends, in turn, on whether it requires typical masculine characteristics, such as task-orientation, or typical feminine characteristics, such as cooperativeness.

About fifteen years ago a friend informed me that when I telephoned people to ask them something I should first inquire how they were. I protested that it was a time-consuming and transparently phony practice, since I obviously didn't care at that moment how they were; moreover, when people called me I preferred for them to get right to the point. She explained that people knew you weren't interested in how they were right then, but that the formalities made the interchange less abrupt and brusque. (So now I *usually* remember to say, "How are you?") The data suggest that a man's getting down to business would be perceived as consonant with his greater task-orientation and instrumentality and therefore would not be offensive.

Women and men are held to different standards of politeness. Both sexes expect women to be polite in every situation. College students view women who do not say "please" in making a request as behaving less appropriately than women who do (Kemper 1984). It doesn't matter whether the woman is addressing a man or a woman, or whether her request concerns a neutral subject (such as asking for directions), a "feminine" concern (such as asking someone to make tea), or a "masculine" matter (such as asking for a hammer)—a woman should always say "please."

The same students' views of men, on the other hand, depended on the nature of the request. A man making a neutral request was seen as behaving equally appropriately whether or not he prefaced his request with "please." In making a "feminine" request, he was seen as behaving more appropriately if he used "please." Finally, in making a "masculine" request, he was seen as behaving more appropriately if he did *not* say "please."

Women, then, must always be polite, no matter what sort of request they are making, while the demands of courtesy for men vary according to circumstances. Not all cultures, however, require women to be the politer sex. Among the Malagasy, women are abrupt, direct, and confrontational, while men are more delicate and indirect (Ochs 1992).

One day I went to Lincoln Center to buy theater tickets. I couldn't remember where the theater was, so I stopped at the Metropolitan Opera box office to get directions. A woman, perhaps twenty years older than I, was at the ticket window. I stood behind her. When there was a lull while she searched her purse for a credit card, I made eye contact with the clerk and asked him, "Where is the Mitzi Newhouse Theater?" The woman turned around and told me where the theater was. I nodded and went on my way.

As I was going out the door I heard the woman say to the clerk, "I'm sure that woman has no idea how rude she was." Whoa! My intention had been to disrupt her proceedings as little as possible, to slip in my request without interfering with her transaction. Since I was in a hurry, I didn't go back to explain myself but went to the theater, bought my tickets, and walked to the bus stop. When the bus came, I got on after a number of other people had boarded and sat down. The woman next to me said, "Did you get your theater tickets?"

Surprised, I turned and saw that my seatmate was the woman I had seen at the Met. "Yes," I said, "I did." Since she seemed friendly, I asked her, "Why did you think I was rude?" She explained that I had not said "excuse me" before asking for directions nor said "thank you" after receiving them. I explained my motivation, she accepted it, and we chatted amiably as the bus made its way across town. I have no way of knowing whether she would have reacted in the same way if I had been a man, but the experimental data suggest that women will be considered rude in circumstances where men will be seen as neutral. Alternatively, we can say that rudeness is acceptable and sometimes appropriate in men but never is in women.

The Cost for a Woman of Being Perceived as Feminine

We have seen that the more masculine a woman appears to be the more antagonism she will arouse. But it is also true that the more a woman is perceived as a woman the less likely it is that she will be perceived as professionally competent (Heilman 1980; Heilman & Stopeck 1985). The qualities required of leaders and those required for femininity are at odds with each other.

Physical Attractiveness

Take the case of attractiveness. Attractive people of both sexes are seen as better representatives of their gender. An attractive man is more masculine than an unattractive man, and an attractive woman is more feminine than an unattractive woman (Gillen 1981). It should be a professional advantage for a man to be considered attractive, because people associate masculinity with professional competence. By the same token, being an attractive woman should be a professional disadvantage, because people associate femininity with incompetence. Those expectations are borne out by an experiment in which working men and women were participants (Heilman & Stopeck 1985). Four different groups of participants were asked to account for the success of a fictitious company executive they believed was a real person, an assistant vice president who was career-oriented and interested in advancement. The executive's starting salary and current salary were supplied, as well as a xerox of a fictitious identification card, which included a photograph supposedly taken when the executive had joined the company. Each group of participants saw a different photograph. One group saw an attractive man, another an unattractive man, a third an attractive woman, and the fourth an unattractive woman. All the participants received the same written description of the executive; only the photographs varied.

The participants evaluated the executive in several different ways. One important question tested whether the participants' perceptions of the attractiveness of the people in the photographs coincided with those of the experimenters. They did. The photographs the experimenters had designated as attractive were in fact seen as more attractive than the ones designated as unattractive. In addition, the attractive male was seen as more masculine (and less feminine—two scales were used) than the unattractive one; and the attractive female was seen as more feminine (and less masculine) than the unattractive one.

Participants also answered a number of questions about the reasons for the executive's progress, in particular, the executive's ability, effort put forth in attaining her or his position, and luck. Whereas attractiveness helped a man be perceived as competent and able, it hurt a woman. Ability was rated as a more important reason for the success of the attractive male than it was for the unattractive male, but the reverse was true for females. Ability was seen as a more important element in the achievement of the unattractive female than of the attractive one. Luck, which participants saw as more important for the unattractive male than for the attractive one, was considered more important for the attractive female than for the unattractive one. The participants also saw the attractive male as more capable than the unattractive one but the attractive female as less capable than the unattractive one.

Male and female participants were affected in the same way by attractiveness. In both groups' judgments, attractiveness was a plus for men and a minus for women. Participants were unaware that the attractiveness and gender of the person in the photograph affected their evaluations. Women's and men's evaluations of others appear to be very similar; both are subject to influences they are unaware of, influences that reveal the impact of gender schemas.

It appears, then, that attractiveness works differently for men and women because it intensifies masculinity and femininity. Attractive men are seen as more masculine and therefore as more deserving of their success and more capable than unattractive men. Attractive women are seen as more feminine and thus less deserving and less capable than their unattractive colleagues. In a professional setting, then, being attractive helps men and hurts women. The heightened awareness of an attractive man's maleness leads to impressions of competence and ability. Awareness of an attractive woman's femaleness, by contrast, leads one to see her as lacking in competence and ability.[5] People of both sexes want to be considered attractive, but women who are seen this way are at a distinct disadvantage.

An example from Wall Street, however, suggests that attractiveness has more complicated effects than the experiment just described can demonstrate. Alice, a recent college graduate, told me this story of her internship at a major investment banking firm. Her group of interns had few women, and about half of them dropped out during the program because of the stressful working conditions. One woman, whom I will call Jane, was beautiful. Jane received a lot of attention from the men who were her superiors. At the end of the training period, a senior man who usually had nothing to do with the interns personally invited her to be a member of his team, which was the most prestigious one in the firm. Alice thought that his personal invitation—a hitherto unheard-of event—was directly due to Jane's beauty.

I asked Alice how people viewed Jane's ability. Alice thought the other interns attributed Jane's success to her beauty rather than to her competence, perhaps partly out of envy. In their opinion, Jane had only average ability. Alice herself wasn't sure how capable Jane was. She believed that the others downgraded Jane's ability because of her beauty but also thought that Jane would never have succeeded to the extent she did solely on the basis of her competence.

Alice's story is compatible with the research on attractiveness, but it illustrates a dimension the research does not investigate. Attractiveness can indeed help women advance, especially in a male-dominated field, because men want to be around attractive women. Alice thought that she herself had been invited to some meetings simply because she was a woman; a woman softened the atmosphere a little and pleased the clients. But attractiveness carries a price, because it undermines the impression of competence.

When decisions are made purely on the basis of competence, less attractive women may fare better. A professor told me the following story about her department in a large urban university. All her department's introductory and survey courses meet in an auditorium that holds about four hundred people. It is an alienating environment, with steeply raked seats and poor acoustics. No one enjoys teaching in the room, but most of the faculty do so at one time or other. Graduate assistants also teach a certain number of undergraduate courses, including those held in the auditorium.

Yet, the professor noticed, with one exception, the women graduate students were never assigned to teach courses there. The exception fit in with the experiment reviewed earlier: this woman wore shapeless and outmoded clothing, was somewhat overweight, and had an almost neuter appearance, neither feminine nor masculine. The professor's analysis was that the faculty—both male and female—did not see the other women graduate students as able to hold their own in the large room, which they perceived as requiring the more commanding presence of a male. (Chapter 1 tells a similar story.) The exceptional woman did not violate the faculty's unconscious perception of what was appropriate for women, because she did not seem very feminine.

What brought the situation to the professor's attention was her experience writing letters of recommendation for students applying for jobs. She noticed that when she wrote for male students she could point to their experience teaching large lecture courses but could not say the same thing when she wrote for female students. Prospective employers want to know about students' teaching experience and regard it as a plus if they can lecture to large groups. With one exception, the female students were at a disadvantage compared to the male students, both in terms of landing jobs and in how well they would handle the jobs they got. The female students' femininity seemed at odds with the demands of the job.

Size of Pool

Attractiveness is an obvious way of highlighting someone's gender, but other conditions also contribute to making a woman's gender noticeable. The number of women in an occupation is one such condition. Perhaps counterintuitively, the more numerous women are, the less important their gender is. Two studies dramatize the consequences of numbers.

One of them examined how positively supervisors rated the performance of men and women in 486 different blue-collar and clerical work groups. The ratings were recorded in an archival data base of the U.S.

Employment Service (Sackett, DuBois, & Noe 1991). The researchers found that women's performance ratings were more negative than men's when women were only 1 to 10 percent of a work group; they were somewhat less negative when women constituted 11 to 20 percent of a group and shifted to being more positive than men's ratings when women were 50 percent or more of a group. (The gender of the supervisors who rated the workers was unknown.)

The women's lower ratings were also affected by their cognitive-test scores, psychomotor-test scores, and length of experience in the firm. The women tended to score worse than the men in each of these areas, and each variable explained some of the difference between overall male and female performance ratings. Even when all those effects were taken into account, however, the proportion of women in the group had an independent effect on how positively they were evaluated. Women who were in a small minority were judged more negatively than women who were part of a large minority or were half the staff.

The results suggest that being in a minority increases a woman's likelihood of being judged in terms of her difference from the male majority, rather than in terms of her actual performance. Her minority status highlights her gender and, accordingly, makes her seem less appropriate for the job, which seems more masculine because of the large number of men filling it. Evaluators appear to conclude that if women had the appropriate characteristics for a job they would be present in greater numbers. When there are large numbers of women in a job there is less disparity to be explained; undistracted by gender, the evaluator can then judge on the basis of merit. (See the discussion in chapter 6 about gender schemas as a rationalization for an unequal division of labor.)

That the phenomenon occurs at the professional level as well as at blue-collar and clerical levels is apparent from a laboratory study (Heilman 1980). Students in an M.B.A. program were asked to evaluate a female applicant for a managerial job. The students were given eight applications filled out on standard forms in different handwritings; the forms provided information about each applicant's academic background, work experience, and interests. The application to be evaluated was rotated from one student to another. Students were told to read all the applications before evaluating the target applicant, so that they could compare her to all the other candidates.

Students evaluated the target applicant on the basis of how qualified she was, whether she should be hired, and how much potential she possessed. In addition, they rated her on four dimensions: ambitious-unambitious, emotional-rational, decisive-indecisive, and tough-soft.

The hypothesis was that if the candidate pool contained a small minority of females the applicant would fare worse than when the pool was totally female, half female, or had a large female minority. One basis for that hypothesis is the reasoning I applied to the results of the performance rating study. (Heilman herself has a slightly different basis.)

Each application existed in two versions, carrying either a female or a male name. That allowed the experimenter to vary the gender composition of the applicant pool. For one group of students, the female applicant was the only woman out of the eight applicants; thus, women were 12.5 percent of that applicant pool. For a second group, the female applicant was one of two women and six men, so that women were 25 percent of the pool. For a third group, women were 37.5 percent of the pool; for a fourth, 50 percent; and for a fifth, 100 percent.

When women were 25 percent or less of the applicant pool, the female applicant was evaluated more negatively than when women made up 37.5 percent or more of the pool. Being in a small minority made a female applicant appear less qualified, less worth hiring, and less potentially valuable to the firm. Even more interesting were the results of the adjective ratings: when women made up 25 percent or less of the applicant pool, the female applicant was perceived as more stereotypically feminine—that is, she was rated as being closer to the unambitious, emotional, indecisive, and soft ends of the scales—than when women made up 37.5 percent or more of the pool.

Again, there were no differences between the evaluations by female and male students; both were affected to the same degree by the number of women in the pool. Being female does not exempt one from the power of gender schemas. And, as usual, the students were unaware of what was affecting their evaluations; they had no idea that they were being influenced by the small representation of women in the smaller pool. They no doubt believed that they were carrying out their evaluations objectively and impartially. The intent to evaluate people fairly does not protect one from nonconsciously rating men higher than women.

We can conclude from this study that personnel decisions are very likely to be affected by the composition of the applicant pool and that women will fare significantly better if they are in at least a sizable minority. They will fare better because they are less likely to be perceived in terms of their gender and more in terms of their qualifications. They will not be women applying for a man's job, but people applying for a person's job.

In addition to the studies just described, there is statistical evidence supporting the notion that women do better when there are more women in an organization. Women law professors, for example, are more likely to be granted tenure in faculties with a higher proportion of tenured women than in faculties with a very low proportion of tenured women (Chused 1988). Men's tenure rates are unaffected by the proportion of women.

The statistical data can explain some of the difficulty women have entering heavily male-dominated professions. The very small number of women in them means that new women are likely to be perceived more negatively than they would if there were more women. They also find it difficult to advance in such professions, because their evaluators can see the small number of women as a justification for their negative evaluations. Only women who are both exceptional and lucky will advance, and their advancement will help other women very little.

Accumulation of Advantage and Disadvantage

In the foregoing sections I highlighted the differences in our perceptions of male and female performance. We do not, however, always discount women's performance, nor always judge a woman's performance as worse than a comparable man's. If we did, there would be no women in professional life. Everyone can think of occasions when they evaluated a woman very positively. Everyone can think of times when they rated a woman more highly than a man. Everyone can think of notable female successes. Our evaluations are not determined purely by gender schemas. We are inaccurate judges, but our judgments do not completely exclude reality.

Because our evaluations are not determined purely by gender, because we are often unaware that our evaluations are gender-based even when they are, because a number of women are modestly successful, and because a few women are extremely successful, it is difficult for us to appreciate the full extent of biased evaluations of women, and similarly difficult to appreciate their impact.

If we want to believe that advancement is determined by merit, as most of us do—especially if we are ourselves successful—we can easily interpret the available data as confirming our hypothesis that we live in a "just world" (Lerner 1975). In a just world, bad things do not happen to good people and good things do not happen to bad people. We interpret the fact that some women make it to the top as showing that evaluations are basically fair and that truly able women succeed. The fact that we admire the competence of some women is evidence to us that we are free of gender bias, or at least free enough. Our interpretations make it hard for us to see that we are in error. We have the beliefs we do because we see ourselves as fair and impartial. That view of ourselves allows us to place the rule governing our behavior in the background and to put the exceptions to it in the foreground. We fail to see just how often the rule—that we inappropriately judge women more negatively than men—operates.

More important than the invisibility of our everyday evaluations is their cumulative effect on the advancement of the people we judge, even when each individual effect is minor. The importance of the accumulation of advantage and disadvantage, as pointed out in chapter 1, is that even small imbalances add up.

John and Joan, new lawyers hired at the same pay and at the same level by the same firm, may start off completely equally. According to the data just discussed, the following scenario is a likely one. On Day 2 of the new job, John's suggestion receives a positive reception in one office; Joan's equally good suggestion is ignored or gets a negative reception in another office. That initial difference sets off a chain of consequences. John's excellent first impression will cast a slight halo over whatever he does next. He is also in a slightly better position to be thought of positively when the next opportunity to excel arises and to obtain, in turn, the next organizational reward. John has done a small thing and gotten a small reward, on which he can build a professional future. Further, he will be perceived as having earned his opportunities, because his superiors will remember his good suggestions and good performances and feel sure that their evaluation procedures are fair and meritocratic.

Joan, in contrast, has not made a good first impression. She has either made no impression at all or a bad impression (for example, she is "bossy") and so is not in a good position to obtain the next organizational benefit. At the end of Day 2 she is already very slightly behind John. Her evaluators, who failed to register the quality of her suggestion, will rank her slightly below John and feel justified in doing so.

Naturally, Joan can still go on to do stunning, brilliant work that, combined with superior interpersonal skills and an in-depth understanding of how institutions work, will guarantee her a partnership. Only a tiny percentage of people, however, turn out stunningly brilliant work, have extensive interpersonal skills, and understand thoroughly how to exploit institutional procedures. Most advancement comes from having a small to medium edge over other employees. Our way of evaluating women puts them at a disadvantage, compared to men, in acquiring that edge.

Fairness does not consist in letting the tiny percentage of exceptional people succeed, but in making sure that no one has an edge because of the group they belong to. Exceptions should not reassure us that we are fair. On the contrary, they are evidence of our unwitting lack of fairness.

Some writers (e.g., Cole 1979) have speculated that women, compared to men, may be less interested in exploiting or less willing to exploit the tacit structure of organizations, to figure out whom to impress or befriend or aid, and to understand what alliances to form. The line of argument I am developing suggests that one reason women do not exploit organizational structure is that others' perception of them makes it difficult for them to use that structure to their own advantage. Women cannot exploit opportunities that are not genuinely open to them. On the surface, everyone is in the same organization, but the underlying reality is that men and women work in different organizational environments. Women work in an environment that is less likely to offer them the rewards they deserve.

8
Effects on the Self

Even if women were completely indifferent to the reactions of those around them, they would be negatively evaluated as professionals. Even if women maintained their high performance, unaffected by lack of attention and lack of positive attention, they would probably be underrated. But women, like men, are influenced by the reactions of those around them. People's expectations of us lead us to perform in a way that meets those expectations. Even when no one is approving or disapproving of us at the moment, our conceptions of ourselves are based in part on a history of other people's views.

Expectation Effects

One summer day, during a U.S. presidential campaign, J, a male companion, and I are taking a taxi to a restaurant. The male driver asks, "What do you think of Clinton's chances—". I am all set to give my opinion—indeed, my mouth is open—when the driver adds, "sir?" J offers his opinion. I say nothing.

Nothing prevented me from expressing my views. I could have ignored the "sir," or I could have stated my opinion when J was finished, even though that might have been considered socially inappropriate. Nothing prevented J, who had also noticed the "sir," from saying afterward, "And I am sure my friend has a view." That would have been within the bounds of social appropriateness. Yet neither of us thought of responding in a different way; we responded as the driver expected us to.

In another summer, J and I are renting a house together. A storm has damaged a large tree in the back yard, and a tree surgeon has come to look at it. The three of us are clustered beneath the tree. As I ask the tree expert various questions about the damage and what needs to be done, I feel there is something a little odd about his responses. Finally, I realize that I am looking at him when I ask my questions, but that he is looking at J when he answers them. For his part, J is mostly looking abstractly out into space, reflecting his lack of interest in the proceedings. For the entire consultation, in fact, J is silent. I continue with my questions, and the surgeon continues to direct his answers to J. Perhaps he is riveted by J's virtuosic ventriloquism.

I got the information I wanted, but I don't know what modifications I might have made—speaking louder? asking longer questions? being more assertive?—to get the tree surgeon to talk to me instead of J. I can imagine the surgeon saying to his crew afterward, "Did you see that woman? She didn't let that guy get a word in edgewise." J himself has noticed nothing, because he has been thinking about something else the whole time. (Smith 1989 tells an almost identical story about talking to a male representative of the gas board.)

The two incidents illustrate several features of expectation effects.

First, the "targets" of expectations may or may not be aware of the expectations. In the taxi, the word "sir" overtly excluded me, and both my companion and I realized it. In the yard, the tree surgeon's gaze covertly excluded me, but I was initially unaware of exactly what was odd about the interaction, and my companion never noticed.

Second, targets and other observers have a tendency to behave in line with the expectations. Even if expectations are only covertly communicated, they can effectively influence behavior. If your opinion is not wanted, you will tend not to express it.

Third, the tendency to behave in accord with expectations strengthens them. If someone expects women not to have and hence not to express political opinions and women do not in fact express them, the core of the expectation is confirmed. The person who has such an expectation of women then feels justified in thinking of women as apolitical. Further, the person holding the expectation does not entertain the possibility that the expectations themselves have kept women from expressing their opinions.

Fourth, targets of expectations can come to devalue the areas they are supposed not to be interested in. If women cannot express their political interests they may become genuinely apolitical, completing a vicious circle (Crocker & Major 1989; Spencer & Steele 1992.)

Fifth, targets *can* resist the expectations, especially if they are pursuing a meaningful goal. It mattered relatively little to me whether I told a stranger that I thought Clinton would win, but I cared a lot about the possibility of a split branch coming down on my head.

Sixth, in resisting expectations, a target might modify his or her behavior without being aware of it, and the modifications themselves might create negative reactions. I might, for example, have spoken more forcefully to the tree surgeon than I normally would, in order to redirect his gaze to me. That, in turn, may have led him to view me negatively, as the experiments discussed in chapter 7 would suggest.

Conversational Effects, Sight Unseen

An experiment with male and female college students asked to have telephone conversations with each other, sight unseen, illustrates dramatically how expectations can affect behavior in young adults (Snyder, Tanke, & Berscheid 1977). Half the male students were shown a picture of a very attractive woman and told, incorrectly, that she was the woman they would be talking to; half were shown a picture of an unattractive woman. The women students received no information about the men they would be talking to.

A second group of male students, unaware of the design of the experiment, listened only to the female half of the conversations and rated the women's warmth and responsiveness, among other qualities. The "attractive" women (that is, the women the first group of men believed were attractive) were perceived by the second group of males as warmer and more responsive than the "unattractive" women. The first group of men spoke to the women differently, depending on whether they believed they were talking to an attractive or unattractive woman. The women, in turn, responded differently.

In another example of expectation effects, college students who were strangers were tested in male-female pairs. They sat in different rooms without seeing or hearing each other and communicated with a light-signaling system (Skrypnek & Snyder 1982). Their task was to divide between them a group of jobs, some of which were stereotypically masculine and some of which were stereotypically feminine.

In one condition the male was told that his partner, who was in reality female, was male. The partner was described as independent, athletic, assertive, competitive, and ambitious. In another condition the male correctly believed that his partner was female but she was incorrectly described as shy, soft-spoken, gullible, gentle, and conventional. In the third condition, the male was given no information about the gender or traits of his partner. The female students received no information about their partners. In all conditions, the light system of communication made possible only a limited negotiation process.

The results showed that the males' beliefs about the gender of their partners affected the men's own choice of jobs. Males picked masculine jobs most often when they believed their partner was female and least often when they believed their partner was an assertive male. They made more room for their partner to express masculine preferences when they believed the partner to be a male or when they did not know the partner's gender. That is not surprising. Both men and women believe that men like and excel at "masculine" jobs, while women like and excel at "feminine" jobs. A man who thinks he is dealing with another man will assume the other man has the same preferences and skills that he has and think they should share the masculine tasks, especially when that man is described as stereotypically masculine. A man who thinks he is dealing with a stereotypically feminine woman will assume he can have all the masculine tasks to himself.

A more surprising finding was that the females were affected by the males' beliefs. Women who were treated as men, or who were not identified at all by gender, chose masculine jobs more often than women who were treated as women. Thus, given the opportunity to express a preference, women choose masculine tasks more often than they did if given no such opportunity.

Both of the experiments just described were primarily interested in how expectations affect women. They demonstrate that women react more warmly and responsively if they are perceived as attractive and show more interest in masculine activities if they are treated as if they were male.

Gaze

Other experiments have looked at how expectations affect both men and women. One of them—by studying how and when people look at each other during conversations—provides a subtle example of how expectations work. In an experiment involving male and female college students in face-to-face conversations, the investigators measured who looks at whom, and when (Dovidio, Ellyson, Keating, Heltman, & Brown 1988). Previous research had demonstrated that gaze reveals social power. For example, researchers looking at same-sex conversations in the military found that when higher-rank people speak to lower-rank people, the superiors either look at their subordinates more while speaking than while listening or look at them the same amount whether speaking or listening. Subordinates, by contrast, look at their superiors more when listening than when speaking.

Looking at the other person carries a different message, depending on whether one is speaking or listening. Looking expresses power when you are talking; you are actively soliciting the other person's attention. Looking expresses deference when you are listening. You look at the other person to assure her or him that you are paying attention. Those with high social power use gaze to express their dominance. Those with low social power use gaze to acknowledge their subordinate status.[1]

The question the investigators asked was what happens in male-female conversations when two people have unequal amounts of expert knowledge (Dovidio et al. 1988). Before the experiment began, the students filled out a questionnaire in which they indicated areas of high and low expertise. The experimenter chose topics from that list for pairs of students to talk about, avoiding topics that other students had rated as either particularly masculine or particularly feminine.

Each conversational pair had three conversations. In one, the woman was the expert and therefore more powerful. In another, the man was the expert. In the third conversation, neither student was the expert, so that the students were equal in informational power.

The experimenters found that the male and female students behaved similarly when they were the experts. They looked at their partner for a little over half of their speaking time and a little over half of their listening time. Both behaved like people with power, looking at the other person for the same amount of time, whether talking or listening. Expertise does confer social power.

The men and women behaved very differently, however, in the role of nonexpert. When the male students were nonexperts they looked slightly more at their partner when listening than when speaking. They thereby showed a small amount of deference. When the female students were nonexperts, however, they looked much more when listening than when speaking, thereby showing a great deal of deference.

The experimenters also found that, for men, the main impact of being a nonexpert was that they looked at the other person a little less while speaking. Men, it seems, acknowledge their lack of power not by being more deferential when listening but by being less commanding while speaking. For women, however, being a nonexpert increased gaze considerably when they were listening. Women acknowledge their lack of power by being much more deferential when listening.

The most interesting result was the pattern of looking when neither sex was designated as the expert. In that situation, men behaved as if they were experts and women behaved as if they were nonexperts. Men looked the same amount when speaking and listening, just as they did when they really were experts and the women were nonexperts. But women looked much more when listening than when speaking, just as they did when they really were nonexperts. That result suggests that, in a "neutral" situation, men will use the dominating pattern characteristic of those with social power and women will follow the deferential pattern characteristic of those with less social power (Dovidio et al. 1988). A "neutral" situation is not genuinely neutral because there is a social power imbalance between the genders. Men correctly expect to have social power unless they get information to the contrary. Women correctly expect to lack social power unless they get information to the contrary.

Both genders modify their behavior when they obtain clear information and behave in the same way when they are the expert. When the genders have low status, however, inherent status differences persist. Women display considerably more deference when they have low status than men do in that situation.

Looking is not simply a signal of deference. It also provides information above and beyond the content of the speaker's message. People in low-status positions need more information about their conversational partners than those in high-status positions do (Wilden 1972). A low-status person needs to know where he or she stands and needs to be more perceptive of subtle clues to the more powerful person's reactions.

The experimenters concluded that status differences determined by gender are not entirely eliminated by differences that are relevant to a particular task (Dovidio et al. 1988). A woman, no matter how expert she is, will not command the same deference from men that an expert man commands from women. That is because a woman enters the situation with lower status, especially in traditionally masculine areas. People act, and are reacted to, in light of long-standing status differences as well as in terms of differences relevant to the particular situation. (The studies of leadership perception and the development of gender schemas reviewed in chapters 6 and 7 confirm this conclusion.)

How people look at each other matters. The direction of gaze at the beginning of an interaction helps to shape the rest of it by setting up a pattern of dominance and deference that participants are not consciously aware of (Rosa & Mazur 1979). In the case of gender, both participants expect the male to be dominant and the female to be deferent. Each conforms to the other's expectations. Gaze maintains and reinforces gender roles (Dovidio et al. 1988).

Gaze is thus simultaneously a subtle but highly reliable cue to status differences and a subtle reinforcer of status differences. Its subtlety makes it difficult to notice, let alone control—if one is the high-status person— or respond to effectively—if one is the low-status person. That subtlety also leads us to underestimate its importance, because it is hard to appreciate the power of processes we are not aware of.

Women who are conscious of the effect of gaze and who try to counteract the expectations of deference implicit in it may find their attempts backfire. As the experiment described in chapter 7 demonstrates, women who behave assertively receive more negative than positive facial reactions, while men who behave assertively receive more positive than negative reactions (Butler & Geis 1990). Women who do not make consistent eye contact while listening are similarly likely to disturb their interlocutor, who will register that something is wrong but not know exactly what it is.

Women are not likely, however, to reduce gaze while listening. People who receive more negative than positive reactions will find themselves avoiding the behaviors that elicit negative reactions. Women are thus likely to perpetuate a deferential and submissive style in situations of nominal equality. Similarly, people who receive more positive than negative reactions will find themselves repeating behaviors that elicit positive reactions. Men are thus likely to perpetuate a dominant and assertive style in situations of nominal equality. Each member of the mixed pair thereby contributes to solidifying the power imbalances.

Self-esteem and Goals

The effects of expectation are more far-ranging than what happens in a single conversation or interaction. Others' expectations may shape the interests and goals of people's lives. Several lines of work suggest that people come to devalue activities and talents in which the group they are part of does badly or is expected to do badly; by the same token, they tend to value highly areas in which "their" group does well or is expected to do well (Crocker & Major 1989; Eccles 1987; Josephs, Markus, & Tafarodi 1992; Spencer & Steele 1992). Groups become specialized in distinct interests and activities. In the case of women, achievement in male-dominated areas like mathematics and sports is devalued, and achievement in female-dominated areas like interpersonal skills is valued. In the case of men, the converse holds. Several investigators have hypothesized that women "turn off" mathematics in part because of subtly communicated expectations that they will not do well in the subject (Crocker & Major 1989; Eccles 1987; Spencer & Steele 1992).

The underlying motivation seems to be our desire to think well of ourselves and the particular group to which we belong. Being told that the group we belong to is deficient in some area, or perceiving that our group fares badly in society, is a threat to our self-esteem. To salvage our self-esteem, we devalue the area in which we are deficient and compare ourselves to similar others, rather than to those who fare better (Crocker & Major 1989).

Studies that measure overall self-esteem, or people's sense of their self-worth, consistently show no differences between males and females. Both groups show the same levels of self-esteem, even though women are objectively worse off than men on a variety of economic and political measures. The two mechanisms for maintaining self-esteem—comparisons with similar others and devaluing areas of deficiency—seem to succeed (Crocker & Major 1989).

Comparing oneself with similar others is a mechanism in widespread use, not just to prop up self-esteem but also to make meaningful comparisons. When people in the United States compare their health system with that of other countries, for example, they restrict the comparison to industrialized countries. In deciding how well-read I am, I compare myself not with literature professors but with psychology professors.

If our group tends to perform badly in a given area, it helps us maintain self-esteem to compare ourselves only to members of our own group. Women may compare their achievements with those of other women, rather than with those of both men and women, because they see themselves as most like other women. If women as a group perform worse than men do in certain areas, such as mathematics, women will tend to be satisfied with a lower performance than they might otherwise be, because they have done well for their group.

I recall the results of the Graduate Record Examination (GRE) quantitative test that I took when applying to graduate schools in the 1960s. My score was at the 79th percentile, a disappointment to me. At that time the percentiles were also broken down by gender. I felt better when I saw that my score among women was at the 89th percentile. The comparison with other women increased my self-esteem. I *should* have said to myself, "You're competing mostly with men, so what's relevant is how badly you're doing compared to men, not how well you're doing compared to women." It was as if I had accepted the idea that women were bad at math. Given my "handicap," I felt I was doing well. The first mechanism for maintaining self-esteem, then, is to restrict comparisons to one's own group; for most people, gender is a natural grouping.

The second mechanism is also a self-protective strategy, one that any individual, regardless of group membership, may engage in. Someone who knows little about wines, for example, may devalue wine knowledge. The person may say, "All wines taste the same" or "Really, you can drink any wine with any food." The person may regard people who are wine connoisseurs as phonies. Derogation of an ability reassures someone who lacks the ability that it is not worth having.

Although any individual may use the devaluing strategy to bolster self-esteem, group membership influences which areas we are likely to devalue. Few men will devalue professional achievement, because achievement is prescribed for men. Because professional ability is a principal component of men's self-esteem, men with high self-esteem are committed to thinking that they can excel professionally. They will therefore be less concerned about whether they excel in their personal relationships. That does not mean that men are completely unconcerned about their relationships with other people, but that their self-esteem hinges more on their professional role.

For women, the converse holds. Few women will devalue interpersonal skills, because they are prescribed for women. Women with high self-esteem will be committed to thinking that they can excel in their relations with other people and will be less concerned about whether they excel professionally. That does not mean that women have no interest in professional achievement, only that their self-esteem hinges more on interpersonal skills.

Men and women with low self-esteem will not have the same investments as their counterparts with high self-esteem. They have already demonstrated to themselves that they are unable to adopt a successful strategy and thus will not be committed to thinking well of themselves either professionally or interpersonally.

This complex hypothesis has some experimental evidence in its favor (Josephs et al. 1992). A study compared male and female college students who were either very high in self-esteem or very low in self-esteem. At the beginning of the experiment, students took a test that was described as measuring two abilities. One ability was for independent thinking and individual achievement; the other was for interdependent thinking and group achievement. In fact the test measured nothing. After they took the test, the students were given bogus information about their performance. Half the students were told they had scored high in independent thinking and low in interdependent thinking. The other half were told they had scored high in interdependent and low in independent thinking. All the students were asked to estimate their scores in each of the two areas if they were to take the test again at a later date.

The experimenters reasoned that students would predict higher scores in the areas that were important to them. If that were so, male students with high self-esteem should predict higher scores on the retest for independent thinking but not for interdependent thinking. The basis of the researchers' reasoning was that men with high self-esteem would see independent thinking as a core component of their self-esteem and could not afford to think they might do badly in that area. Such men would not, however, predict improved performance in interdependent thinking, because interdependent thinking is less important to their self-esteem.

For men with low self-esteem the researchers had a different analysis. Such men would have already relinquished a positive image of themselves as achievers and would not, therefore, predict higher scores for themselves on the retest for independent thinking. Nor would they predict higher scores for interdependent thinking, because of the lesser importance of that skill.

For women, the researchers reasoned that female students with high self-esteem would predict higher scores on the retest for interdependent thinking, because interdependent thinking is a core component of women's self-esteem. They would not predict higher scores on independent thinking, because that is not a core component of their positive self-image. For women with low self-esteem the prediction was similar to that made for men with low self-esteem. Such women would already have relinquished a positive image of themselves as social beings and so would not predict a higher score on the retest. They also would not predict higher scores for independent thinking, a skill less important for their self-image.

The results were consistent with the researchers' analysis (Josephs et al. 1992). Of the students who were told they had scored low in independent thinking, only the men who were high in self-esteem estimated that they would score higher on that dimension on a retest. All the others—men with low self-esteem, women with high self-esteem, and women with low self-esteem—estimated that they would score the same on the retest as on the original test. Of the students who were told they had scored low in interdependent thinking, only the women who were high in self-esteem estimated that they would improve in that area on a retest.

As gender schemas would suggest and the results confirm, individual achievement is a more important component of men's self-esteem than of women's, and interpersonal achievement is a more important component of women's self-esteem than of men's (Josephs et al. 1992). The results also suggest that people selectively attempt to acquire skills and abilities in areas important to their self-esteem and do not attempt to acquire them in less important areas.

High self-esteem is a mixed blessing. People can achieve and maintain high self-esteem by restricting the people or groups they compare themselves to and by derogating abilities and achievements they find difficult. Both mechanisms limit the accuracy of their perceptions of the social world and prevent them from working harder in areas they might ultimately find fulfilling. I was not doing myself a favor by comparing my math GRE score with those of other women. I was distorting reality and failing to work as hard as I could have in an area that repays work.

Expectations and Alternatives

Even when people have acquired skills in "unexpected" areas, and even when those skills are important to them, their performance may be affected by others' expectations. That fact is demonstrated by a study of male and female college students who scored well on the quantitative part of the Scholastic Assessment Test (SAT) and reported that doing well in math was important to them (Spencer & Steele 1992). Both the male and female high scorers were given a math test. Before the test, half the female students were told that women typically scored lower on it than men did. The other half of the female students were told that the test was one in which no gender differences had been found. The women who had been told that women typically did worse than men scored lower on the test than the male students who were taking the test at the same time. The women who were told the test showed no gender differences scored the same as the male students.

The underlying mechanism is understandable. People's reaction to a difficult problem depends in part on whether they think the problem is soluble. If I give you a set of problems to solve and tell you that some of them can only be solved by a computer, you will be likely to classify the problems you have initial difficulty with as computer-soluble problems and go on to the next problem. That is a rational strategy. If, instead, I tell you that you can solve all the problems if you just work hard at them, you will be much more likely to keep working and to find the solutions.

Part of what contributes to your judgment of whether or not you can solve a set of problems is information about how your group performs on them. If I tell you that the group you belong to does worse on some of them than another group, you will probably classify a difficult problem as an example of that type. You are then likely to put forth less effort into solving the problem and be correspondingly less likely to solve it.

Even though females are seldom told bluntly that they have lower ability in math and science than males, they are aware of those expectations and of the fact that few women enter fields requiring a strong background in these subjects. Many women, consequently, devalue stereotypically male areas of achievement and put greater value on stereotypically female areas of excellence before they have a chance to fail. Even women who persist in mathematics remain at a higher risk of failure than their abilities would predict, because their expectations lead them to limit their efforts when they encounter difficulties. Instead of trying harder, they try less hard, or give up.

Another experiment looked at the comparative effect of expectations on the performance of male and female students on tests of mental-image rotation (Sharps, Price, & Williams 1994). Mental rotation (as we mentioned in chapter 5) is a task that males typically perform much better on than females do. The experiment contrasted two types of implicitly gendered instructions to the students. The "masculine" instructions told the students that success on the test correlated well with achievement in tasks requiring good visualization abilities, such as "in-flight and carrier-based aviation engineering, in-flight fighter weapons and attack/approach tactics". The "feminine" instructions said that success on the test correlated well with success in "clothing and dress design, interior decoration and interior design," and related skills (Sharps et al. 1994: 424–25).

Under the feminine instructions, there were no differences in the performance of males and females, whereas under the masculine instructions the males significantly outperformed the females. The males also significantly outperformed the males who took the test with feminine instructions. Men seem to be galvanized to perform well when a task is associated with stereotypically male activities. (Alternatively, males' lower performance under feminine instructions may indicate a desire not to do well, in order not to be associated with femininity.)

Females' performance did not differ under the two types of instructions. The feminine instructions did not galvanize women to perform well, perhaps because most college women are not interested in doing well at stereotypically feminine tasks. The experiment demonstrates that performance on a task where males usually perform better than females is affected by the expectations and affiliations of the people performing the task. In this case, males were more affected by instructions than females were. In other cases, females have been more affected than males.

The careers of premedical students provide a good example of differences in the ways young men and women respond to the difficulties encountered in their course of studies (Fiorentine 1988). At the northeastern university studied, the premed attrition rate was much lower for men than for women. Thirty-six percent of the men dropped out, compared to 56 percent of the women. For both groups, as one would expect, grades were related to attrition rate. The higher the grades, the lower the attrition rate. One reason for the sex difference in attrition was that the women, on average, performed worse in required courses, such as organic chemistry, than the men did. Grade differences, however, did not completely account for the differences in attrition.

Another contributor to the drop-out rate was the difference in how the students rated themselves on several abilities, including overall academic ability, mathematical ability, writing ability, and popularity. On *every* measure—including how well they thought they would perform as physicians—women rated themselves lower than men rated themselves. The combination of grades and self-ratings accounted for about half the sex difference in attrition rates (with grades accounting for twice as much as self-ratings). That still left half the difference in drop-out rates unaccounted for.

A closer look at the students showed that among those with high grades there were no gender differences in attrition. Men and women with high grades remained in the premed program to the same extent. It was only among those with lower grades that the attrition rates differed, with women dropping out at higher rates than men. The women drew a different conclusion from doing poorly in their coursework than the men did.

One proposed explanation is that current gender roles continue to require men to excel in masculine roles like physician but allow women a wider range of possibilities, ranging from masculine to feminine roles

(Fiorentine 1988). A male student who is doing badly cannot devalue a traditionally masculine area like medicine, exactly because it is part of the male self-concept to achieve in such areas. For better or worse, male students persevere. A man cannot say, "Forget medical school, I'll get married." Nor will anyone suggest that alternative to him; it is ruled out from the beginning. A man can *slightly* more easily—but not much—say, "Forget medical school, I'll be a nurse." Or, "Forget medical school, I'll be a social worker." Men who do not excel in their high professional ambitions are given few alternatives. Since they lack alternatives, they continue to try to achieve, if not in their original choice, in one of equivalent status.

On the other hand, a female student who is not doing well can devalue medicine, because she has feminine alternatives she values highly. She is not too surprised to be doing badly, because medicine (in the United States) remains male-dominated. Instead of trying harder, she can drop out. Dropping out is not a cause of unbearable shame, because her self-esteem is not solely dependent on achieving in a masculine domain. A woman can say, "Forget medical school, I'll get married." If she doesn't say it to herself someone else will say it to her. She can very easily say, "Forget medical school, I'll be a nurse." Or, "I'll be a social worker." She might find those professions less fulfilling, and they might not meet her human aspirations, but they are available alternatives. Women with high professional ambitions have many nonprofessional and low-status alternatives.

How much perseverance is the right amount? The odds are that we have too many male physicians who should have become nurses or medical technicians and too many female nurses or technicians who should have become physicians.

Equity, Entitlement, and Perceptions of Bias

Expectations also shape what people believe they are entitled to. Imagine that you and a partner of the other sex perform a task together under the direction of an experimenter. Afterward, the experimenter tells you that you performed better than your partner did and gives you a small reward, say $5, to divide between the two of you. Your partner apparently does not know how much money you received, so it's up to you to decide how much you will keep and how much you will give your partner. How will you divide it up?

In that situation, men tend to divide the money equitably, that is, according to how well each person performed. If he performed better, he will keep more than he gives his partner, whereas a woman will divide the money equally (Kahn, O'Leary, Krulewitz, & Lamm 1980). She will split the reward in half, even when she has performed better. If the situation is reversed—with one's partner performing better—both men and women divide the money equitably, but men still take more for themselves than women do.

At first glance it may seem simply that women are nicer than men. That is not a sufficient explanation, as a variation of the experiment demonstrates (Major 1987). In the original experiment, people had to split the money with their partner; if they gave themselves more they gave their partner less. That might suggest that women take less so that other people can have more. In the variation of the experiment, however, participants are not asked to divide the reward. They are simply asked to say either how much they think their partner should be paid, or how much they themselves should be paid.

When asked how much their partner should be paid, men and women proposed similar amounts. They both made the award equitably, to the same degree. Both men and women awarded a partner who performed well more money than a partner who performed badly. In that situation, women are no "nicer" or more generous to others than men.

Males and females do differ, though, in how much they think they themselves should get. When asked only to say how much of a reward they should get, women award themselves less than men award themselves, regardless of how well they (supposedly) performed. They also award themselves less than they would award a partner who performed well.

A series of experiments demonstrates that women frequently behave as if they think they are entitled to less than men believe themselves to be entitled to (see Major 1987 for review). When male and female college students were asked to pay themselves as much as they thought was fair for an experiment, women paid themselves significantly less than men paid themselves. When asked how much they thought other males and females would take, both groups of students estimated, correctly, that males would take more than females. Moreover, how much females took was highly related to their guesses of how much other females, but not males, would take in that situation. Similarly, how much males took was highly related to their estimate of what other males, but not females, would take. Expectations about how much payment different groups of people will take affect both males' and females' ideas of what they personally should take. In another experiment, participants were told that they would receive a fixed amount of money for performing a task and had to decide how long they would work. In that situation, women worked longer than men.

Earlier I pointed out that people are likely to compare themselves to similar others and that gender is a powerful determinant of similarity. Women appear to spontaneously compare themselves to other women and to see their labor as worth less than men's. Men similarly appear to compare themselves to other men and to see their labor as worth more than women's. Men's and women's ideas about how much they are entitled to differ significantly.

In 1991 professional tennis player Monica Seles argued that men and women should compete for equal prize money in tennis tournaments. Two other players responded publicly. Steffi Graf was quoted as saying, "We make enough, we don't need more," and Mary Joe Fernandez reportedly said, "I'm happy with what we have; I don't think we should be greedy" (Bailey 1991). A lack of entitlement thus interprets equality as greed.

A few years later, in 1995, Seles, Graf, and other top players wrote to the organizers of the Australian Open, to protest the organizers' decision to substantially increase the size of the men's purse for 1996, so that it was $390,000 more than the women's prize (Gallo 1996). Although the players protested, they also pledged not to boycott the tournament—for the good of the game. Naturally, the Australian organizers saw no reason to equalize the prize money, and the women played for less. (See chapter 10 for more data and discussion about women in sports.)

Under certain circumstances, people do change their frame of reference and, instead of comparing themselves with people of the same gender, compare themselves with the average person in a given job. In one variation of the experiments described earlier, students were shown a fictitious list of previous participants who had signed their names and the amounts they had taken after completing the experiment (Major 1987). Both male and female names appeared on the list, with larger amounts, on average, next to the male names than the female names. The students who saw the list took the same amount—apparently an average of the amounts on the list—regardless of their gender.

In sum, when males and females must determine for themselves how much their labor is worth, they implicitly compare themselves with their own gender and pay themselves what they think others of their gender would take. But when they learn how much the job is worth, by being told how much others make, they change their standard of comparison. People now think about what the job is worth and pay themselves accordingly.

The studies on pay suggest that people are most likely to shift from a gender-related to a job-related standard of reference if the job itself appears gender neutral and if half the people doing the job are female (Major 1987). Both aspects should reduce the importance of gender as a category. As chapter 7 reported, the presence of a goodly proportion of women in a group of candidates reduces the tendency of evaluators to downgrade women's credentials (Heilman 1980). A similar effect should occur when candidates themselves consider what they are entitled to receive. If women think of themselves not as women but as people doing a job, they will feel more entitled to good pay. If men think of themselves not as men but as people doing a job, they will feel less entitled to overpayment.

Unless jobs are gender-balanced, it will be difficult for either sex to assess what a job is worth. Female-dominated jobs tend to be paid less than male-dominated jobs, even when the jobs are comparable in terms of the skills and training they demand (see papers in Reskin & Roos 1990). A woman in a female-dominated job will think of her job as worth less than it is because most of the people who hold jobs like hers are women. Similarly, a man in a male-dominated job will think of his job as worth more than it is because most of the jobholders are male.

We can understand the women tennis professionals who said they didn't need to receive equal prize money in terms of the research on entitlement. Since the sexes play principally against other members of their own sex, women compare themselves with other women and feel they are doing well. Thus, sex segregation in jobs helps maintain gender inequalities in pay: people see the jobs in terms of the dominant gender of those who do the job.

Even a woman in a male-dominated job will tend to underestimate how much she should earn if she compares herself primarily with other women in the job. If women who are chief executive officers compare themselves with other female CEOs, they will be satisfied with lower salaries than they would be if they compared themselves with CEOs in general. Similarly, a woman who is a full professor at a university may call to mind only her female peers in thinking about her salary. If she is doing reasonably well, relative to her female peers, she will not notice that she is disadvantaged vis-à-vis male full professors.

Women in general express relatively little dissatisfaction with their earnings, a fact that is explicable if women are comparing themselves with other women rather than with other jobholders. A striking demonstration of women's view of their own situation comes from an early 1980s survey of men's and women's job satisfaction (Crosby 1982). The men and women who were surveyed were equal in the prestige of their job, their education, training, and experience, their age and marital status, and the average number of hours they worked each week. The main variable on which they were not matched was salary. The women earned 60 percent of what the men earned. One might expect these women to express a great deal of dissatisfaction with their jobs. Both men and women were asked a number of questions: for example, Taking your training and abilities into account, is your job as good as it should be? How satisfied are you with your present job? How do you feel about the salary you'll be earning in the next five years or so? The women's and men's answers to those questions were the same. Despite the fact that their qualifications entitled them to the same pay as the men received, the women did not see themselves as deprived.

Yet when the respondents were asked similar questions about the situation of women in general, there were differences between men and women on almost every question. The women accurately portrayed women as less well off than men. The puzzle, then, is why women who—when faced with an explicit comparison between women as a whole and men as a

whole—correctly perceive that women are worse off, do not spontaneously make the same comparison in assessing their personal situation.
The best hypothesis is that the relevant others to whom the women implicitly compared themselves was other women, not men. Researchers
have coined the term *denial of personal disadvantage* to describe this phenomenon, in which a group member accepts the notion that the group as
a whole is treated unfavorably but denies that she or he has been treated
unfavorably (Clayton & Crosby 1992).

Crosby tells a story about her experience giving talks on gender discrimination in academia. At the beginning of each talk she asks members
of the audience (usually mostly women) to raise their hands if they think
there is sex discrimination in the nation. They all raise their hands. She
then asks whether they believe there is sex discrimination in academia.
Fewer people raise their hands. The next question is whether there is sex
discrimination at the particular institution where she is lecturing. Still
fewer people raise their hands. Then she asks whether there has been sex
discrimination in their own department. Still fewer hands go up. Finally,
she asks whether anyone in the audience has personally experienced professional gender discrimination at their present institution. At that point,
not one hand is raised.

The phenomenon is not restricted to women (Clayton & Crosby 1992).
Members of many different groups report that their group experiences
discrimination or difficulties but that they personally have not. It is, of
course, entirely possible that a given individual has not experienced discrimination. (It is also possible that people believe they have experienced
discrimination but are unwilling to say so, especially in a public forum.)
What is not possible is that no individual has experienced discrimination
even though the group as a whole has. Everyone, it appears, sees herself
or himself as an exception.

It is easy to understand why people would be unwilling to say that they
benefit from discrimination. A white man, for example, will be loath to
acknowledge that he owes a large part of his promotion, or his career, to
the overly positive evaluations he has received because of his race and sex.
What is more surprising is that women are similarly loath to consider that
they suffer from overly negative evaluations. Yet some of the same reasons
lie behind the lack of awareness of both men and women. First, men

largely compare themselves with other men, and women compare themselves to other women. Second, both groups may be unaware of how much money or status the other group has or may be ignorant of others' qualifications.

For professional women, there are additional reasons for failing to recognize that their negative evaluations and slow advancement are due to inaccurate perceptions of them as women. Women who choose to work in male-dominated fields are faced with a painful conflict between aspiration and accuracy of perception. On the one hand, realizing that women are likely to receive lower evaluations than they should and to accumulate advantage at a lower rate than they deserve can salvage women's self-esteem. In that case, their failure (relative to men) is not their personal fault. On the other hand, that realization will cause anger, resentment, bitterness, hopelessness, and helplessness. No one wants to play against a stacked deck.

Some women, faced with a clear picture of their personal situation, devalue the field they originally aspired to and relinquish a professional career or relinquish their high aspirations. They resolve the conflict by valuing other areas of their lives more highly. Others who perceive their situation accurately may maintain their aspirations and tolerate the negative emotions. Those feelings, however, can distract women from their goals, interfere with their collegial relationships, and reduce their chances for achievement. Women who make this choice can live in a constant state of conflict.

The other option open to women is to ignore the evidence of unfairness or to deny that what applies to women in general applies to them in particular. This second option is intellectually unjustified, since unfairness exists, and the odds are that all women will experience inaccurate evaluations of their work and abilities. Still, the option allows them to feel personally effective and optimistic, to believe that hard work and merit will win the day, and to work toward their goals without conflict.

Very successful women are more likely than others to take the second option. As exceptions, very successful women may actually have experienced less unfairness and may then, inappropriately, generalize from their own limited experience to the experience of women in general. It also seems not to have occurred to some very successful women that they might have been even more successful had they not been female. Both very successful women and those observing them may take the women's success as evidence that unfairness does not exist. They fail to recognize that exceptions are just that—exceptions to a rule—and that the rule is that inaccurate, overly negative evaluations are likely and few women escape them.

One irony concerning the conflict between perception and aspiration is that exactly those women whose training best fits them to recognize the objective nature of their situation are most likely to ignore it. In one survey women with Ph.D.s in science reported that they had experienced little or no discrimination (J. R. Cole & Singer 1991). Women in science identify strongly with the goals of science and have high aspirations for their performance—as they should. Because they are committed to science and to their ambitions, they cannot take the option of acknowledging the bias they experience. To do so would require them to relinquish some of the feelings of personal control and efficacy they need to try to live up to their aspirations.

Women thus face a cruel set of choices: make an accurate intellectual evaluation of the situation and feel helpless; or make an inaccurate evaluation and feel in control. Many women, not surprisingly, prefer to take the latter course. They risk experiencing the low self-esteem that their relative lack of achievement entails but find the risk a worthwhile trade-off for the feeling of being in control of their progress and remaining in a field they love. (See discussion in Clayton & Crosby 1992 and Crocker & Major 1989.) If a life in science—or business, or government, or law—is a woman's goal, lower self-esteem plus a feeling of personal responsibility for failure may be preferable to an acknowledgment that unfairness exists, and exists for her as well as other women.

There is a third way out. Women can learn how gender schemas work, recognize instances of disadvantage, and develop methods of correcting imbalances. Knowledge is power.

9

Interpreting Success and Failure

Gender schemas, as we have seen, influence what information we pay attention to, our interpretations of that information, and the predictions we make about ourselves and others. Because our schemas of males and females include expectations directly related to their professional competence, they also influence the way we view people's actual job performance. Our schemas about men tell us that they are instrumental and task-oriented; as a consequence, we expect them to do well and see their performance as better than it actually is. Our schemas tell us to expect less of women—because they are primarily nurturant, expressive, and communal—and so we judge their professional performance as worse than it actually is.

Explaining Others' Successes and Failures

Together, three interrelated processes involving our social beliefs and the way our memories work account for our tendency to discount women's good professional performance: (1) hypothesis confirmation; (2) gender-based interpretations of success and failure; (3) the way we encode and retrieve events in memory.

The first process, hypothesis confirmation, is at work in the professions and in academia, where white men have been, and still are, numerically dominant. The sheer numerical imbalance leads us to associate men with successful performance and women with its opposite, and to see successful performance as a masculine characteristic (Kiesler 1975).[1] Our attempts to explain and justify the imbalance in the sexual division of labor (as described in chapter 6) result in our positing that men and women have different abilities. The professional world, we assume, requires the abilities we associate with men—instrumentality and task orientation—rather than the nurturing, emotionally expressive, and communal qualities our gender schemas attribute to women. We conclude that women do not belong in the professional world. We therefore perceive women professionals as acting "out-of-role".

We interpret the information we receive about women professionals in the light of our beliefs. Because a woman's good performance is incompatible with our gender schemas, we either ignore it when we see it—literally fail to perceive it—or we treat it as an exception. And, since job performance is often ambiguous, we can interpret it in positive, negative, or neutral terms. Our beliefs about women and men color our evaluations of their performance.

Such evaluations bring into play the second, interpretive process, often called *attribution*. It concerns what we view as the causes of success and failure. In interpreting a person's performance we can attribute it to, primarily, four major causes: ability, effort, luck, or the nature of the task (Weiner, Frieze, Kukla, Reed, Rest, & Rosenbaum 1971; also see Weiner 1983, for other types of attributions). Although the list is certainly not exhaustive, it includes the causes that most laboratory-based studies of conceptions of success and failure have concentrated on.

In thinking about our own successes and failures, we may intuitively and unconsciously assign weights to the four causes in proportion to their contribution to the outcome. For example, I will probably attribute finding a parking space on a busy street right in front of the shop I'm planning to visit to luck, but I will see finding the same space after driving around for thirty minutes as a matter of effort. In the professional arena, success and failure are most frequently attributed to ability and effort.

The third, final component of our performance evaluation is a memory process that operates on both cognitive and social perceptions. It links together events and experiences on the basis of their similarities. The way that we encode or interpret an event initially affects not only how we store our memory of it but also how we retrieve that memory and what we retrieve along with it (Ashcraft 1994). Similarly encoded events are likely to be associated in our memory, so that thinking of one event will prompt our memory of the others. (See relevant discussion of content-addressability in Potter 1990.)

Together, these three processes shape observers' perceptions of men's and women's success or failure on the job.

Job Success

The literature on professional achievement suggests that when a man succeeds, observers tend to attribute his success to his ability and to the effort he put forward (Deaux & Emswiller 1974; Deaux & Farris 1977). His behavior is consistent with what is expected of men (Deaux 1984). Success redounds to his credit and is seen as a sign that he can succeed in the future. (This is, obviously, a generalization, not a law.)

Each time a man succeeds, observers encode in their memory a picture of him as competent and effective and add it to other similar pictures. The man's present success reminds people of his past successes—which were also encoded as the result of his ability—and consolidates further a picture of him as competent. The success brings to mind not just the fact of his past successes, but also, more importantly, the observers' own interpretations of his success. The man accumulates advantage, molehill by molehill. With each new molehill, he is increasingly seen as having high ability and his observers' hypothesis becomes a little more highly confirmed and more likely to influence subsequent interpretations.

For men's successes, then, observers' interpretations amplify the importance of ability and effort and attenuate the importance of luck and the ease of the task.

When a woman succeeds in a male-dominated domain, attributions and memory interact differently. Observers are less likely to attribute her success to her ability, since they have already assumed that she has less ability than a man does (Deaux & Emswiller 1974; Bar-Tal & Frieze 1977). She has succeeded against their expectations. In order to maintain their hypothesis of male-female differences, people seek an explanation for her success that would neutralize it. Observers can attribute her success to luck, to the task's being easy, to the great effort she expended, or to all three, depending on the task. Attributing her success to these causes enables observers to preserve intact their original schema about women.

Moreover, if the success a woman achieves is looked upon as singular, it is less likely to call to mind her other successes. Each performance may be perceived and interpreted as a unique event. Even if a woman's success causes people to recall her other successes, observers may still fail to evaluate her positively. Only if the interpretation of her achievement includes ability as well as effort will people view her as competent. Otherwise, they will consolidate a picture of her as an extremely lucky person (and some people *are* very lucky); as one who attempts only easy tasks (and some people *do* confine themselves to easier tasks); or as such a hard worker that she is labeled an "over-achiever."

For women, then, the social-cognitive processes described result in an attenuation of the importance of ability and an amplification of the importance of causes other than ability.

Although working hard is a virtue, labeling a woman a hard worker can be damning with faint praise. If someone is not considered able to begin with, working hard can be seen as confirmation of his or her inability. Thus, a woman's success not only does not especially redound to her credit, it fails to be interpreted as a sign of future success. Successful experiences that are encoded in observers' memories as lucky shots or the result of an especially easy task or an extraordinary effort provide no assurance of future success. Two of those causes are unstable, and only one of them—high effort—is under the woman's own control. The woman does not, therefore, accrue the advantage from her successes a man would.

The two patterns of attribution just sketched are equally consistent with the available evidence. The man could have been lucky, and the woman could have had high ability. But observers—both men and women—are more likely to adopt one pattern when evaluating women's success and another when evaluating men's success. All observers are likely to emphasize ability in interpreting men's success and to stress other factors in interpreting women's success. And all observers draw long-lasting conclusions about others on the basis of those patterns of attribution.

A meta-analysis of fifty-eight experiments that focused on interpretations of men's and women's achievements concluded that the predicted effects of sex on evaluations of success and failure were present, although small in magnitude (Swim & Sanna 1996). On masculine tasks, men's success was more likely than women's to be seen as due to ability, while women's success was more likely than men's to be seen as due to effort.

Even if there is only a slight bias against attributing women's success to ability, they will accrue advantage at a slower rate than men will and will benefit less than men from each new success.

Recall also that the extent of a woman's success appeared to affect observers' judgments of her ability (Greenhaus & Parasuraman 1993). The study looked at 748 ratings of male and female managers in three different companies; the managers were rated by their supervisors as moderately to very successful in their job performance. Supervisors were asked to evaluate how much a manager's ability contributed to his or her effectiveness. They saw ability as a more important contribution to the success of highly successful male managers than of comparably successful female managers. When explaining the reasons for the performance of moderately successful managers, however, they saw ability as equally important for men and women. A very successful performance by a woman is slightly less credible than a very successful man's performance.

Job Failure

Failure is bad; it is costly for everyone, no matter what the cause. But here too an asymmetry in our evaluations of men and women is likely. A man's failure is less likely than a woman's to be interpreted as primarily due to lack of ability and is therefore less likely to be viewed as predictive of future failure. People nonconsciously look for face-saving ways to explain men's failure.[2]

If employers and peers attribute a man's failure to causes other than lack of ability, its long-term implications will be less negative. If they encode his failure as a result of attempting to accomplish a very hard task, observers can draw one of two conclusions. They may question the judgment he displayed in tackling such a hard task, especially if he has done so too often in the past. A supervisor might then decide to have a helpful talk with him, suggesting that he avoid such high-risk situations. Alternatively, more senior colleagues may remind him that it often takes many efforts to succeed at a challenging task and encourage him to keep at it. Professional achievement, they may remind him, does not come easily.

If observers encode the failure as the result of lack of effort, the situation will be more serious. The failure will call to mind other occasions when the man did not try hard enough; others may criticize him for lack of effort. His superiors may worry about whether he is going to change, but at least the remedy is clear. Finally, if they attribute his failure to bad luck they will probably be sympathetic; bad luck can happen to anyone. The meta-analysis cited earlier found that observers were more likely to attribute a man's failure to bad luck or low effort than to explain a woman's failure in those terms (Swim & Sanna 1996). Men who fail, of course, can be and often are perceived as having low ability, but the gender schema for men slightly attenuates this possibility.

If my hypothesis is correct, the converse should hold for women who have failed at male-defined tasks. The gender schema for women should slightly amplify attributions of low ability and slightly attenuate attributions of other causes. If a woman's failure is encoded in observers' memories as due to her lack of ability, it is likely to remind them of other failures that were encoded as due to that cause. Those memories will arouse pessimism about her prospects for future success, because we see ability as something people cannot control. (In fact, that perception is incorrect; people can become more capable with experience and effort.) The meta-analysis found limited support for the suggested pattern of attribution (Swim & Sanna 1996). For very masculine tasks, a woman's failure was more likely than a man's to be seen as due to low ability and a difficult task.[3]

Omnicompetent Men

The intricacies of the attribution process are illustrated by a study that asked college students to account for male or female performance on masculine or feminine tasks (McGill 1993). In some of the scenarios that the students judged, a male protagonist failed; in others he succeeded. The same was true for the female protagonists. The question of interest was what types of explanations people would give for a protagonist's success or failure. In particular, would a person's performance be attributed to their sex or to their individual characteristics?

For example, a man was described as failing at a feminine task like sewing. Students had the choice of rating him as lacking in the qualities that women who succeeded on the task possessed, or as lacking qualities that men who succeeded on the task had. If the students perceived the man as failing because he was different from women who succeeded, they would be attributing his failure to his sex; he couldn't succeed at sewing because sewing is something that only women are good at. But if they perceived him as failing because he was different from other men who succeeded, they would be attributing his failure to a lack of the requisite set of individual characteristics.

Similarly, students were asked to judge a woman who failed at a masculine task like bargaining for a better price on a car. If the students perceived her as failing because she was different from men who succeeded, they would be attributing her failure to her sex; she couldn't succeed at bargaining because bargaining is something that only men are good at. But if they perceived the woman as failing because she was different from other women who succeeded, they would be attributing her failure to the absence of necessary individual characteristics.

Given previous research, we know what to predict. Men are seen as the norm, as good at everything. Therefore, students would tend to see the cause of a male's failure—regardless of the task—as an individual failure of that particular man, not as a built-in sex-related flaw. A woman's failure, according to this analysis, would be interpreted differently, depending on the task. If the task is sewing, the woman who fails will tend to be seen as lacking important individual characteristics, rather than as being the wrong sex. But if the task is bargaining, the woman who fails will be seen as being the wrong sex.

The results confirmed the prediction. The male character was always compared with other males, whether the task was masculine or feminine. Even when a man failed at a feminine task, the students compared him to other males who had succeeded rather than to females. Had the males who were performing a feminine task been viewed as disadvantaged by their sex, they would have been compared to females who succeeded. The pattern was different for judgments of females who failed. On feminine tasks, the students compared the female character to other females. On masculine tasks, however, they compared her with males rather than with other females who had succeeded at the task. The results suggest that women as a group are seen as lacking the characteristics needed to succeed at a masculine task.

More broadly, the results suggest that men are always their own comparison group. They are seen as omni-capable. Women are their own comparison class only when the tasks they perform are viewed as feminine (McGill 1993). On tasks that are viewed as masculine, women as a group are seen as unlikely to succeed. A woman's failure does not contrast her with other women who succeed but with men who succeed. When she fails, she is seen as doing what is normal for women and as failing *because* she is a woman.

As in most experiments that ask people to evaluate or make judgments about male and female characters, there were no differences between men and women student evaluators. The female participants in the experiment made the same judgments as the male participants. Gender schemas affect the perceptions and interpretations of both men and women.

Men are more likely than women to be seen as deserving their successes, and women are more likely than men to be seen as deserving their failures. One reason that women are less successful than men is that our implicit hypotheses about women and men do not allow us to give women the same credit for their achievements that we give men. When we are evaluating women and men professionally, we have difficulty detaching our gender schemas. The evidence of our senses is that men and women are different, and it is difficult to go against that evidence, even when it is irrelevant to a particular task.

Understanding Our Own Successes and Failures

It is possible that people do not judge themselves the same way they judge others.[4] Many investigators have hypothesized that the more specific information we have about a person the less likely we are to see her or him schematically and the more likely we are to treat the person as an individual (e.g., Locksley, Borgida, Brekke, & Hepburn 1980). If so, we would seldom apply gender schemas to ourselves, because we know ourselves best of all.

Yet, for several reasons, it is doubtful that we can simply leave gender schemas at the doorstep in evaluating ourselves. One limiting factor is that, with rare exceptions, people are emotionally committed to their gender, even if they do not conform to gender norms in every respect, or accept everything that goes along with being prototypically masculine or feminine. (For discussion, see Aube & Koestner 1992; O'Heron & Orlofsky 1990; Spence & Sawin 1985.) A second limiting factor is the nonconscious nature of gender schemas' operation. Although consciousness does not guarantee freedom from a schema, nor nonconsciousness slavery to it, it is hard to avoid ways of thinking that one is unaware of. A third limiting factor is others' expectations. As we saw in chapter 8, it is possible for people to behave independently of others' expectations, but their view of themselves is inevitably influenced by others.

We should thus expect gender schemas to affect our judgments of ourselves, even if the effects are modulated by self-knowledge.

A further point is that it is very difficult to accurately apportion the causes for our successes and failures, since we are seldom in possession of all the facts. The causal ambiguity of success and failure allows us interpretive latitude in understanding our performance. Without doing gross violence to reality, we can maximize how much of our success we attribute to ability and effort, as the following story of my encounter with Dr. X illustrates.

Dr. X

Two men who are seated in the same row with me on a plane going south begin talking to each other as we wait to take off. The man on my right, Dr. X, is a physician; the man on his right sells pasta sauce. Dr. X, who is on his way to a conference, greets other men going to the same conference as they board. Between greetings, Dr. X tells the salesman about his experiences at various resorts, hotels, and restaurants. As far as I can tell from his comments about places I too have visited, he is knowledgeable.

Shortly before takeoff, Dr. X asks his acquaintances around the plane for that day's *New York Times* crossword puzzle, since he has forgotten to bring along his newspaper. When he succeeds in getting a copy of the paper, the salesman asks him if he always does the puzzle. "Oh, yes," Dr. X says, taking out his pen, "every morning. I start at the top and work my way down."

Dr. X's arrogance has intrigued me from the start. I have already completed that day's puzzle and have found it unusually easy and boring for a Thursday. "It's a bit too easy today," I say to him. He looks at me, surprised, and I add, "I did it at home."

I am curious to see how Dr. X will respond. By labeling the puzzle easy, I have reduced the explanations at his disposal. Should he succeed, he cannot attribute his success to his ability. Should he fail, he cannot attribute his failure to difficulty or to bad luck. He is momentarily taken aback, but then says, "I can always tell how tired I am by whether or not I finish."

Good going! I laugh to myself and mentally congratulate him on his clever and creative neutralization of my comment. He may not be able to take any credit if he succeeds, but he has made it impossible to be saddled with any blame if he fails. If he fails he is tired; failure is a diagnostic test of latent tiredness. (Why, I ask myself, wouldn't *I* have thought of something like that, and having thought of it, why wouldn't I have been able to say it without embarrassment?)

There is more than a bit of face-saving to his reply, but he has good reason to know, from myriad past experiences, that he is good at doing crossword puzzles. He may not be as good as he thinks he is, and tiredness would be a lame excuse for failing with this puzzle, but his strategy is functional. (It also demonstrates how one can escape from attributions of the four classic causes of failure or success.)

The puzzle *is* easy, however, and Dr. X succeeds handily. When he finishes, he puts his pen away with a flourish and says to me, "You were right. It was too easy."

My hat goes off to him. (As should be clear, I'm more than a little jealous of Dr. X, even while I'm laughing at his self-serving behavior, and even though I disapprove of it.)

Understanding Dr. X

Why might a man respond as Dr. X did? As I have reiterated throughout, men are a heterogeneous group. Not all men would respond as Dr. X did. Further, no one man responds the same way all the time; on other occasions, Dr. X might be less self-serving. What I am suggesting is that Dr. X's response is more likely to be found among men than among women. Men's methods of fine-tuning the attributions for success and failure are slightly differently from women's.

From what we know about gender schemas, we can develop some reasons for Dr. X's response, starting with a need to feel masculine. Men who see themselves as less masculine than other men, and who see themselves as having few instrumental traits, are more likely to feel socially anxious and depressed than more masculine men (O'Heron & Orlofsky 1990). Men appear to require a certain number of stereotypically masculine traits and behaviors in order to feel adequate as men. The range of socially acceptable characteristics is relatively narrow for men. The gender schema for men is constricted, compared to the gender schema for women, and transgression is more costly for men, both in terms of their feelings of well-being and of observers' reactions to them.[5] (We may recall, in this regard, the data from chapter 3 about fathers' reactions to their sons' play interests and boys' reactions to their male peers.)

Professional competence and success is not just compatible with masculinity, it is required. The more agentic and instrumental and successful a man is, the more he can see himself as masculine. For a man, professional success is an unambiguous, unambivalent, unalloyed pleasure. It not only assures economic well-being and meets his human aspirations, it strengthens his masculine identity. We would therefore expect a man to amplify the role played by ability when interpreting his own professional success.

Explanations of success that focus on internal qualities like ability and effort are cognitively as well as psychologically advantageous. If we see ourselves as responsible for our success, we will be encouraged to analyze it in order to increase the chances of future success. We will learn from what we did right. We often speak of learning from our mistakes, but it is equally important to learn from success. Although a man's self-enhancing strategy is partly unrealistic, and is forced upon him by his commitment to feeling masculine, it has many functional benefits. Learning from his successes is one of them.

Another advantage of attributing success to ability and effort is the accumulation of psychological advantage. Each time a man attributes his success to his merits, he encodes a picture of himself as competent and effective, adding it to other such pictures and consolidating a picture of himself as competent. That picture gives him confidence about his future effectiveness and makes it more likely that he will persevere in the face of future setbacks. The accumulation of psychological advantage will lead to the accumulation of objective advantage, because perseverance is necessary for long-term success.

Earlier in the chapter, we saw that observers are more likely to attribute men's successes to their abilities than they are women's. Experimental studies suggest that women's and men's self-concepts follow a similar pattern. The difference between them is small—but significant. (See the meta-analysis by Whitley, McHugh, & Frieze 1986.)[6] The difference is to be expected, given the importance of gender schemas. To live up to gender norms, a man *must* take the credit for his success; he must see himself as having earned his achievement by his merits.[7] (There are obviously cultures with different norms, where such a generalization would not hold.)

Depending on the importance of an achievement, we would expect men to interpret their own behaviors as they would interpret other men's. If the success is in an important area, men should credit themselves with ability. If the failure is in an important area, they should try to evade the blame. Professional failure is one of the most devastating events a man can experience. In addition to causing economic hardship and hindering his human aspirations, professional failure destroys masculinity. It is a disaster. We would therefore expect men to try to neutralize failure, even in areas that have no direct professional impact, if those areas are psychologically important. For Dr. X (and for me), doing crossword puzzles successfully is important. (We probably both, absurdly, see them as mini-IQ tests.) He cannot afford to attribute a failure at a puzzle to a lack of ability and therefore invokes a tiredness whose hitherto-unsuspected existence will be demonstrated if he fails.

The Downside of the Male Attribution Pattern

Because of its importance to men's conceptions of themselves, most men aspire to high-level professional success. But most men cannot and will not succeed at a high level, because there are very few positions at the top. Middle-income white men with modest, rather than major, successes have always had to accommodate to their failure to meet these unrealistically high expectations.

Many different accommodations to modest success are possible. For example, a man can continue to aspire and to see major success as just around the corner. Or he can trade in his dream of being a large fish in a large pond for being a large fish in a small pond. He can also denigrate other men's major successes by attributing them to their privileged backgrounds, a plausible explanation in many situations. That explanation also nourishes a man's hope that his children will achieve the great success he did not.

Yet another way to accommodate a lower than hoped for level of achievement is to accept the superiority of those who are powerful and align oneself with them. That is what people commonly see heterosexual women doing through marriage; unable to achieve their own goals, they obtain gratification from being married to someone who can. That same mechanism can hold for men; by working in someone else's shadow, they can obtain the gratification of being allied with a powerful man.

Men's early training in sports, which provides objective measures of ability and success, may accustom boys and men to acknowledging the objective superiority of others and to deriving gratification from being on the same team as someone who is extremely talented. In addition, there is no shame in losing to someone who is very able. Shame only comes from losing to someone who is clearly your inferior.

Modest success, then, is much better than outright failure, but also always less desirable than major success. Until the early 1970s, middle-income white men had a unique position in the United States. Overt discrimination against women and minorities protected white men's access to the best educational opportunities and the most prestigious jobs. Moreover, from the late 1930s through the 1970s the economy was either expanding or stable. One result of managed competition in a favorable economy was a higher success rate for middle-income white men than their abilities alone would have brought them in a completely open market or an unfavorable economy. Statistically, that had to be the case. With their competitors roughly half as numerous as they would have been without discrimination, their own chances for success were doubled.

When regulated competition and discrimination were reduced, however, and white men stopped being an overtly protected group, competition sharpened. An expanding economy might have absorbed the influx of new competitors; in a stable or contracting economy, however, the larger pool of competitors with the same range of abilities inevitably caused white men to fail at a higher rate than before, a rate that—

although it was more closely related to their real abilities—would have been inconceivable earlier. (That argument assumes, of course, that people's success is genuinely related to their abilities.) Since white men's expectations did not change, the gap between their expectation and their achievement grew much larger than it had been earlier.

Even so, white men are not yet failing at the rates the situation suggests that they should. People continue to have high expectations for white men as a group, which biases observers into overrating their performance relative to women's (as detailed in chapter 7). The acceptance of gender schemas by both men and women gives men a leg up on the ladder of success, a leg up that their abilities alone would not guarantee them. The centrality of the gender schema to men's own self-concept prevents them from questioning their expectations and encourages them to focus on internal explanations—ability and effort—for success.

Failure, however, is a different matter. Since the unrealistic nature of white men's expectations has not been acknowledged, and since the implications of gender and race schemas have not been appreciated, many white men are unable to understand or come to terms with their failures. They perceive that they are losing out to some women and minority men, but they cannot see the loss as justified because they are in the grip of race and gender schemas portraying non-whites and women as professionally inferior to white men. For many white men, losing out to a minority person or a woman engenders shame and anger and also compromises their masculine identity. Some then invoke the explanation of "reverse discrimination" to claim that those who are less able and qualified receive unfair advantages.

Since it is part of the male gender schema that men are realistic and objective (while women are unrealistic and subjective), it is difficult for men to recognize that their expectations are intellectually unjustified. A further contribution to their difficulty is the fact that everyone holds the same gender schemas. Men's unrealistic expectations for themselves are shared and reinforced by the men and women around them. Our tacit acceptance of gender schemas provides men with few opportunities to discover that their high expectations are unrealistic and based not on their actual abilities but on their sex.

Gender schemas do men a disservice. They prevent men from being realistic and objective and require men to be successful in order to maintain an essential aspect of their self-concept—their masculine identity. They lead men to think that they are more capable than they are and encourage them to have overly high aspirations.

Professor Y

Professor Y is a full professor in a prestigious department at a prestigious university. She is a successful and productive academic, as well as the chair of her primarily male department. She tells the following story. She applied for a small grant that was not directly in her area of expertise. She did not expect to get it. When she did, her first thought was, "Oh, I lucked out."

The next day, while talking to her colleague, Joan, she discovered that Joan had received one of the same grants. She then thought, "Oh, so they gave them out to everybody."

Understanding Professor Y

Why might a woman respond as Professor Y did? Why was luck her first explanation for her success? Why did another woman's success make her think that the task was easy? We have to agree with her that it *could* have been the case that she was lucky, and it *could* have been the case that, that year, the grants were easy to obtain. But it also *could* have been the case that she wrote a superior proposal, thanks to her ability and effort, and that Joan did too. Why did she only entertain the hypotheses of luck and ease of task, not the hypotheses of superior ability and effort? If she does not even entertain the latter hypotheses, her success can give her no confidence about her future effectiveness. She can't count on being lucky and she can't count on grants being easy to get.

As with the story of Dr. X, I do not mean to suggest that every woman would respond as Professor Y did, nor that she herself would respond the same way on every similar occasion, nor that a man would never respond as she did. Instead, I am suggesting that Professor Y's response is more likely to be found among women than men. It is that higher likelihood that needs to be explained.

Gender schemas apply less straightforwardly to women's interpretations of success and failure than to men's, because some women feel adequate as women even if they lack many feminine traits and have many masculine ones. For some women, feelings of well-being are not related to having many feminine traits (O'Heron & Orlofsky 1990). In fact, women who see themselves as having many instrumental traits—traits stereotypically associated with men—are well-adjusted, regardless of whether or not they also have feminine traits and behaviors.

In general, violations of the female gender schema are more acceptable than violations of the male schema. Although the reason for that greater flexibility—the prevailing view that masculine characteristics are more desirable than feminine ones—is unfortunate, the result is that women have more psychological freedom than men do. They can adopt masculine characteristics more easily than men can adopt feminine ones. Success and failure should thus affect women more variably than they do than men, which might be why researchers have found it difficult to characterize women's interpretations of success and failure (Whitley et al. 1986).

The more agentic and instrumental a woman is, the less she can see herself as feminine. Depending on her self-concept, that may or may not concern her. If it does, then highlighting luck, task ease, or other external factors will let her resolve the contradiction between success and the female schema.

Even when seeing themselves as feminine is not a particular concern of women, they are still more likely than men to react as Professor Y did. As we have shown in previous chapters, people perceive women as less able than men and give women negative evaluations when they should give positive ones (for example, for assertive leadership). Women have more experiences than men do in which good performance does not lead to success. As a result of the lower evaluations they receive, women may correctly perceive that ability and effort do not pay off. Professor Y may see herself as intelligent, competent, and hardworking but nevertheless attribute her success to other factors, because ability and effort have not been reliably associated with success in the past.

If the usual mechanisms of success do not work for women, it is rational for them to perceive their success, when it does arrive, as due to luck or some other unstable, uncontrollable factor (as described in chapter 1). Women are faced with a situation in which the same performance with the same effort and ability behind it sometimes succeeds and sometimes fails. That happens to men as well—since all evaluation systems are imperfect—but less often. Normal cause-and-effect relationships hold more often for men than for women; men live in a more lawful world.

Again, that does not mean that women never attribute their successes to ability, only that they invoke ability less often than men do and invoke luck more often. The experimental data are consistent with that generalization (see the meta-analysis of Whitley et al. 1986). A recent study of male and female scientists who had obtained federally sponsored post-doctoral fellowships found that the women were considerably less likely to perceive themselves as having above-average scientific ability than the men were: 52 percent compared to 70 percent (Sonnert & Holton 1996), even though they were above-average. The women were correspondingly almost twice as likely to perceive themselves as having average ability: 35 percent compared to 18 percent.

The second part of Professor Y's reaction is also easy to understand. She applied the female gender schema to Joan and, therefore, did not identify Joan's success as due primarily to her ability. The success rendered the task easy, rather than rendering the colleague able, because the colleague was antecedently viewed in the light of the female schema.

The Downside of the Female Attribution Pattern

To the extent that women see success as due to random or uncontrollable factors, they will profit from it less. Seeing success in those terms is particularly disadvantageous because it leaves women with nothing to analyze, nothing to learn from success. People cannot build on an experience they attribute to luck. To benefit cognitively from a success and increase the chances for the next one, a person must figure out what was causally relevant. Successes are linked to each other. Each success teaches a lesson that can be used to advantage for the next attempt. There *is* a causal chain from one success to another, even if that chain is harder for women to construct.

I have said that it is rational for women to attribute more of a role to luck than men do, because cause-and-effect relations hold less strongly in their world. But it is even more rational for women to understand how the inaccurate evaluations of their success weaken the causal chain between ability and success. That understanding will, in turn, allow women to perform a more sophisticated analysis of their situation and develop a more sophisticated strategy to deal with it. Perhaps the single most important factor in success is flexible perseverance—"flexible" because simply doing more work in the same way may not be enough. Long-term success requires having a strategy and refining it in the light of short-term successes and failures.

Professor Y had a success when she was expecting a failure. But it is the opposite experience, a failure where one could reasonably expect a success, that can engender feelings of hopelessness and helplessness. Women are more likely than men to have such experiences, because of the way they are evaluated. If they feel that their efforts are unavailing, and that factors over which they have no control are operating, they will be less likely to persevere. Women may have a sense of futility without knowing its origin, especially if they do not realize that gender schemas affect others' evaluations of them.

The experience of things going wrong when one's best judgment says they should have gone right undermines not just feelings of effectiveness but also confidence in one's judgment. If women do not entertain the hypothesis that they are being inaccurately evaluated, their failures may lead them to think that there is something wrong with them and that they are not fitted for professional life.

Learning how to deal flexibly with failure is essential for everyone's professional achievement. Both men and women are bound to experience failure at some point; it is an inescapable feature of professional life. Both men and women also need perseverance to get ahead. But perseverance requires a belief that one's actions will be effective and that effort can make a real difference. If you feel effort is futile, you will not persevere. Indeed, you will feel like a fool if you persevere in a hopeless quest. Yet, flexible perseverance is exactly what is necessary.

Good Attribution Patterns for Men and Women

How should we understand our successes and failures? Some aspects of our understanding should be common to men and women, but some need to be different. Everyone should understand that small successes lead to major successes and that, therefore, it is worthwhile to work hard for even a small success. Advantage does accumulate and multiply.

Everyone should recognize that ability is not a fixed entity but can be developed through effort. Because ability and effort reinforce each other, everyone should persevere. People of both sexes also need to develop flexible strategies, based on analyses of what went right in the successes and what went wrong in the failures.

Everyone should have high aspirations—though not necessarily high expectations. High expectations for women are unrealistic, because men are evaluated somewhat too positively and women somewhat too negatively. Because those different evaluations reflect different expectations about the sexes, men and women also have to be able to integrate information about likely evaluations into their analyses of success and failure.

For men, the dangers are an unrealistically strong belief that effort and achievement are wholly responsible for their successes, a failure to recognize that some of their successes are unearned, and insufficient respect for their competitors. Men are so committed to professional success that it is difficult for them to perceive their situation accurately. Too much of their self-worth is at risk. For women, the dangers are a feeling of futility, a failure to recognize that some of their failures are unearned, and an inappropriate devaluation of their own abilities.

The Costs of Effort

Men have little to lose, psychologically and objectively, by trying hard; they simply get closer to their goal. For women, however, there are certain costs attached to trying hard.

Effort strengthens ability, as I said earlier; but there is also something of a trade-off between the two. I am a better writer than my companion, J. As a consequence, I do not have to work as hard as he does to create clear, readable prose (though I probably have higher standards and, in the end, exert more effort). I am also better with machines than he is; I can troubleshoot a problem more quickly and easily than he.

We are all accustomed to the idea that being talented at something lets us accomplish it with less work. By contrast, working very hard at something for a modest return can be taken as evidence that the effort is needed to compensate for lack of ability. Seeing work this way entails a psychological cost that women are more likely than men to incur, because they have to work harder for less.

Expending great effort for a small reward can make women feel helpless, rather than instrumental, because their efforts do not buy them enough. Their achievements are too few and too far between, and their progress is too slow. Women—and their colleagues—may perceive women's expenditure of effort as evidence of lack of ability. The disproportionate effort women have to make could thus arouse feelings of humiliation rather than pride and trigger a vicious cycle: women may prefer to expend less effort, in order to see themselves as able. Women who work in male-dominated professions will naturally have the issue of their abilities at the forefront, because their abilities are so frequently being subtly questioned by those around them. Reality conspires with gender schemas to make the accumulation of advantage more difficult for women, both objectively and psychologically. Women can thus fail to see that there is, nevertheless, an underlying pattern over which they can exert some control.

Women *can* do something to change their objective and psychological conditions. One important ingredient in making that change is understanding how gender schemas work. That understanding can help women develop strategies for handling the negative effects of gender schemas (as chapter 14 details).

Learning how gender schemas and attributions interact should also allow women to reconceptualize effort so that the expenditure of effort will not undermine their belief in their abilities. If women understand the importance of effort for success, the role of effort in increasing ability, and the relation between short-term and long-term goals, making a great effort should entail less psychological cost. Questions of ability can take a back seat to questions of goals. From that perspective, the clear benefits of expending effort are more visible.

10

Women in the Professions

From the data reviewed in chapters 6 through 9 about how people judge men and women and how they judge themselves, we would expect women to fare worse than men in the professions. Women, we would predict, will be evaluated less positively and therefore accumulate advantage more slowly than men. In fact, women *do* fare worse than men. Long-standing and continuing inequalities between women and men exist in salary, promotion, and ability to reach the top, regardless of profession. There has been some progress over the past twenty-five years; more women have entered the professions, and entry-level salaries are closer to parity. That progress, however, is not uniform across the professions or within subfields of a given profession.

The focus of this chapter is data on high-status positions in business, medicine, and law. The women and men who are considered are college-educated and usually hold a professional degree as well. They have invested time, money, and energy in acquiring high qualifications. I do not consider here the plight of working women in general, who earn less than working men, even though their lower earnings are undoubtedly related to women's slow advancement in the higher-status professions.

Understanding the Data

Aggregate and Cohort Data

To assess women's achievements in business, law, and medicine, I look at two types of data. The first type, *aggregate data,* ignores the particulars of an individual's age, date of degree, time spent in a field, area of specialization, type of institution, and so on. Aggregate data are valuable for demonstrating overall trends, but they have a limited value for comparative purposes. They might show, for example, that the average pay of female law partners is less than the average pay of male law partners but fail to take into account the fact that male law partners are on average older than female partners and have been in the firm longer.

The second type of data—*cohort data*—presents data for subgroups that are similar along an important dimension, such as age, number of years of work experience, or number of years post-degree. Some data for lawyers, for example, subdivide groups according to year of admission to the bar. Such data are valuable because they maximize the similarities among the males and females being compared and avoid some of the problems of aggregate data. They cannot, however, answer the question of whether the particular subgroup being investigated is representative of all the people—or women, or men—in the profession.

The two types of data complement each other. The aggregate data allow us to demonstrate that a given finding is indeed general, while the cohort data allow us to determine whether the aggregate data are replicated within a given cohort. In the findings I report in this chapter, the aggregate and cohort data support each other.

Within-rank Comparisons

To establish whether a disparity exists, comparisons by rank are preferable to overall comparisons. To return to the situation of lawyers, it is easy to see that comparing male and female partners is preferable to comparing male and female lawyers as a whole. Females are likely to be more highly represented at the associate level than at the partner level, simply because they are on average younger than male lawyers. Since associates make much less money than partners, an overall comparison would exaggerate the income differences between men and women lawyers. Data divided by rank help us to compare like with like.

Unfortunately, within-rank comparisons are not perfect; they can lead to either overestimation or underestimation of income disparity. The overestimation was considered earlier in discussing comparisons of partners. Now consider how an underestimation of salary disparity could arise from data on law associates. If there are a number of females at this level who should have made partner but were retained as associates, they will be more experienced and, therefore, likely to earn higher salaries than their younger male colleagues. Their presence in the rank will therefore artificially increase the apparent salary of junior women and could give an impression of parity where it does not exist. At least some of the female associates should not be associates but partners making much more money.

Equal Pay

Deciding what counts as equal pay should be a simple matter, but it isn't. If someone makes 70 percent as much as someone else, it is clear that the two people are not paid equally. But if someone earns 95 percent as much as another person, it is less clear. To determine whether people are paid equally, it is necessary to examine trends over time and across different contexts. Even a small disparity, if consistent, represents inequality.

If men and women were paid equally, then on average half the comparisons would show women being paid more than men, and half would show men being paid more than women. The extent of the deviation from equality would be equal in each direction. If, for example, male and female executives were paid equally, one would expect that in some firms women would average more than men, whereas in other firms men would average more than women. It would not be commensurate with equality to find, instead, that in firm after firm men were paid more than women (or women more than men), even if the extent of the extra payment were minimal. A consistent small difference is a real difference. It indicates that factors other than chance are operating.

We therefore need to know not only what the average pay of males and females is, but also how much variation there is. Data on variation, however, are seldom available. Some comparisons by year are available, and we can use the same reasoning there. If over a period of ten years women were to earn on average 98 percent of men's salaries, that fact alone would not be good evidence of salary parity. We would also have to know how much variation there is from year to year. If in every year women's average earnings were somewhat lower than men's, that small consistent difference would indicate the presence of a factor that was systematically depressing female salaries.

A final issue in salary equality is the political importance of a small disparity. If women earn 95 percent of men's salaries, some might think that that is close enough. In dollar terms, it would mean that women earning $47,500 a year would have male peers earning $50,000 and that women earning $95,000 a year would have male peers earning $100,000. My position is that there is no political justification for a systematic disparity, no matter how small. Over a lifetime small differences mount up to a large difference. No one would voluntarily take a pay cut of 5 percent. If, of course, women's performance could be demonstrated to be 95 percent as good as men's—using agreed-upon objective criteria—and if performance were the sole determinant of salary, that would be another matter. But, barring such a dual justification, only 100 percent parity is equality, and only equality is good enough. The demands of justice are clear. No difference based on sex is acceptable.

Qualifications

One prominent theory about women's lesser position in the professions holds that women begin their careers with less *human capital* than men and therefore reap fewer rewards than men do (see, e.g., Becker 1957; O'Neill 1991). Human capital—education, experience, and certain other qualifications—is undeniably necessary for success. Whether women and men have equal access to qualifications is a separate issue. The human capital hypothesis only concerns the outcome once equal qualifications are in hand.

According to some proponents of this view, when women acquire the appropriate qualifications, they will be paid and promoted equally (assuming that overt prejudice is absent). One way economists and sociologists have addressed the issue is to ask whether the same qualifications benefit males and females equally, or whether males receive an additional benefit simply from being male. There is considerable evidence that human capital is only part of the story of the difference between women's and men's advancement in the professions. Even when human capital is equal, women advance more slowly than men. Women accumulate advantage less easily than men. (I discuss the wider issues of sex differences in preferences and in on-the-job performance in chapter 12.)[1]

Business

Scarcely a month goes by without some mention in the press of the small percentage of women who hold executive positions in corporations. Women in management are overrepresented in lower-status positions and underrepresented at the top, as many different figures show.

In 1980, a group of fifth and sixth graders bought six shares of stock in the Mohasco Corporation as part of a school economics project (Ferretti 1980). They then attended a stockholders' meeting, where an eleven-year-old girl asked the company's president and chief executive officer: "What are you doing to improve the role of women in your company?"

He replied, "Heh, heh. Learning very young, isn't she?" He went on: "As a company we have promoted—that didn't come out quite like I intended—we have encouraged the expanded use of young ladies in various parts of our company. We have no officers who are young ladies, though we have them moving up the ranks. We have very brilliant young ladies in management roles, in the area of computer programming. We'll have a place for you in a few years" (Ferretti 1980).

Mohasco subsequently experienced a number of reverses and is now a private company, so its record of promoting women to upper-management positions cannot be examined. We can, however, look at the overall figures for corporations in the United States. In 1978, two years before the eleven-year-old asked her question, there were two women heading Fortune 1000 companies; in 1994 there were also two; in August of 1996, sixteen years after the question, there were four (Foster 1995; Brooks & Groves 1996).

In 1985, 2 percent of top executives were women; IBM, where 7 percent of the executives were women, was exceptional (Powell 1988, summarizing data from Korn/Ferry International). In 1990, women were less than one half of 1 percent of the most highly paid officers and directors of 799 major companies (Fierman 1990). In 1992, 3 percent of senior executives were women (Blau & Ferber, 1992). On Wall Street in 1996,

8 percent of managing directors of major investment banking and broker-
age houses were women (Truell 1996). Perhaps most telling, a 1996 review of the thousand largest firms in the United States shows that only 1
percent of the top five jobs in these corporations (sixty out of five thousand)
were filled by women (Greene & Greene 1996). The percentages reported
for different samples of the business world vary, but they all demonstrate
a continuing problem for women who aspire to top positions.

By themselves, those figures demonstrating inequality do not demonstrate inequity. If, for example, the cadre of managing directors on Wall
Street is composed of many older men, a few younger men, and a few
younger women, the small percentage of women is due to the lack of
older women. Further, it is possible that there are only a few women with
the necessary qualifications to choose from. We need cohort data to determine whether women who are as qualified as men achieve the same professional success as men.

College Graduates

An interesting study based on human-capital theory hypothesizes that
early sex discrepancies in college graduates' salaries result from differential investment in mathematical skills (Paglin & Rufolo 1990). Occupations in fields that pay particularly well, such as engineering and the
natural sciences, are dominated by people with strong mathematical
skills. Because of women's lower scores on standardized mathematical
tests like the SAT, their lower interest in math and science, and their inaccurate judgments of their mathematical abilities (see chapters 3 to 5), few
women become engineers and natural scientists.

Within each occupation examined in the study, female college graduates earned almost 98 percent as much as male college graduates. Thus,
unequal pay was observed, but the differences were small. In dollar terms,
a man hired at $30,000 a year would have a female counterpart whose
starting salary was $600 less. Larger sex discrepancies occurred between
different fields. That is, women are underrepresented in high-paying fields
that require strong math skills and overrepresented in low-paying fields
that do not. That form of sex segregation produces an across-the-board
difference between male and female salaries. The findings suggest that

when men and women invest equally in the relevant training, they are paid almost equally in entry-level positions (Paglin & Rufolo 1990).

That 2 percent gap is smaller than the sex differentials found in other studies. A study of college graduates who had majored in business and graduated between 1983 and 1985 found that females were paid lower starting salaries—about 7 percent lower—than males. That was so despite the fact that the females as a group had better credentials than the males. They had higher grade-point averages, more internship experience, and more of a tendency to major in high-income subfields like accountancy (Fuller & Schoenberger 1991). When females' higher qualifications were taken into account, the gap in starting salaries was even greater than it initially appeared to be.

A complex study examining beginning and current salaries within one firm found a difference in starting salaries that favored men, even when comparisons were restricted to those with college degrees (Gerhart 1990). Combined differences in human capital—such as college major—explained some, but not all, of the discrepancy. Further analyses showed that among those who remained with the company, men benefited more from receiving a particular performance rating and a given job title than did women. Again, human capital differences were important, but did not explain all of the difference in salary. Men gained more from their achievements than women did.

On balance, it is clear that differential investment in math and science skills distinguishes male and female college graduates overall and that those differences contribute to higher starting salaries for males. But it is also clear that differences in human capital do not account fully for the differences. Men appear to profit more from their investments in human capital than women do.

Careers of MBAs
A review of data from several studies conducted primarily in the 1980s looked at the first jobs and later jobs of business school graduates (Olson & Frieze 1987). Holders of masters' degrees in business administration (MBAs) are not fully representative of men and women in business; overall, they are a prestigious minority. Exactly because of their

roughly equal and high human capital, however, they provide the best comparisons of the careers of women and men in business.

The data from the 1980s and earlier do not allow us to reach any firm conclusions about sex differences in salary on the first job (Olson & Frieze 1987). When differences are found, they are in the expected direction. Women earn less than men, and sex is a negative contributor for women. But women also tend to have less work experience than men; once differences in prior work experience are taken into account, the salary differences for the first job become minor. That reduction in salary disparity shows the importance of human capital: lack of prior work experience is clearly costly. Whether women can acquire relevant work experience as easily as men can is a separate issue. Given the influence of gender schemas, we would expect women to have more difficulty than men getting such experience.

Data about later jobs, however, show clear, often substantial, sex differences in salary. In some studies, differences are eliminated when relevant factors like experience are taken into account, but in others differences favoring men remain. The review concludes that female MBAs are paid less than males, even after other factors have been taken into account (Olson & Frieze 1987).

The review also examined the extent to which various characteristics were correlated with higher or lower earnings (Olson & Frieze 1987). Work experience, as mentioned, was strongly positively related to earnings, whereas job interruptions or part-time work were strongly negatively related. Women managers are paid less than men in large part because they have, on average, less work experience and more job interruptions. (Whether such differences genuinely contribute to work productivity is a separate question.)

People in "line" positions—that is, those responsible for the overall policy and functioning of an organization—are more likely than those in "staff" positions—people who carry out or supervise the carrying out of specific functions—to earn more and have more opportunities for advancement. In addition, some business sectors pay better and have more advancement opportunities than others. Women's lack of advancement could be related to either or both factors. Here the evidence concerning women MBAs is less clearcut, although there is a tendency for women to be employed in staff positions in lower-paying sectors. That characteristic could be the result of sex differences in employees' preferences, employers' preferences, or both.

A 1991 study of 502 MBAs who graduated from one of the top ten business schools in the United States between 1976 and 1986 shows that women earned less than men did. Even when the groups were equated on variables such as type of position, starting salary, level of their initial job, experience, age, job performance rating, and type of industry, the disparities remained (Cox & Harquail 1991). Women also received fewer management promotions than their male peers did and so had not reached comparable levels of management.

Managers
Perhaps the most important survey of managers to date is due to Jacobs (1992), who investigated salaries of close to fifteen hundred male and female managers in 1969 and 1986. His analyses show that even when education, training, experience, hours worked, occupational specialization, supervisory status, and job preferences are accounted for, a substantial unexplained discrepancy in the salaries of women and men remains. Men have the advantage of being men.

Another study of managers in twenty Fortune 500 corporations attempted to assess the extent to which differences in human capital and other areas might affect salary differences between men and women (Stroh, Brett, & Reilly 1992). It examined the effects of years of work experience, amount of education, attitudes toward moving for one's job, and differences between industries. Each factor accounted for a substantial amount of the differences in how much male and female managers' salaries increased between 1984 to 1989. Above and beyond those factors, there was also a small but significant effect of sex: men's salaries increased more than women's did.

The authors note that it behooves women to obtain work experience and education; those attributes help everyone. Yet even women who had amassed as much human capital as men still suffered slightly because of their sex. Although the disparity was small, as the authors note, it should not have existed at all (Stroh et al. 1992). A further point is that the effects of gender may well have entered earlier into the process without being visible at the time of the study. If women cannot accumulate advantage as easily as men can, they are less likely to have as much relevant work experience. Work experience itself, then, is a factor that can be influenced by gender schemas.

International Business
A 1991 survey of United States professionals working in international business found that the males and females were similar on most dimensions but differed in four ways (Egan & Bendick 1994). The men held more graduate degrees and were less likely than the women to have liberal arts degrees; their highest degrees were also less likely than women's to have an international focus. More of the men were the sole earner in their household, and fewer of them had limited their careers for the benefit of their spouses' career. On other measures, including range of occupations, years of experience, strategies for career advancement, being designated as "fast track," and number of hours worked per week, there were no differences. In human capital terms, then, the men had invested only minimally more than the women in preparation for and commitment to their profession.

The investigators analyzed which factors contributed to determining the men's and women's salaries. The factors that helped men make higher salaries also typically helped women, but to a lesser extent; fourteen of the seventeen factors examined helped men more than they helped women. That result is what gender schemas would lead us to expect: women's achievements, qualifications, and professional choices were worth less than men's.

Here are some of the more striking examples. A bachelor's degree contributed $28,000 to a man's salary but only $9,000 to a woman's, and a degree from a high-prestige school contributed $11,500 to male salaries but subtracted $2,400 from female salaries. Not constraining one's career to benefit a spouse's career added $21,900 for men but only $1,700 for women. Being designated fast track added $10,900 for men but only $200 for women. Experience living outside the United States added $9,200 to men's salaries but subtracted $7,700 from women's. Similarly, deliberately choosing international work added $5,300 for men but subtracted $4,200 for women. Finally, speaking another language added $2,600 for men but subtracted $5,100 for women.

Only two factors helped women more than they helped men: negotiating for one's salary subtracted $5,600 for men but added $3,500 for women; frequent travel added $3,200 for men and $6,300 for women.

Women's average salary in this area of business ($54,800) was not significantly lower than men's ($63,700), but only 5 percent of women, compared to 14 percent of men, made over $100,000 a year. About a third of the salary gap could be accounted for by sex differences in qualifications; the remainder was due to differences in the way identical qualifications were rewarded. In general, investment in human capital accounted for the variability in male salaries better than it did for female salaries.

As we have now seen repeatedly, women tend to have lower human capital, which hurts their ability to advance. Above and beyond human capital, however, is the fact that women benefit less from their qualifications and credentials than men do. One reason for that may be that women's credentials are discounted, making it difficult for them to accumulate advantage. In the international business study, the investigators conjectured that the assets of speaking another language and living outside the United States are interpreted differently for males and females (Egan & Bendick 1994). They suggest that employers only interpret such qualifications as career preparation when men have them. The gender schema for men would not see men as choosing to live abroad or learn a language for the intrinsic pleasure of those activities but for the professional benefits they can bring. The gender schema for women, on the other hand, would picture them as pursuing such activities for their own sake. When men go abroad, the choice signals career commitment; when women go abroad, it signals indifference to a career. Men can accumulate advantage because their decisions are interpreted as being made for the right—instrumental—reasons.

The CIA

Although the U.S. Central Intelligence Agency (CIA) cannot be categorized as a business, it possesses a hierarchical structure similar to that in most businesses. In 1993 the director of the CIA reported to the House of Representatives that "women and minorities [have been] concentrated in the lower grades. Promotion rates in the period 1985–1990 ran higher for white, professional men than for women or minorities at the same starting grades. This is not our vision of where the agency should be"

(Weiner 1994). Similar patterns have been reported for the FBI and the U.S. State Department (Weiner 1994).

Engineers

The situation of engineers in industry is an interesting one, because male and female engineers have very similar training. In one study, the background and job history of a cohort of female and male electrical and mechanical engineers who graduated from two public universities in southern California between 1976 and 1985 were compared (Robinson & McIlwee 1989). The engineers differed little in experience or educational background, but women tended to be overrepresented in lower-prestige ranks and men in higher-prestige positions. Women also went backwards in their careers at a much higher rate than men did: 22 percent of women, compared to 2 percent of men, went from higher- to lower-prestige positions. As in several other studies, years since graduation and experience with their current employer predicted men's salaries, but not women's. Thus, even in a field where qualifications are identical, men's experience benefits them more than women's comparable experience. In engineering, as elsewhere, men accumulate advantage more easily than women do.

To sum up, in almost all types of business women fare worse than men. Sometimes women and men start out on an equal salary footing, but disparities arise as their careers progress. The disparities exist even when qualifications are equivalent.

Law

Structure of the Profession

Lawyers, once they have been admitted to the bar by successfully passing an examination, can practice law in a variety of settings. A majority of lawyers work in private practice, which covers both solo practice and practice in a law firm of any size. About half of private practitioners are in solo practice, and a little over half of those in group practices work in firms with ten or fewer lawyers. Although smaller firms often do not distinguish among different ranks, most larger law firms do. In 1980, somewhat more than half of the lawyers in private practice were in firms with two ranks—associate and partner (Curran, with Rosich, Carson, & Puccetti 1985). There is some variation, but most firms have either the same number of partners as associates or more partners than associates; only in firms of more than a hundred lawyers are there slightly more associates than partners (Curran & Carson 1991). Promotion from associate to partner can take from seven to ten years, with longer periods becoming more common, especially in large law firms. An associate who does not make partner within a given period typically leaves the firm.

Other settings for lawyers include industry or business (as in-house counsels), the state or federal judiciary, state or federal government, public defender offices, nonprofit organizations, and law schools. Corporations generally employ in-house counsel at nine different ranks: three in nonsupervisory, junior-level positions (attorneys I and II, and senior attorney) and six in supervisory positions, with corporate general counsel being the highest level. Nonsupervisory positions are equivalent to the associate level in private law firms.

Within the judiciary, there is a three-part distinction: at the lowest level are support personnel (e.g., clerk of court, court administrator, law clerk, staff attorney, marshal); an intermediate level includes other court officials who are neither support personnel nor judges (e.g., magistrates, referees, or judges in bankruptcy); at the highest level are the judges.

Women's Representation in Law

In the 1970s and 1980s women flooded into the law. In 1970 women were 3 percent of all lawyers. By 1980, they were 8 percent; in 1985, 13 percent; in 1995, 23 percent (American Bar Association 1995). Those overall figures represent the impact of women's admissions to the bar. Of those admitted to the bar between 1961 and 1970, only 3.5 percent were women. Between 1971 and 1974 8 percent were women; between 1975 and 1979 24 percent were women (calculated from Curran, with Rosich, Carson, & Puccetti 1985, Table 1.3.3). In 1987, women were 36 percent of new admissions to the bar (Curran & Carson 1991).

A statistic that brings out women's lower status in law firms, and that cannot be explained by female lawyers' youth, is the fact that in 1988, 66 percent of law firms of two or more lawyers were composed solely of men, even though by that date there were more than enough female lawyers for every law firm to employ at least one woman. Another 12 percent of firms had female associates but no female partners. Thus, in 1988, only 22 percent of large law firms included women at both the associate and partner levels. By 1991 the figures had improved slightly, so that 61 percent of law firms were all male and 26 percent had women as both associates and partners (ABA 1995). One percent of firms were all female.

Associates and Partners

Overall gender percentages for 1980 show that 86 percent of women were associates and 14 percent were partners (calculated from Curran et al. 1985, Table 1.7.4). In comparison, 37 percent of men were associates, and 63 percent were partners. That disparity in part reflects the fact that most of the women lawyers were young. By 1988, the percentage of women who were partners had risen to 20 percent and the percentage of men at the partner level had fallen to 60 percent (Curran & Carson 1991). Again, the lower average age of women lawyers partially accounts for the disparity. In 1980, 19 percent of the lawyers who were twenty-nine years old or younger were women, but only 4 percent of those aged 45 to 54 were women (Curran et al. 1985, Table 1.3.2). Since the overwhelming percentage of women in law were young, one would not expect equal gender percentages from comparisons of the profession as a whole.

Gender percentages are different from rank percentages. Gender percentages take each sex separately and ask what percentage of the sex has achieved a given rank or salary. Rank percentages look at each rank and ask what percentage of that rank is female and what percentage is male. Rank percentages for 1980 show that women were 15 percent of associates but only 2 percent of partners (Curran et al. 1985). In 1988 women were 30 percent of associates and 7 percent of partners (calculated from Curran & Carson 1991). In 1994, 13 percent of partners were female (ABA 1995). Again, the small percentage of women partners can be partially accounted for by the influx of young women into the profession that began in the late 1970s. The pool of female associate-age lawyers is much larger than the pool of female partner-age lawyers.

The cohort data show, however, that women's youth does not fully account for the disparities in achievement of partner status. Those data allow us to compare attorneys who were admitted to the bar before 1971 with those admitted between 1971 and 1979 (Curran et al. 1985). If men and women made partner equally easily, most of those lawyers admitted before 1971—at least 90 percent—should either have reached partner by 1980 or left their first firm. The gender percentage for men conforms to what is expected: 94 percent of the men admitted before 1971 were partners in 1980; only 6 percent were still associates (calculated from Curran et al. 1985, Table 1.7.14). In contrast, only 67 percent of the women admitted before 1971 were partners in 1980; 33 percent were associates (similarly calculated). Men in this cohort fared five times better than women did.

The next age cohort included those admitted to the bar between 1971 and 1979. In that cohort, 7 percent of the women in law firms were partners in 1980, compared to 26 percent of the men. The cohort data are not perfect, however, because the admission of women to the bar was not constant throughout the 1970s; many more women were admitted in the second half of the decade.[2] We would thus expect that by 1980 a smaller percentage of women than of men from that decade would have achieved partnership.

To adjust for the changing percentage of women across the decade, I assumed that none of the 1975–1979 cohort (male or female) had achieved partner status by 1980 and recalculated the gender percentages. A disparity remained: 63 percent of the males from the 1970–1974 cohort achieved partner status by 1980, compared to 41 percent of females (from Curran et al. data 1985).[3] Data from later cohorts are not available, but there is some evidence of progress in the overall gender percentage of women who are partners. From 1980 to 1988 that percentage rose from 14 to 20 percent.

An in-depth study of eight large Manhattan law firms found that women were 3 percent of the partners in 1980 and 12 percent in 1994 (Epstein, Saute, Oglensky, & Gever 1995). Similar data on the nation's top 250 firms show that women were only 3.5 percent of partners in 1981 and 11 percent by 1992 (Epstein 1993). Although the increase in partnerships from 3 to 12 percent in the eight New York firms represents obvious progress for women, it should be seen in relation to the fact that after 1984 35 percent or more of the associates in those firms were women.

Their 12 percent share of partnerships in 1994 must be contrasted with that of men—who were 65 percent of the associates in 1984 and 88 percent of the partners in 1994. Men and women at these firms were not being promoted equally.

The extent of the inequality can be determined by looking at gender percentages by age for males and females (calculated from data in Epstein et al. 1995, Tables II.11A and B).[4] In 1994, of the attorneys born between 1948 and 1953, 85 percent of the men, compared to 26 percent of the women, were partners. Of those born from 1954 to 1959, 50 percent of the men, compared to 23 percent of the women, were partners. Thus, even among relatively young attorneys, males were much more likely to be partners than females were. Nor can the differences be explained by the prestige of the lawyers' law school or undergraduate school, or by the area of law in which they specialized. Further, cohort data for the eight firms showed that from 1975 to 1985, men were twice as likely to be promoted from associate to partner as women were. Even among those hired in 1985 there were different promotion rates: 16 percent for male associates but only 5 percent for females.

Another way of examining the route from associate to partner is to look more broadly at cohorts. One study of two different samples of lawyers presents strong evidence that women do not achieve partnership at the same rate as men (Spurr 1990). The first group—2,116 lawyers—entered law firms between 1969 and 1973. The second group—293 lawyers—consisted of all the lawyers who entered firms of 40 or more members in New York City and Chicago in 1980. Both groups were followed until 1987. By then, twice as many men (39 percent) as women (18 percent) had become partners. The absolute rate of success was actually higher than in the New York study, probably because of differences in sampling. In all the groups, however, the comparative rate of advance was the same: men were more than twice as successful as women.

The men and women in the study did not differ in their law school ranking or in the honors they garnered in law school. A statistical model was used to estimate whether the same standard was used for the promotion of males and females. The standard for women was estimated to be more than 50 percent higher than the standard for men. Women were required to meet a higher criterion for promotion than men (Spurr 1990).[5]

Similar data on 1986 partnership rates were reported for 337 women and 1,435 men at private law firms in Los Angeles (Scott 1987). This study found that fresh lawyers admitted to the bar between 1981 and 1985 did not differ by sex in the percentage who were partners by 1986— 6 percent of the women and 5 percent of the men. Of those admitted to the bar between 1976 and 1980, however, only 32 percent of the women were partners, compared to 69 percent of the men. Again, the absolute numbers differ from the studies cited earlier, which presumably reflects geographical differences. The relative success rate, however, is consistent. Again, men are twice as successful as women, except for very young lawyers. One interpretation of the data is that the early identification of exceptional lawyers is not biased by sex, but the normal process of determining partnership works to women's disadvantage.

Salary in Law Firms
In 1993 the starting salary of that year's law school graduates nationwide was $38,000 for men and $35,000 for women; young women thus averaged 92 percent of men's salary (Foster 1995). Comparative data for private practitioners in two-rank firms are meager. The *National Law Journal* occasionally publishes figures comparing incomes by sex for associates at some of the country's largest law firms. The 1992 salaries reported for males and females admitted to the bar between 1986 and 1989 were equal: women averaged 99 percent of men's salaries (calculated from *National Law Journal* 1993). Figures for the 1981 to 1985 cohort, however, show a salary discrepancy, with women earning 95 percent of men's salaries. (Whether smaller firms, which are not included in the survey, showed the same pattern is unknown.) Since men are promoted to partner at a faster rate than are women, the 95 percent figure is worse than it appears. That is because what is being compared are salaries for men and women of the same admission year who are both still at associate level. What is left out is the salaries of partners. That would not matter if men and women were promoted equally. Since they are not, what remains in the pool are women who would have been making considerably more money as partners.

The salary data for lawyers in major law firms are roughly similar to data for MBAs. Women lawyers and MBAs currently start out on an equal salary footing with their male peers. Presumably because of differential promotion rates, the equality does not last for more than a few years.

More fine-grained salary data resulted from a telephone survey of almost eight hundred lawyers in 1989 (Dixon & Seron 1995). The investigators attempted to determine the relationship between human capital—for example, the prestige of the lawyer's law school and his or her years of experience—and salaries. In the private sector, law school prestige, being married, and having children added to men's salaries but not to women's. Years of experience contributed to both men's and women's salaries. Above and beyond these professional and personal factors, however, was the effect of sex: being male helped. Similar findings, showing earnings disparities after accounting for a range of human capital factors, hold for Canadian attorneys as well (Kay & Hagan 1995).

The data about private law firms—both gender percentages and rank percentages—consistently demonstrate that women are overrepresented at the associate level and underrepresented at the partner level. At major law firms, entry-level salaries for men and women are equal, but later disparities favor men. Differences in representation and salary are partially due to human capital differences and partially due to sex.

In-house Lawyers

There are three reports on the salaries of lawyers who work in business and industry.[6] The first examines the 1989 salaries of attorneys in nonsupervisory positions (low ranks) who were admitted to the bar between 1984 and 1988 (Resnick 1990). According to this report, women who were admitted in 1988 were better paid than their male peers; they earned 105 percent of men's salaries. Those admitted between 1984 and 1987, however, averaged 96 percent of their male peers' salaries in 1989. The younger women appear to have entry-level jobs for which they are paid equally as well or better than men, but they may not retain that level.

The second report examined five hundred corporate law departments employing seven thousand lawyers by comparing the 1992 salaries of male and female lawyers employed in each of nine ranks (Franklin 1992a, 1992b). The women's salaries relative to men's vary a great deal from rank to rank; the higher the rank, the greater are the sex disparities in income.

Thus, in the three lowest ranks women earned an average of 94 percent of men's salaries, whereas in the three highest ranks they earned an average of 78 percent of men's salaries. At the highest ranks, the sex discrepancy amounted to a very large dollar figure. For example, male general counsels averaged $205,097, while females averaged $152,412—a difference of more than $50,000.

In their very first jobs, men and women are frequently equally paid, but they appear to become unequal as a result of differential promotions. One analyst claims that corporate sex discrepancies in salary exist in firms of all sizes even during the first six years after admission to the bar (Franklin 1992a, quoting Robert J. Berkow of Ernst and Young).

Success as measured by place in the hierarchy can also be computed from the 1992 study of corporate law departments. Rank percentages show that women were overrepresented in the two lowest ranks, attorneys I and II, where an average of 42 percent of the ranks were women. They were underrepresented at the three highest ranks, comprising an average of 15 percent of the ranks of general counsel, group general counsel, and chief assistant/deputy general counsel (calculated from data in Franklin 1992a). The data are similar to the data reported for private law firms.

Gender percentages can also be computed. They show that 52 percent of the women employed by businesses are in the lowest two ranks, compared to 27 percent of the men. Since the women are on average younger than the men, we would expect to find a higher percentage of women in the junior ranks; the actual figure, however, appears disproportionately high, especially when taken in conjunction with the rank percentages.

The third report presents survey results of almost 4,500 attorneys who worked for 151 U.S. corporations in 1994 (France 1994). As in the earlier studies, salary differences were greatest at higher ranks (reflecting in part the larger percentage of older men), but also existed at low ranks, where women are most highly represented. Fifty-five percent of the women in these firms were clustered at the lowest rank, junior attorney. At the three lowest ranks, women earned 94 percent of what men in those positions earned.

At the highest level represented, chief legal officer, there were no women among the 151 corporations surveyed. At the next highest level, general counsel, there were a hundred men and eight women (France

1994). At that level and the next two highest, women earned 86 percent of what men earned. The salary disparities were also present in every subarea of the law. At the high salary level of these lawyers, even a small percentage difference is worth thousands of dollars. The male general counsels in the survey averaged $262,000; their female counterparts averaged $210,750. Other data for 1994 show that only one woman was among the hundred most highly paid general counsels in 1994 (Davis 1995).

In short, in-house women lawyers face the same situation as women attorneys in law firms: they make less money and advance more slowly than men.

The Judiciary
The overrepresentation of women in junior positions is also apparent in the judiciary. There are data on the 1980s for the three judicial categories of support personnel, non-judge positions (such as magistrate), and judges (Curran et al. 1985). In 1980 less than 1 percent of all lawyers were employed in the federal judiciary, and about 3 percent were employed in state or local courts. Cohort data for 1980 show differences between the federal and state/local levels and between lawyers admitted to the bar before 1971 and those admitted from 1971 to 1979.

The number of women lawyers in the judicial system is somewhat disproportionate to their representation in the law as a whole. In 1980 women were 3 percent of the total pre-1971 cohort of lawyers, but 5 percent of the judiciary. Similarly, women were 15 percent of lawyers admitted to the bar between 1971 and 1979, but 26 percent of both federal and state/local judiciary.

Gender percentages for the lawyers of the pre-1971 cohort serving in the federal judiciary show an unusual pattern (calculated from data in Curran et al. 1985, table 1.7.15). Men and women were equally represented at the judgeship level: 56 percent of males in the judiciary were judges, compared to 58 percent of females. The figures do not reveal whether males and females achieved judgeship at similar points in their careers, but they do show that women in the federal judiciary were as likely as men to become judges. At the same time, however, women were much more highly represented in the lowest rank: 9 percent of the males in the system were support personnel, compared to 25 percent of the females. In the later, 1971–1979, cohort, 94 percent of the males and almost all of the females (99.6 percent) were support personnel. Taken together, the data for the two cohorts suggest that support personnel positions are entry-level positions, that women move beyond those positions less rapidly than men, but that the same percentage of women as men eventually become judges.

There is less inequality in the federal judiciary than in state and local judiciaries. At the state/local level, gender percentages for the pre-1971 cohort show men to be more highly represented among judges than women: 91 percent of men in the system were judges, compared to 78 percent of women. Women were correspondingly overrepresented among support personnel. Gender percentages for the 1971–1979 cohort show the same pattern: 30 percent of the men were judges, compared to 8 percent of the women; 66 percent of the men, compared to 89 percent of the women, were support personnel.[7] Differences between the federal and state/local judiciaries may reflect a heightened sensitivity to equal rights for women on the part of those appointing judges to federal courts.

Rank percentages demonstrate progress in the judiciary as a whole. Between 1980 and 1991, women's representation in the courts went from 4 percent to 9 percent. At the federal level, dramatic improvement began during the Carter administration. Prior to 1976, less than 2 percent of the federal judges were women and less than 2 percent of every president's appointments went to women. Under Carter, the percentage of women on the federal bench rose to 7 percent, and 16 percent of Carter's appointments went to women. That figure is especially notable because women were only 8 percent of new bar admissions from 1971 to 1974, and 24 percent from 1975 to 1979. Carter actively and successfully sought out women candidates.

From 1981 to 1988, under Reagan, the percentage stayed roughly constant, rising only to 9 percent; only 8 percent of Reagan's appointments went to women. Between 1989 and 1992, during the Bush administration, the percentage of federal female judges rose to 12 percent. By 1995—three years into the Clinton administration—18 percent of federal judges were women. (All percentages were calculated from figures supplied by the Federal Judicial Center for Art. III judges.) Although 18 percent is still an underrepresentation of women, the increase of women in the federal judiciary demonstrates the power of the president to promote or retard the advancement of women.

In summary, data from private law firms, corporations, and the judiciary converge well. They show that women in all three sectors of the law are overrepresented in junior positions and underrepresented in senior positions. Women advance more slowly than men do, even when their qualifications are equal. Available salary data also suggest that although some women and men are paid the same in their first jobs, women's salaries rise more slowly than men's. Women in law and women in business have similar career paths.

Medicine

The situation of young women in medicine is somewhat more encouraging. Income data for 1990 are available for physicians under the age of 45 with two to five years of experience (Baker 1996). When incomes were unadjusted for factors like number of hours worked per week and specialty, women earned 70 percent as much as men. One factor contributing to that difference was that the women physicians worked fewer hours than the men did—51 compared to 62 hours per week. When hourly rates were calculated, women made 87 percent as much as men did. Some of the income disparity is thus due to the fact that women worked less than men.

In addition, women had less-remunerative specialties. Fifty-five percent of the women—compared to 42 percent of the men—practiced in the three lowest-paying fields: general practice, pediatrics, and general internal medicine. Moreover, only 14 percent of the women, compared to 27 percent of the men, worked in the four highest-paying fields: radiology, general surgery, anaesthesiology, and subspecialty surgery. When the rates per hour were corrected for specialty and practice setting, women earned 98 percent as much as men. Thus, most of the disparity in earnings per hour was due to the field of practice. The remaining 2 percent disparity was eliminated when other factors—including AMA membership and personal characteristics like marital status—were taken into account.

The data for 1990 contrast with the 1986 data. In 1986, even after adjustments were made for all the factors mentioned above, young male physicians earned more per hour than did young females. The change between 1986 and 1990 indicates progress for women. Young women's medical credentials were worth more in 1990 than they were in 1986.

But the progress in young women's income was not paralleled by progress for somewhat older women physicians—those with six to nine years of experience. Even after adjustments for all other factors, the more experienced women made 96 percent of men's income in 1990. The disparity was larger still for doctors with ten years or more of experience; in this cohort, women earned 85 percent of men's income (Baker 1996).

These data are similar in several ways to those we have seen for other professions. First, differences in human capital are often an important component of women's lower income. Second, women and men are equal or nearly equal very early in their careers, but, third, men's advantage increases over time. An equal starting point does not guarantee equal professional progress. This result is not unexpected. If, as we have suggested in earlier chapters, men accumulate advantage more easily than women do, increasing disparities over time are inevitable.

Analyses of the data by medical specialty revealed that in some fields women earned more per hour than men did and in others earned less, even after all other variables were taken into account. For example, the incomes of women in general practice averaged 14 percent more than men's, and in pediatrics averaged 7 percent more. Women in internal medicine subspecialties and emergency medicine, however, had incomes of a little less than 80 percent of men's. In surgery, women's average income was 93 percent of men's.

The differences in women's position vis-à-vis men is understandable if we consider them in terms of gender schemas. In general practice and pediatrics, a doctor's manner and interpersonal skills are as important as his or her medical skill. Indeed, the two interact: an accurate diagnosis requires sensitive questioning of a patient. In emergency medicine and surgery, on the other hand, manner is almost irrelevant and medical skill is everything. No interpersonal skills are needed to deal with an unconscious body. Since gender schemas represent women as more nurturant and expressive and as less technically skillful than men, their relative advantage in general practice and relative disadvantage in emergency medicine is not surprising. Women look and act right for general practice, and men look and act right for surgery.

We can conjecture that three factors operate. First, men and women both prefer specialties that are congruent with gender schemas. Second, senior physicians encourage younger ones to practice in specialties congruent with gender schemas. Third, once a physician has chosen a specialty, he or she can garner more income if that specialty is gender-congruent.

Sports

Participation

Female participation in sports in high school and college skyrocketed in the 1970s but has increased minimally since then. In 1971, 7 percent of the high schoolers participating in sports were girls; by 1977–1978 32 percent were girls (Women's Sports Foundation 1992). By the 1990–1991 school year, however, the percentage had only risen to 36 percent. The pattern for college students was similar but appeared earlier. In 1966–1967, 9 percent of NCAA athletes were women; in 1971–1972, 16 percent were women; and by 1976–1977, 27 percent were women. In 1989–1990, 33 percent were women. Gender percentages for interscholastic sports in high school also show a dramatic initial spurt followed by minimal growth in girls' participation. In 1971, 49 percent of high school boys participated in interscholastic sports, compared to 0.4 percent of girls. By 1977–1978, 56 percent of boys and 27 percent of girls participated. By 1990–1991 the percentages were, respectively, 55 percent and 31 percent.

One reason for the large increase in female participation in the 1970s may be the 1972 enactment of Title IX as part of the Educational Amendments Act modifying the Civil Rights Act of 1964. Title IX stated that "no person in the U.S. shall, on the basis of sex, be excluded from participation in, or denied the benefits of, or be subjected to discrimination under any educational program or activity receiving federal aid." It had policy implications for girls' and women's sports at all educational levels. Compliance with Title IX was not, however, required until 1978, so it is unclear how much of the increase can be attributed to it. Further, the increase in college women's participation predated Title IX, suggesting that the same climate that fostered the increased enrollment of women in Ph.D. programs, law schools, and MBA programs was at work in the gym.

Coaches and Administrators

Where Title IX did have a clear effect was on women's status as coaches and sports administrators. In 1972, before Title IX, women are estimated to have been 90 percent of the head coaches of women's teams. By 1978 their rank percentage had decreased dramatically, to 58 percent; it reached 48 percent in 1992 (Acosta & Carpenter 1992). Thus, Title IX reduced women's status as head coach. At the assistant coach level in 1992, women were 59 percent of those who were paid and 53 percent of those who were unpaid. Women are now a somewhat higher percentage of assistant coaches than of head coaches. A detailed analysis of the state of Ohio shows that there were 974 women coaches in 1974–1975, 640 in 1981–1982, and 542 in 1988–1989; their proportional representation slipped from 93 percent to 43 percent to 33 percent (Stangl & Kane 1991).

Nationwide, Title IX increased the number of sports programs available to women and thereby increased the number of coaching positions for women's sports, from 4,208 in 1978 to 5,952 in 1992. Men were the principal beneficiaries of that change; 75 percent of the new jobs went to men. Of the twenty-four sports we have separate tabulations for, twenty showed a smaller percentage of women coaches in 1991–1992 than in 1977–1978. Declines range from a high of 50 percentage points in archery to a low of 1.5 points in skiing, where women had only been 23 percent of the head coaches in the earlier year. Although Title IX helped men become head coaches of women's teams, it did not work the other way around; women are estimated to be only 2 percent of the head coaches of men's teams at the college level (Acosta & Carpenter 1992).

Moreover, directors of women's intercollegiate athletics programs, like the coaches, are now predominantly men. In 1972 an estimated 90 percent of athletic directors of women's programs were women; by 1984 only 17 percent were women, a percentage that remained essentially stable through 1992 (Acosta & Carpenter 1992). By then, 28 percent of women's programs had no women administrators. Thus, women's representation among coaches and athletic directors has seriously declined since the early 1970s.

To determine whether differences in male and female coaching salaries could be explained by differences in human capital, a survey of head coaches at NCAA Division I schools queried coaches on their current salaries and their backgrounds (Knoppers, Bedker Meyer, Ewing, & Forrest 1989). The women in the sample made less money overall than the men. Further, men who coached females made less money than men who coached only males. Of the women surveyed, 95 percent coached only female teams, and none coached only male teams; of the men, 24 percent coached only female teams, and 53 percent coached only male teams.

Human capital included factors like varsity athletic status as an undergraduate, type of undergraduate institution attended, college major, win/loss record, and years of coaching experience. The women coaches, on average, had fewer years of higher education and job experience than the men but were more likely to have been a college athlete and to have majored in physical education. Human capital factors explained more of the variation in women's salaries than in men's but contributed relatively little to either—perhaps because other, unmeasured, variables are better reflections of human capital. Overall, the differences in human capital apparently were not major determinants of the salary disparity (Knoppers et al. 1989).

The history of college coaching has brought a new dimension to the data on women in the professions. Even though coaching women carries lower status than coaching males—as seen by the lower salaries of men who coach only females compared to those who coach only males—men are more successful in obtaining such coaching jobs than women are and earn more money from them.

Professional Tennis

In part because of the paucity of women in most moneymaking sports, there are few comparisons of top-level male and female athletes. There are no major league women's baseball teams, no women's football teams, and very few professional female basketball teams. In professional tennis, however, we can compare the women's and men's prize purses in the four

Grand Slam tennis tournaments: the Australian Open, the French Open, Wimbledon, and the U.S. Open.

Before 1973 none of the championships had equal-sized purses for men and women; in 1996 only one of them—the U.S. Open—did. One of the most intriguing sports stories is how the U.S. Open came to award equal prizes to the male and female winners. In 1972 the women's first prize was 40 percent of the men's award. Equality came about in 1973 when Billie Jean King, the 1972 women's champion, said that she would organize a boycott of the tournament unless the male-female disparity was eliminated (Kahn 1991). The change testifies to the power that one important and determined individual can wield.

In 1989 the Australian Open also equalized its prize money. In 1995, however, tournament officials announced that the 1996 men's purse would increase by 17 percent but the women's purse would rise by only 6 percent (Cart 1995). The officials based their decision on the higher television ratings of men's matches, data that reports of other Grand Slam events contradict. For example, in most years the French Open's women's events have had higher ratings in the United States than the men's matches (Elmore 1996). One reason for the lower ratings of the Australian Open's women's matches may be that women are frequently scheduled to play at times when television networks in different time zones do not cover the events (Cart 1995). Women's matches cannot reap high viewer ratings if they are not televised.

Wimbledon and the French Open also continue to pay women less. In tennis, women are staying the same or going backwards. In 1996 the U.S. Open was the only Grand Slam tournament awarding women and men equal prizes. What (scanty) data there are suggest that women draw more viewers than men and thus should, if anything, win slightly larger prizes than men (Kahn 1991).

Men and women do not play against each other, except in mixed doubles. Nor could they, because the men's power would overwhelm the women's game. Skill and strategy are a part of both players' games, but the men's game is less balanced than the women's: the men rely more on the power behind their strokes. Men serve a much larger number of aces than women do and have fewer and shorter rallies. Both styles of play are interesting in their own way, and spectators seem equally interested in both.

Tennis is a good illustration of the important role that physical sex differences play in our assessments of women and men. Since men are taken as the norm and would overpower women if the sexes played against each other, the men's game is seen as the game that women are deviating from and doing worse at. But the two games can be seen as equal in interest though different in kind.

In tennis and in other sports, enthusiasts appear increasingly interested in women's games. At the 1996 Olympics, for example, the finals of the women's soccer event attracted 76,481 stadium viewers, the largest live audience ever gathered for a women's sporting event (Vecsey 1996). The potential television audience, though, was largely deprived of the opportunity to watch the game; the commercial broadcasters' failure to televise the complete game is an example of the difficulty women athletes have in demonstrating the public appeal of their sports.

In my discussion of various topics I have stressed that women and men are much more similar than they are different, which is true. In sports, the sex differences are more pronounced. But viewers are spontaneously discovering the pleasures of watching a game played a different way. Difference does not by itself justify unequal payment.

Summary

In every field and profession examined in this chapter, men earn more money and achieve higher status than women do. In business, women are overrepresented at the bottom and underrepresented at the top. Starting salaries for MBAs tend to be roughly equal, especially if experience is factored in, but advancement is slower for women. In law, too, whether working in private firms, corporations, or the judiciary, women are overrepresented in junior positions and underrepresented in senior positions; they also make less money. Women physicians tend to be concentrated in lower-earning specialties and, with increased experience, earn less than men physicians. In college sports, women's status as coaches and administrators was once high, but has declined since 1972. In professional sports as well, women continue to lag behind men in earnings. Differential investment in human capital sometimes explains part of the sex disparity in income and rank, but gender always explains an additional portion. Women are required to meet a higher standard.

Gender Schemas

In 1940 the ceiling for female office workers was made of marble, not glass. In many companies women were explicitly barred from positions of authority and responsibility. Even more interesting are the data showing that men stood on an elevated marble floor: they were prevented from taking jobs, such as that of a stenographer, lacking in advancement possibilities (Goldin 1990).

The situation of office workers in 1940 is very different from that of professional women in the 1990s. The marble ceiling and the marble floor are now made of glass, but the present is continuous with the past. Women receive a lower rate of return from their investments in education and experience than men do. It is as if women were asked to accept lower interest rates on a savings account. Gender schemas discount women's achievements. Women receive less interest because they are seen as investing less than men, even when their investments are equal. In a sense, that is not surprising. Attitudes that were expressed openly and unconstrainedly through the 1960s are unlikely to disappear in forty years, even if they are not longer articulated.

Two different questions can be posed. The first is, Why have women advanced as much as they have? The second is, Why have they advanced so slowly? The second question is easier to answer than the first. Schemas change slowly, especially if people do not know how schemas operate. Even when they do know, they may require frequent reminders, as I have reluctantly acknowledged from my own reactions.

After buying a laptop computer by mail I telephoned the company about a keyboard problem. The person who answered my call was a woman. My first reaction was surprise and my second was faint dismay. She's not going to be able to help me, I thought. And she wasn't. I was frustrated and impatient and asked her to connect me with someone who could answer my question. She transferred me to a man, who told me that the problem could not be solved. Afterward, I realized that my reaction to the woman had been dictated solely by gender schemas. If I weren't careful I would draw a faulty conclusion from my encounter that would perpetuate my schemas.

The first question—Why have any women succeeded?—is more difficult. One answer is that women reconceptualized themselves. Another is that at least some employers accepted women's new role. In the early 1970s, white, educated, middle-class women radically reconsidered their place in the world, with long-term and wide-ranging consequences. They were able to do so in part because they *were* educated and middle-class. Those women *could* flock to professional schools: they already had college educations and had sources of funding. In addition, the democratic, egalitarian beliefs of many contemporary political groups gave women a set of ideas and a language they could use to critique the antidemocratic, inegalitarian behavior that those very groups displayed toward the women in their midst. Women then pursued those ideas and their implications for the wider world, in particular the workplace. The development of the women's movement is a testament to the power of ideas to change the thinking of both women and men.

Where do we go from here? The statistical data on women in the professions and in academia (see chapter 11)—along with the data on how children are reared and women are perceived that we reviewed in earlier chapters—suggest that women will not advance faster without a better understanding of gender schemas and how they hinder women's accumulation of advantage.

It is not that conscious understanding guarantees freedom from a schema, nor that nonconsciousness guarantees slavery to it. But it is harder to challenge beliefs and attitudes we do not know we possess. The "consciousness-raising" discussions that occurred in the late 1960s and early 1970s can be interpreted as an attempt to develop an explicit, if initially informal, understanding of the gender schema for women, in order to challenge it. The discussions were a raising *to* consciousness of implicit beliefs and attitudes. Making what is implicit explicit can be difficult, because it involves recognizing in ourselves attitudes or beliefs we do not want to possess, as was the case for me when I spoke to the woman on the computer help line.

Unless we—women and men alike—understand how gender schemas disadvantage women professionally, women will not receive the positive evaluations their work merits, women will get less than their fair share, and women's advancement will continue to be slow.

11

Women in Academia

The facts concerning men's and women's achievement in academia echo, in many respects, the data for business, law, and sports reviewed in chapter 10. The academic data are more plentiful and more reliable than the information we have about other employment areas and, hence, are even more convincing. Like the data for the other professions, the data for academia are of two types—aggregate data and cohort data. Taken together, they show that in almost every field and subfield, in almost every cohort and at almost every point in their teaching and research careers, women advance more slowly and earn less money than men. The history of the profession in the past few decades suggests that the problem of women's lower status in academia will not dissipate in the fullness of time.

We saw in chapter 10 that comparing male and female salaries for high ranks can inflate apparent income disparities. In academia as well, the interaction between salary and rank can lead to invalid comparisons. A true picture should compare peers. But if male full professors are—like male law partners—on average older than female full professors, they will have more experience and earn higher salaries. Comparisons within a rank, therefore, can be only partially successful at equating people if the rank contains people of disparate ages and experience.

In junior ranks, comparing apparent peers may have the opposite effect: it can underestimate income disparities. If male professors are promoted at a faster rate than female professors, the people in a lower rank will include not only young men and women but also older women who should have been promoted out of that rank. Independent evidence that women *are* promoted more slowly than men confirms that underestimation of income disparities occurs when gender comparisons are confined to junior ranks. Data tabulations comparing the incomes of males and females who are the same number of years post-degree, or who have the same number of years of experience, regardless of rank, are preferable and are used here when available.

The Status Structure of Academia

There are three basic ranks within academia: assistant professor, associate professor, and professor (or full professor). An opening as an assistant professor may be designated a tenure-track position, meaning that a person hired as a beginning-level assistant professor can be considered for tenure.

The most common successful career path in academia begins by being hired as an assistant professor in a tenure-track line. The initial contract is often for three or four years but may be for as few as two or as many as five. It has become common for departments to review assistant professors in their second or third year before offering another three- or four-year contract. An assistant professor is reviewed for tenure in the sixth year and, if successful, becomes tenured in his or her seventh year.

At many institutions, promotion to the next rank, associate professor, is considered concurrently with tenure; in others, promotion is considered earlier, in the fifth year; in a very few universities, promotion is considered after tenure has been granted, and is almost automatic. The timing of promotion to full professor depends on the academic's continuing productivity but usually occurs within twelve to fourteen years post-Ph.D. Because a full professorship is typically the final academic rank, there are usually more full professors in a department than associate and assistant professors combined.

The tenure decision is the most important decision an institution makes about a faculty member, because a tenured professor can only be fired for gross incompetence, legal or moral malfeasance, or because his or her research or teaching program has been eliminated. Otherwise, a tenured faculty member leaves an institution only by resignation (for example, to take a job at another school), by retirement, or by death. Getting tenure is similar to becoming a partner in a law firm.

The requirements for tenure vary somewhat. Prestigious universities—institutions that award Ph.D.s and professional degrees in addition to bachelor's degrees—demand that the candidate make significant contributions to knowledge in her or his field. Scholarly contributions are measured by both the quantity and quality of peer-reviewed publications and presentations, by success in obtaining research grants, and by other evidence that the professor is an active scholar. The more prestigious the institution, the more significant the research must be. Competence in teaching is demanded too, but is less important than research at the most prestigious universities. At colleges, which primarily award bachelor's degrees, although research contributions are increasingly demanded, teaching skills are more highly valued than they are at universities.

Most tenure-track or tenured positions require a Ph.D., but exceptions are made, usually for individuals, such as writers or political figures, whose credentials are their achievements outside academia.

People still working on their Ph.D.s may be hired as instructor or lecturer. Such positions are usually not tenure-track and are one-year appointments renewed at the institution's discretion. An instructor who finishes his or her degree in a timely manner and has a prior agreement with the institution may become an assistant professor.

Other instructors or lecturers may already have their Ph.D.s. A person with a Ph.D. who has a non-tenure-track position is at a professional dead end. Nonetheless, one member of a couple may accept such an appointment when his or her partner is offered an attractive position, in hopes that a better job will open up at the same or a nearby institution. Or, a Ph.D. may have no better alternatives immediately available.

The positions discussed thus far are full-time positions. Academia also has part-time positions, which are generally designated as *adjuncts,* for example, adjunct assistant professor or adjunct lecturer. An adjunct is typically paid by the course—very poorly paid, usually between $1500 and $3000. Institutions have no stake in adjuncts and seldom provide them with more than a desk or a part-time office in which to meet students.

The range of status within academia can be seen by comparing the salary and teaching load of a full-time scholar at a prestigious university with those of an adjunct. A beginning-level assistant professor at a highly regarded institution will teach two courses per semester and earn about

$35,000 to $45,000 per year. In contrast, an adjunct assistant professor typically earns $1500 to $2500 per course; he or she makes far less money for far more teaching and has little time and few facilities to conduct research. Since research productivity is the key to advancement in academia, an adjunct has virtually no chance of advancing.

In my earlier example of a successful career path, progress from assistant to full professor and from tenure-track to tenured status all occurred within a single institution. An individual may also move to a new college or university as a result of receiving a better offer elsewhere, not being reappointed, being denied tenure at the original institution, or for personal reasons.

There are important differences in the career paths of male and female academics. The data show that women are considerably less successful in academia than men are. Women earn less money, are promoted and granted tenure more slowly, and work at less prestigious institutions.

Salary

Across Disciplines

Regardless of their discipline, women at universities and colleges at each rank have lower average salaries than men do. Moreover, the inequalities are progressive: the disparity at the assistant professor level is smaller than it is at the full professor level. The American Association of University Professors (AAUP) data in figure 11.1 compares 1996–1997 salaries for all ranks in terms of the percentage of men's salaries that women earn at universities and colleges nationwide. Figure 11.2 (a,b, and c) shows salary data for each rank at four selected samples of elite institutions (AAUP 1997). I include the selected samples as well as the overall data to determine whether the same pattern is apparent in elite institutions as well as in institutions as a whole. One might hypothesize that elite institutions would lead the way in equitable treatment of women and that other institutions would follow.

The first sample of elite institutions is made up of five northeastern private universities: Harvard, Yale, Princeton, MIT, and Columbia. The second is a group of five public universities: Michigan, Wisconsin, California–Berkeley, California–Los Angeles, and Texas. The five small north-

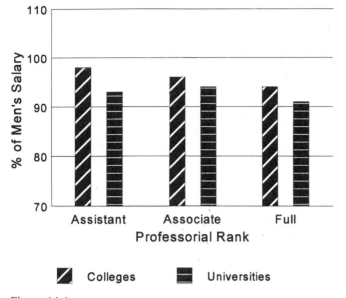

Figure 11.1
Percent women earned of men's salary, 1996–1997: universities and colleges nationwide. (Data from AAUP 1997)

eastern coeducational colleges in the third sample are Swarthmore, Amherst, Williams, Wesleyan, and Haverford. The final sample is made up of five small northeastern women's colleges: Wellesley, Smith, Mt. Holyoke, Bryn Mawr, and Barnard.[1]

The figures allow us to test the hypothesis about elite institutions by comparing the averages for the two university samples with the averages at universities nationwide (AAUP's Category I). We can also compare the averages for the two college samples with those for all undergraduate colleges without significant numbers of higher-degree programs (AAUP's Category IIB).

Figure 11.1 shows that average salaries for women at each rank are lower than men's. At universities, women average 91 percent of men's full professor salaries and 93 percent of their assistant professor salaries. At the colleges, the comparable figures are 94 percent and 98 percent. Comparison of the two university samples in figure 11.2 (a, b, and c) suggests that elite private universities pay men and women slightly better at these two ranks (91 percent and 95 percent) than elite public universities do

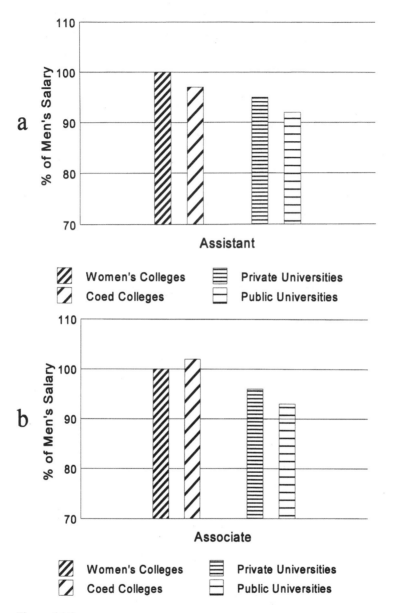

Figure 11.2
Percent women earned of men's salary, 1996–1997: selected elite institutions.
(Data from AAUP 1997)

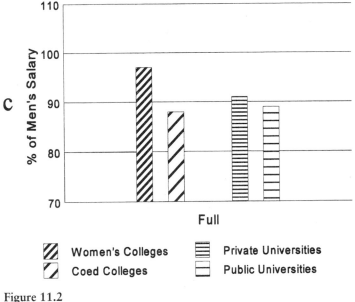

Figure 11.2
continued

(89 percent and 92 percent). The averages for the two college samples in figure 11.2 (a, b, and c) show that women's schools pay men and women roughly equally at both ranks (97 percent and 100 percent), in contrast to private coeducational schools, which pay assistant professors equally (97 percent) but women full professors only 88 percent of men's salaries. Since women hold lower positions longer than men do, the salary figures at the ranks of assistant and associate levels are misleadingly positive and underrepresent the gender disparity.

Some of the discrepancy in current salary figures may be due to the fact that there are fewer women in more highly paid disciplines (such as computer science). However, even when data are reported by discipline, they show that women earn less than men in almost every field.

Humanities
Consider, for example, the figures for a sample of men and women Ph.D.s in the humanities compiled by the National Research Council (NRC) (Ingram & Brown 1997). These 1995 figures are the most current ones available and are less than ideal, in that they include Ph.D.s employed outside

as well as inside academia, though approximately 80 percent were employed in educational institutions. An important virtue of the NRC data is that they are subdivided by number of years post-Ph.D., allowing us to compare male and female Ph.D.s at the same level. Such cohort information is especially useful because it maximizes the likelihood of comparing individuals with the same training and background at the same point in their careers.

In 1995, the median salaries of full-time male and female humanists who were zero to five years post-Ph.D. were equal, at approximately $34,000 (Ingram & Brown 1997, table 19).[2] At all further intervals post-Ph.D., however, women's salaries lagged behind men's: they averaged 95 percent of men's at six to fifteen years post-Ph.D., 96 percent at sixteen to twenty-five years, and 89 percent at over twenty-five years. Overall, women humanists earned 84 percent of men's salaries ($40,500 compared to $48,000). Earlier figures from the NRC (e.g., 1987) had shown women lagging behind men in salary even during the first five years post-Ph.D. The current data are thus encouraging: they suggest that women and men start out on an equal salary footing. At the same time, they are discouraging: they indicate that the later salary inequalities found in earlier surveys are continuing.

Science and Engineering

1993 salary data for samples of scientists and engineers with Ph.D.s were gathered by the National Science Foundation (NSF) (NSF 1996).[3] The disciplines represented include mathematics, computer specialties, psychology, and social science (such as economics and sociology), as well as physics, chemistry, biology, and traditional engineering fields. The average income of women from all fields combined was 78 percent of the men's average: the median salary for women was $48,400, compared to $61,500 for men (NSF 1996, table 38). Within each individual field, women also earned less than men; the percentages ranged from 76 percent of men's salaries in environmental science to 93 percent in mechanical engineering.

Even among the newest Ph.D.s—those with degrees earned in 1991–1992—women fared worse than men. In 1993 the average female in that cohort earned 89 percent of the average male's salary, $37,600, compared to $41,900 (NSF 1996, table 54). The lack of parity for new graduates, however, is due to nonacademic employment sectors. Of scientists who earned their degrees in 1991–1992, females at universities and four-year colleges earned 99 percent of males' salary (NSF, unpublished data, NSF table 14).

But academia does not provide salary parity for even slightly more experienced women. In 1993, women whose degrees were awarded between 1985 and 1990 earned 92 percent of men's salaries; women with degrees from 1980 to 1984 earned 90 percent; and those with degrees from 1970 to 1979 earned 86 percent (calculated from unpublished NSF data, NSF table 14). Overall, women scientists in universities and four-year colleges earned about 80 percent of men's salaries: women's average salary was $43,300, compared to $54,000 for men (NSF 1996, table 44).

In sum, the picture for science and engineering in academia is similar to that for the humanities. The most recent female graduates start out on an equal salary footing with males but lose that equality as early as three to eight years post-Ph.D. The salary disparity increases with years post-degree. The salary discrepancies between men and women in science and engineering are greater than they are in the humanities.

Rank and Tenure

Salary is only one aspect of status in academia; rank and tenure are, if anything, more important measures. As will be seen, women in all fields are overrepresented in low-status and untenured positions, according to the data available for humanists, scientists and engineers, and for academics in general. My discussion of academia presents both rank and gender percentages, as they tell us different things about women's and men's career patterns.

Rank Percentages

For each rank or status level, rank percentages reflect the numbers of female and male occupants at that rank. Although rank percentages tell us how far away we are from equality within each rank, they do not tell us the source of the inequality. The numbers of each sex that make up the candidate pool constrains the rank percentages. If, for example, only 5 percent of the Ph.D.s in a given field were women, we would not expect any rank to be composed equally of males and females. Thus, in trying to determine what the percentage of women "should" be in any rank or status, we must take into account the size of the pool, while also acknowledging that the composition of the pool could itself reflect prior inequalities.

Gender Percentages

Gender percentages express separately for women and men what percentage of each group occupies a particular rank. Gender percentages are useful for tracking the careers of people who received their degrees at about the same time and are therefore in the same cohort. The figures are independent of the size of the pool. For example, we can take males and females in the 1980 cohort (that is, those who received their degrees in 1980) and ask what percentage of the males were full professors in 1990 and what percentage of the females were full professors that year. We would expect that, in the absence of other differences, males and females from the same cohort would have the same profiles ten years later. Gender percentages thus provide another measure of equality.

Gender percentages are less useful for comparing groups that are not in the same cohort, because the groups may vary on dimensions other than gender. If, for example, we found that only 10 percent of all women in a discipline were full professors, compared to 40 percent of all men, that might be explained by the fact that the women are on average much younger than the men and, therefore, are less likely to be tenured. Cohort data control for that possibility.

Rank and Tenure

Rank Across Disciplines

Women are a minority in every rank. They are only 13 percent of full professors at universities and 21 percent at colleges (calculated from AAUP 1997, table 11). Figure 11.3 shows the 1996–1997 rank percentages for institutions nationwide, and figure 11.4 (a, b, and c) shows the comparable rank percentages for the elite samples in the same year.

The long-standing and continuing commitment of women's colleges to hire and promote women is clearly visible in figure 11.4. Women at the five colleges in the sample are 42 percent of full professors and 55 percent

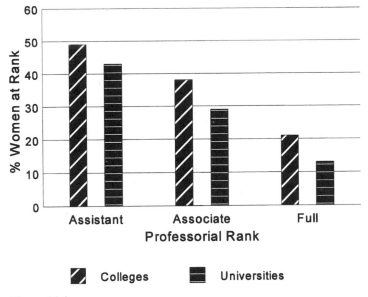

Figure 11.3
Percent of women at each professorial rank, 1996–1997: universities and colleges nationwide. (Data from AAUP 1997)

of assistant professors. The contrast with the record of the coeducational colleges (18 percent and 49 percent) is especially noteworthy, because the two types of institutions are similar in the academic courses they provide. Although universities may offer courses in fields few women teach in (e.g., engineering), the curricula in women's and coeducational colleges differ little.

Earlier I mentioned the need to know the composition of the candidate pool in order to determine whether there are gender imbalances in hiring and promotion. If the pool includes very few women, very few women can be promoted. Often, however, the pool is difficult to establish, because it is constantly changing: both the number of Ph.D.s awarded and the gender composition of the recipients shift each year.

In the past few decades, the number of women Ph.D.s has increased tremendously. In 1964, for example, women were awarded 11 percent of all doctorates; in 1974, 20 percent; in 1984, 34 percent; and in 1994, 39 percent (Simmons & Thurgood 1995, table 2, p. 21). When recipients from outside the United States are excluded, women earned 39 percent

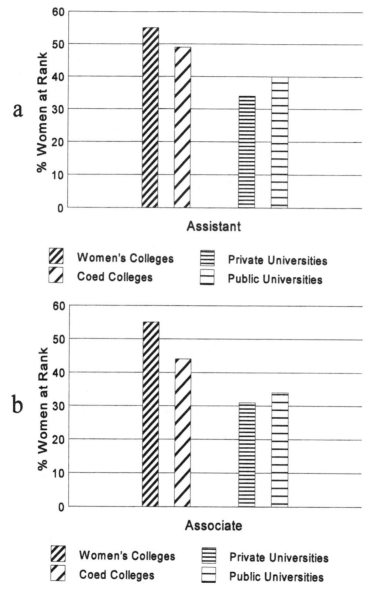

Figure 11.4
Percent of women at each professorial rank 1996–1997: selected elite institutions. (Data from AAUP 1997)

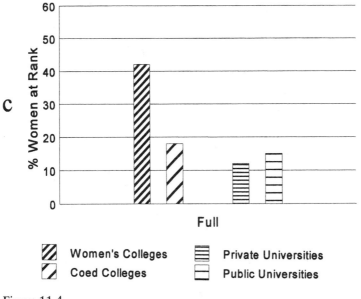

C

Figure 11.4
continued

of the doctorates awarded in 1984 and 46 percent in 1994 (calculated from Appendix table B-2, Simmons & Thurgood 1995). A disproportionate percentage of women receiving Ph.D.s has been and continues to be white: in 1994 only 9 percent of the doctorates awarded to women went to black and Hispanic women (calculated from Appendix table B-2, Simmons & Thurgood 1996).

The influx of white women into higher education that began in the 1970s was paralleled by an influx of white women into law schools, medical schools, business schools, and sports (see chapter 10). The women's movement of the early 1970s appears to have been a galvanizing force behind white women's entry into fields dominated by men.

The constantly changing sex composition of the pool complicates estimates of how many women should be represented at each rank. In addition, the representation of women in the different fields varies widely. Overall, as stated earlier, women earned 39 percent of the doctorates awarded in 1994. That year, 42 percent of all doctorates in the life sciences, 49 percent of the social science doctorates, and 48 percent of the humanities doctorates were awarded to women. In contrast, women received only 11 percent of the engineering doctorates and only 20 percent of the physical science doctorates—including mathematics and computer science (Simmons & Thurgood 1995, table 2, p. 21). If we assume that universities hire roughly proportionately to the numbers of doctorates available each year, then we would expect at least 39 percent of assistant professors in 1996–1997 to be women. On that basis, elite private universities appear to hire fewer women than appropriate at that rank, while elite public universities hire at the correct level (see figure 11.4a). Universities as a whole (averaging both elite and nonelite institutions) hire slightly more women at the assistant professor level than the assumption would predict (see figure 11.3).

Colleges probably do not hire as heavily as universities in fields where women are least well represented, such as engineering and the physical sciences). More of their courses involve the social sciences and humanities—where women received 42 percent of the doctorates in 1984 and 49 percent in 1994. If we assumed that colleges hired roughly proportionately, we would expect (IIB) colleges in 1996–1997 to have between 45 and 49 percent women assistant professors. As figures 11.3 and 11.4a show, the elite coeducational colleges and colleges overall seem to hire women at the correct rate, and the women's colleges exceed that rate.

Tenure Across Disciplines

In 1996–1997 the gender percentages show that 96 percent of men at universities nationwide were in tenured or tenure-track appointments, compared to 85 percent of women (AAUP 1997, table 11). At colleges that primarily award bachelor's degrees, the figures are 94 percent for men and 88 percent for women. These percentages for both types of institutions show that men are more likely to be tenured than women are; but as the data are not organized by cohort, the reasons for the imbalance are not clear.

At all universities combined, 15 percent of full-time women worked as instructors, lecturers, or in no-rank positions, compared to 4 percent of full-time men. At the (IIB) colleges combined, 13 percent of the women and 6 percent of the men were in these bottom categories (AAUP 1997, calculated from table 11). Thus, at both universities and colleges, women appear to be underrepresented in tenured or tenure-track positions and overrepresented in nontenure positions.

Because such aggregate figures could be skewed by the large percentage of older male full professors, I computed new values excluding full professors and compared the distributions of the remaining full-time men and women in the other ranks. The asymmetry remained. At the universities 39 percent of the women and 57 percent of the men were associate professors; 43 percent of the women and 34 percent of the men were assistant professors; and 19 percent of the women and 9 percent of the men were instructors or lecturers or held no rank. The figures for the undergraduate colleges were comparable. When full professors were excluded, 36 percent of the women and 48 percent of the men were associate professors; 50 percent of the women and 43 percent of the men were assistant professors; and 16 percent of the women and 9 percent of the men were instructors or lecturers or held no rank. Women continue to be overrepresented at the bottom ranks. Moreover, across all fields, ages, and institutions, figures for 1995–1996 showed that 72 percent of academic men were tenured, compared to only 48 percent of women (AAUP 1996).

To sum up, the rank and tenure data across all disciplines demonstrate that women in academia fare considerably worse than men.

The Humanities

To evaluate whether academic women's opportunities to attain rank and tenure were affected by the disciplines they specialized in, I looked at data for the two broad areas of the humanities and sciences. In 1995, 35 percent of the employed Ph.D.s in the humanities were women (Ingram & Brown 1997). According to the NRC (1997), in 1995, women in the humanities who were zero to five years post-Ph.D. fared less well in rank than men, despite their overall equality of salary. That statistic suggests that the salary data are misleading. Women advance through the ranks more slowly than men, leaving more older women than older men in the lower ranks. That imbalance makes the salary figures appear more comparable than they actually are.

The gender percentages show that 3.1 percent of employed new male Ph.D.s compared to 2.2 percent of females became full professors within six years (Ingram & Brown 1997). To become a full professor in such a short period of time is a major achievement in academia. The data thus suggest that men are slightly more likely than women to be perceived as stars, something we would expect on the basis of gender schemas. (I note, though, that women lawyers in one study mentioned in chapter 10 were as likely as men to receive early partnership.)

More telling are the data for the lowest ranks—instructor, lecturer, adjunct, and positions that carry no rank. Not quite 26 percent of employed men who were five or fewer years post-Ph.D. occupied such positions, compared to 29 percent of employed women (calculated from Ingram & Brown 1997, table 14, p. 42). Women were overrepresented at the bottom and in the ranks of the unemployed. Figures for new Ph.D.s who were unemployed and seeking work in 1995 show that 1.7 percent of men were in that category, compared to 4.4 percent of women. Again, these are data that gender schemas would lead us to expect: women carry an implicit minus sign that helps keep many of them at the bottom or out of work.

The figures for the humanities are particularly important, because they demonstrate that even the newest Ph.D.s have differential success rates. In 1995 new women Ph.D.s were 82 percent as likely as men to achieve associate or full professor status within six years, but 114 percent as likely as men to end up in the least advantageous positions and 259 percent as likely to be involuntarily unemployed.

Six to fifteen years post-Ph.D., the situation is considerably worse. Only 10 percent of women were full professors, compared to about 21 percent of men. Approximately equal percentages of men and women were associate professors, and more women (21 percent) than men (14) were still at the assistant professor level. In the bottom ranks were 17 percent of men and 24 percent of women.

As would be expected given their overrepresentation at the bottom, a smaller percentage of women than men in the humanities have tenure. Although at five years post-Ph.D. an approximately equal percentage of women and men—about 12 percent—had tenure, by six to fifteen years the equality had disappeared: 65 percent of men and 51 percent of women were tenured (Ingram & Brown 1997, table 16). Data for positions without tenure are similar: 21 percent of men, compared to 30 percent of women six to fifteen years post-Ph.D. lacked tenure (Ingram & Brown, table 16, p. 44).

Science and Engineering

In 1993 women were 19 percent of all employed doctoral scientists and engineers (NSF 1996, table 3), and 22 percent of faculty at universities and four-year-colleges (NSF 1996, table 17). Women ranged from 4 percent of faculty in engineering departments to 30 percent of faculty in social science and related fields (NSF 1996, table 17).

Gender percentages for 1993 show that 61 percent of the men in science and engineering were tenured, compared to 35 percent of women. We would expect some imbalance, because there are more older men than older women. If differences in the age distribution fully accounted for the disparity, however, the combined tenure plus tenure-track percentages should be equal for men and women. They are not. Overall, 60 percent of women were in tenured or tenure-track positions, compared to 77 percent of men. And, like women in the humanities, women in science were disproportionately represented in non–tenure-track positions: 14 percent of women, compared to 8 percent of men. The remainder of each sex were in positions to which tenure does not apply; here too women were overrepresented. (All data were calculated from NSF 1996, table 18).

New women Ph.D.s in science fields fared better in tenure-track status than older women Ph.D.s, but even new women lagged behind new men. Of those who graduated between 1985 and 1992, 57 percent of the males were tenured or in tenure-track positions in 1993, compared to 50 percent of the females. Of those who graduated before 1985, 85 percent of the males, compared to 69 percent of the females, were in tenured or tenure-track appointments.

The plight of women who earned degrees before 1985 is seen most sharply at the levels of full professor and assistant professor. In 1993, 14 percent of women compared to 6 percent of men were still assistant professors. Only 31 percent of the women, but 59 percent of the men, were full professors that year (calculated from unpublished NSF data, table 23). Women scientists are moving through the ranks in academia at a slower rate than men.

A different sample of men and women scientists, intended to represent those who show high levels of achievement early in their career, was studied from 1987 to 1990 (Sonnert & Holton 1996a, 1996b). The participants had received postdoctoral fellowships from either the National Science Foundation or the National Research Council between 1952 and

1986. Because those national fellowships are prestigious, the men and women who earn them are roughly equal in terms of human capital and performance at the start of their academic careers. Nonetheless, with the exception of biologists, women with such fellowships were less successful at moving through the ranks than men were. For example, women who had earned their Ph.D.s in the physical sciences, mathematics, and engineering after 1978 were almost a full rank behind their male peers; women in the social sciences were more than three-quarters of a rank behind (Sonnert & Holton 1996a).

The women in this sample were somewhat less productive than the men; but even when productivity was taken into consideration, the women (except the biologists) held lower ranks than comparable men. Thus, even women who have obtained a prestigious credential profit from it less than men do. Moreover, women do worse in sciences like physics— where we might think the possible existence of objective criteria would benefit them—than they do in the social sciences.

Women also did less well than men in terms of the relation between their rank and the prestige of their institution (Sonnert & Holton 1996a). For women, the more prestigious their institution the lower their rank, whereas for men, there was no relation. Thus, although women were as likely as men to be represented at high-prestige institutions, they suffered in rank to obtain that representation. Again, the results from women in biology did not fit that pattern.

Finally, a number of human-capital variables, ranging from the time men and women spent earning a degree to their relationship with their dissertation director, were assessed (Sonnert & Holton 1996a). Some of the characteristics had similar consequences for men and women; others had different effects. For example, although men and women were equally likely to have an influential advisor, that helped men more than women. Productivity also helped men more than it helped women; even though the men and women were not equally productive, a given amount of productivity helped men more than a comparable amount helped women.[5]

A striking demonstration of the overvaluation of men comes from a study of postdoctoral fellowships awarded by the Swedish Medical Research Council in 1995. Women were 46 percent of the applicants but only 20 percent of the winners, having been rated below men on scientific competence by the senior scientists who had judged the applications. An analysis showed that females had needed 100 or more "impact points"— a combination of productivity and journal prestige—for a rating equal to that of males with 20 or fewer impact points (Wennerås & Wold 1997). Men thus had five times the edge over women.

An Apparent Contradiction

The overall data from universities and colleges might appear to contradict the specific data for humanists and scientists. The overall rank percentages suggest that colleges and universities have about the right proportion of women assistant professors, given the percentage of new Ph.D.s who are women. The specific data show that early in their careers women humanists and scientists are disproportionately employed in marginal positions.

The two sets of data can be resolved. Taken together, they suggest that colleges and universities are not in fact hiring and promoting women correctly. Although the rank percentages of women at the assistant and associate levels seem proportional, they are not. Instead, the percentage of women at the assistant professor rank is inflated by the presence of women who should have higher ranks. The rank thus includes both very new women Ph.D.s and more experienced women but, among men, includes a higher percentage of very new Ph.D.s than more experienced men. The combination of the two phenomena—the disproportionate representation of female Ph.D.s in marginal jobs and the disproportionately lower rate of promotion for more experienced female Ph.D.s—accounts for the seemingly appropriate percentage of women assistant professors.

Prestige of Institution and Teaching Load

Women professors are underrepresented on the faculties of high-prestige institutions and overrepresented at low-prestige schools. If we broadly define universities as higher-prestige institutions and colleges as lower-prestige institutions, we can see evidence of women's lower prestige in the 1996–1997 AAUP figures, when women were 27 percent of university faculty but 38 percent of (IIB) college faculty (table 11, AAUP 1997). As noted earlier, faculty at many colleges teach more courses than their peers

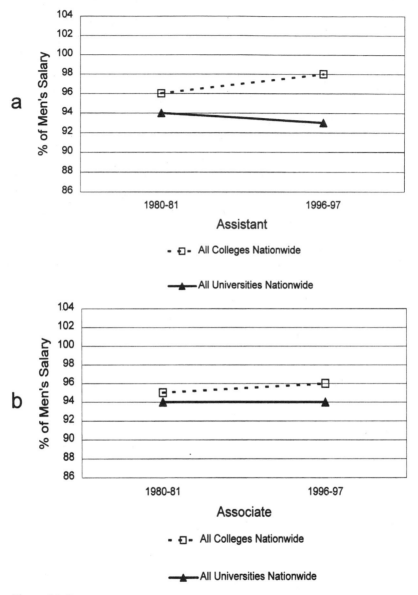

Figure 11.5
Progress between 1980–1981 and 1996–1997 in percent women earned of men's salary: Universities and colleges nationwide. (Data from AAUP 1981, 1997)

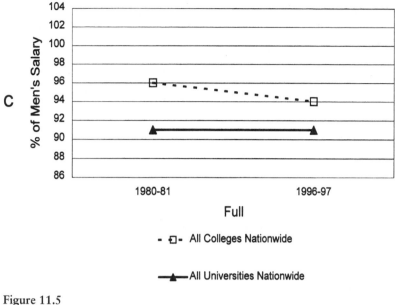

Figure 11.5
continued

at universities. Partly as a consequence of women's greater representation in colleges, then, women teach more than men, even taking into account rank, discipline, and Ph.D. cohort.

Progress in Academia

How much progress has there been in salary, rank, and tenure? The results are mixed. With respect to salary, for example, we have seen that the very youngest male and female professors in the humanities were on a par in 1993, which represents clear progress compared to the 1980s. But for those more than five years post-Ph.D., women's salaries continue to lag behind men's. For scientists and engineers there has been less progress: younger and older women alike are still paid less well than their male peers.

Overall salary data for universities and (IIB) colleges show almost no progress between 1980 and 1996, as figures 11.5 and 11.6 illustrate. In some samples there has even been regression. Some of the reverse progress could be explained if the largest increases in new appointments occurred

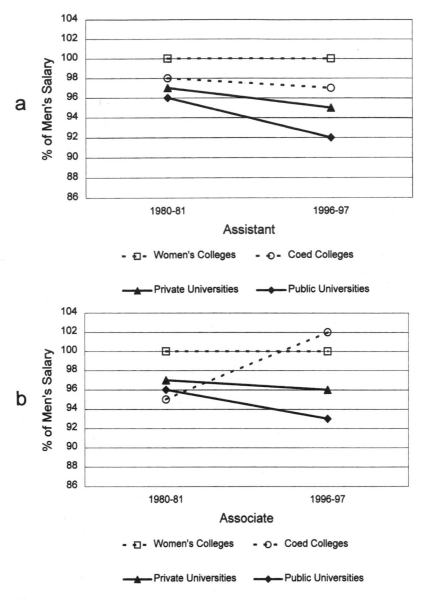

Figure 11.6
Progress between 1980–1981 and 1996–1997 in percent women earned of men's salary: selected elite institutions. (Data from AAUP 1981, 1997) (Missing cell due to lack of data)

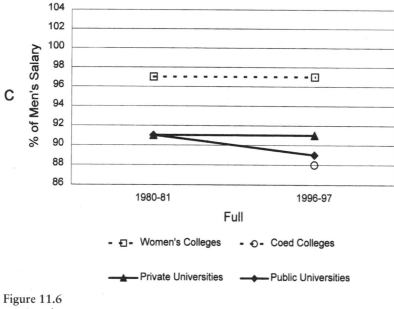

C

Figure 11.6
continued

in disciplines that pay less. For example, English faculty earn less than computer science faculty: $46,000 for English professors in 1995 (Ingram & Brown 1997, table 19) but $60,800 for computer scientists (NSF 1996, table 38). Further, there are larger percentages of women in literature than in computer science. In 1993, 57 percent of Ph.D.s in English and American literature were earned by women, compared to 15 percent of doctorates in computer and information science (Simmons & Thurgood 1995, Appendix table A-1). If most new female appointments were in lower-paying disciplines, women's salaries would be, on average, lower than men's. That asymmetry might contribute to the regression, but it cannot be the whole story, since there is considerable gender inequality among even young scientists and engineers.

Women's progress in occupying more positions is clear. The percentages of women at all tenure-track ranks at both universities and colleges were greater in 1996–1997 than in 1980–1981 (see figures 11.7 and 11.8). At the same time, however, there were more women in marginal positions than ever before. Compared to men, women are still much more likely to

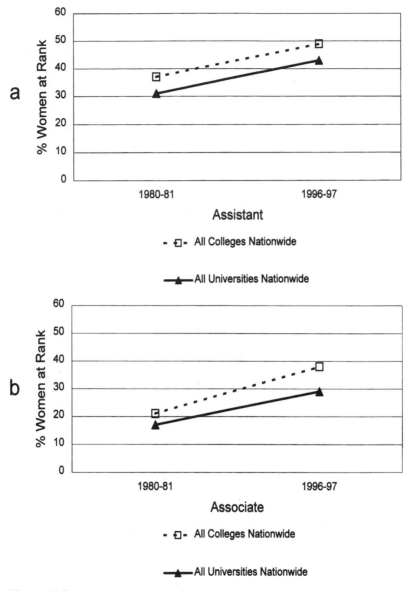

Figure 11.7
Progress between 1980–1981 and 1996–1997 in percent women at each professorial rank: universities and colleges nationwide. (Data from AAUP 1981, 1997)

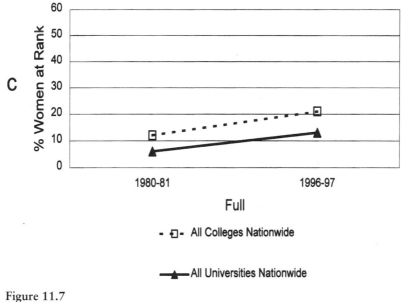

Figure 11.7
continued

hold marginal jobs or to be involuntarily unemployed. In sum, women remain overrepresented at the bottom and at the margins and underrepresented at the top, though less extremely so than in the past.

Finally, since 1976 there has been zero progress in closing the tenure gap between men and women. Although the percentage of women who are tenured increased from 44 percent in 1976 to 50 percent in 1994, the tenure rates of men also increased, from 64 percent to 71 percent. Figure 11.9 shows those figures for all institutions nationwide, and figure 11.10 illustrates the tenure disparities in universities and colleges separately. Since 1980 there has been a consistent gender gap of 28 percentage points at universities and 22 percentage points at four-year colleges (National Center for Education Statistics 1992, 1996).

The data for institutions that grant tenure also show that there has been no progress in reducing tenure disparity.[5] In 1995–1996, 48 percent of women and 72 percent of men were tenured (AAUP 1996). The comparable AAUP figures for 1976–1977 were 44 percent for women and 64 percent for men. At private universities in 1995–1996 only 47 percent

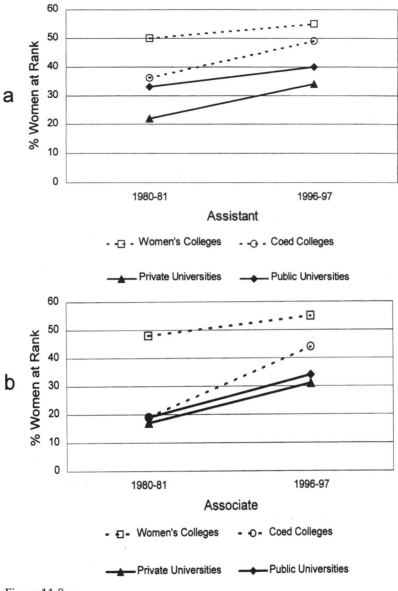

Figure 11.8
Progress between 1980–1981 and 1996–1997 in percent women at each
professorial rank: selected elite institutions. (Data from AAUP 1981, 1997)

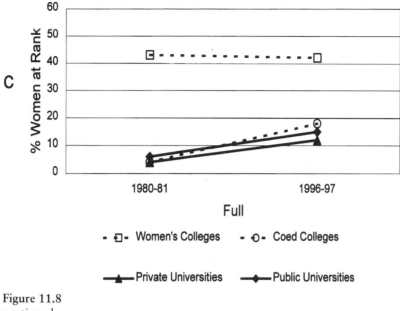

Figure 11.8
continued

of women, compared to 71 percent of men, had tenure; at public universities the proportions are 50 percent and 74 percent (AAUP 1996). The tenure situation is probably even worse than it appears, because women are unlikely to be moving through the ranks as fast as men are.

Somewhat more women are being tenured, however, as are more men. What percentage of women "should" be tenured? We cannot definitively determine the answer with the available data, but the best estimate is that a considerably higher percentage of women should be tenured than are at present. The lack of progress in tenure does *not* seem attributable to the ever-increasing percentage of women assistant professors, a rank that rarely carries tenure. We can eliminate that possibility on two grounds.

The first can be dealt with quickly. The data for humanists who are sixteen to twenty-five years post-Ph.D. show tenure disparities that are similar to the overall figures. Since those male and female academics are roughly balanced in years of experience, there should be no differences.

The second reason involves gender percentages for humanists and psychologists. From 1977 to 1989, a *decreasing* percentage of women in the

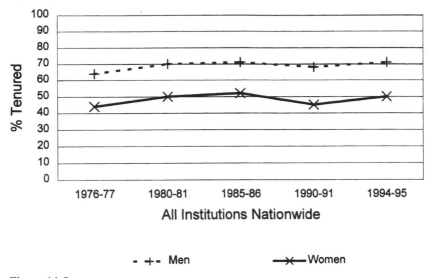

Figure 11.9
Percent men and women with tenure at all institutions nationwide. (Data from
AAUP 1981 and from Digest of education statistics, 1992, 1996)

humanities occupied the rank of assistant professor; that is, 36 percent
were assistant professors in 1977 but only 27 percent were assistant professors in 1989 (NRC 1991, table E-7). The percentage of women who
were associate professors stayed constant over that period, while the percentage of those who were full professors increased from 19 to 25 percent. Thus, if we looked just at women, we would expect to find a larger
increase in the proportion who are tenured than the figures reflect.

The same pattern holds for women psychologists. In 1981, 44 percent
of women psychologists in academia were assistant professors; in 1991,
only 30 percent of them were. The percentages at the associate professor
level stayed constant, and the percentage of women who were full professors increased from 19 to 25 percent (American Psychological Association 1995). Again, since a smaller percentage of women are at the
assistant professor level and a larger percentage at the full professor level,
we would expect a greater percentage of women to be tenured. A final
sobering comment is that, here too, the tenure situation is worse than it
appears, because women seem not to be moving through the ranks at a
speed comparable to men's.

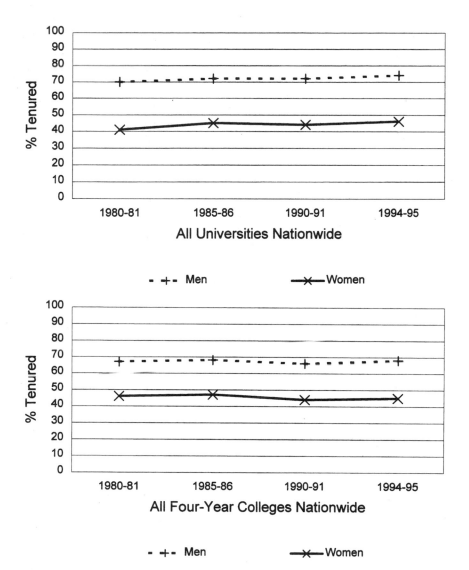

Figure 11.10
Percent men and women with tenure at universities and colleges nationwide.
(Data from Digest of education statistics, 1992, 1996)

The AAUP report also includes data for men and women who are tenured or in a tenure-track position. Naturally, someone who is not on a tenure track cannot achieve tenure as long as she or he stays in that position. Since women are overrepresented in the ranks of instructor, lecturer, and adjunct, we would expect to find fewer of them in tenure-track lines. And that is the case: 92 percent of the men at all institutions reporting tenure information in 1995–1996 were either tenured or on the tenure track, compared to 81 percent of women (AAUP, 1996).

Overall, progress in the standing of academic women is mixed. Salary equality has come to only the newest members of academia and is most visible in the humanities. In sheer numbers, progress has been clear: there are more women in the total academic population than ever before. Yet women are still markedly underrepresented at the top and grossly overrepresented at the bottom and among the involuntarily unemployed. Women are also still disproportionately untenured, and the disparity vis-à-vis men has not changed since the early 1980s.

Most academics probably have the impression of more progress than the facts indicate. One likely reason for that perception is that more women than ever are walking the halls of academe. Because there were such small percentages of tenure-track women at most campuses in earlier years, even small increases are very noticeable. The difference between five women in the faculty dining room and fifteen seems a large one, even if fifteen is still too few.

Other reasons suggest themselves as well. Some institutions—notably, women's colleges, and, to a lesser extent, coeducational colleges—are doing better than others. Women may also be more active professionally and hence more noticeable than before. Women may be serving on committees in disproportionate numbers. The institutionalization and development of women's studies programs may be making women more visible.

Still, the data indicate that perceptions of progress in academia are rosier than the facts support. It is clear that parity will not be achieved without special effort.

A Case Study: Psychologists

Thus far we have reviewed data about academics as a whole and about such broad groups as humanists, scientists, and engineers. All show a similar pattern of career development. In data collected by Rosenfeld (1984) we can get an in-depth look at the academic careers of one group of scientists—psychologists.

The study sample of 207 men and 207 women psychologists received their degrees between 1955 and 1962 and held academic appointments in 1970.[6] The men and women were roughly matched for the age at which they received their doctorate, for the prestige of their Ph.D.-granting institution, and for their specialization within psychology. By matching the individuals in this way one can rule out extraneous factors, such as variations among particular subfields. More importantly, the matching attempted to equalize the quantity and quality of people's work skills.

The research illustrates a very important point, one that has been documented in other work (e.g., Reskin & Hargens 1979 and studies cited in chapter 10). That point is this: men's salaries are usually well predicted by the variables one expects to be relevant—prestige of their Ph.D.-conferring institution; prestige of their current institution; their own productivity, experience, and public service and administrative contributions. Women's salaries are not. (For a summary of relevant data, see Finklestein 1984.) Men's achievements buy them more than women's achievements buy them, a result that confirms the experimental data on evaluations of men and women I present in chapter 6. Not only is there a residual disparity between male and female incomes even when relevant factors are controlled for, but the factors that should predict salary levels do so much better for males than for females. Men accumulate advantage more easily than women.

In returning to the data, we look first at the nature of the psychologists' first job post-Ph.D. (Rosenfeld 1984). In their first job, women were underrepresented at assistant professor positions and overrepresented at instructor, postdoctoral fellow, and non-tenure-track positions. As the data we reviewed earlier showed, the same pattern holds for women in the humanities and for women in general. The prestige of the psychologists' Ph.D. institution was less important for determining whether the women's first job would be tenure-track than it was for the men's. Data for natural scientists have similarly shown that the prestige of the scientist's postdoctoral institution increased the likelihood of gaining a tenure-track position for men but not for women (Reskin 1978). Again, men accumulate advantage more easily than women.

In addition, when the men and women psychologists acquired new positions, men fared better. Among men and women whose first job was non-tenure-track, women were twice as likely as men were to move to another non-tenure-track job—38 percent versus 16 percent. Women were correspondingly less likely than men were to move from a non-tenure-track first job to an appointment at the associate professor level—10 percent versus 31 percent. Most shocking of all, women went backwards at twice the rate of men: 13 percent of the women whose first job was at the assistant professor level went on to a second job of instructor or other non-tenure-track position, compared to 6 percent of men; 12 percent went from associate professor to a lower rank, compared to 6 percent of men.

Later data on women and men in psychology show that, in 1991, 55 percent of faculty who were not tenured or on the tenure track were women (American Psychological Association 1995; Pion, Mednick, Astin, Hall, Kenkel, Keita, Kohout, & Kelleher 1996). Moreover, women were 46 percent of the assistant professors, a smaller number than would be expected from the number of new women Ph.D.s.

As of 1991, women psychologists were also underrepresented on the editorial boards of the twenty journals published by the American Psychological Association. Women were only 15 percent of journal editors, 24 percent of associate editors, 25 percent of consulting editors, and 27 percent of reviewers (Pion et al. 1996). These figures represent a modest improvement from 1981, where the comparable numbers were 10, 15, 22, and 20 percent, respectively.

Summary

The data demonstrate that women in academia are substantially underrewarded. They are paid less, promoted more slowly, and tenured more slowly. Except for the number of women in assistant and associate professor positions, progress from 1980 to 1996 was slow and slight in every area. Nor can women's slower advancement be accounted for by a lower standard of performance. Even when productivity is controlled for, women earn less and achieve tenure more slowly than men do. And, as chapter 12 shows, although women publish less than men, what they publish is of higher quality—as measured by the number of times their work is cited by other scholars in their field.

12

Professional Performance and Human Values

The first question many people raise when they hear about the gender differences in salary, rank, and promotion described in chapters 10 and 11 is whether the inequalities are inequities. If, for example, women have lower expectations than men and therefore do not negotiate for good salaries and promotions to the extent men do, they may fail to receive equal rewards. Or women could have less background, education, and experience—human capital—than men, which would justify their initial lower status. A third possibility is that women's performance on the job is worse than men's, so that they deserve their slower advancement. Finally, perhaps men and women do not want the same things from their professions. If women are less motivated by salary and advancement than men are, they may choose jobs that pay less but are more interesting or choose career paths that result in slower advancement. If so, there is no injustice.

The status inequality between men and women cannot, however, be completely accounted for by any of these four factors, which I analyze in the following sections of this chapter. Nor, I argue, will the status inequality between men and women professionals go away by itself, or be eliminated by normal economic processes or women's acquisition of more and better work skills. Excellent work skills are necessary for success, but they are not sufficient to guarantee equality; even when women and men are shown to be equal on all job-related criteria, men are, on average, better rewarded for their efforts.

A hidden obstacle to determining whether inequalities are indeed inequities is the way performance is measured. Unbiased measures of performance must meet four criteria. First, they must be objective and established in advance as good measures of performance. Second, each evaluation must take place without systematic error. Third, standards must apply to everyone equally. Fourth, everyone must be given equal opportunities to perform. Creating conditions under which the four criteria can be met is not easy, expressly because of the influence of gender schemas and the unequal opportunities to accumulate advantage they give rise to.

Consider first the problem of insuring that measures of performance evaluate the determinants of success in a particular job. Institutional policy makers tend to establish and maintain measures of performance that they themselves have previously met. In this way, every organization comes, over time, to mirror the beliefs of the people in charge, even if those beliefs are not adequate bases for judging competence. Although there are many ways to get a job done, some methods become ritualistically enshrined over time.

One example of the power of such long-established ways of thinking is the case of the Virginia Military Institute (VMI). The college, which trains young people for military leadership, receives one-third of its funding from the state of Virginia (Greenhouse 1996). VMI's training methods are "adversative": that is, they purport to develop cadets' military character by making them overcome the adversities of humiliation, hazing, and personal torment, as well as rigorous physical discipline. VMI officials argued against a U.S. Justice Department demand that it accept women by claiming that they would be unable to continue their training program in its current form if women were admitted: "The system would have to be fundamentally changed" (Greenhouse 1996).[1]

As it happens, the U.S. military academies, such as West Point, do not use adversative methods, a fact brought out when Supreme Court justices hearing the case questioned VMI's lawyer. When the lawyer asserted that VMI would have to change its procedures if women came to campus, Justice Stephen Breyer responded, "I take that as a given, but so what?" Justice Breyer said, "Maybe you don't have exactly the same rat line or the same hazing. The answer to that is, so what? You have to show why it's important, what it is that's so important about this hard-to-grasp, adversative kind of thing that enables you to say to women who want to go there, you can't come" (Greenhouse 1996). It may well be that VMI's methods do produce a distinctive sort of person; but if they do not produce better officers—and military leadership is the point of the enterprise—they do not justify excluding women.

The fact that other successful programs use different training methods seemed to weigh heavily in the Court's decision that VMI had to admit women. In effect, the justices ruled that arbitrary standards that exclude women do not qualify for public support. The successful record of other military schools makes the arbitrary and unnecessary nature of VMI's procedures obvious.

In most work environments, however, there are few or no alternative systems to point to. It may be difficult to demonstrate that an organization's procedures are, like VMI's, arbitrary and unnecessary. People may find it difficult even to imagine the possibility of other procedures. An existing state of affairs defines a norm, and norms tend to be invisible. Moreover, few employees who argue for changes have the power or financial resources of the Justice Department.

Thus, the first criterion—making sure that performance is measured objectively and validly—will be difficult to meet. Although evaluating how well different types of performance achieve desired outcomes would be the best test of a measure's validity, such an experimental approach is almost never adopted.

Next, consider the second criterion, the problem of applying performance standards fairly. In chapter 1, I described an experiment in which participants estimated the height of male and female students photographed in doorways or near other indicators of height. Although each male was paired with a female of the same height, observers consistently underestimated the females' height and overestimated the males'.

By analogy, if observers believe that males are in general more competent than females, they will be likely to overestimate the males' performance, compared to the females', even when evaluating males and females matched in competence. The data on gender schemas suggest that such evaluations are usually biased against women. It is difficult to find measures that are impervious to the subjectivity of the beholder; when subjectivity enters into professional judgments, it operates to women's disadvantage. Gender schemas are especially likely to favor males when evaluators are busy with other tasks or doing evaluations under time pressure, as frequently happens (Martell 1991).

Expectations

The objection that women anticipate lower entry salaries than men do has some merit (see McFarlin, Frone, Major, & Konar 1989; Blau & Ferber 1991). But women are also more realistic than men are about entry-level salaries; both men and women expect higher salaries than they are likely to get, but women's expectations are less exaggerated. Women may also expect lower salaries because they know men usually are better paid than women.

College students who are asked to assign a salary to a well-qualified applicant assign higher salaries to applicants who expect more money (Major, Vanderslice, & McFarlin 1984). Further, the students reacted differently to the salary requests of male and female candidates. When applicants requested salaries that were either low or high—as opposed to moderate—students assigned women lower salaries than men. When applicants requested moderate salaries, however, students paid women more than men. That finding suggests that women will get more money if they ask for it, as long as the requested figure is in the moderate range. We do not know whether real employers would respond the way the students did, but the data suggest that women—like men—should request moderately high salaries.

The influence of gender schemas may also explain women's lower salary expectations. Like the woman tennis player quoted in chapter 8—"I'm happy with what we have; I don't think we should be greedy"—gender schemas may lead women to interpret equality as greed (Bailey 1991). Before women can get their fair share, they will have to believe that they are entitled to equality and learn how to negotiate.

Human Capital

Many of the rank and salary gender comparisons of professionals cited in chapter 10 indicated that women accumulated less human capital than men.[2] Women had less education, less profitable college majors, and less work experience than men did. Those differences in human capital do explain some of the salary and rank discrepancies between men and women. Obviously, it behooves everyone—male and female alike—to obtain as much education and experience as possible.

Nonetheless, in almost all of the comparisons, differences in human capital failed to account completely for disparities between male and female earnings, rates of promotion, and status. A gender disparity in rank remained—for example, between male and female scientists who had obtained prestigious fellowships—even after a large range of human capital variables was considered (Sonnert & Holton 1996b).[3]

In general, a woman's education and experience buys her less than a man's buys him. Men have a net advantage. Normal economic processes, such as employers' desire to maximize profits by hiring productive workers, will help equalize women's status vis-à-vis men's, but will not be sufficient. Women have a problem that is reflected in economic inequalities but is neither itself purely economic in origin nor purely accounted for by insufficient human capital. Women's problem is also a social and psychological problem: men benefit from gender schemas that portray them as more competent than women.

The studies on performance evaluations and on people's responses to women's attempts at leadership (described in chapters 6 and 7) provide an interpretation of the data on women's slow advancement in business, law, academia, and other professions. Women benefit less than comparable men do from investments in human capital, from good performance, and from traditional marks of prestige. Even when women's qualifications are equal to men's, they are not evaluated equally positively.

Gender schemas and the accumulation of advantage also provide an interpretation of women's lesser human capital. Some economic models assume that women choose to invest less in acquiring marketable skills. For example, a heterosexual woman might calculate that she could do better economically by investing in household skills and benefiting from her male partner's salary. In that case, her lower human capital results from a rational choice (Becker 1993; see also note 2). But her choice might be rational in part because it is more difficult for women to acquire human capital than it is for men. A woman cannot acquire human capital if people do not hire her and give her the opportunity to develop her skills. (See discussion in Madden 1985 and England & McCreary 1987.)

Consider again the findings on doctors discussed in chapter 10. Perhaps women choose the lower-paying fields of family practice and pediatrics because those specialties are closer to their interests. On the other hand, gender schemas may make it easier for women to obtain training in one specialty rather than another. Women may be readily accepted for residencies in pediatrics—because children are seen as requiring nurturant doctors and gender schemas portray women as nurturant. In contrast, women may find it difficult to receive training in high-paying surgical specialties—because surgery is seen as requiring a cool impersonal focus and gender schemas portray men as task-oriented and instrumental. Gender schemas may thus lead both medical schools and medical students to see women as better suited to family practice and pediatrics and men as better suited to the operating room.

The concept of statistical discrimination used in economics can apply to hiring, promotion, training, or salary issues but is most often invoked to explain hiring or promotion decisions (see discussion in Madden 1985). If I, as an employer, must choose between two job candidates who look equally good on paper, I may make my decision on the basis of group membership in order to maximize my chances of getting the best employee. My decision is an example of *statistical* discrimination, because I am basing my decision about an individual on data about the average tendencies of two groups. If I am hiring a research assistant and have two candidates who have equally good research experience, undergraduate grades, letters of recommendation, and test scores, I may hire the candidate with an Ivy League degree over the graduate of a public university. My past experience may or may not have given me a reason to think that Ivy League graduates are on the whole more competent than graduates of public universities. Either way, I am engaging in statistical discrimination by hiring the Ivy Leaguer, because I am using group membership to predict the future performance of an individual. I need not be at all prejudiced against public university graduates; I can simply be trying to get the best odds for future performance.

Similarly, if I as an employer believe that men stay on the job longer than women do and therefore hire a man—even though a woman candidate looks just as good on paper—I may have no particular bias against women. I am simply seeking to maximize my chances of choosing a productive worker. But if women do not stay in jobs as long as men do, it may be because they are given worse jobs and promoted more slowly. Under those circumstances, statistical discrimination, no matter how "benign" an employer's motives may be, can create the very differences that appear to justify it. Statistical discrimination, then, can give rise to objective differences in human capital and work commitment that favor men.

Even if the group differences employers are responding to are real and unrelated to employers' practices, statistical discrimination makes life harder for individuals, especially individuals who do not fit the norm. A woman who plans a professional lifetime will, if employers engage in statistical discrimination, have more difficulty getting a good job than will an equivalent man. Employers' motivations may be benign, but the consequences of statistical discrimination may be harmful.

Statistical discrimination differs from personal preference or outright bigotry. If, as an employer, I preferentially hire men because I dislike the idea of women in professional jobs—independent of my beliefs about their competence—I am being discriminatory but I am not practicing statistical discrimination, because my response is not based on a real or perceived group difference that I think will affect candidates' work. On the other hand, the college students' estimations of the heights of the young men and women in the photographs was an example of statistical discrimination. The generalization which they had made was correct: men are on average taller than women. But the generalization did not fit the particular individuals they were judging. As this example demonstrates, statistical discrimination is an automatic consequence of schemas that represent two social groups as different on essential dimensions.

Thus, competent people can be harmed when their productivity is judged on the basis of group membership, even if the generalizations about the group are accurate. When prospective employers or instructors choose or reject individuals on the basis of group membership, they help perpetuate an imbalance in the ability to accrue human capital. In the case of women, the result is likely to be a strengthening of gender schemas and a reduction of women's ability to accumulate advantage in the professions.

Performance Issues

Several considerations make it impossible to know for sure whether men's and women's professional performance is equal. Every professional job requires a variety of skills and can be performed in a variety of ways. No one person is equally good at all aspects of a job, and at different times different skills are called for. Few measures of performance are objective, and even when they are, they might not be valid measures—that is, they may not measure what we think they do. In addition, professions vary in the constraints they place on individuals. Those working in organizations with a clear hierarchy and with frequent periods of evaluation have relatively little autonomy, compared to those who run their own businesses, work in academia, or work as free-lancers.

Law

The law profession provides a good case study of the difficulties involved in judging performance (see discussion in Epstein, Saute, Oglensky, & Gever 1995). In terms of sheer legal ability (if such a thing exists), there is general agreement that men and women are equal (Epstein et al. 1995). In major law firms, however, two other characteristics (neither of which directly involves legal ability) are just as important in determining which associates become partners: the number of billable hours—the hours of work put in that can be billed to a client—and the new business the associate is expected to bring once he or she becomes a partner. Law firms also take into account such intangible characteristics as personal style, which may weigh heavily for or against an associate.

Although the number of billable hours is a function of how much time someone puts in, and is thus an objective measure, it has nothing to do with legal ability and may be even inversely related to it. One might argue, as some women have, that they are penalized for completing a job efficiently (Epstein et al. 1995). One woman tells me that in her law school class, the people with 4.0 averages were women with children. Those women had both excellent legal ability and the ability to figure out how to use their time to best advantage.

Time also measures something else: dedication and commitment to the firm. It is, of course, to a law firm's financial advantage to have a large number of associates who bill an average of fifty to fifty-five hours a week and others who routinely bill sixty-three hours or more. Similarly, it is to a firm's advantage to have employees who are prepared to work more hours when they are needed (Epstein et al. 1995; Harrington 1993). Since lawyers have "down time," cannot always be at peak efficiency, and also perform tasks that cannot be billed to a client, the figure of fifty to fifty-five hours per week underestimates how much time lawyers actually spend on the job. From all accounts, sixty to sixty-five hours seems to be a typical work week, especially for young lawyers.

It is also to a law firm's financial advantage to have its associates and partners constantly at the beck and call of its clients, which is the norm at major law firms (Epstein et al. 1995; Harrington 1993). That instant and constant availability, however, is something that law firms have themselves defined as the clients' right; in no other field do clients expect twenty-four-hour access. As one lawyer put it, "If you think about it rationally, there are very few situations in a commercial context that are real emergencies. . . . The trial is the exception" (Harrington 1993, p. 188).

Some young attorneys have raised the question of whether profitability really requires law firms to be organized as they are. Although partners assert that the present system is necessary (Harrington 1993), critics have implied that an equally profitable institution could operate under very different work norms. Many comments by young lawyers suggest that younger men, as well as women, would prefer a different structure (Epstein et al. 1995).

The question of whether law firms organized on a different basis would be successful is largely moot, because few of them try anything different. Similarly, whether a less ruthless, driven personal style than the one popular in large law firms could be successful is largely unknown. There are reports that women who have started their own firms and run them under different procedures are successful. As one lawyer commented, "There's no real reason for this crazed approach to work. It happens because it's valued, not because it has to" (Harrington 1993).

Long and unpredictable time requirements obviously have different effects on people who value their personal lives, compared to those whose professional lives are all-important. Neither the number of hours nor their unpredictability and uncontrollability is an insurmountable problem for lawyers who are totally career-oriented. They are, presumably, working long and hard because they want to. As one young woman said, "I don't have anything to do with the rest of the day that's more important than what I'm doing here" (Epstein et al. 1995). When I repeated that comment to another lawyer, though, she chuckled and said, "Pathetic!"

For people who want a fuller personal life, and for those with children who take their family responsibilities seriously, the long hours and the lack of control over their time is a problem. Because women are more likely than men to value their personal lives and to take their child-care responsibilities seriously, they are more likely than men to work part-time (Chambers 1989; Epstein et al. 1995).

Women who work full-time at large law firms, however, appear to average as many work hours as men who work full-time, regardless of whether they have children. For full-time men and women, therefore, performance as measured in billable hours is equal (Epstein et al. 1995). Promotion to partnership, however, is not equal. Men are much more likely to make partner than women are.

With respect to bringing in business, few new associates of either sex are in a position to do so. Associates with six to eight years of experience, however, are increasingly expected to bring in new business. Partners estimate the value of potential partners on the basis of both their current success and the personal characteristics that promise future success. Among partners, the few who are extremely successful at bringing in business—the "rainmakers"—tend to be men (Epstein et al. 1995). The stage is thus set for partners to judge individual women associates in terms of gender schemas—and they do so judge them. Women associates are judged less likely than men to be successful rainmakers.

After they become partners, women face a variety of problems in developing new business that men do not. They may, for example, have less access to people in powerful positions at companies that could be sources of business, because they have fewer ways to meet such people. Their ability to develop new business is also limited by the likelihood that potential clients are themselves subject to gender schemas and may not respond equally positively to women and men.

To sum up, in major law firms, the most important factors determining whether an associate becomes a partner are not directly related to legal ability. Men's and women's legal ability appears to be equal, and full-time men and women spend equal hours on the job. Estimates of how much future business they will develop, however, favor men. Among partners, women do bring in less business than men do, because of limited access and because of the operation of gender schemas, but few lawyers of either sex are rainmakers. Performance differences, then, do not fully account for women lawyers' lower rate of success in achieving partner status.

Academia

In academia, too, measures of performance are not and cannot be applied to everyone equally. Different people have different contributions to make. Some professors excel in research but perform badly in the classroom and neglect their committee work. Others shine in the classroom and perform valuable services to the department and the institution as a whole but may perform little research. Ambiguity therefore enters in whenever someone is judged; there is considerable latitude in how the various areas of performance can be weighted.

Nor do all faculty members have equal opportunities to perform. The junior faculty member described in chapter 1 who was not permitted to teach a large introductory course probably had, as a consequence, less time for her research. Other women may not be allowed to teach important or higher-level courses or be given the most responsible committee assignments, and may therefore have less opportunity to demonstrate their competence.

In academia, the two primary measures of research performance are quantity and quality. Of the many possible measures of performance, the data on quantity are most abundant. It is easier to measure than quality, because it can be measured by dividing the number of publications by a unit of time. Nevertheless, the count is not completely straightforward. Book reviews, for example, are publications, but they are minor publications. Books are major publications. How many articles equal one book? Are all articles equal? Researchers studying the role of productivity in academia have developed various techniques for resolving such issues. In general, the sheer number of pages is not taken into account. Thus, a long article reporting on many experiments, or analyzing many literary or historical documents, does not count for more than a short article describing one experiment or only a few pieces of evidence.

Quality is usually measured by citation rate; that is, by how often others in the field cite an article or book. Such a measure is not, obviously, foolproof—people can, and do, ignore unfashionable work of high quality—but it is a rough guide to how useful and important peers find a person's work. It is also a good measure of an article's influence. Another way to judge the quality of an article is the prestige of the journal in which it is published. That measure has the advantage of being less likely to reflect prevailing fashions; unfortunately, it has seldom been used in studies of sex differences in publishing. (Sonnert 1995, however, found that the most productive biologists were also likely to publish in the top biology journals.)

Quantity of Publications   Women academics publish fewer articles than men, with the possible exception of those at elite institutions. During the 1970s and early 1980s, studies in all disciplines showed consistently that women published about half as many papers as men (J. Cole & Zuckerman 1984). The median number of papers written over a twelve-year period in the 1970s by male chemists, biologists, psychologists, and sociologists was eight, while the comparable figure for females was three (J. Cole 1979). Over a three-year period in the mid 1970s, men psychologists averaged 1.7 papers, compared to 0.7 for women (Helmreich, Spence, Beane, Lucker, & Matthews 1980).

Most figures from the 1980s and 1990s show smaller discrepancies, suggesting that productivity differences between men and women are declining (Zuckerman 1987). In the mid-1980s, full-time male faculty in a social work department reported that they had published or had accepted for publication an average of 2.1 articles in a two-year period; the figure for women was 1.63 articles (Fox & Faver 1985). A more inclusive study of social work faculty found no sex differences (Rubin & Powell 1987). In an early 1990s study of scientists who had received prestigious fellowships, men averaged 2.8 papers a year, while women averaged 2.0 (calculated from Sonnert & Holton 1996a). In economics and sociology, studies from the 1990s show no sex differences in productivity (Kolpin & Singell 1996; Stack 1994). Taken together, studies measuring productivity in terms of quantity find that women typically publish 50 to 80 percent as much as men.

The average difference in productivity between men and women is partly, but not completely, due to the fact that there are more men than women with extremely high publication rates (J. Cole and Zuckerman

1984). In most fields 10 to 15 percent of the scholars account for 50 percent or more of the publications. Even when these very productive scholars are removed from the samples, however, women are still less productive than men and are more highly represented among those who do not publish at all (Long 1992).[4]

One reasonable hypothesis would be that women's lower productivity is responsible both for their slower rate of promotion and their overrepresentation in nontenured positions and at institutions that provide less opportunity for research. Although that would seem to make sense, it is difficult to confirm. Indeed, if anything, the data suggest the reverse: the prestige and resources—such as equipment, library holdings, support staff, and internal research grants—of a scholar's academic institution influence productivity more than productivity influences the chances of getting a job at a prestigious institution (Long 1978; Long & McGinnis 1981).

Moreover, the culture at prestigious universities does not just help scholars be more productive than they would be at less elite institutions, it forces them to be. If women are less successful than men at getting tenure-track jobs at elite institutions—as they are—more women than men will be unproductive. Conversely, if the prestige of the institution plays a role in determining productivity, then men and women in similar ranks at elite institutions should be roughly equal in productivity.

We can find some confirming evidence for that hypothesis in a study of psychologists (Helmreich et al. 1980). Although men overall published more than women, there were no productivity differences at elite universities. As described earlier, however, a study of scientists with prestigious postdoctoral fellowships did show small productivity differences in favor of men (Sonnert 1995). In that study, although there were no differences in the percentage of men and women at elite institutions, the women had lower ranks than men and, as a result, probably had less access to resources.

Institutional factors thus account for part of women's lower productivity. The concept of the accumulation of advantage and disadvantage may explain another part of the difference between men and women in academia (e.g., J. R. Cole 1979; J. R. Cole & Singer 1991; Fox 1985; Long 1992; Zuckerman 1987, 1991). If Lee Smith's first job is a tenure-track appointment at an elite institution, and Robin Jones's is not, Smith will have access to facilities and resources that give him an advantage relative to Jones. If Smith takes advantage of his benefits, over time he can expect to become richer, figuratively and literally. Jones does not have the same initial benefits to take advantage of. She can therefore expect the disparity between her position and Smith's to increase over time. Yet even when a woman's first job is equal to a man's, she may be less likely to gain access to the institution's resources.

A final important point about productivity differences is that at the beginning of their careers, men and women have similar rates of publication. The disparity between them increases toward mid-career (J. R. Cole & Zuckerman 1984; Finklestein 1984; Long 1992; Zuckerman 1987). That result may be an artifact of the relatively few publications very young scholars produce, but later in the chapter I suggest an alternative explanation—that men and women respond to publication success and failure differently (Cole & Zuckerman 1984).

The lower quantity of women's publications does not account fully for the inequalities between academic men's and women's salary and promotion rate reported in chapter 11. Quantity predicts male success better than it does female success. Even when men and women produce the same amount of work, women are paid less than men and promoted less rapidly. (See Kolpin & Singell 1996; Rosenfeld 1984; Sonnert & Holton 1996a; Stack 1994 for examples.) The differences in productivity between men and women are smaller than the differences in compensation, advancement, and tenure. Women deserve more than they receive, even if quantity is the only measure of performance.

Quality of Publications   An even more important finding about women's lower status in academia is the fact that the quality of their publications, as measured by citation rate, is on average higher than that of men's. In studies of quality differences, papers by male researchers were cited 60 to 98 percent as often as papers by female scholars (Sonnert 1995; Long 1992; Zuckerman 1987). Women's lower productivity thus appears to be related to producing work of higher quality.

Quantity appears to be an important criterion of performance, while quality, as measured by citation frequency, seldom influences promotion, salary, or tenure decisions. In the studies mentioned above that report citation rates, women fare, on average, less well in salary and status than men; the high quality of their scholarship thus does not benefit women as much as it should. No studies have been performed, however, to determine the correlation between citation rate and rank in either sex. Nonetheless, if we assume that quality should be rewarded, the gap between men's and women's salaries, rank, and tenure status cannot be accounted for in terms of lower performance by women.

Since scholars' reputations are built on the influence of their ideas, and citation rates reflect that influence, we might expect women to accrue higher prestige than men. They do not, however, because men's overall citation rate is considerably higher than women's, even though each paper is cited less often. Men increase their overall citation rate by publishing more often. The more papers you publish, the more likely you are to be noticed, and the greater the total number of citations you can accrue (Long 1992). If the goal is to become well known, a researcher will be better off publishing more articles of a slightly lower quality than fewer papers of a slightly higher quality. Prestige in the scholarly community is largely a function of the quantity of published work (Finklestein 1984).

To summarize, women in academia publish somewhat less than men, and produce work of somewhat higher quality. The overall productivity differences are partially but not completely explained by structural inequalities that give men easier access to resources. The productivity differences themselves do not fully explain women's lower salary and promotion rates, because women have lower status and salary even when productivity is accounted for. Women do not benefit from the higher quality of their work.

Teaching   The data on students' evaluations of instructors are mixed; women do not, on the whole, receive higher evaluations than men. One large study examined the evaluations of four hundred faculty by nine thousand students. As might be expected on the basis of gender schemas, women professors received lower ratings on competency than men did (Sidanius & Crane 1989). Since competence is the main contributor to judgments of overall effectiveness, students also perceived the women as less effective. Men students tended to give lower competence ratings overall than women students did, but the two student groups' comparative evaluations of male and female instructors did not differ. Thus, at least at some institutions, women should be concerned about how competent they appear to students. They need to work harder simply to be perceived as equally good teachers.

What Do Men and Women in the Professions Want?

A justification for women's slower progress that is sometimes advanced is that women and men do not desire income and status to the same degree. In the language of economics, differences in men's and women's *nonpecuniary tastes* could result in their placing different emphases on earnings. According to this hypothesis, women might value aspects of life that men do not, or value to a lesser degree—such as personal relationships. For women, such values may be equal to or more important than high earnings and status. Alternatively, women may find it more profitable to invest in household experience than in labor market experience. For men, the lack of important personal relationships or nonwork interests could result in attaching greater importance to a high salary.

Preferences on the Job
By and large, studies looking at these issues suggest that men and women want the same things from their jobs: earnings, autonomy, recognition, and the opportunity to help others (Dipboye 1987; Olson & Frieze 1987). Most such studies have examined future or current business people. In one study, male and female undergraduate business majors ranked the same three job characteristics—salary, opportunity for advancement, and intellectual challenge as most important (Blau & Ferber 1991). More men rated salary as very important than did women, and more women rated intellectual challenge as very important than did men. The students also ranked the same three job characteristics as least important: having an undemanding job, earning acclaim, and getting an opportunity to travel.

Data from close to 1500 managers collected in the 1970s and 1980s showed that men and women were alike in ranking meaningful work as the most important job feature, followed by chances for advancement, high income, job security, and shorter hours (Jacobs 1992). There was little change over the two time periods. Women managers ranked meaningful work as more important than men did (though both groups ranked it first), and men ranked income as more important than women did (though both ranked it third). In a survey of people in nine Western European countries there were few if any sex differences in employees' values or their orientation to their jobs (De Vaus & McAllister, 1991).

In a study of dual-career couples with managerial or professional jobs, both men and women reported work as an equally important source of psychological distress, although women also reported more satisfaction with their jobs (Barnett, Marshall, Raudenbush, & Brennan 1993). The finding that problems at work distressed men and women equally suggests that at least some groups of men and women value their work equally.

It is not surprising that men and women who plan to have or do have careers in the business world want largely the same things from their jobs. Although it seems plausible to think of women as considerably less interested in money than men are, and therefore considerably less well paid, that plausibility derives less from empirical evidence than from our notions of what women and men are like. The data suggest that men and women who enter the same field have very similar values and that differences in their incomes cannot be explained by reference to differences in their values.

A Well-Rounded Life
Nevertheless, value differences do exist. Women value a well-rounded life, which includes work, love, friendship, and other interests (Eccles 1994). As we saw in chapter 10, women attorneys with children who work in major law firms were more likely than men with children to work part-time. That pattern would be expected if men and women have different values. The desire for a well-rounded life is so patently human that it is men's lack of expressed interest, rather than women's interest, that needs to be explained. Why don't men value a well-rounded life as much as women do? Why don't they take part-time jobs as often as women do?

From the standpoint of gender schemas, men's values and behavior are not difficult to understand. To maintain self-esteem, people can come to devalue activities others do not expect them to like or do well in. I described that process in chapter 8 to partially explain women's lack of interest in math. It can also help explain some men's lack of interest in living a fuller life. To the extent that others expect men to be less interested in and less capable of love, friendship, and other nonwork activities, men may place less value on those aspects of life. Many heterosexual men pay less of a price for neglecting those values than they otherwise might because their female partners ensure that they have at least a modicum of a full life. Further, because the gender schema for men is more restrictive than the gender schema for women (as we saw in chapters 3 and 9), men who actively pursue a full life violate the norms of masculinity and risk appearing feminine.

The result, for many men, is a strong commitment to earnings and prestige, great dedication to the job, and an intense desire for achievement. If the arenas in which people can attain satisfaction are narrowly circumscribed, they will invest their energy in the arenas that are open to them. Obviously, some men do lead full lives. More and more men—both because they are pushed by their female partners and because they independently want the satisfactions of a richer life—are trying to achieve a better balance in their commitments. Many others, however, constrained by the male gender schema, are at risk of overinvestment in salary, prestige, and achievement.

One small example is the following anecdote about a couple who were vacationing in Italy with their two children. The father, an academic, and the mother, a lawyer, were expecting a visit from another family with two children. The father in the second family was also an academic and the mother was also a lawyer. The first father told a colleague that he was a bit worried about the visit, because he and the other father would be talking shop all the time, which would be a problem for the women.

It didn't occur to this man that he could spend part of each day in professional conversation with his colleague while his wife took care of the children, part of it taking care of the children while his wife did whatever work she might want to do or went sightseeing, and part of it wholeheartedly enjoying the pleasures of Italy. Instead, he saw Italy as no more than the backdrop to an extended professional conversation, slightly marred by wives' protests. Both fathers are extremely productive scholars, and neither is likely to voluntarily reduce his work time in order to lead a more varied and balanced life.

Child Care

The issue of child care looms over every discussion about working men and women. Almost all women with children—no matter what their profession—talk about the conflicts between spending time caring for their children and spending time performing their work (see, e.g., Aisenberg & Harrington 1988). They see child care as the single most important issue facing women (see Harrington 1993; Okin 1989).

In both law and academia, part-time work is a more common option for mothers than for fathers, as the data in chapters 10 and 11 show. Indeed, it is more common for working women than working men in every area of employment. Child care is at the heart of the female gender schema. Both men and women expect women to take the primary responsibility for children.

For parents who work full-time, it is more difficult to evaluate the differences between men and women because of the lack of objective indicators of performance and the absence of comparative studies. In law, the little research that is available suggests that full-time men and women work the same number of hours, as detailed in chapter 10, whether they have children or not.

In academia, the relation between parenthood and number of publications has been studied in detail, and the results are surprising. Although women are less productive than men, women with children are not less productive than women without children. To take one example, a study of productivity among full-time faculty in graduate social work programs found that women's productivity over a two-year period was significantly *positively* correlated with having young children (Fox & Faver 1985).[5] As the researchers note, the correlation could well be due to other factors. For example, it could be that the women with young children had arranged to have them immediately after receiving tenure; tenure was positively related to productivity for women. (There was no relation between productivity and having children for men.)

Other researchers have found no evidence of a negative relation between productivity and either marriage or motherhood. The one exception is in graduate school, where being married and having children increases the time to degree much more for women than for men (Long 1990; Sonnert & Holton 1996a). Among women who are full-time faculty, however, having children is either unrelated to productivity or is positively related.

Nor are married women with children promoted more slowly. A study of academics who received their Ph.D.s between 1970 and 1974 found that married women with children were more likely than women in other categories to have reached associate professor rank by 1979 (Ahern & Scott 1981). Of the married women with children, 51 percent were promoted, compared to 41 percent of married women without children and 37 percent of single women without children.[6] Thus, those with the fewest outside responsibilities—single women without children—fared considerably worse than those with the most outside responsibilities—married women with children. Marriage with children was also a positive promotion factor for men. Of the married men with children, 66 percent were promoted, compared to 51 percent of married men without children and 53 percent of single men without children.[7] Overall, as the data on promotion in chapter 11 would suggest, more men than women in each marriage category reached the level of associate professor within the five-year period.

Most women with children will find such results hard to believe or understand. The data seem to fly in the face of our knowledge of the roles of women and men in heterosexual relationships. Working women, including academic women, perform a much larger share of domestic and child care responsibilities than do their male companions (as reported in chapter 2). How can it be that women's research does not suffer from domestic inequities?

It may be that the method of sampling in some studies works against uncovering the actual relation between productivity and motherhood (Long 1987). Since women academics are overrepresented in part-time and non-tenure-track positions, they are not included in productivity statistics for full-time faculty. Were they taken into account, the correlation between productivity and motherhood might well be strongly negative.

Mothers who remain in full-time positions may be those who have found solutions to child care, such as more equitable domestic arrangements, reduction or elimination of leisure time, or outside help. Women may also cope by exploiting the flexible work hours and work location of academia. Academics can work outside the normal daytime hours and some of them can do significant portions of their work at home. Women academics are also likely to marry men academics. The study of scientists holding prestigious fellowships reported that 62 percent of the married women, compared to 19 percent of the married men, were married to other academics (Sonnert & Holton 1996a). Academic couples understand each other's professional needs and have flexible schedules that maximize their ability to meet those needs. Such factors could explain why married women with children do not fare worse than single women without children.

In short, the full-time women with children who are active researchers are a highly selected, nonrepresentative group. They are women who have found individual solutions—and were lucky. If the full sample of women who began with research aspirations were included, we might well find that those with children are much less productive than those without.

None of those considerations, however, explains why single women and women without children publish less than men do. Although the time that women spend in child care is a very noticeable factor, its very salience may hide the operation of other factors determining women's productivity.

Four anecdotes reveal some of the connections that women academics see between work and child care.

During the discussion following an afternoon talk I gave on women in academia, one woman mentioned that she would have to leave soon to pick up her child. Her child-care responsibilities, she implied, curtailed her work day. Although the woman's description of where her time was going was accurate, her assumption that she would have worked longer hours were it not for those responsibilities might have been mistaken. For different reasons—conversations with colleagues, meetings with students, casual reading of journals, or other activities—she might still have spent her time doing something other than work. Indeed, there she was at my talk instead of at her desk!

Another woman told me in a private conversation that, at the beginning of her career, she had not published much but what she had produced was important and had received a great deal of positive attention. After she achieved tenure, she and her husband decided to have children. Although she felt very committed to her work, she arranged to take an administrative job at her university. She anticipated that she would have little time for research in the first few years of her children's lives and would therefore write few papers. As an administrative position is often correlated with a reduction in publications, her vita would suggest a choice of administration over research rather than the demands of parenthood. Once her children were in school, she planned to leave administration and resume her research. She had her first child. To her surprise, her work suddenly seemed much less important. She wondered whether she would ever regain her former enthusiasm for research.

My impression was that this woman's attitudes toward research and publishing had been ambivalent from the start. She had not considered other arrangements, such as discussing with her husband the possibility of his working part-time in order to share the child care responsibilities equally, or getting outside help. She had not tried for a solution in which she would maximize her productivity despite having less time at her disposal.

Another female academic told me, only half-jokingly, that benign neglect had seemed to work fairly well with her four children. She thought people exaggerated the amount of time parents needed to spend with their children. She had spent less time performing and publishing her research than she thought she should have, but she didn't think she would have spent more time on research even if she had had no children.

Yet another woman said that having a child forced her to be more disciplined about how she used her time. The result was that she became more productive after her child's birth. She knew that once she got home she would not do any work, so she was careful to make good use of her time in her office. Before motherhood, she had wasted a lot of time during the day, telling herself that she would make up for it at night. Usually, though, she didn't use her evenings to good advantage, either. Once she became a mother, she could no longer fool herself with unrealistic plans.

The women in the first two stories attributed their lack of work time to child care. The woman in the third story knew that taking care of her children was time-consuming, but thought she would have spent that time on something other than work had she been childless. The woman in the fourth story eliminated the other activities that had reduced her productivity.

The data I have reviewed suggest that the last two women have a better understanding of the role of child care. Since women without children publish less than men, and the same amount as women with children, child care by itself cannot be the determining factor.

Instead, women and men appear to make different trade-offs in allocating their time. First, as the stories of the last two women suggest, women spend, on average, more of their potential work time on other activities than men do. Many women with children spend that time on child care and household maintenance; other women spend it on other nonwork activities. Second, women appear to emphasize quality over quantity, while men do the reverse. Sex differences in time allocation are best documented in academia but probably occur in all the professions.

The Role of Gender Schemas

The role of gender schemas in a person's self-definition helps explain why women and men would allocate their time differently. Women are expected to have interests external to work, and expected to want to lead a full life. They probably come closer to realizing such a life than men do, whether or not they have children and whether or not they are involved in a romantic relationship. A woman who puts her work in second or third place is in harmony with the female gender schema.

A related explanation, offered for women's greater attrition in pre-med programs (mentioned in chapter 9) may also play a role in academic women's lower productivity. Women who dropped out had a wider range of socially acceptable alternatives than men did (Fiorentine 1988). That explanation can cover the cases of academia and other fields where there is no direct supervisor. Women in those fields have more nonwork alternatives compatible with their gender schema than men do. As one male academic put it, "For a man to decide not to take his career seriously is like admitting he takes drugs. For a woman to say she puts her family ahead of her career is considered a virtue; the pressures are all in that direction" (Etzkowitz, Kemelgor, Neuschatz, & Uzzi 1992).

Gender schemas also determine who people compare themselves to. As mentioned in chapter 8, women compare themselves with other women and men compare themselves with other men. People tend to measure themselves against similar others, and sex is a prominent cue to similarity. Thus, women's notion of what a job entails is probably gleaned more from other women's performance than from men's. The converse holds for men. Once a sex-linked pattern is established, it will take effort to change it.

The research on entitlement discussed in chapter 8 demonstrates that when a job is clearly spelled out to them, women tend to work harder and more efficiently than men do for the same amount of money (Major, McFarlin, & Gagnon 1984). Women also expect and accept less pay for the same amount of work (Major et al. 1984). Women, in other words, typically work hard at whatever they conceive their job to be, and their conception is determined in part by how similar others behave.

So, one explanation of women's lower rate of publication is that they do not conceive their jobs primarily in terms of quantity, even though it is the most important determinant of academic success. Women may see their jobs more broadly, in terms of research quality, teaching, and institutional service, and divide their time accordingly. On that interpretation, women's performance is at least the equal of men's and should be equally rewarded.

Gender schemas may, in addition, make it difficult for women to be successful in competition. It is hard to determine whether women actively and consciously eschew a competitive role because of different values, or whether they are discouraged from behaving "out of role" and thus left with no way of succeeding. As we saw in chapter 7, women who behave "like men" elicit negative reactions. Women may feel forced into a less competitive stance because they are punished for being competitive.

As we have seen, gender schemas affect people's evaluations of others and themselves. Everyone finds the prospect of a negative evaluation aversive. In organizations with a clear hierarchy, evaluations cannot be avoided. In academia, however, evaluations of one's research and writing can be postponed; in fact, the less an academic produces the longer the evaluation can be put off. If women have the (perhaps latent) idea that they are likely to be judged more negatively than men are, they will emphasize quality over quantity in order to increase the chances of a favorable evaluation. Since women *are* more likely to be judged negatively, it is a reasonable expectation.

The pattern of women's attributions discussed in chapters 8 and 9 suggests an additional reason for their caution and concern about quality. Women are at risk for drawing the wrong conclusion—their own incompetence—from the rejections they experience. There are two ways of avoiding rejection and its negative message. The easiest way is not to submit one's research to public scrutiny; you can't be rejected if you don't submit a manuscript. Women are overrepresented among scholars who do not publish their work. They may berate themselves, but their failure to submit a manuscript is, in principle, a failure they can control and correct. A rejected manuscript is harder to cope with.

The second way to avoid, or at least delay, rejection is to set unrealistically high work standards, to be a perfectionist. A perfect paper cannot be rejected. But a perfect paper also requires ever more data and analysis and ever more revision. Taken to its logical extreme, perfectionism means that nothing is ever good enough. Men as well as women may suffer from perfectionism, but they are less likely to succumb to it because they lack acceptable alternatives to trying hard for success.

I have focused the discussion on academics' productivity because we have solid data on it. But the analysis holds equally for any professional activity that requires initiative. According to the research reviewed earlier, women are less likely than men to attribute successes to their abilities and more likely to implicate luck whether they succeed or fail. The fact that women are not rewarded for their good performance to the same extent that men are makes those attributions eminently reasonable. As a result, however, women are less likely than men to react to rejection in a way that benefits them. They may conclude that success is hopeless and stop trying. Or, to retain a feeling of being effective, they may inflate their idea of an acceptable performance and spend even more time on each initiative.

Failures and setbacks are inevitable in every line of work at every juncture. Success requires perseverance. Women need to know both that they are likely to receive more than their fair share of rejections and that their response may make productive work more difficult. As I suggest in chapter 9, women can change the way they think about success and failure. If women can reinterpret failures as normal, and reinterpret rejections as par for women's course, they might find work easier and more satisfying. If men can reinterpret their focus on work as a less-than-completely-desirable legacy of the male schema, they might find life easier and more satisfying.

In conclusion, women's slower advancement in the professions does appear to be an inequity. It cannot be fully accounted for by differences in performance, preferences, or values. Attaining a happy medium for men and women requires changing in gender schemas.

13

Affirmative Action and the Law

.

Equal opportunity statutes prohibiting discrimination in employment, affirmative action procedures designed to implement them, and lawsuits against organizations that do not promote women have had at least a modestly positive effect on the representation of women in various professions. The psychological effects, however, are harder to assess. For example many people—both men and women—perceive being hired under affirmative action as evidence of lower ability; if the person were competent, they believe, she would not have needed affirmative action. (For discussions of affirmative action and perceptions of it, see Binion 1987; Clayton & Crosby 1992.)

Affirmative Action Procedures

Affirmative action and equal opportunity procedures are intended to create employment conditions in which women and minorities are hired and promoted according to their qualifications. They are designed to rectify unjust imbalances and to provide, at least in principle, redress for the negative consequences of inaccurate race and gender schemas. Successful lawsuits brought under federal and state antidiscrimination statutes provide back pay and legal fees and, in some cases, awards for damages.

Procedures for implementing affirmative action goals acknowledge that people are not hired and promoted purely on the basis of their known qualifications and that some individuals are favored because of their membership in a particular group. Some people have been and continue to be preferentially hired according to job-irrelevant characteristics, characteristics that prevent women and minorities from getting their fair share of good jobs. The goal of affirmative action, then, is to ensure that female or minority job candidates who are more qualified than white male candidates will be hired or promoted, and that female or minority candidates who are as well qualified as white male candidates will receive preference until no group is overrepresented.

Affirmative action procedures implicitly acknowledge the social psychological facts described throughout this book, and directly address the overt discrimination that has existed in many professions. If women are systematically underrated in professional life—and the data show that they are—a mechanism is needed to compensate for employers' faulty judgments. Affirmative action is one such mechanism.

Unfortunately, affirmative action is widely misunderstood as a procedure that gives hiring preference to a female or minority candidate over a better qualified white male. That misunderstanding arises from two sets of beliefs. The first is our faith that hiring procedures are normally meritocratic, so that the best person gets the job. Even though we all have ample evidence that the "best person" does not always get the job, we cling to the idea of a "just world" (Lerner 1980). In a just world, the deserving are rewarded and the unrewarded are undeserving. What supports that erroneous belief is our own explicit espousal of principles of meritocracy and fair play and our explicit use of such principles to justify our decisions about others. Our commitment to equality makes it difficult for us to perceive the extent to which we make unfair, nonmeritocratic evaluations that are based, implicitly and unconsciously, on gender and race schemas.

The second set of beliefs behind the misunderstanding of affirmative action is gender and race schemas themselves. The nonwhite or nonmale candidate is perceived at the outset as having fewer qualifications and therefore as less deserving than the white male; affirmative action is needed in order to compensate for the candidate's poor qualifications. (For historical discussion and political arguments for and against affirmative action, see Bergmann 1996; Bolick 1996; Eastland 1996; Skrentny, 1996.)

The Impact of Affirmative Action

How Has Affirmative Action Changed Organizations?

Misperceptions to one side, the objective impact of affirmative action policies is difficult to measure. To do so, we need to ask two questions. The first is, Have more women and minorities been hired and promoted into positions traditionally held by white men as a result of affirmative action? In other words, has affirmative action had the desired effect of increasing the representation of women and minorities? The second question is, Have the institutions that adopted affirmative action policies paid a price in lower worker productivity, lower work quality, or lower profits?

Even the first question is hard to answer, because the statistical problems are formidable (see Clayton & Crosby 1992; Kellough 1990). How, for example, do we separate the consequences of affirmative action from the consequences of a generally more progressive organizational climate? In principle, we could settle the matter by comparing institutions that have affirmative action policies with similar institutions that do not. In practice, however, that is difficult, because institutions within a given category, such as universities, all receive federal funds and thus must all have affirmative action programs. Institutions that have such policies often differ along many other dimensions from those that do not, and so are not comparable.

In government agencies the explicit requirement to increase the numbers of women employees does appear to have been effective. Before 1971, although equal employment opportunity laws existed, there were no numerical goals or timetables. After 1971 there were. A comparison of the percentages of women and African Americans hired in the higher civil service grades of twenty-two federal agencies reveals the impact of numerical goals (Kellough 1990). On balance, it appears that the position of women in the higher grades improved more between 1971 and 1980 than it did from 1966 to 1971, even when problems such as the rate of improvement already underway before 1971 were controlled for.[1]

Another study examined employment patterns in engineering in California by comparing large aerospace firms that had received federal contracts (often Department of Defense) to smaller, high-tech firms that had no government contracts and so were not obliged to have affirmative action programs (McIlwee & Robinson 1992). The firms in the study varied in several other respects as well. The small firms, computer-oriented technology companies, had lower percentages of women in high-status, high-responsibility jobs than did the aerospace firms. At the same time, the women in the aerospace firms reported encountering more attitudes that denigrated female competence than did the women in high-tech firms.

There is, in sum, some evidence that women are objectively better off as a result of affirmative action policies. In industries and areas where affirmative action has not been enforced, however, there is no difference between companies with such policies and those without them (Leonard 1989).

The second question, whether firms that hire and promote women are better or worse off, is even harder to answer. One national study of police departments in 1981 compared forces that had less than 1.5 percent female officers with those that had 9 percent or more (Steel & Lovrich 1987). Policing is a particularly interesting area, because the schema for females and the schema for police officers are so much at odds, and because male police have resisted the entry of women. The national study found no difference between the two types of forces in the number of crimes reported and solved from 1970 to 1980 and no difference in expenditures. We can conclude that hiring women police officers neither decreases a department's productivity nor adds to its costs.[2]

Another study, of employees in a wide variety of jobs in North Carolina, concluded that women and African Americans tended to be better qualified than their white male peers (Tomaskovic-Devey 1993). Although such findings are surprising to observers who are operating on the basis of gender and race schemas, they are not surprising to observers who are aware of the inaccurate perceptions that gender and race schemas promote. Gender and race schemas overrate white men and underestimate women and African Americans. Procedures like affirmative action, then, which increase the representation of women and minorities, should provide workers of equal or even slightly higher caliber.[3] At a minimum, no study suggests that a higher representation of women negatively affects an institution's achievements—a conclusion reached by Leonard about both women and African Americans (1984, 1989).

Another factor that makes it difficult to assess the impact of affirmative action procedures is that they are often embedded in a set of progressive policies, such as provision of day care facilities, family leave policies, flexible working hours, and easier transfer and promotion within the firm. Progressive firms tend to have happier and more productive workers (Kanter 1983). We do not know whether affirmative action plays an independent role. We can, however, conclude from the data available that institutions that implement affirmative action programs suffer no apparent ill effects.

We can, in fact, reasonably go further. The federal mandate to increase the proportion of women and minorities has probably had a number of more-distant effects, such as helping spur the introduction of generally progressive policies and increasing the awareness of some senior executives of the benefits of hiring women. Since the views of institutional leaders have a major influence on an organization's climate (see chapter 14), those who take a strong egalitarian stand improve their organization's policies toward women. Without affirmative action, then, institutional commitments to increasing the representation of women and improving women's internal progress might never have come about.

Finally, to the extent that affirmative action does result in more women in high positions, gender should become a less salient category and jobs should be seen in terms of gender-neutral qualifications. When women are in a small minority, as the studies reviewed in chapter 7 show, they are evaluated more negatively. That effect seems to be a joint function of two processes: jobs that are predominantly occupied by men appear to require masculine characteristics; and women who are in the minority are more likely to be perceived in terms of their gender. Policies that increase the representation of women should thus help shift the focus from a person's gender to the individual's actual performance.

Gender Schemas as Barriers to Affirmative Action
Given the findings reviewed in earlier chapters—especially that women work more than men for the same pay and that their contributions are evaluated more negatively than men's—we would expect that women, on average, will be better employees than men. They have had to overcome more obstacles in order to remain in an organization and are therefore

more highly selected than their male peers. Yet even those who might agree that women are qualified for low- and middle-level jobs may remain skeptical of their qualifications for high-level positions. Affirmative action may seem appropriate only for junior levels. Senior executives are thought to require characteristics, such as leadership ability, that run directly counter to the female schema.

As we saw in chapter 7, male businessmen perceive women in general, women managers, and even successful women managers, as possessing less leadership ability than their male peers (Heilman, Block, Martell, & Simon 1989). Another study reviewed in chapter 7 demonstrated that people respond to the same characteristics more negatively when displayed by a woman than a man (Butler & Geis 1990). Women who act like leaders, especially if their leadership style is highly assertive, receive more negative responses than do men who act like leaders. Affirmative action will be perceived as counterproductive if it promotes people seen as lacking leadership ability.

There is, however, no evidence to suggest that women actually deserve high position less than men do, or that they are less capable than men when they attain such positions. There is only evidence that women's merits and abilities are systematically devalued by both men and other women. Since gender schemas portray women as less competent in traditionally male areas than men, it is easy to misperceive the underrepresentation of women at senior executive levels as due to women's lack of fitness for those "male" positions, despite the lack of objective evidence.

In such situations, where evidence about women as a whole is either lacking or unknown, observers tend to rely on single examples. An employer might, for example, say that a woman appointed to a particular position in the past didn't work out, and conclude that women aren't suited to that job. Although a single example is worthless unless one knows how typical it is, people rely on single examples even in emotionally neutral areas. In fact, people can rely on a single example even when they know it is not in accord with the general rule.

The classic case is someone whose automobile is a lemon and who vows never to buy Brand X again, even though Brand X has the best rate-of-repair record (Tversky & Kahneman 1973). How much more likely, then, we are to rely on unrepresentative but vivid examples if we lack objective data and are also being asked to adopt beliefs opposite to those we have held nonconsciously since early childhood. Affirmative action cannot directly overturn those beliefs.

What Impact Does Affirmative Action Have on Beneficiaries?

Such is the force of gender schemas that both those who observe others being hired under affirmative action guidelines and those who are hired may react negatively. Women hired under those guidelines may feel diminished, seeing themselves as hired not for their competence but to fill a "quota." That, in turn, may call into question their own estimate of their competence.

This reasoning, however, is flawed. Even if a woman were being hired simply to satisfy affirmative action guidelines (an implausible scenario, since people are seldom hired for a single reason), that would have no logical bearing on her competence. She might be competent and she might not be. Similarly, a competing white male might or might not be competent; the fact that he has an edge because of his color and gender is independent of his actual qualifications. Neither gender can be presumed to be competent or incompetent.

But, because women and men hold similar theories about women's professional ability, women are likely to be psychologically undermined if they think they have gained a position because of their gender. This possibility bothered a professor who was discussing her tenure case with me. We agreed that she had an objectively good case, but she regretted the fact that her department had no tenured women, and therefore "needed" one. She believed that would affect her department's decision and didn't like that; she wanted to be judged on merit alone.

I suggested a different way of looking at the situation—that her department's "need" of a woman would increase the chances of a fair outcome. The minus sign that was attached to her achievements because of her gender would be neutralized by her department's recognition that there was something wrong (at least in the eyes of the world) with a department that had no tenured women when 30 to 40 percent of the people in the field were women. Whatever the views of others in the department, she at least should welcome affirmative action considerations, because they made fairness more likely.

In chapter 8 I noted that a white man would be unlikely to attribute a raise or promotion to his race and gender. Gender schemas both result in men's being more successful than their objective performance warrants and encourage men to think that they deserve their sometimes undeserved success. Conversely, gender schemas result in women's being less successful than their objective performance warrants and lead women to think that the successes they do have are undeserved. Affirmative action interacts with gender schemas to give women—and their observers—an explanation other than ability for their success. Since the gender schema for men includes professional competence, the informal affirmative action of which white men are the beneficiaries has no negative effect on them. Gender schemas render men immune to the perception that the benefits they enjoy are partly due to their gender. Even men who are aware that men in general benefit from their gender are likely to credit their success to their competence.

Two laboratory experiments confirm that men perceive their successes in this light. One study found that women students' self-perceptions are undermined when they think they are selected for a leadership position on the basis of gender rather than merit but men's are not (Heilman, Simon, & Repper 1987). The women in the experiment rated their performance more negatively than was objectively appropriate, took less credit for a positive outcome than was objectively warranted, and had less interest in continuing as a leader than did women supposedly chosen purely on the basis of ability.

The male students who were supposedly chosen because of their gender responded differently. They rated their performance equally highly whether they had been told that their selection was based on merit or on gender. Gender schemas favor a negative view of women's leadership abilities and a positive view of men's, ensuring that men's feelings of competence are not undermined by their being chosen on the basis of gender.

Findings from the second, similar study show that women who believe they are chosen for a leadership position because of their gender subsequently pick a less challenging task to perform than those who believe they are chosen because of their abilities (Heilman, Rivero, & Brett 1991). The men, in contrast, picked the more challenging task, regardless of the reason for their selection.

Again, the sex difference appears to spring from differences in beliefs about ability. In neither experimental condition were the students given any direct assessments of their ability. Thus, any differences in self-ratings were jointly due to the affirmative action information and the students' prior views of themselves. Men and women who thought they had been chosen on the basis of merit rated their abilities equally highly (Heilman et al. 1991). Like the men in the earlier study, the male participants who thought they had been chosen on the basis of gender rated themselves just as highly as the men who believed they had been selected on merit. But women in that situation rated their abilities much lower than did the women who believed their selection was based on merit.

Thus, when supposedly selected by merit, both groups inferred high ability; when supposedly selected by gender, only men assumed high ability. The experiment demonstrates the low opinion women have of their ability and the high opinion men have of theirs.

For both genders, understandably, the students who chose the more challenging task were those who rated themselves high in ability. As the authors of the second study point out, what is particularly disturbing about the results is the implication that women who believe they obtained their jobs because of affirmative action are likely to attempt less challenging assignments than those who think they earned their jobs purely on merit (Heilman et al. 1991). Choosing less challenging assignments will create a vicious circle in which women fail to give themselves opportunities to demonstrate their competence and ability and so will be less likely to be promoted. The women will therefore be unable to accrue advantage.

A laboratory study explored what happens when students are given direct but bogus information about their ability, along with bogus information about the selection process (Heilman, Lucas, & Kaplow 1990). First, male and female students individually performed a task that was described as a test of leadership ability in communication but that in fact tested nothing. Afterwards, some students were told that they had been chosen to be a leader in a second task because they had performed well in the communication pretest. Others were told that they had been chosen as a leader in the second task because the experimenters needed more male or more female leaders. The second group of students was further subdivided into three groups of males and females. One group received bogus information that they had performed above average on the leadership pretest; another group learned that they had performed below average; and the third group received no information at all.

Each student then performed a communication task with a stooge designated as the follower. Afterwards, the students were asked to assess themselves on a number of qualities, including competence.

Male and female students supposedly chosen on the basis of merit and given no other information about their ability rated themselves as equally competent, replicating the results described earlier. Of those supposedly chosen on the basis of gender and given no information about their ability, males rated themselves highly but females did not. That finding also replicated the results of the other experiments.

When chosen by gender and given negative information about the pretest, males and females rated themselves as equally low in competence. That result shows that men are not immune to negative information about their ability; they do not assume that their ability is low in the absence of information to that effect, but they do accept negative information when it is explicitly communicated to them.

The crucial results of this study come from the group of males and females who were told that they had been chosen by gender and were also given positive feedback about their pretest scores. In that condition, males and females rated themselves equally highly. Thus, selection on the basis of gender, if combined with information that affirms people's competence, allows both men and women students to see themselves as competent. Being told that they were effective leaders reduced the women's tendency to draw the unwarranted inference from gender-selection to low ability.

In summary, women supposedly chosen on the basis of gender rated their competence at the same low level whether they received no information about their ability or negative information. Men chosen on the basis of their gender showed a different pattern. When they received no information about their ability they rated it as high as they did when they were told that they possessed superior leadership ability.

Neither the women nor the men in this experiment had any actual grounds for drawing inferences about their ability; the pretest that purportedly measured their ability supplied no genuine information. Any views that they had about their competence had to come from self-evaluations that were in place before the experiment began. It is as if, in the absence of direct information, the men said to themselves, "I will think well of myself unless I receive explicit information to the contrary. Yes, I was chosen on the basis of my gender, but I probably did well on that pretest." But the women appeared to tell themselves, "I will think ill of myself unless I receive explicit information to the contrary. I was chosen on the basis of my gender and probably did badly on the pretest."

The implication of this experiment and the others I have cited is that the negative psychological effects of affirmative action are caused not by affirmative action itself but by the already-existing negative views that men and women hold about women. The very process that makes affirmative action necessary—men's and women's underestimation of women's performance because of gender schemas that selectively attribute professional competence to males—also makes affirmative action psychologically costly for women.[4]

Should Affirmative Action Procedures Be Abolished?

Some have argued that the objective benefits of affirmative action are so uncertain, and the psychological costs so high, that affirmative action policies should be discontinued (e.g., Sowell 1990; S. Steele 1990). Others have objected that affirmative action targets groups for advancement, not individuals.

Although it is difficult to measure definitively the objective benefits of affirmative action, we have seen that there is some evidence that it has benefitted women and minorities, both directly and indirectly. And, while it is true that the psychological costs of affirmative action can be high, we are not helpless when it comes to psychology. When we understand that the psychological costs originate in a set of false beliefs about the world and the nature of women, we can take steps to reduce those costs and help individuals correctly perceive their situation.

The argument that affirmative action targets particular groups—and is thus not color-blind or gender-blind—is also true, in a sense. But groups are targeted only because they would otherwise experience unfair evaluations. Affirmative action thus seeks to nullify the disadvantages that people of certain groups experience sheerly due to their membership in those groups.

To attempt to abolish affirmative action is to accept the faulty theories about social differences that gender and race schemas represent. It is to deny the plenitude of data reviewed throughout this book, data showing that women are underpromoted, undervalued, and underrecognized. The world of professional advancement is not a just world, however much we wish it to be so, but affirmative action could bring us closer to justice.

Individual women and minority group members might wish to disaffiliate themselves from affirmative action procedures in order to assert their own merit. That attitude, though understandable, is ignorant at best, given the evidence already reviewed. At worst, it is an attempt to see oneself as exceptional, to say, in effect, "*I* will succeed on my own merits"—as if most other women are as professionally incompetent as gender schemas portray them. Most women would probably be horrified by such an accusation and aver their belief that all women can succeed on the basis of their merits. But the data are clear: most women cannot succeed on merit alone. The goal of affirmative action is to create a world in which they can.

Can We Neutralize the Psychological Costs of Affirmative Action?

The Role of Institutions

The laboratory experiments described earlier illustrate the costs of implementing affirmative action procedures, but they also suggest how employers can reduce those costs to the intended beneficiaries. First, they can make sure that both people who are hired and those already employed by an organization understand that the goal of affirmative action is an equitable deal for everyone (Arthur, Doverspike, & Fuentes 1992).

Second, they can help everyone understand that there are no data to suggest that people appointed under affirmative action guidelines are less competent than others in an organization. Most people are ignorant of the facts of affirmative action, and ignorance can be dispelled (Jackson-Leslie, 1995; Kravitz & Platania 1993).

Third, the people who do the hiring should explicitly tell new employees which positive aspects of their record made them attractive to the organization (Arthur et al. 1992; Pettigrew & Martin 1987). New people should be aware of what employers see as their specific strengths, and the organization should keep those strengths in mind. Were it not for affirmative action, those abilities might well have gone unnoticed.

Not all people involved in a hiring decision may think it appropriate to mention the person's strengths, especially if they believe those strengths are not the primary reason for the hire. One benefit of affirmative action, however, is that it can draw attention to and emphasize positive qualities that are otherwise likely to be ignored.

General comments about a person are less useful than specific information about his or her abilities (Pettigrew & Martin 1987). It is probably not a good idea simply to reassure a new person that others in the organization see him or her as competent; that may or may not be true, even if the person is perceived as having certain strengths. People may be uncertain. One can believe strongly in the value and importance of affirmative action without believing that it picks out a superior candidate every time. Judgments are fallible and are based on a number of desiderata, some of which are difficult to quantify. Every organization has a range of competencies among its employees, and affirmative action will not change that. Sometimes people who are less competent than average are hired, perhaps on affirmative action grounds, perhaps on other grounds.

What is important to remember is that, no matter what selection procedure is used, by definition some people will be less competent than the average of those who are hired, some will be average, and some will be above average. It is worth noting again that no data suggest that affirmative action hires are less competent on average than other employees.

In addition, since evaluations are skewed by gender schemas, the prudent person will have reservations about the accuracy of his or her evaluations of others. The prudent person will recognize that a negative evaluation of a woman could be due in part to gender schemas. It might not be, but it could be, and it is best to keep that in mind. Gender schemas operate even in within-gender comparisons. Nonstereotypical men, for example, are likely to be underrated compared to men who are more stereotypically masculine.

Another reason not to reassure the new person of his or her perceived competence—rather than describing his or her strengths—is that such reassurance lends credence to the improper equation of affirmative action with incompetence. In effect, it implies that the person is an exception to the purported rule that affirmative action hires are less competent than others, a rule for which there is no evidence.

Finally, people in leadership positions at institutions need to understand and control the tendency to draw the wrong conclusion from occasional incompetent hires (see chapter 14). Some affirmative action appointments will be failures. Since failure is what is expected on the basis of gender schemas, such people will be salient and memorable, especially when there are relatively few affirmative action hires in an organization. Their numerical infrequency makes such people stand out. In contrast, the incompetents who are not affirmative action hires are simply seen as mistakes in a selection process that cannot be perfect every time.

The Role of the Individual

Women, as we have seen, are at risk for drawing false conclusions about their abilities when told that affirmative action pressures played a major role in their hiring. It is therefore incumbent on women themselves to understand what affirmative action is, how gender schemas work, and how those schemas can undermine their belief in their own abilities. Institutions need to dispel the ignorance of their employees, but women need to dispel their own ignorance.

Affirmative action is a corrective; it exists, in part, because women's abilities are undervalued—by employers and co-workers of both genders. Of course, we all prefer to be accepted purely for our merits. Yes, we want our abilities to be recognized and valued. But affirmative action is needed because people tend not to recognize women's merits. If there were no problem there would be no need of a solution. To accept the false idea that affirmative action entails lower professional competence is to deny the data about gender schemas detailed in chapters 6 through 9.

Women and men both have responsibilities. For women, it is the responsibility of thinking well of themselves, of developing their own realistic evaluation of their abilities, and of putting first things first. The goal is to be in a position to do the best work possible. Similarly, men must accept the responsibility of understanding the evaluation procedures from which they unwittingly benefit and of developing a more realistic evaluation of their actual abilities. Both women and men need to educate themselves about their own psychology.

Lawsuits

Partnership: A Case Study

Perhaps the most famous case involving gender discrimination is the one I have referred to at several points throughout this book, the case of Ann Hopkins, an associate of Price Waterhouse, a large international accounting firm. The case is famous, first and foremost, because it is such a clear instance of unfair denial of partnership (Fiske, Bersoff, Borgida, Deaux, & Heilman, 1991). In 1982 Hopkins was the only woman being considered for partnership, along with 87 men. At the time, Price Waterhouse had 662 partners, of whom 7 (a little over 1 percent) were women. By 1990 Price Waterhouse had 900 partners, of whom 27 (3 percent) were women. Hopkins had brought 25 million dollars' worth of business to the firm and had billed more hours that year than anyone else being considered for partner. She was a superlative candidate. She was rejected.

The Hopkins case has to be considered in the light of the leadership versus ladyship issues discussed in chapter 7. According to the court proceedings, Hopkins's senior colleagues apparently objected to the fact that she was too much of a leader and not enough of a lady. Her style was assertive, task-oriented, and instrumental. She had all the qualities that gender schemas dictate successful men should have. Her problem was that she wasn't a man.

Price Waterhouse didn't see it that way. They claimed that Hopkins didn't get along well with people and that they were within their rights in denying her partnership on that basis.

Hopkins claimed gender discrimination and sued the firm in federal district court in 1984. She won. Price Waterhouse appealed the decision to the federal appellate court. Hopkins won again. Price Waterhouse then appealed to the U. S. Supreme Court. On the most important issue raised there, Hopkins won again.

The important issue raised before the Court has been called the mixed-motives issue. Baldly put, it asks whether employers can discriminate against someone if they would not have hired or promoted that person for other reasons (see discussion in Fiske et al. 1991). According to the mixed-motives defense, if the person's competence can be separated from her gender and she is proven insufficiently competent, then the fact that the employer also opposes her because of her gender has no additional consequences. The employer's preference for men, in that case, is innocuous.

One problem with that way of evaluating the possible presence of discrimination is the difficulty of separating the employers' judgment of the person's competence from their attitudes toward women in general. As we have seen, observers discount women's merits and perceive them as less competent than they are—because they are women. It is especially difficult for employers who are unaware of the power of gender schemas to evaluate women fairly. The Price Waterhouse partners who voted against Ann Hopkins may sincerely have believed that her style of social interaction was so offensive that it more than offset her objective strengths, such as her ability to bring in $25 million in new business. (Their claim does, however, raise the question of why her style did not offend the people whose business she successfully sought.) The data in chapter 7 suggest, instead, that the partners perceived her style as offensive because it failed to conform to the norm for women dictated by gender schemas. She was not nice; she was not a lady.

A second problem with the way Price Waterhouse framed its defense is the difficulty of determining the level of competence required for a given position (Fiske et al. 1991). No employee is perfect. One could come up with reasons that any employee should not be in his or her present position or should not be promoted. If a plaintiff had to present evidence of flawless performance, no one could ever prove discrimination. If mixed motives are accepted as innocuous, then employers could discriminate freely and defend their action by pointing to one or more of the employee's shortcomings.

Price Waterhouse did not deny that some partners might be biased against women; they argued that if bias existed, it was irrelevant. Hopkins did not deserve partnership because of her personal style. Since their motives were mixed and not purely discriminatory, they argued, they were within their rights to deny her partnership. But if Ann Hopkins, an extraordinary executive by any objective measure, was viewed as unworthy of partnership, no employee would ever be able to win a discrimination suit. She came as close to perfect as any employee could.

The Court ruled that employers cannot discriminate on the basis of gender, even though an employee is not perfect. The employee does not bear the burden of proving that she is flawless. Instead, if there is evidence of discrimination, employers must prove that the woman would not have been promoted in the absence of any discrimination. The employer would have to demonstrate, for example, that men whose level of assertiveness was similar to or greater than Ann Hopkins's were typically denied partnership because of their abrasive personal style.

Educating the Judiciary

From a remedial point of view, a noteworthy feature of Ann Hopkins's march through the courts was the role that evidence about gender schemas played in the various decisions (Fiske et al. 1991). Susan T. Fiske, testifying at Hopkins's first trial, summarized the social psychological literature on sex stereotyping, the circumstances that promote or reduce stereotyping, and its consequences. She also interpreted many of Price Waterhouse's comments about Hopkins within the framework provided by research on stereotyping. Although the firm's lawyers tried to dismiss Fiske's testimony as speculation, the judge was convinced; his ruling in favor of Hopkins specifically referred to the data on sex stereotyping.

For the Supreme Court appeal, the American Psychological Association filed an *amicus curiae* brief reviewing the research on sex stereotyping (1991). Price Waterhouse again had the poor judgment to try to cast doubt on the scientific legitimacy of the psychologists' summary of the data. When referring to sex stereotyping, for example, their lawyers put quotation marks around the phrase (Fiske et al. 1991). The Court's majority decision in favor of Hopkins specifically referred to that practice, commenting that "such conduct seems to us an insinuation that such stereotyping was not present in this case or that it lacks legal relevance. We reject both possibilities" (cited in Fiske et al. 1991).

What is heartening about this case is the judiciary's receptivity to facts of the sort reviewed in this book and its willingness to see sex stereotyping as a form of discrimination (Fiske et al. 1991). The data are convincing to people who are charged with making fair decisions that will withstand close public scrutiny. Lawyers who try to win by derogating the research findings are pursuing a losing strategy.

The judiciary's commitment to fairness can also be seen in decisions concerning the presence of gay men and women in the military; federal judges have ruled in several cases that the military has no legitimate grounds for barring homosexuals. A judge from federal district court in Seattle, Thomas S. Zilly, ruled that Washington's National Guard had improperly discharged Colonel Margarethe Cammermeyer after having learned she was a lesbian. Her commanding officers had not wished to dismiss her but were forced to do so by the Pentagon. Zilly's ruling noted that the military "conceded that their justifications for the policy are based on heterosexual members' fear and dislike of homosexuals. Mere negative attitudes, or fear, are constitutionally impermissible bases for discriminatory governmental policies" (Schmitt 1994).

Benefits of Successful Suits

Suits like Ann Hopkins's bring many benefits to the community at large. They heighten awareness of the bias that affects the professional evaluation of women and of the difficulties women face in trying to reap the rewards of excellent performance. When an Ann Hopkins wins, people begin to accept that miscarriages of justice occur, and that they occur because of implicit theories about what is appropriate behavior for women. Ann Hopkins goes from being regarded as a possibly deluded termagant to a woman with a legitimate grievance. She becomes a woman whose grievance is that she was judged as a woman and not as a person. Although lawsuits that reach the public eye are rare, their effects are far-reaching.

In 1982, the year Ann Hopkins was denied partnership, I had a conversation with an undergraduate at a women's college about women and achievement. At the time, neither of us knew anything about Ann Hopkins. The student, whom I will call Carol, said she was sure an able woman who played by the rules would succeed. Perhaps, she commented, that hadn't been true twenty years earlier, but she was certain it was now. Women, Carol thought, should stop complaining and start working. Her denial of gender disadvantage was echoed fourteen years later in a 1996 article spotlighting seven successful businesswomen (Sellers 1996).

Hopkins's case is extraordinary in part because she did exactly what Carol recommended: she didn't complain, she worked hard and well; yet she was subject to discrimination because she was insufficiently feminine. Here was a woman whose work could not be devalued. How could having more billable hours than any other candidate for partner be devalued; how could $25 million be devalued? And yet her work *was* devalued—it was considered less important than wearing makeup and behaving in a traditionally feminine way. As the Supreme Court pointed out, Hopkins was placed in an impossible position. Her job demanded that she act assertively in order to succeed, yet she was rejected for that behavior. In essence, the Court declared that businesses do not have the right to demand that women be ladies.

Hopkins's victory fosters both a recognition of the power of gender schemas and a hope that—by education—their power can be understood and neutralized.

Limitations of Successful Suits

Other aspects of the Hopkins case, however, suggest that the beneficial effects of lawsuits may be limited. Ann Hopkins cannot inspire the mass of women. Because her talents and efforts are so exceptional, she cannot be emulated by 99 percent of executives—male or female. Her case could therefore arouse profound pessimism: if this is what can happen to someone who was virtually perfect, what hope is there for the rest of us? Moreover, despite the clarity of her case, it took seven years from the denial of partnership to the Supreme Court's ruling in her favor. Very few people crave justice intensely enough to spend the time, energy, and money that is required for seven years of litigation against a powerful, wealthy, and dogged adversary. Very few people believe in themselves strongly enough to sustain such a craving for justice.

Gender Schemas and Mixed Motives

Here, again, is where women's own psychology becomes important. Everyone's performance (as Fiske et al. 1991, point out) is mixed. We excel at some things; we perform less well, perhaps even poorly, at others. One reason, I believe, that the mixed-motives defense was ill-received by the courts in Hopkins's case was that her performance was unassailable. She lacked a traditionally feminine style, but she had no objective flaws. Thus, the idea that she might have been rejected independently of her employer's preference for men was not credible. In almost all other cases in which people are promoted or rejected, however, there are objective flaws. How serious they are is a matter of judgment—employers' judgment.

Employers cite those flaws to justify their decisions not to promote certain people. Employers may genuinely believe that those flaws are the reasons for their negative decisions. Exactly because most evidence is subject to interpretation, employers—and the women who are denied promotion—can be convinced that the women did not deserve to be promoted. Most women who fail in their attempt to reach the top are aware of their flaws. Especially since gender schemas operate so subtly, and motives are mixed, the women involved may accept the explanation that their flaws were a sufficient cause of their failure, whether or not discrimination also played a role.

The mixed-motives defense may thus win in women's psyches and in observers' judgments, even if it does not win in the courts' decisions. The desire to believe in a meritocracy and the desire to feel in control of their own lives may lead women to accept negative evaluations of themselves and to deny that the disadvantage of gender affects them. The negative evaluations they receive are, in some sense, true. Work is seldom as good as it could be.

Both women and their employers need to adopt a better-informed perspective. The development within the organization of objective criteria for success will help, for several reasons (Tomaskovic-Devey 1993). Such criteria make the standards of judgment explicit; they allow employees to know what is expected for success and allow employers to guard against the tendency to use irrelevant criteria. They also enable employers and employees to make relevant comparisons. If someone is to be promoted, his or her performance should fall within a range of the average of others who have been promoted.

A woman being considered for partnership or tenure under such criteria need not be better than everyone else who has made partner, nor as good as the best who have made partner, nor even better than the average of those who have made partner. She—like her male peers—only needs to be within the average range.[5]

Naturally, everyone should try to excel. But a woman who is not promoted should not compare herself to the best people in her organization in order to determine whether or not she deserves promotion; she should compare herself to the average. Whether gender discrimination is at work may, in any individual case, be impossible to determine; many are the reasons that people do not get what they deserve. But a woman does not need to know all the reasons; she simply needs to know where she is relative to the average. Employees need to know whether they merit promotion, because that knowledge gives them good grounds to argue their case if they do not get it. They may or may not then conclude that bias was the reason for their failure.

My discussion here has assumed that the organization does not actively prevent certain people from performing well, but that assumption does not always hold. Some work environments are so inimical to women that they are unable to perform at an average level. Other environments, while not actively hostile, may prevent women from acquiring the experience they need, because that experience is seen as incompatible with women's characteristics.

Recall, for example, the university department I described in chapter 7, where female graduate students were not assigned large lecture classes. Without intending to, the faculty prevented the women from gaining experience they needed to be competitive in the job market. It is highly unlikely that those young women, if they do badly with their first large lecture class, will recognize the role that gender schemas played in their current difficulties. They are much more likely to blame themselves for their poor performance.

Tenure: A Case Study

While the case of Ann Hopkins was clear-cut, the case of mathematician Jenny Harrison was not (Selvin 1993). In 1986 Harrison was an assistant professor at the University of California at Berkeley. At that time the mathematics department had seventy-one tenured professors, of whom one was a woman. The department voted against giving Harrison tenure, although the vote was split. The higher-level university committees ratified the no-tenure decision. Following the logic I have recommended for dealing with a mixed-motives case, Harrison argued that both the quantity and quality of her work was at the average of the eight men who had been tenured during her time at Berkeley. She had published as much work as three of the men, and its quality equalled that of four of the men.

In 1989, when Harrison had to leave Berkeley, she brought suit against the university, charging gender discrimination. She taught for one year at Yale and was then unemployed. In 1993 she and the university agreed to an out-of-court settlement in which an independent committee of seven people (two Berkeley mathematicians, three from elsewhere, and two nonmathematicians) would go over her case and determine whether she deserved tenure. Under the terms of the settlement, the committee was to decide whether she currently deserved tenure, not whether she had deserved tenure when it had been denied seven years earlier. The committee recommended that she be given a tenured full professorship, and she returned to Berkeley in 1993 as a tenured full professor. She was not vindicated—there was no review of the 1986 decision—but she did get tenure.

Harrison's situation is more typical of women's experiences than Hopkins's is. Harrison's performance had not been outstanding relative to the male mathematicians who had recently been granted tenure; it was in the middle range. What makes her case noteworthy is that she understood that being in the middle range of those who had been promoted was, or should be, good enough. To merit promotion one should not have to meet higher standards than others do.

What is perhaps most insidious about the biased evaluations women receive is that people see as reasonable the idea that women who want to get ahead should perform better than men. Men and women adopt higher standards for women, and women adopt those standards for themselves. But having to prove that you are equal by proving that you are better guarantees that most women will fail, just as it would guarantee that most men would fail were that standard applied to them.

Again, I am not saying that women should not aspire to excellence. Everyone should. I am saying that the standard of comparison for deciding whether people deserve a job, partnership, tenure, or a high salary, is the performance of other people who have such positions and salaries, rather than the ideal to which one aspires. One may fall far short of one's aspirations but still deserve promotion, partnership, or tenure.

School Admission: Two Case Studies

In 1993 Shannon Faulkner applied for admission to the Citadel, a small all-male, state-supported military college in South Carolina. Faulkner had asked the people who wrote letters of recommendation for her not to mention her sex. Since her high school record, test scores, and letters of recommendation were all of sufficient quality for admission, the Citadel admitted her. Upon learning that she was a woman, the school reversed its decision. There was no question about her ability; her record had already passed muster. She was the wrong sex.

Faulkner sued on the grounds that, as a state-supported school, the Citadel could not discriminate against her on the basis of sex. Her case fell under the equal-protection provisions of the Fourteenth Amendment. Each court on Faulkner's march to justice affirmed the validity of her claim. The most notable response, again showing the judiciary's sense of fairness, came from Federal Court of Appeals Judge Kenneth Hall. He was quoted as saying: "The daughters of Virginia and South Carolina have every right to insist that their tax dollars no longer be spent to support what amounts to fraternal organizations whose initiates emerge as full-fledged members of an all-male aristocracy. Although our nation has through its history discounted the contributions and wasted the abilities of the female half of its population, it cannot continue to do so" (Applebome 1995).

Hall's reference to Virginia concerns a separate case begun in 1990, in which the Justice Department sued the state of Virginia, which partially supported the Virginia Military Institute (VMI), another all-male military college. In an effort to resist sex-integration, VMI tried to create an equivalent program at a women's school. The Justice Department responded by taking its case to the Supreme Court, claiming that the alternative program was not equivalent to VMI's own program. In 1996 the Supreme Court ruled in favor of the Justice Department, stating that women had to be admitted to VMI. That ruling also applied to the Citadel, which immediately made plans to accept several women.

The Citadel and VMI contrast with Norwich University, a small private military college in Vermont. Norwich went coed voluntarily in 1974, and in 1995 had an entering class of 245 men and 65 women (Rimer 1995). Male students at Norwich were reportedly surprised by attitudes at the Citadel. One male student, the second-highest-ranking cadet, was quoted as saying, "I never thought about it, really, until this Shannon Faulkner thing. No matter where you go, unless you make your own club, you're going to have to deal with women." The colonel at the college said, "I tell these young men, 'You're going to work for, and work with, women. The sooner you understand that the better.'"

The attitude at Norwich seems to be—it doesn't matter whether you like it; a sex-integrated professional world is a fact of life; accept it and adjust to it. Norwich's experience is evidence that all-male military institutions can become sex-integrated with little fuss.

Leadership was the critical element in Norwich's smooth transition. Institutional leadership can either facilitate or thwart the achievement of fairness. At Norwich, leaders instruct cadets to be matter-of-fact about the inclusion of women and to acknowledge women's competence. At the Citadel and VMI, the leaders condoned and tacitly encouraged anti-woman comments and attitudes among cadets. At the Citadel, cadets harassed Faulkner (who withdrew shortly after arriving at the school). At VMI, cadets bought T-shirts inscribed "Better Dead Than Coed" (Allen 1996). If the officials of those institutions had been doing their job properly, such behavior would not have existed. Students at VMI get demerits for accepting delivery of pizza (Allen 1996), but they do not receive demerits for overt antagonism toward women.

Early in 1997, two of the four women who had been accepted into the first-year class at the Citadel charged male cadets with harassment. The interim president of the Citadel (himself the father of one of the two other female students) announced that one cadet was being dismissed for at least a year and nine others were being disciplined (Nossiter 1997). The discipline suggests that the male cadets' behavior went beyond tolerable hazing.

The events demonstrate both that getting in the door of a previously closed institution is only a first step and that the Citadel's previous leadership was a failure. Making women's entrance into male fields a success requires a more sophisticated understanding of attitude formation and maintenance than the school's early attempts have displayed.

Effects of Lawsuits on Employees and Observers

The ability to sue on the grounds of sex discrimination—both as individuals and in class-action suits—has clearly helped women to prove that discrimination has occurred and to obtain redress. In addition, such suits have helped increase awareness of the fact that discrimination occurs and is unacceptable. Instead of remaining something that women must accept as a fact of life, discrimination is becoming something that women can effectively counteract. In addition, the kinds of arguments that are made in lawsuits—such as Harrison's claim that she need be only equal rather than superior to men receiving tenure—help educate observers about legitimate grounds for evaluations of men and women.

Effects of Lawsuits on Employers

There is some evidence that employers too are affected by lawsuits—and by the threat of lawsuits—and that those effects are helping to equalize women's and men's professional opportunities. For example, the CIA was reportedly influenced by the threat of a class-action suit charging discriminatory assignment and promotion practices into taking steps to ensure equal opportunity (Weiner 1994). If employers learn that discrimination is costly, they are likely to take steps to avoid discrimination suits. Successful suits can bring an organization unwelcome publicity, and can cause financial losses from damage awards, back pay, and legal fees.

Some employers, however, try to avoid discrimination suits by evading the intent of antidiscrimination laws: they demand that employees sign agreements that take away their ability to sue. Elaine L. Williams is an African-American partner in a Chicago law firm, Katten Muchin & Zavis. In 1994, she attempted to file suit against the firm in federal court, charging that she had received less bonus money than other partners even though her performance was superior to theirs (Holmes 1994). Katten Muchin & Zavis denied her charges and also argued that an agreement she had signed in 1991, when she had made partner, prevented her from suing. That agreement stated that employee disputes had to be submitted to binding arbitration. A federal judge agreed with the firm and dismissed her suit.

Katten Muchin & Zavis is only one of numerous corporations, such as ITT, Hughes, Rockwell International, NCR, and Travelers, that, as of 1994, required employees, as a condition of employment or promotion, to forfeit their right to sue for discrimination (Holmes 1994). It is cheaper to forbid suits against discrimination than to ensure that discrimination does not occur. Whether such agreements can be legally enforced remains to be seen. (Collective-bargaining agreements ensure that unionized employees never forfeit their right to sue.)

The Future

It seems clear that affirmative action programs and legal cases, while important tools for increasing justice for women, are only one way to remedy the inequities produced by gender schemas. Legal remedies invite counterresponses based on narrow legal points and deflect attention from the underlying mechanisms responsible for discrimination in the first place. To bring about more thorough change, employers and employees alike need remedies that will directly and indirectly alter gender schemas. In the next chapter, I review several remedies of this kind.

14

Remedies

My explanation for why women are underrepresented at high levels of professional achievement has focused on gender schemas and the accumulation of advantage. Gender schemas influence evaluations to women's detriment, in turn making it difficult for women to accumulate advantage at the same rate as men. The goal of this chapter is to suggest several ways to nullify the negative professional consequences of gender schemas and to equalize men's and women's ability to accumulate advantage.

Toward Accurate Evaluations

The most common professional outcome of gender schemas is the undervaluation of women's performance. Evaluations favoring men occur because evaluators do not know how to protect themselves from the inaccuracies that gender schemas give rise to. Evaluators need help in neutralizing the effects of gender schemas. Both formal and informal remedies are possible.

Evaluators also need to understand that every evaluation is important, because evaluation contributes to the accumulation of advantage or disadvantage. No one in authority can comfort himself or herself by dismissing small differences in their treatment of others as unimportant over the long haul. To the contrary, small differences add up to considerable disparities in advantage and disadvantage over time. People need training both in the concept of the accumulation of advantage and disadvantage and in how to recognize examples. The university department chair described in chapter 1, who did not allow a new female faculty member to teach a large lecture course, can learn how and why his refusal put the woman at a disadvantage.

Learning about Gender Schemas

Men's and women's beliefs about themselves and others are powerful. Becoming knowledgeable about the origins and consequences of gender schemas is an important step toward correcting inaccuracies. For several reasons, however, knowing that one's impressions of oneself and others are subject to systematic error will not automatically correct those errors.

In order to correct our errors we have to perceive them as mistakes. A woman whom I will call Karen told me the following story about going shopping with her husband a few weeks after reading about my encounter with the tree surgeon (see chapter 8). They went to a store that was demonstrating a particular brand of food processor that her husband was very interested in buying; Karen herself was indifferent.

The husband asked the demonstrator many questions about the processor, ranging from the power of the motor to the various functions it could perform. Karen stood by, bored but patient. She then began to notice that the demonstrator—a woman—looked at Karen's husband when she was answering one of his technical questions but shifted her gaze to Karen when the question was culinary.

No doubt the demonstrator was completely unaware of her shifting glances and, probably, of the underlying beliefs that they reflected. Karen doubted that she herself would have noticed the changing direction of the woman's gaze had she not read chapter 8.

Karen had no way of bringing the demonstrator's behavior to her attention. First, it would have seemed intrusive and rude. Second, unless the woman already knew that gaze signals and maintains nonconscious perceptions of power, she would have been incredulous that anyone would draw conclusions about her gender beliefs from whom she looked at while answering questions. Third, her conscious beliefs about women's and men's roles may have been so much at variance with her nonconscious beliefs that she would have been unable to recognize that she harbored the beliefs she did. Fourth, people prefer to ignore bias, whichever end of it they experience. We all want to think that we treat other people as individuals and that they treat us the same way.

Changing behavior is a complex process. First, we must understand the import of subtle cues like direction of gaze and be willing to examine our own and others' behavior for the presence of those cues. We must accept that we may have expectations and attitudes we are unaware of. Even then, we may find it difficult to change. The demonstrator's attention, for example, was focused on communicating the virtues of the food processor. Keeping an eye on her eyes, as it were, might have siphoned attention away from her sales pitch. Change does not happen automatically. It requires us to pay attention to a host of behaviors and expectations, as the data presented throughout this book confirm.

Because gender schemas are such fundamental ways of perceiving and understanding the social world, they resist change. But even well-entrenched hypotheses are not immutable. We can modify them and, in time, replace them with new ones.

Challenging Hypotheses

To evaluate other people more accurately we need to challenge our implicit hypotheses about men and women and recode items in memory. There are two ways we can do that. First, we can inform ourselves about our biases by forming explicit explanations of the reasons for individual examples of success and failure. That is, when we hear about an individual's success or failure we can examine our own reactions to discover and state explicitly what we implicitly see as its causes. Why did X not get tenure? Why did the people at this morning's meeting not discuss Y's suggestion? Why did Z make that mistake in sales projections?

We can go further by recalling objectively similar events that have happened to men and women we know and comparing our reactions to the events. If, for example, we negatively evaluated a woman in some situation, we can try to find a comparable behavior by a man to test whether we saw his behavior in the same light. Or, if we have positively evaluated a man for some action, we can think of a woman who behaved in a similar manner to see whether we evaluated her in the same way.

Second, we can conduct thought experiments in which we switch the sexes. For example, we can consider how we would rate someone who did not fulfill a responsibility in a timely manner—first thinking about a woman and then about a man. We might discover that we would assume that the woman who did not complete the job on time was incompetent but that the man needed an assistant to cope with a job that was too big for one person (Geis, M. Carter, & Butler 1982).

I conducted a switch-the-sexes thought experiment on myself recently, after going to a bookstore to see if they had some books I wanted. I had asked a tall young man with glasses and long hair if the books were listed in their computer. As he was searching the list, the phone at his desk rang. He answered it and began apologizing almost immediately. I could tell that he was interrupting the person who was talking to him in order to apologize. He kept saying, "I'm sorry, yes, I know what I'm supposed to say, I usually do, I'm sorry."

Wow, I thought, what in the world has he done? I also thought, "Hey, shape up, don't be so craven, it can't be that bad."

When he hung up, he found one of the books I was looking for in the computer, along with the category it should have been shelved under—sociology. "Ah," I said, "so it should be in sociology."

"Might," he said. "I have to say that it *might* be there, that we *might* have it. That's what the phone call was about. I told a customer we had something, because it was in the computer, instead of saying we *might* have it."

That's what all that was about? *Might?*

Afterwards, I reflected on my reaction. I doubted that I would have been so surprised by his apologies or would have thought him so craven had he been a woman. His apologies probably would have seemed natural to me.

In both the thought experiments and the comparisons of actual similar events, the mechanism is the same: to change our implicit hypotheses we need to become explicitly aware of them, to catch ourselves in the act of operating with them, and then to explicitly entertain evaluations that run counter to our hypotheses. This will not be easy. It may take several people working together on many examples to make progress. Nor will change occur overnight, as my own reaction to the book clerk makes all too clear.

Our hypotheses are long-standing explanatory devices: without them we feel lost. Further, as we become aware of our hypotheses, we replace our belief in a just world with a view of the world in which bias plays a role. Since this is a state of affairs we wish were otherwise, we prefer not to acknowledge it. But we can learn.

by an unbiased, higher authority, they are more likely to form accurate ones. The underlying mechanism may be that evaluators incorporate another perspective from the start. They may ask themselves questions like, "How would I evaluate this performance if the person were a man rather than a woman?" "How did I evaluate a man who performed in this way?" "How closely did this person meet the objective requirements of a good performance?" In other words, accountability is apt to encourage people to challenge their hypotheses about gender differences.

Increasing the Number of Women in a Candidate Pool   One message of many studies reviewed in preceding chapters is that women receive less favorable professional evaluations when gender schemas are invoked. Thus, conditions that highlight a woman's femininity, especially if she works in a traditionally male area, put her at risk of being considered unsuited to the "male" job and therefore devalued. One remedy for the salience of sex, then, is having adequate numbers of women and men in any group being evaluated. That will make any given woman's sex less distinctive.

The data suggest that women will be more fairly evaluated if they are at least 25 percent of the group. That percentage of women not only reduces the availability of the female gender schema but, just as significantly, it alters perceptions of the job itself. A job held by both males and females in reasonable numbers appears to be a human job rather than a male or female job (Hoffman & Hurst 1990).

Thus, an important goal of organizations should be to increase, as quickly as possible, the number of women in responsible positions or positions that are entry points to such jobs. Ann Hopkins probably would not have been judged on the basis of her lack of femininity had she not been the sole woman being considered for partner along with eighty-seven men. As it was, her situation was maximally unfavorable.

Only recently have women been 25 percent of associate professors at major universities. That percentage should help create fairer evaluations of women being considered for tenure and promotion to associate professor. At law schools, as the data reviewed in chapter 7 indicate, women are more likely to be successful candidates for tenure on faculties that have a higher proportion—rather than a very low proportion—of tenured women (Chused 1988). It is not that women judge other women more fairly than men do, or show a preference for women. We know that women's judgments of other women are very similar to men's (see data in chapter 7). The reason is, rather, that evaluators at these schools have stopped seeing the job of tenured professor as a male job, thanks to the relatively high number of female tenured professors.

Data from other contexts confirm that numbers are important. Both men and women who observe a range of women in positions of authority and subsequently take part in a group discussion view the women in the group as higher in leadership than those who had only observed men in authority roles (Geis, Boston, & Hoffman 1985). Seeing a variety of women in leadership positions encourages people to see leadership not as a masculine trait but as a human trait.

Learning to Reason   Even without the influence of schemas, evaluators make mistakes in judgment. Cognitive psychology has pinpointed various errors in human reasoning, including weighting extreme examples as more typical than they are, ignoring information about how frequently different events occur, and giving too much weight to one's own personal experience. Social schemas exacerbate reasoning errors. Thus, evaluators need to learn how to avoid reasoning pitfalls.

The first stage of a program to improve reasoning would give evaluators problems to solve that had nothing to do with judgments of women. Evaluators would learn what kinds of errors they make and how to improve their reasoning. The second stage would introduce similar reasoning problems involving judgments of members of different social groups. Three important reasoning errors, to be discussed in turn, are failure to appreciate covariation, blocking of relevant hypotheses, and illusory correlation.

Failure to appreciate covariation is nicely demonstrated in a study showing that women are more likely than men to correctly analyze statistical information demonstrating hiring bias against women (Schaller 1992). College students were asked to imagine that they were the president of an aerospace company that employed forty executives and office workers, each of whom had taken a test of leadership ability. In tabular form, the aggregate results would have looked like this:

Leadership Ability Data

	Executive		Office Worker		Aggregate	
	hi	lo	hi	lo	hi	lo
Men	12	3	1	4	13	7
Women	4	1	3	12	7	13

The participants were asked to look at each employee's test result and note his or her sex, status in the company, and leadership ability rating. The participants' task was to judge whether sex was related to leadership ability and decide whether to hire a man or a woman as a new executive or a new office worker.

Overall, more men (13) than women (7) were rated as high in leadership ability. But those data are misleading, as a look at the figures for executives and office workers shows. There are more women than men office workers and more men than women executives. Within the executive category, however, exactly the same ratio of high to low leadership ability—4:1—exists for each sex. Similarly, within the office worker category, exactly the same ratio of high to low leadership ability—in this case 1:4—exists for each sex. In this company, status and sex covary; that is, all the variation in leadership ability can be accounted for by the distribution of the sexes into the two status groups. There happen to be more men than women in the executive category, but 80 percent of each sex in that category displayed high leadership ability. That covariation means that the overall data cannot be accepted at face value. The overall data are uninformative about the relationship between leadership ability and employees' sex. So, the correct answer to the first question is that there is no demonstrable relation between sex and leadership ability.

The correct answer to the second question is, similarly, that there are no grounds for preferring either sex for either job category. The data at hand give no reason for thinking that men and women differ in leadership ability. Of course, it could be the case that fewer women than men occupy the executive category because women in general have less leadership ability than men. But that interpretation would be based on prior beliefs; it is not a valid conclusion from the data presented.

The investigator hypothesized that female participants would be more likely than men to spot the spurious relation between sex and leadership

(Schaller 1992). They would be more motivated to perceive the fact that within each status category men and women show the same leadership potential. The results showed that female participants indeed had a better appreciation of the fact that status and sex covaried, thus rendering the aggregate data uninformative.

A further study explored the implications of these results and revealed that training in the logic of covariation reduces the likelihood that people will draw the wrong conclusions about differences between social groups (Schaller, Asp, Rosell, & Heim 1996). Employers can evaluate potential employees more fairly if they have learned how to recognize the presence of covariation and to understand the faulty conclusions that unnoticed covariation can lead to.

A related experiment—on *blocking*—shows that both males and females are unlikely to perceive causes that might genuinely contribute to a person's performance if a prior hypothesis—such as a gender schema—independently predicts that performance (Sanbonmatsu, Akimoto, & Gibson 1994). In the experiment, participants learned a number of facts about four fictitious students who had passed a welding course and four who had failed. Many of the facts were irrelevant to the student's success or failure, but one piece of information—about course load—was important. Students with a light course load passed and those with a heavy course load failed. Some participants also received information about the students' gender. In one condition, as would be expected on the basis of gender schemas, all the passing students were male and all the failing students were female. In another condition, half the students who passed were male and half the students who failed were male. Participants were asked to say why some students had passed and others had failed.

The experimenters reasoned that participants would expect males to be more likely than females to pass a welding course. If the gender information supported such an expectation, the participants would be unlikely to notice the other characteristic that predicted performance, namely course load. The division of success and failure along gender lines, the researchers hypothesized, would block students from seeing that gender covaried with course load. In contrast, participants given information that did not support expectations based on gender schemas should be more likely to see that course load was an explanation of students' performance.

As predicted, participants who were told that half the males passed and half failed were more likely to perceive that course load was related to passing or failing than did participants who were told that only males passed and only females failed. In this experiment, there were no differences between male and female participants in detection of covariation. Both sexes seem to have equally strong beliefs about women's unsuitability for welding, but—given the data from the previous experiment—different beliefs about leadership ability.

The welding experiment has obvious implications for judgments about women in professional settings. People who see a woman fail at a task that they expect her to fail at, because of the influence of gender schemas, will be unlikely to perceive other possible causes of her failure. They will attribute her failure to her sex rather than search further for other reasons, even if those other reasons are the actual causes of her failure. It may even seem to observers that a search for other causes is a search for excuses. Evaluators who understand that their own gender-based expectations may conceal the real causes of people's performance will judge employees more fairly and accurately.

Another important aspect of this experiment is the link the researchers established between their results with gender schemas and similar results from purely cognitive tasks (Sanbonmatsu et al. 1994). For example, in one such task, participants classified different letter sequences into two types. After they had developed a rule based on one differentiating property of the sequences, they classified new sequences. The participants continued classifying according to their rule, failing to notice that the new sequences contained additional properties providing the same classification. The old rule blocked perception of the new regularities. An established hypothesis tends to block people's recognition of valid alternative hypotheses. That blocking occurs even in tasks that have no association with gender schemas shows that it is a general cognitive phenomenon.

The third type of reasoning error that helps create and maintain negative evaluations of others is *illusory correlation,* or seeing a relation that does not exist between two distinctive and relatively infrequent conditions (Hamilton & Gifford 1976; see review of related studies in Fiske & Taylor 1991). Like blocking, illusory correlation is a cognitive process that occurs even in socially neutral tasks. It could have a particularly negative influence on evaluations of women in male-dominated professions.

Illusory correlation requires, first, two groups, one of which is more frequently encountered in certain situations than the other. In the professions the two groups are males and females, with males being the more numerous. The second requirement is the presence within each group of the same proportion of positive to negative behaviors. Males and females in the professions are likely to exhibit the same proportion of competent to incompetent behaviors.

In that type of situation, observers overestimate how often the less frequently encountered, and therefore more distinctive group—women— perform the less frequent and therefore more distinctive behaviors—incompetent ones. Women will thus be linked with incompetence, because both are seen relatively infrequently in the professions, and because infrequent, distinctive events are seen as causally related to each other. The correlation is illusory, since the same proportion of incompetent behaviors appears in both groups. The phenomenon of illusory correlation also helps explain why increasing the number of women in a candidate pool makes it more likely that they will be evaluated positively. If women are numerous, they are less likely to be paired with infrequent events like incompetence.

In the classic demonstrations, illusory correlation occurs if one group is encountered twice as often as the other and if the distinctive behavior is half as common (Hamilton & Gifford 1976). Thus, women are at risk in settings where they are less than one-third of job occupants, a figure compatible with the findings of studies cited in chapter 7.

Awareness Training

The remedies I have offered thus far emphasize the cognitive changes that people can make to increase the accuracy of their evaluations of others and decrease their reliance on gender schemas. An obvious question is whether accuracy would also improve if people underwent training in articulating the content of their gender schemas. A major component of many programs aimed at increasing diversity in the workplace is awareness training, in which people are encouraged to explore together their nonconscious beliefs about gender, ethnic, and other differences. The effectiveness of such programs is unknown because there are no established methods of evaluation (Rynes & Rosen 1995).

In the case of gender, I think awareness training may be counterproductive. As the research reviewed in this book has shown, males and females share a core of nonconscious beliefs about gender, even if they differ in their explicit beliefs. That similarity is unlikely to come out when people exchange personal anecdotes, because many aspects of how gender schemas work are not available to consciousness. Most males and females are not very knowledgeable about gender schemas. For example, the fact that male and female evaluators will rate a woman's suitability for a management job more positively if there are other women in the candidate pool (Heilman 1980) is not common knowledge, nor could any single individual easily become aware of it through introspection.

People need well-documented information about sex differences and evaluations of others, information based not on single examples but on systematic observation and experimentation. Although examples are personally meaningful, they are no substitute for representative data. People need not, I think, bring out in public their discoveries about their own biases. They need only understand that they are likely to have such biases, and that they must work out procedures to protect themselves and others from bad judgments based on them.

Institutional Policies

Institutions play a critical role in social equality. Through their policies institutions can hurt or help the advancement of women and minorities. The procedures I have described, if incorporated into training programs for administrators, managers, and executives, should increase the percentage of qualified executive-track appointments. The fewer the errors in hiring and promotion decisions, the better off an organization is.

Effective training programs will help evaluators identify inaccurate judgments and the role that gender schemas play in those judgments. Perhaps most important, evaluators who understand that even small imbalances in treatment add up to large imbalances in outcome can then establish procedures to eliminate imbalances.

The Roles of Committed Leaders

In order for organizations to institute effective training programs—and other changes described below—they must have leaders who are committed to increasing fairness. Leaders naturally have a disproportionate impact on organizations because of their status as authorities. They can play two roles in equitable treatment of men and women. First, they can establish and publicize policies designed to increase fairness; second, they can legitimize and support the leadership of both women and men.

One piece of evidence for the influence of institutional leaders comes from a survey of personnel professionals whose work involves managing human resources (Rynes & Rosen 1995). Asked to rate the success of diversity training programs in their organization, they particularly cited the importance of the support of top management and the provision of rewards for increasing diversity. Although diversity training differs in several important respects from the educational program I have described, it is likely that a committed leadership is equally necessary for any set of procedures designed to increase fairness.

Research on personal persuasiveness suggests several reasons—aside from their obvious power to initiate change—that leaders are influential (Fiske & Taylor 1991). When people are asked to adopt new attitudes, they first assess the credibility of the person who is doing the persuading. One characteristic of a credible persuader is neutrality. A credible persuader appears to have nothing personal at stake and to have no antecedent biases; even more credibility attaches to someone who expresses a view at variance with the one we would expect him or her to advocate. A second characteristic of a credible persuader is knowledgeability; a credible persuader appears to know the facts.

Richard Nixon's overtures to China in the 1970s demonstrate credible persuasion. As a conservative president with an anticommunist pedigree and a reputation for expertise in foreign policy, Nixon was well positioned to establish diplomatic relations with China. He could not be dismissed as a liberal who was soft on communism, nor as acting out of ignorance.

Institutional leaders similarly derive their credibility from their appearance of neutrality and knowledgeability. That credibility can be used against fairness as well as for it. When General Colin Powell argued against allowing homosexuals to serve in the military, he was a more persuasive voice against fairness than a white general would have been. First, as an African American who defended a racially integrated military, he would be expected to hold other egalitarian views. His willingness to deny equality to homosexuals thus went against the bias people would have anticipated. Second, his role as head of the Joint Chiefs of Staff made him, on the face of it, knowledgeable about what would be best for the armed forces. He was thus both credible and persuasive, despite the lack of any evidence in favor of his views.

Leaders use their credibility in another important area: they legitimize other leaders by vouching for their abilities. In one study, undergraduate evaluators watched different versions of a videotape of five graduate students holding a group discussion (Brown & Geis 1984). On the tape, a male faculty member introduced one of the students as the leader. In one version the professor vouched for the student's expertise by mentioning the student's theoretical knowledge and performance ability; in another version he simply introduced the student as the discussion leader. The two videotapes were otherwise identical. After watching the video, the undergraduates evaluated the discussion leader on a number of dimensions, including leadership ability, value of contributions, desirability as an employee, and salary deserved.

The leader scored higher on all those measures if the faculty member had vouched for his or her expertise. The same effect occurred whether the student leader was male or female, and there was no difference in how positively male and female leaders were rated. (And, as usual, there was no difference in the responses of male and female evaluators.) A credible authority figure can successfully legitimize females as well as males.

In such a situation, evaluators appear to interpret the information they get directly from a potential leader's actual performance in the light of whatever information they already possess. If the prior information legitimizes the leader, his or her behavior is seen as an example of good leadership. If the prior information is not legitimizing, judges see a leader in less positive a light.

A subsequent study showed that both male and female authority figures can legitimize others' leadership (Geis, Brown, & Wolfe 1990). Using the same set of videotaped group discussions, the experimenters prepared one version with a male authority endorsing the leader and another with a female authority doing so. The two versions were equally effective in establishing the students as leaders, demonstrating that women in positions of authority can help competent aspiring women as well as men can. Authority figures can thus counteract the tendency of both women and men to judge women leaders less positively than men leaders (as reported in chapter 7).

The student evaluators were later queried about what the authority figures said about the leaders (Geis et al. 1990). Although they correctly remembered the gist of the authorities' statements, they believed that the statements had had no effect on their own judgments. People believe that their judgments are independent of others' influence, even when that influence has demonstrably contributed to those judgments.

Performance Criteria

Once evaluators have some understanding of the consequences of applying schemas to individuals, they can more readily appreciate the importance of developing and sticking to objective criteria for judging performance. Reliance on objective criteria will help us ignore a woman's femininity and a man's masculinity so that we can judge them both on the basis of their accomplishments rather than their looks.

Here, too, institutional leaders play an important role, both in emphasizing the importance of using clear criteria, and in helping direct a search for valid criteria. Objective criteria that are arbitrary, rigid, or inappropriately favor one group over another are no improvement over no criteria at all. They may even be worse, because they may give an illusion of fairness while calcifying unfairness. As noted in chapter 13, our notions of how to do a job are usually influenced by earlier jobholders' performance. Thus, we are tempted to see the traits of previous jobholders as necessary for doing the job well, rather than seeing them as one set of many that could be effective. Indeed, the incumbents' traits might even have been counterproductive. The recognition that there is more than one way to do a job well should promote a search for criteria that are valid as well as objective. The development of explicit, valid criteria will directly benefit an organization.

It is not enough, however, for organizations to develop sound criteria. For aspirants to advance, they must know what the criteria for success are. Thus, organizations must not only have equally challenging expectations for men and women, but must explicitly communicate those expectations, provide clear and constructive performance evaluations at frequent intervals, and make sure that both the content and implications of the evaluations are understood. Organizations also need to provide accurate information about the inevitability of short-term failures and the need for flexible perseverance.

Johns Hopkins—A Case Study
One example of a successful long-term program—illustrating some of the recommendations described earlier—was developed at the Johns Hopkins University School of Medicine within the Department of Medicine (Fried, Francomano, MacDonald, Wagner, Stokes, Carbone, Bias, Newman, & Stobo 1996). At medical schools throughout the United States, women are underrepresented in full professor positions. A committee at the Johns Hopkins medical school found that women faculty there, too, made less money than men and were promoted at a slower rate. In response to that finding, and to recommendations to medical schools by the American College of Physicians and the Association of American Medical Colleges to develop procedures for improving women's status, the (male) chair of the Department of Medicine appointed a committee to design an effective program.

The committee's first step was to identify problem areas by interviewing women faculty about their perceptions of the department. The material from those interviews formed the basis of a questionnaire sent to the entire faculty. The second step involved developing and implementing procedures to eliminate problems that appeared to be gender-based. The third step was to evaluate the success of the program by examining the changes in the promotion of women and changes in women's attitudes.

The committee found, for example, that women were put up for promotion later than their male peers. The problem seemed to have multiple components, ranging from evaluators failing to identify qualified women, to women themselves not knowing the criteria for promotion. The solution was aimed at all the components. Each female faculty member (and later, each male faculty member) was evaluated annually and given explicit information about her progress. A monthly meeting was begun to provide women faculty with concrete information about how to move through their professional career and how to handle different problems that might arise. Those meetings were necessary in part because mentors of male junior faculty were more likely to pass along that information than were mentors of female junior faculty. Another change was to provide senior faculty with explicit information about how to mentor, in an effort to eliminate disparities in treatment of junior men and junior women. The committee had learned, for example, that mentors invited men junior faculty to chair conferences (and thus receive public exposure) six times as often as they invited women junior faculty.

Within five years, the program became extremely successful (Fried et al. 1996). In 1990 there had been only four women associate professors; by 1995 there were twenty-six. The improvement was not due to changes in promotion criteria. What did change was women's knowledge of what was required for promotion. In 1990, only 26 percent of the women reported that they were advised about the criteria, but in 1993, 46 percent reported being advised. It is likely that knowledge of what is required for promotion helps candidates modify their behavior accordingly. Notice, too, however, that slightly over half the women still had not received information about what was needed to achieve promotion.

More subtle aspects of the women's experience also improved. In 1990, 38 percent of the women said they felt like a welcomed member of the institution, compared to 74 percent of the men. In 1993, 53 percent of the women felt welcome—a dramatic improvement within a short period of time, albeit one that still fell short of equity.

The Johns Hopkins program demonstrates that institutions can, with major efforts, significantly improve the status of their female employees. Yet the limits of the program also suggest the need for interventions that more directly acknowledge the effects of gender schemas, such as those that would train evaluators in reasoning and judging.

Costs and Benefits of Progressive Policies

The commitment of organizational leaders, as well as the specific institutional steps I have recommended in this chapter—the development and implementation of valid and objective performance criteria and of educational programs to help supervisors and managers become more accurate evaluators—all have obvious costs in time and money. We do not yet know whether such costs will be recouped by greater employee productivity, competence, satisfaction, and loyalty. There is, of course, a *prima facie* plausibility to the idea that employees will work better and harder for institutions they perceive as fair. The data we do have show that companies perceived as progressive and fair have more productive, satisfied, and loyal workers than do other companies (Arthur 1994; Grover & Crooker 1995; Hall & Parker 1993; Kinicki, Carson, & Bohlander 1992; Koys 1991). We also know that the intervention program at Johns Hopkins medical school improved both men's and women's attitudes on a variety of measures (Fried et al. 1996).

The benefits of an organization's policies, however, are broader and potentially more far-reaching than productivity gains and professional fulfillment. Every institution implicitly takes a position on its employees' personal and family lives. If employees have children, the institution takes an implicit position about who is taking care of those children.

At Johns Hopkins before the intervention program, meetings were routinely held in the evening and on weekends (Fried et al. 1996). That schedule assumed that faculty members had no important personal life and that, if they had children, someone else was bringing them up. The revised schedule instituted by the intervention program moved all meetings to normal working hours, thereby communicating the implicit assumption that faculty members had a personal life and were bringing up their children themselves.

Johns Hopkins was led to a revised schedule because of the women faculty. Sixty-three percent of the women and 28 percent of the men had reported that meetings held on weekends and after 5 P.M. were a problem. The new policy did not challenge the notion that bringing up children is a mother's job, but, because it applied to everyone, it potentially benefitted not just the 28 percent of men who disliked the old policy, but the 72 percent of men and 37 percent of women who had not complained about the after-hours schedule. With its revised schedule, the institution went on record, implicitly, as saying that a personal and family life was important.

Equalizing the Accumulation of Advantage

What makes successful women successful? This natural question assumes that there are differences, above and beyond their achievements, between women who succeed and those who don't. But the truth of that assumption is unknown. Women executives, for example, are more self-confident than women middle managers or women in general (see review in Ragins & Sundstrom 1989), but it is hard to determine cause and effect. Are women executives successful because of their high self-confidence? Or is their high self-confidence due to their advancement, and the low self-confidence of those who are unsuccessful due to their lack of success (Ragins & Sundstrom 1989)?

Informal observations of only a few cases are even less informative. Popular magazines frequently spotlight a handful of unusually successful women and describe their characteristics. I remember a newspaper article about a successful executive who had dyed her hair bright blue. The implicit message was that there were no barriers to women's success in business. Even a woman with blue hair could succeed; indeed, having blue hair could be a plus, by attracting attention. But the missing information is crucial. How many successful women have blue hair? How many women with blue hair are successful? Unless we know the full range of characteristics we cannot evaluate how typical the few examples are. With just a few examples in hand, we cannot distinguish between the exceptions and the rule.

More importantly, how many unsuccessful women have the same characteristics as the successful women? Unless we know that successful and unsuccessful women begin their professional lives with clearly distinct characteristics, information about the traits of a few successful women is useless. It is worse than useless; it is misleading. It suggests that any woman can succeed if she only goes about it in the right way. The information presented in this book, however, would lead us to expect an enormous overlap in ability and effort between successful and unsuccessful women; we know that women are less likely than men to reap the rewards of their efforts and talents.

No woman should think that if she just does everything "right" she will succeed. No woman should think that any modifications she may make in her everyday demeanor will guarantee success. Observers' views of women as a class constitute an entire structure that no individual woman can change. It is that structure that needs changing.

Each individual woman can, however, learn about the ways she is at risk and what steps she can take to modulate the effects of gender schemas. She can increase her chances of being seen as competent and thereby increase her chances of being effective. (Obviously, taking the steps to actually be competent is a prerequisite.) In the rest of this chapter, I recommend a number of strategies women can use to evade the negative consequences of gender schemas and accumulate advantage. Many of the strategies will also be useful to men.

A final reminder: in the professional world, it will be to women's advantage and men's disadvantage to circumvent gender schemas. Because gender schemas assign women a small professional minus and assign men a small professional plus, it is primarily women who will wish to be perceived and evaluated independently of their sex.

Be Where Women Are Well-Represented
Women should try to work in fields and organizations where women are well-represented. Some women fear a backlash against women as they make strides in areas formerly reserved to men. I do not dismiss such fears, but a backlash can have only limited effects if there are enough women (regardless of the beliefs of those women). In the past few years, women have earned the majority of Ph.D.s in psychology, and there are no signs of a backlash in the field; nor has it become "feminized" (Pion, Mednick, Astin, Hall, Kenkel, Keita, Kohout, & Kelleher 1996). If a woman is one of many, she is less likely to be perceived in terms of her sex and her job is less likely to be perceived as a man's job.

Be Impersonal, Friendly, and Respectful
An impersonal but friendly speaking style that conveys respect for others' opinions can help a professional of either sex be perceived as a leader, as some of the studies reviewed in chapter 7 suggest. Impersonality is less distracting to listeners; it allows them to focus their attention on the ideas being expressed. An impersonal approach is particularly effective for women, because it makes them seem less feminine, and femininity is

incompatible with competence and leadership (Heilman & Stopeck 1985; see also chapter 7).

Yet another reason for women to adopt an impersonal style is suggested by a study examining the qualities needed to be accepted as a leader. Both men and women had to demonstrate their competence, but women, in addition, had to show that they were not seeking status at the expense of other group members (Ridgeway 1982). Attempts at self-aggrandizement by women are particularly negatively perceived. Women must subordinate, and be seen to subordinate, their personal needs to the needs of the group. People do not want women to overtly defy gender schemas; those who appear too interested in their own advancement are actively challenging, rather than evading, notions of nurturance and communality.

A friendly manner and respect for others also takes some of the sting out of being competent and effective. Visible displays of competence and leadership evoke some resentment in observers, male and female alike (Butler & Geis 1990; chapter 7). Most professionals aren't eager to admire and respect others' leadership; they greet assertive behavior by either sex with negative facial expressions. Men leaders, however, also receive enough positive facial reactions to compensate for the negative ones, because leadership is congruent with the male gender schema. No one likes a ruthless martinet who has all the answers and treats other people primarily as means to an end; but we tolerate such behavior more easily in men than in women. A woman who tempers her assertiveness with a friendly, respectful manner, therefore, can counteract some of the negative reactions and thereby maintain her leadership.

We can prize honesty and candor but realize that it is not necessary to tell people exactly what we think of them or exactly what is wrong with their suggestions. A friend of mine told me he is quieter now than he used to be. He'd finally realized that his clever put-downs and witty insults were making enemies, but he usually couldn't think of anything else to say. So he didn't say anything at all, except to tolerant friends. We all alter our behavior somewhat from situation to situation and from person to person; we do not express ourselves in the same way and to the same degree in every milieu. Developing a new style for business purposes can be the best tactic if what comes naturally is likely to antagonize others.

At the same time, as observers, we can become aware of and question our own interpretations of others' personal style; we can try to put in place procedures to prevent ourselves from being overly reliant on our first impressions. Because we are all likely to respond negatively to assertive women, women as well as men can use the facts about gender and assertive leadership to guard against unthinking reactions to women's assertiveness.

Build Power

Men and women can take actions that will increase their power within an organization or group. Men are more likely than women to learn about such methods informally from mentors and colleagues, but women can seek out such information. Kanter (1979) describes several ways of achieving power, which she defines as efficacy in shaping the goals and policies of an organization or group. She suggests that activities build power if they are (a) out of the ordinary, pioneering, or not part of the job description, (b) visible to others in the group, and (c) relevant to current organizational problems.

I inadvertently discovered the accuracy of Kanter's observations when I was placed in charge of a departmental function that was in disarray. I instituted some order, and once it was running reasonably well I wrote a report summarizing what I had done and what I planned to do next. I showed the report to the department head, solicited his comments, and received his permission to circulate it to the faculty as a whole for comments. As I circulated the report I anticipated that my colleagues would react positively, but I could not articulate exactly why. When I read Kanter's article, I saw that I had satisfied her three criteria. My activity was pioneering, in that it had not been done before; by writing and circulating a report I was making the activity visible; my actions solved a current organizational problem.

Kanter also describes how to determine whether a job has the potential for building power. The less routinized the job, for example, the more power potential it has. In addition, a job with few or no predecessors has greater potential, because a new occupant has leeway in defining the dimensions of the job. The more discretion the jobholder can exercise, the more power potential there is. Kanter's (1979) article is a brief manual on how to build power, which anyone interested in advancement and leadership can study with profit (1979). It is, in essence, a lesson in how to accumulate advantage within an organization.

Seek Information

Building power requires access to information about promotion possibilities, job openings, and other opportunities for advancement. Much research indicates, however, that women are less likely than men to seek or receive such information (Ragins & Sundstrom 1989). Thus, individual women need to rectify their informational poverty by making alliances both within and outside their own institutions.

Specific, tangible information about performance criteria is essential for success. If superiors do not spell out those criteria, people must discover them for themselves and assess how well they are meeting them, perhaps with the help of others at their own rank as well as senior people.

It is difficult for newcomers to a field to know what to pay attention to. For example, some academic journals have a much higher reputation than others, yet graduate students tend to see all journals as equal in prestige. It may not occur to young assistant professors to ask where they should try to publish their work. One woman told me she was shocked to learn during her third-year evaluation that a journal's reputation was important; she had known she should publish but not that it mattered where she published.

Become an Expert

People who are knowledgeable in some area make it easier for others to respect them, especially if they convey the knowledge in a friendly fashion. As the research on eye gaze demonstrates, people will accept leaders whose power comes through expert knowledge (Dovidio, Ellyson, Keating, Heltman, & Brown 1988; see also chapter 8). A man will display at least a small amount of deference to his female conversational partner— by looking at her when she is speaking—if she knows more about the topic under discussion than he does. Other studies suggest that women in business implicitly recognize the value of becoming experts and emphasize the importance of acquiring competence, knowledge, and skill (Ragins & Sundstrom 1990).

Get Endorsed by Legitimate Authority

A woman can increase her chances of advancement within an organization by obtaining the endorsement of a legitimate authority. The authority need not be an actual person. In academia, endorsement can be gained by publishing a paper in a prestigious journal or by receiving external funding for research. Similar indirect forms of endorsement are available to women in other professions—for example, by playing an active role in a professional conference or serving on a government study commission.

Negotiate, Bargain, Seek Advancement

Women are more likely than men to behave as if they are less entitled to higher salaries, substantial resources, and promotions (chapter 8). The negotiation process does not guarantee success, but it is hard to get what you want if you don't ask for it. Role-playing with a knowledgeable friend will be good practice for the real thing.

Overcome Internal Barriers to Effectiveness

Although the data suggest that men and women perform roughly equally as professionals, there are internal psychological barriers to women's effectiveness stemming from gender schemas and the failure to appreciate the importance of accumulating advantage. Even though they may appear only sporadically, such internal difficulties may make women less effective than men and may lead to higher attrition rates.

Both women's beliefs about their abilities and women's attributional style—that is, their ways of thinking about the causes of success—can have negative consequences. First, if women underrate their abilities—in mathematics, for example—they may fail to attend to information that those abilities are necessary for success. Rather than trying harder—which they may see as futile—they may avoid acquiring a good understanding of the criteria for success.

Second, women may underestimate how much time and effort are required to do well and may see ability and effort as inversely related. If women routinely attribute their successes to factors other than ability and effort (to luck, for example), they may see the need for great effort—the only factor over which they have control—as evidence of lack of ability. The mere experience of putting forth great effort, of knocking oneself out, can come to feel like an admission of failure, a confession that one is less competent than one's peers. Seemingly paradoxically, then, some women may put in less time than is necessary to do well in order to bolster a sense of themselves as able.

Several ways of thinking about this situation may help rectify it. The first is that the overwhelming fact of achievement is that it is time-consuming. The rule, to which there are few exceptions, is that genuine accomplishment demands time and perseverance—no matter how capable one is. The second thought is that women's attributional style may be costly to the work process itself, especially if the work must be carried out independently. Doubts about one's ability and doubts about how one's work will be received tend to distract attention from the job at hand. That is true for everyone, but women are more likely than men to harbor such doubts. Women may therefore need to work longer hours than men do, not because they are less capable, but because their preoccupations can make them work less efficiently.

Third, women may fail to see that each bit of advantage is useful and is worth spending time to acquire. Women accumulate advantage more slowly than men, but they do accumulate it. Fourth, many women should modify their perceptions of the causes of their successes and failures (see discussion in Dweck 1986). They need to analyze the reasons for their successes, especially their own contributions. Luck and other uncontrollable causes no doubt play a role in success, but those causes should not eclipse the importance of women's own abilities and efforts. When women fail, on the other hand, they also need to analyze both their own possible contribution and the role of external factors, such as the failure of evaluators to judge them properly.

What all these ways of thinking amount to is intervening in one's own psychology—understanding it and changing it.

How Valuable Are Role Models?

Many advocates of gender equality stress the importance of role models, but the research findings cited throughout this book suggest a different perspective. One common conception of a role model is an ideal figure—an Eleanor Roosevelt—that others should emulate. The way to obtain the same high achievement as the ideal is to behave as she did. The problem with that conception is that the few women who are in high positions are unrepresentative, exceptional women. Not only are they very competent and hardworking, but many of them they have had unusual advantages that most women are unlikely to enjoy.

As this book has documented, women are unlikely to succeed by merit alone—because they have to overcome the odds that are in men's favor. The notion that a successful woman can serve as a role model for others is a hoax, the outcome of which is to make many women feel inferior because they are unable to follow the model. Instead of role models, people need concrete suggestions about how to do their best work and how to maximize the chances that their work will be recognized and rewarded.

People who are trailblazers are uplifting and inspirational; they demonstrate courage and a rare reach of the human spirit. In that sense, they are helpful. But observers often reason incorrectly from the example set by role models. To take one case, a letter-writer to the *New York Times* used the victory of the first African-Asian-American in a Masters golf tournament to argue against affirmative action. To quote the writer, "[Tiger Woods] just went out and took on the world and won on his own ability" (Hellmuth 1997).

A more careful reasoner replied, "If the exceptional skills of Tiger Woods . . . prove that affirmative action is unnecessary, . . . then Nelson Mandela's exceptional resilience proves that prison reform in South Africa is unnecessary. [M]aking public policy by reference to extraordinary people is silly. Public policy must address the real problems of ordinary people" (Chang 1997).

Trailblazers also help us by showing that the barriers to success are not completely insurmountable. In another 1997 first, a woman tied for first place in a notoriously difficult mathematics competition (Arenson 1997). For many women, that was an immensely cheering event.

But the more remarkable the achievement, the smaller the likelihood of equalling it. If there is only one woman in a position of authority and you are dissimilar to her, you have no reason to think that there is room for you and some reason to think there isn't. If, instead, you see a number of women with a broad range of characteristics, you have reason to think that you too could fit in. If the job is open to people of different types, it might be open to you even if someone like you is not yet represented.

That doesn't mean examples are useless. In 1977 I published an article about the strategies I had developed to write my thesis (Valian 1977). I had always found it hard to work in a consistent, timely way; working filled me with great anxiety. In the article I laid out the techniques I had developed to cope with the problem. Since then, many people have told me how helpful they found the article. One academic, Ellen, told me she kept it on her desk for the entire time she was working on her thesis and read parts of it every day.

For her, I was a role model, but not in the usual sense. I wasn't an ideal but an anti-ideal. I was someone who, at one time, could not write steadily for more than fifteen minutes a day. People like Ellen said to themselves, "If this unheroic program could help this woman, whose anxieties are at least as severe as mine, perhaps it could also help me." It had not helped Ellen to see the ideal role models among her fellow graduate students, because she was too removed from the ideal.

For women in organizations, the notion of role models communicates the idea that women simply need to try harder. Women should, of course, strive for excellence and persevere in the face of failure. But their individual efforts cannot undo the gender schemas that stand in their way. An emphasis on how an individual woman should behave places women in an impossible position unless there is an equally strong emphasis on broader remedies for what is a broader problem.

The sentiments in the phrase—"to succeed a woman has to be twice as good as a man; fortunately, that isn't difficult"—are wrong. Not only is it difficult, it is impossible. Men and women are, on average, equal in ability. Only a tiny fraction of women could be twice as good as the average successful man, just as only a tiny fraction of men could be twice as good as the average successful woman. Even worse than recommending an impossible course of action, the phrase tacitly accepts the unfairness of having to be twice as good as the price of professional achievement. It tells an individual woman that if she is not twice as good as a man she doesn't deserve success.

Rather than role models, people need equal access to information, opportunity, and recognition. People need fairness. Fairness does not guarantee that people will always be rewarded according to their merits, but that no one will be unrewarded more often than someone else because of membership in a particular group. Fairness means that an average woman has as great a chance of success as an average man.

Personal Lives

More Work and Less Work

Married women with children leave professional jobs at higher rates than married men with children do. Men spend less time than women do on personal activities such as taking care of children. Men are at risk for underrating the importance of a full life, and women are at risk for underrating the importance of the professional side of their lives.

Both groups need to change, but change is more critical for men than for women. Women have already moved into the professional world to a greater extent than men have moved into the personal world. Because of the rigidity of the male gender schema, it will be more difficult for men to change what they want. And, because few workplaces make it possible for employees of either sex to balance a fulfilling professional life with a rich personal life, people who want to change will encounter many obstacles.

Couples who want an egalitarian relationship need to plan in advance how they will create a household in which both adults work and both adults have equal responsibility for nonwork activities like housework and child care. In addition to detailed planning, equality requires a willingness to negotiate, a recognition that neither party can have everything he or she wants, and a belief that each party has something to gain from equality (B. Carter with Peters 1996).

Children

Although there is a great deal we don't yet understand about the sources of cognitive sex differences, we can take steps toward eliminating them. Parents and teachers can begin to reduce differences by having high expectations for all the children in their care, emphasizing the value of effort, and making clear that there is no single right way to approach intellectual problems.

Too little research is currently available to evaluate suggestions that girls and boys be taught in separate mathematics classes. One argument against single-sex education in any subject as a long-term method of reducing sex differences is that it ignores the root problem: we treat boys in ways that give them advantages over girls. Sex segregation temporarily puts girls out of harm's way but does not eliminate the harm.

Parents who are committed to egalitarianism can affect their children's aspirations and expectations. Children of egalitarian parents, especially daughters, have less traditional occupational preferences than children of conventional parents (Weiner & Wilson-Mitchell 1990). They are also less rigid in how they assign objects, such as a hammer, to the appropriate person.

Even among the children of egalitarian parents, girls have more sex-neutral reactions than boys do. Parents who want to bring up children who are assertive, self-reliant, independent, nurturant, expressive, and communal will find it harder to achieve their goal with boys than with girls. That is not because of anything inherent in boys' nature, but because of parents' beliefs, concerns, and fears. Parents may worry about how their son will be perceived by other children and adults if he does not adhere to gender norms. Fathers in particular have a strong commitment to certain features of the male gender schema and exercise a disproportionate influence in gender schema development. At present, fathers are less able than mothers to help their sons grow up with accurate gender perceptions.

Egalitarian parents can, however, bring up their children so that both girls and boys play with dolls and trucks, help care for younger children, are active in sports, learn self-defense, and learn how to cope with others' aggression and ridicule. Both girls and boys can aspire to a satisfying professional life with a meaningful personal life. From the standpoint of equality, nothing is more important.

Notes

Preface

1. In an interview on National Public Radio on January 9, 1993, Donna Shalala, then the newly appointed head of the Department of Health and Human Services, mentioned reading the same series of books. Carol Tavris thanks her father for the books on great women that he gave her to read as a child (1992: 381). These books were clearly salient experiences for some of us.

Chapter 1

1. Bem (1993) and others have used the expression *gender schema* in a different way. In her usage, people who are *gender schematic* tend both to typify the expectations held of their gender (e.g., males have many stereotypically masculine traits and few stereotypically feminine traits) and to apply those expectations strongly in their perception of others. For gender schematics, gender is a very important category in evaluating the self and others. By contrast, *aschematic* individuals do not markedly conform to the expectations of their gender (e.g., males may be either high or low on both masculinity and femininity); nor do they impose gender conformity on others.

In my usage, gender schemas refer to the implicit hypotheses that almost all of us share about the nature of men and women. Gender schemas are beliefs about the sexes that we hold in common—whether we want to or not.

I use the term *schemas* rather than *schemata* because the former is the norm in the psychological literature.

2. Merton (1968) dubbed the phenomenon the Matthew effect, after the following passage in one version of Matthew 13:12: "For whosoever hath, to him shall be given, and he shall have more abundance: but whosoever hath not, from him shall be taken away even that which he hath."

3. Our usual notion of women is that they talk more than men. In fact, there is little evidence for that claim. Two academic women have mentioned to me their impression that women in academia often seem either to say nothing or say too

much. One explanation for this phenomenon, if it is one, is suggested in chapter 7. My own impression, however, is that an equal, if not larger, proportion of academic men say too much.

4. Deaux (1985) and Unger (1990) draw the distinction between sex and gender in a similar way. Terminology concerning sex and gender varies from field to field and from author to author. The following view is typical of work in psychology in the 1990s: ". . . in discussing behavioral differences between human males and females, some authors reserve the term *sex* for distinctions that are biological in origin and *gender* for those thought to have psychosocial origins. . . . However, this convention assumes a great deal more knowledge than actually exists regarding the sources of male-female differences; also, it falsely dichotomizes potential influences, ignoring the possibility that behavior is shaped by a complex interplay between social and biological factors. . . . Therefore, we view the terms as interchangeable, but generally use the term *sex*" (Collaer & Hines 1995).

5. Fiske and Taylor (1991) contrast three different models of the social perceiver: the naive theorist, the cognitive miser, and the motivated tactician. In their division, the *naive theorist* acts normatively, that is, correctly weights and analyzes the information available in order to draw accurate conclusions. The *cognitive miser*, in contrast, takes shortcuts, fails to consider all the data and sometimes fails to correctly analyze the data he or she has collected. The *motivated tactician*'s analyses depend on his or her goals. Under some conditions the tactician correctly analyzes the range of data but under others uses shortcuts or reasons incorrectly.

My own use of the analogy of the perceiver as a theorist cuts across Fiske and Taylor's tripartite division. In my usage, the naive theorist does not consistently obey normative reasoning procedures (nor does the individual scientist). The "lapses" are related both to demands for cognitive economy—as suggested by the cognitive miser model—and to the need for cognition to serve different motivational goals—as suggested by the motivated tactician model. The virtue of emphasizing that social perceivers are theorists is the focus it places on people's need to understand and predict their social world. People do not approach their social world with a set of pre-established heuristics or strategies; they attempt to develop a coherent picture.

6. The performing arts are a possible exception: women earn high salaries as performers.

Chapter 2

1. Subsequent studies of infants from 4 to 16 months in age show that observers respond to infants' actual sex as well as to their gender label, at least in part because children are already responding in sex-differentiated ways to parents and strangers (Burnham & Harris 1992; Lewis, Scully, & Condor 1992). For example, children between 11 and 16 months showed sex differences in the way they reacted to their mothers when strangers played with them. Baby girls tended to stay closer to their mother than boys did and to relate to a female stranger

better than a male stranger. Both boys and girls were likely to choose masculine toys when a male stranger played with them (Lewis et al. 1992). Thus, adult strangers asked to evaluate the children had cues from the children's behavior which affected their evaluations.

A second study showed adults videotapes of infants 4 to 8 months in age who were sitting on their mothers' laps. The study did not, however, measure possible differences in the ways the infants responded to their mothers or the ways their mothers treated them. Thus, the finding that observers generally judged actual boys to be less "sensitive" than actual girls is hard to evaluate. When the college students among the observers were asked to guess the sex of the children, they could not do so at levels better than chance. Of the 4 boys in the study, 2 were correctly identified; of the 4 girls, only 1 was correctly identified (Burnham & Harris 1992). It seems likely that young infants give off few reliable indications of their sex.

A review of studies on perceptions of children finds some inconsistency from study to study but few contradictions with what would be expected on the basis of people's beliefs about sex differences. In general, the effects of labeling a child as one sex or another are small to moderate (Stern & Karraker 1989). Infants begin to show sex-differentiated behavior rather early, and those differences have an effect on adults' perceptions over and above the label applied to the child. Children and college students seem to be more affected by the child's label than mothers are. Children and college students judge 9-month-olds labeled as girls as smaller, nicer, softer, and more beautiful than the same children labeled as boys (Vogel, Lake, Evans, & Karraker 1991). Mothers, in contrast, attend more to a child's actual characteristics and are more accurate in judging children they have never before encountered.

2. Some of the similarities, such as equal discouragement of aggression, whether the aggressor is male or female, may seem surprising. There was a small differ-ence, with parents tending to discourage aggression more in girls than in boys. Lytton & Romney (1991) point out that they combined different measures of the same variable, which—because some measures show no differences at all or show differences in the other direction—would have the effect of reducing the magni-tude of differences (see also chapter 3).

In the specific case of aggression, it is not clear what prediction one would make about parental reactions to aggression. Parents might have different reasons for discouraging aggression in girls and boys. They might, for example, consider aggression in girls as less appropriate but see the potential for escalation of vio-lence as higher for boys. Thus, parents could discourage aggression equally in boys and girls but have different underlying motivations for doing so.

3. Cross-cultural data are lacking, but anecdotal evidence from colleagues in western Europe suggests that other cultures do not penalize women professionally for being stereotypically attractive. Stylish clothing and make-up do not signify a lesser commitment to professional achievement or lesser ability. The difference may reflect a greater interest in clothing among both males and females in western Europe compared to the U.S.

4. For both sexes, duty and a sense of obligation can be important reasons for performing certain tasks.

5. The responses of the children's peers were also observed, but here I describe only the parents' reactions.

6. Some readers have been astonished at the idea of a couple spending 51 hours a week in housework—a little more than 7 hours a day 7 days a week. Since households with young children as well as households with no children are included in such studies, the estimates may include child care. Some studies report lower figures. One estimate for two-earner couples, including both those with and without children, estimated 34–36 hours a week for meal preparation, dishes, shopping, bill paying, laundry, yardwork, repairs, and housecleaning (Ferree 1991, from 1989 data). That comes to 5 hours a day 7 days a week—still a lot of housework!

Chapter 3

1. The meta-analysis by Lytton and Romney (1991), which looked only at parents, shows no overall differences in discouragement of aggression in boys and girls. Fagot and Hagan's (1985) study compared teachers and peers.

2. Not all studies report differences in teachers' treatment of elementary students. One English study, for example, observed 32 elementary school teachers and 38 high school teachers (Merrett & Wheldall 1992). The elementary teachers—males and females alike—gave praise and criticism equally to boys and girls. Further, there were no sex differences in how much the children focused on the class lesson. At the high school level, however, teachers responded about twice as often to boys as to girls, both positively and negatively. Male teachers, in particular, gave more positive responses to boys' academic behavior than to girls'. Like the primary school students, the boys and girls in secondary school were equally focused on classroom activities.

   One study of U.S. college classrooms found no differences in the ways faculty responded to male and female students, and few sex differences in students' classroom behaviors (Cornelius, Gray, & Constantinople 1990). The ubiquity of teachers' differential treatment of students is thus open to question.

3. My interpretation here and in a few other places differs from Langlois and Downs's (1980). I found their categories of distal reward and punishment neither rewarding nor punishing and have therefore largely ignored those results. In addition, I have attended more to the pattern of individual means, while Langlois and Downs attended more to overall means.

4. Thorne (1993) points out that investigators have concentrated on sex-segregation in play, neglecting the times when children play together. She notes that an adequate understanding of children's play and the role of gender in play requires casting a wider net. Sex differences in play are not rigid and omnipresent.

5. Since the study did not ask the children about female-stereotyped abilities like spelling, it is possible that the sex differences reflect attitudes toward academic

work in general rather than toward math in particular. Earlier work (Stipek 1984) showed that 5th and 6th grade girls rated themselves as equally competent in spelling and math, but their self-ratings in math were lower than boys'. Thus, boys' self-ratings seem to be higher in math than in other subjects, while girls' self-ratings tend to be lower in academic work in general than boys' are in math.

6. Some work (e.g., Dweck, Davidson, Nelson, & Enna, 1978) has suggested that teachers praise boys for the intellectual content of their work and praise girls for the form of their work, or that boys are asked higher-level questions than girls are (e.g., Becker 1981). Other studies, however, have failed to replicate such findings. There may be a great deal of variation from one classroom to the next; girls in some classrooms may receive less challenging and less relevant comments than boys do. Those differences may be particularly marked in higher-level math courses (Brophy 1985). But clear, overt, differences favoring boys in grammar school have not been documented.

Chapter 4

1. Most behavioral endocrinologists distinguish between organizational and activational effects of sex hormones. Sex hormones secreted in utero determine the development of the gonads and genitalia and affect brain organization. There are sex differences in brain morphology (see summary in Kimura 1996), ranging from brain lateralization to average size differences of certain structures. Little is known, however, about the mechanism of neural organization or the significance of neural sex differences. After they are born, humans do not secrete sex hormones again until puberty. At that time, the hormones are thought to exert activational effects on brains that are already organizationally different. In discussing the effects of environment, I do not suggest that environmental factors can alter a prior organization of the brain. Rather, I suggest that the activational effects are inherently variable for the behaviors of interest. For an interesting discussion of the conceptual limitations of the organizational-activational distinction, see Moore (1985).

2. Kimura and Hampson (1994) report that males' scores on sex-neutral tests—tests on which males and females typically score equally well—do not fluctuate as a function of season. That suggests both that males are not inherently more variable than females and that the variability they do demonstrate is linked to testosterone.

3. Hall and Kimura (1995) and Kimura (1996) also speculate that early-arising neural organizational differences between male heterosexuals and homosexuals may underlie differences in the ability to throw accurately. At present, there are no data to either confirm or refute this possibility. Practice cannot be definitively ruled out, since homosexual males tend to be less involved in sports than heterosexual males; controlling for childhood sports history reduced but did not eliminate the differences. A further complication is that homosexual females' skill at throwing does not differ significantly from that of heterosexual males,

homosexual males, or heterosexual females, though they tend to perform some-what better than the latter two groups.

4. Although brain morphology probably cannot be changed, its significance is in part determined by the activating effects of hormones. For example, as noted in the text, individual males' spatial performance varies as a function of circulating testosterone level, even though their brain morphology is unlikely to change diurnally or seasonally. As also noted, females with higher than average testosterone levels are indistinguishable in their spatial performance from males with lower than average levels, even though the circulating testosterone levels differ by a factor of 2. Thus, what would be a very small amount of testosterone in a male is a large amount in a female, and has similar effects, despite—or because of—differences in brain morphology. Finally, the role of early childhood experience in modifying the development of brain morphology is largely unknown. We can conclude that observable sex differences that are mediated in part by sex differences in brain morphology are also mediated by hormonal and social factors.

5. The definition does not require that every female be capable of giving birth, just as the definition of humans as bipedal does not require that every human be born with two feet.

6. My conclusion here differs from that of several authors (e.g., Berk 1989; Maccoby & Jacklin 1980), who note that some activity studies show no sex differences; those authors also emphasize aggression rather than activity differences. The meta-analysis cited here, however, is more reliable than a partial narrative review, and I have relied on it for that reason.

Chapter 5

1. The decline does not appear to be due to inclusion of more "gender-neutral" test items over time (Feingold 1988).

2. The male-to-female variance ratios—the extent to which male scores are more variable than female scores—have fluctuated fairly widely across samples and across time, showing no clear trend. The NAEP data more uniformly show slightly increasing variance ratios over time. Several studies have commented on the existence and significance of greater male variability (Hedges & Nowell 1995; Lubinski & Benbow 1992; Feingold 1992; Geary 1996). To summarize the data, greater male variance is found in most cognitive areas, but not all (e.g., the SAT-Verbal and PSAT-Verbal show no male-female differences in variability (Feingold, 1992), in most cultures but not all (Feingold, 1994), and at some time periods but not others. There is no clear pattern to the differences, suggesting the influence of unknown social and environmental factors. Finally, no one has correlated male variability with time of year to see what role seasonal variation may play in calculations of greater male variance.

Although some authors have used the finding of greater male variability in some test areas to suggest an inherent sex difference between males and females (e.g.,

Lubinski & Benbow 1992), the cross-cultural and cross-temporal variability does not support such an interpretation.

3. The children from the U.S. do not seem to have been more variable in their scores than the Taiwanese or Japanese groups, so differences are unlikely to be due to the relatively greater ethnic or class homogeneity of the Japanese and Taiwanese samples.

4. Mills et al. (1993) performed a factor analysis which divided the problems into three types. Because it is difficult to provide a conceptual definition for the factors, and because there was relatively little difference in children's performance on them, I have ignored the separation.

5. Not all studies indicate that teachers and parents have lower expectations of girls than boys. There seems to be considerable variation from one classroom to another and from one family to another. When there are differences in expectations, however, they are always in the same direction, that boys will do better than girls. It is likely that both boys and girls encounter such expectations in some situations. However, attitudes alone do not explain all of the sex differences in math.

6. One study (Casey, Pezaris, & Nuttal 1992) found that adding spatial performance improved prediction of the mathematical achievement of eighth-grade boys and girls only slightly after general scholastic aptitude and verbal performance were taken into account. Scores in the latter two areas accounted for 49 to 69 percent of the variance in scores; spatial ability accounted for only another 3 percent. Like the data cited in the text, these findings suggest that spatial ability makes only a small, independent contribution to mathematical ability. (Casey et al. found differences in girls as a result of handedness patterns, but those differences are incidental to the main point being made here.)

7. The lack of correlation for males could not be explained by the restricted range of scores.

8. Criticisms of studies with girls with CAH have included their exposure to cortisone, their sometimes prolonged surgical history and its concomitant physical problems (such as salt-wasting), and the possibility that parents treat them differently (Bem 1993; Fausto-Sterling 1985). More recent studies have eliminated some of the problems by more selective sampling of children and by use of better control groups. It seems unlikely that the particular pattern of traits and behaviors seen in girls with CAH is unrelated to androgen (Collaer & Hines 1995).

9. Especially if rotations are difficult, women remain less accurate than men, even though they improve (Delgado & Prieto 1996). With easier rotations, at least one study found similar accuracy but slower times for women (Kail, Carter, & Pellegrino 1979). In the same study, women's scores were more variable than men's, with about 30 percent of the women taking longer than any of the men. The aggregate data on mental rotation may thus give a misleading picture of sex differences (Favreau & Everett 1996). It is possible that a subset of females, whose other characteristics are not known, are largely responsible for the overall differences.

Chapter 6

1. See footnotes 1 and 5 in chapter 1.

2. Gilligan (1982) has been interpreted as suggesting that males and females tend to have different moral codes. The evidence, however, does not support that hypothesis; it suggests that males and females have the same moral codes (Beal 1994 and Tavris 1992). A recent, well-designed study of undergraduates showed that males and females made the same types of moral judgments and used the same types of moral reasoning to the same degree (Wark & Krebs 1996). The only sex difference was in what sorts of moral dilemmas males and females spontaneously reported. Women tended to report dilemmas involving conflicting demands or others' needs, while men tended to report dilemmas involving transgressions or temptations. Queried about a dilemma of the same type, however, men and women reasoned similarly.

3. I first read this passage in Barnett, Marshall, Raudenbush, and Brennan (1993).

4. People also often speak of the sun coming up or going down, even though they know that they live in a heliocentric universe; such usage is simply a *façon de parler*. Reference to the opposite sex, however, does not seem merely a figure of speech but a reflection of an underlying belief that only gods can be simultaneously masculine and feminine.

5. Many theorists have attempted to explain the ubiquity of the sexual division of labor and the higher value placed on male activities (e.g., Chodorow 1978; Dinnerstein 1976; Mitchell 1984; Ortner 1974; Rosaldo 1974). The cognitive approach I adopt here is compatible with those interpretations, which seek to explain a range of phenomena outside the scope of this book.

6. No questions have been raised about homosexuals' competence; indeed, military brass have gone on record asserting homosexuals' competence (Herek 1993). Since homosexual males' sexual orientation violates the male military schema, how could they be adjudged competent? What seems to have happened is that secrecy has allowed them to be evaluated on the basis of their performance.

Chapter 7

1. The main focus of the Greenhaus and Parasuraman study (1993) was race differences in evaluations. Supervisors were less likely to rate African-Americans as highly successful compared to whites. They were also less likely to attribute blacks' success to ability, compared to their ratings for whites. In general, male-female differences were smaller than black-white differences in the supervisors' ratings.

2. Carli, LaFleur, and Loeber (1995) report similar results in a experiment in which people rated the performance of other (trained) students on a number of dimensions. The male and female trained students adopted different postures and

speaking styles but conveyed the same content. Male raters found women who spoke quickly, firmly, and confidently more threatening and less likable than men with the same characteristics. Most important, male raters were less influenced by women with the confident style than they were by men with the same style.

3. One meta-analysis came to a different conclusion about the importance of bias against women. It looked at 123 studies concerned with evaluations of material, often prose passages, sometimes job applications, supposedly produced by either a male or female (Swim, Borgida, Maruyama, & Myers 1989). The effects of evaluation bias effects were very small when averaged across studies, but from study to study, the findings varied a great deal, suggesting the possible influence of other variables. For example, material that was sex-neutral tended to be judged more negatively when produced by a woman than a man, while material that was stereotypically feminine showed no such tendency. Evaluators of job applications showed larger biases against women than evaluators of ordinary prose passages did. In both cases, however, the effects were relatively small.

Taken at face value, the meta-analysis (Swim et al. 1989) would suggest that bias is present only to a small degree. I think, however, that the meta-analysis presents certain internal problems because of the experiments it reviewed. A general difficulty with meta-analyses, on which I rely heavily in this book, is that some behaviors and characteristics are easier to measure than others. Cognitive skills like reading and solving word problems, for example, are relatively easy to measure, and there is great similarity in the measures used from one study to another. Meta-analyses based on such studies are highly trustworthy.

Evaluations of professional competence are more difficult to measure, because there are no agreed-upon, standardized measures. Many studies thus use a variety of measures, with the aim of determining which judgments reflect expectations of competence and which do not. In addition, there is variation from study to study in the measures used. When meta-analyses average all the measures (as in Swim et al. 1989), the result can easily be a wash (see relevant discussion in Lytton & Romney 1991).

For example, Swim et al. refer to a study in which experimental subjects evaluated men's and women's requests for a leave of absence (Rosen, Jerdee, & Prestwich 1975). The participants were more likely to grant a woman's request based on family responsibilities than they were to grant a similar man's request. That result is consistent with stereotypes about women as less professionally committed than men. In the meta-analysis, however, the result would be coded as indicating a positive bias toward women and thus would help to average out other findings showing a bias against women. (In fact, that particular study was excluded from the meta-analysis because its results made it an outlier; still, the point of the example is clear.)

There is no easy solution to the problem. It would also have been inappropriate for the reviewers to look only at measures that show a difference in evaluations of men and women. What is needed is agreement about which measures reveal attitudes about male and female competence, and that agreement is lacking.

4. Laboratory studies probably underestimate the extent of inaccurate perceptions of women in the workplace (Eagly et al. 1992). Most laboratory studies

use college students or business students as experimental subjects, and students' evaluations tend to show less bias than those of nonmanagerial employees.

5. Not all studies of attractiveness have come up with the same results. A different study asked college students to evaluate six college-age men and women who were fictitiously described as management trainees (Spencer & Taylor 1988). The people to be rated varied both in attractiveness and in the positiveness of their supervisors' performance ratings. There were no sex differences in the students' attributions of ability to high-performing attractive or unattractive trainees. Attractive females were, however, perceived as owing their success to luck and supervisory bias. Because of the many differences in procedure between this study and Heilman and Stopeck (1985), it is difficult to directly compare the results.

Another study found that college students evaluated attractive male and female candidates for the job of police officer more highly than unattractive males and females (Drogosz & Levy 1996). It is possible that the cost of attractiveness for women is decreasing. Again, however, differences between this experiment and the one described in the text make them difficult to compare. For example, although the job of police officer is held predominantly by males, it requires different characteristics than the job of assistant vice president. Nor did the police-ratings experiment require participants to rate such characteristics as ability. Finally, one aspect of the procedure used in the police study may have reduced the likelihood that participants would base their decisions on either sex or attractiveness. Each participant evaluated four fictitious employees—one attractive female, one attractive male, one unattractive female, and one unattractive male. Given the data on the effects of the candidate pool described later in this chapter, a pool of two males and two females, half attractive and half unattractive, could have reduced the impact of each variable. The research design could also have made the variables of interest known to the participants; in such an experiment, it is generally preferable not to show participants each item.

Finally, a study looking at ratings of potential job candidates by personnel professionals found no differential effects of attractiveness due to sex (Morrow, McElroy, Stamper, & Wilson 1990). As the investigators point out, however, the participants in their experiment also rated more than one person, which, again, could have made the variables the experimenters were interested in salient to the participants. In addition, professionals in human resource management would probably be on guard against making differential ratings.

Chapter 8

1. Gaze has culture-specific meanings. In Korea, for example, it is considered presumptuous for a social inferior to look at a superior.

Chapter 9

1. The word *men* is used without modification, but the statement may hold only for white men. We do not know whether observers have the same expectations of

professional black men, compared to white or black women, that they have of white men. Salary patterns in computer-related fields (Robinson & McIlwee 1989) suggest gender and race interact: black men receive higher salaries than white or black women but lower salaries than white men. At the same time, white women are more highly represented, proportionate to their number, in professional life than are African-American men or women (Sokoloff 1992).

2. Men are, of course, usually evaluated and ranked according to their ability. But when there is ambiguity about someone's performance, observers give men the benefit of the doubt.

3. It is not clear why task difficulty is more frequently invoked to account for women's failure than for men's. One possible explanation is that ability and task difficulty are linked in people's minds and that the nature of the link depends on the kind of ability being considered. If I am very able in some domain and you are not, a task that is easy for me will be difficult for you. If I see you as low in ability and you fail at the task, I can indicate a belief in your low ability by labeling the task as too hard. It is too hard *for you*. But if I see your ability as high in some domain, and you fail at the task, I will infer that the task was too hard, period. In the experimental studies, where few tasks are extremely hard, attributing failure to task difficulty may be another way of indicating low ability.

Swim and Sanna (1996) point out a methodological difficulty that complicates interpretation of the attribution studies. In some of them, experimenters pitted some attributions against each other by, for example, forcing the attributions to add up to 100 percent. In such a case, if one attribution is very prominent, all the others have to be less so. Studies using measures that pit one score against another gave different results for failure than studies where the scores were independent of each other. Scores for low ability, difficult task, and bad luck were all affected by the use of dependent measures. Only lack of effort showed the same pattern in both ways of measuring attributions. Thus, the one secure finding from the pattern of results on failure is that lack of effort is more likely to be used to explain a man's failure than a woman's.

4. There are conceptual and methodological problems with studies that examine people's explanations of their own successes and failures. The attribution process is a complicated and subtle one, difficult to simulate effectively in a laboratory setting and difficult to probe via questionnaires. Moreover, few studies of gender and attribution were performed in the 1990s. For those reasons, I have made only limited use of attribution studies. Some of the problems with this research are detailed in this extremely long note.

First, most studies allow respondents to choose only a narrow range of causes for success and failure. Few of them allow people to attribute their success or failure at a task to their gender, thus limiting the conclusions that can be drawn. A related problem is that people have at their disposal a host of reasons to explain their successes and failures.

Most people have a reasonably accurate picture of their abilities, if not in absolute terms, at least in relative terms. Joan, for example, is likely to know that she is better at softball than basketball. She also knows how much effort she typically puts into a game and knows something about her competitors. If Joan plays especially poorly in a particular softball game, her self-knowledge should prevent her from chalking up her poor performance to a lack of softball ability. If, in addition, she perceives herself as trying hard and as having an average set of conditions to contend with, she is likely to see luck as a minor component of her poor play. How then does she explain her performance? She may come up with a variety of reasons, such as preoccupation with other matters, clutching, fatigue, or just an off day. The limitations imposed on the answers people can give in a laboratory experiment cannot capture that variety and, hence, give us only partial insight into people's attributions.

Another explanation for success most studies ignore is interpersonal relationships. When they are included as possible reasons, male and female senior administrators accord them—especially professional contacts—considerable weight, though less weight than they accord ability and effort (Russo, Kelly, & Deacon 1991).

A second problem with most studies is that they look at single tasks or at exam grades in courses, where relatively little is at stake. Relatively few studies, as Fiorentine (1988) points out, examine actual professionals or natural settings. Experiments focusing on grades in one course or on performance of a single task may tap only a diluted vein of attributions. People are unlikely to care much or be deeply involved in a single task or course (unless it is critical to their professional future). As a result, genuine differences between groups of people may not show up.

The few existing studies of actual professionals have yielded mixed results. One study of junior and middle managers asked them to describe one of their successful performances and one of their unsuccessful ones (Rosenthal, Guest, & Peccei 1996). For each performance the managers rated four different explanations. In the case of success, the possible explanations were the person's skills and abilities, hard work, positive circumstances (luck), or the relative ease of the task. In the case of failure, the possibilities were the person's deficiencies in skill and ability, lack of effort, and so on. The only sex differences appeared in interpretations of success: women attributed their success to their ability less often than men did. Since the managers were free to describe any incidents they chose, we would expect them to choose successes that would showcase their ability and failures that would highlight external factors over which they had little control. In that context, it is perhaps revealing that women nevertheless did not attribute a successful performance to ability as often as men did. It is impossible to know whether women were realistic and men boastful in rating their abilities or whether women were overly modest and men were appropriately proud.

A third problem with these attribution experiments is that they seldom measure or manipulate expectations, which often affect attributions. If people do not expect to succeed in a task, they are less likely to attribute a subsequent success to their ability than if they expect to succeed, because expectations reflect estimates of ability (Deaux 1976; Deaux & Farris 1977).

In one experiment that did manipulate expectations, groups of men and women were asked to complete an anagram task (Deaux & Farris 1977). One group was told that men typically performed better than women, and the other group was told that women typically performed better than men. When the task was described as one in which men typically outperformed women, men were assumed to have more of a stake in doing well. If they failed, they would see themselves as less masculine. For that reason, we would expect men to be unwilling to ascribe their failure to lack of ability. As predicted, the men who performed poorly on the "male" anagram task were less likely to blame their lack of ability than men who performed poorly on the "female" anagram task. Men seem particularly likely to avoid explaining their failures as due to a lack of ability in areas where they believe men do better than women. Deaux and Farris also found that men invoked lack of ability less often than women did in explaining failure, contrary to the results of one meta-analysis (Whitley, McHugh, & Frieze 1986). Women in the experiment were particularly likely to attribute their failure to lack of ability when the task was defined as one on which men typically scored better. In such a study, therefore, knowing about participants' expectations would help us evaluate the results. Yet most attribution studies do not contain that information.

Fourth, the rating scales used in the studies are ambiguous, leading to methodological problems in measuring attributions (Deaux 1976). Three experiments illustrate problems with the instructions given to participants. In the Deaux and Farris (1977) experiment, the experimenters asked college students to solve anagrams and then to rate their overall success or failure in the task, their ability (presumably at the task), the effort they expended, the task difficulty, and the role of luck, among other ratings. The ability scale ranged from 1 to 10, with 1 representing very low ability and 10 very high ability. A participant could interpret that scale as asking how much ability they *have in general* at anagrams or how much ability they *demonstrated* on that particular occasion.

A participant who received easy anagrams and therefore solved a large number of them, might think his or her ability in general was relatively low, say, 3, and thus check 3. Alternatively, the participant might check 7, because he or she solved so many anagrams on that particular occasion. A participant who received very difficult anagrams and therefore solved very few, might still rate his or her general ability as relatively high, say, 7, even though that level of ability was insufficient to guarantee a good performance on that particular occasion. On the other hand, the person might be affected by that day's poor performance and thus rate his or her ability as fairly low, say, 3. A rating of 7 could thus mean different things to different people.

In another experiment, Travis, Burnett-Doering, and Reid (1982) asked participants to estimate, on a 15-point scale, the extent to which a success resulted from the person's ability. Although stated in causal terms, the question conflates estimates of ability and causation. A participant could rate his or her ability as not very high but still consider it the critical factor in his or her success; the participant would, therefore, check a high number. If the same person saw ability as unimportant to the task, she or he would check a low number. Another participant might see her or his ability as very high and either think it had played a small role in being successful—in which case he or she would check a low number—or think it played a large role—in which case he or she would check a high number.

Because the actual basis of participants' choices is unknown, it is hard to draw any firm conclusions from the data.

In a third experiment, Sweeney, Moreland, and Bruber (1982) asked college students to say how important ability was in explaining an examination grade, again a request for a causal evaluation. But if a participant is asked to explain a poor examination grade and is faced with a 7-point scale for ability, with "unimportant" at one end and "important" at the other end, it is hard to know how to interpret the results. Someone who thinks her ability is high might check "unimportant," in the belief that the grade did not reveal her ability, making that ability unimportant. Or the same person might check "important," in the belief that her high ability enabled her to do as well as she did, given, say, lack of background, lack of sleep, or high test anxiety. Someone who thought his ability was low could check "important," seeing low ability as responsible for his poor grade. But he could also check "unimportant," if he sees his low ability as irrelevant to the grade. Thus, one cannot unequivocally interpret a rating of "important": the person who checks "important" might see her or his ability as either high or low, and similarly for "unimportant."

As these three experiments demonstrate, the instructions are so open-ended that participants can give them a wide range of interpretations. That problem—combined with the problems of a restricted choice of attributions, use of successes and failures of relatively low importance, and lack of knowledge of participants' expectations—makes it hard to rely on attribution experiments.

5. I am concentrating here on the dominant culture in the U.S. Within certain subcultures, masculinity can work differently.

6. Whitley et al.'s (1986) meta-analysis includes 28 studies published between 1971 and 1982; no more current meta-analysis of self-attributions exists. I have included references to later studies, as well as to some studies that appeared between 1971 and 1982 but were excluded from the meta-analysis for reasons that are irrelevant to my purposes. Whitley et al. divided the studies into two main types, those that used informational wording (7) and those that used causal wording (21); they reported results both for the 28 studies as a whole and for each of the two types.

My analysis ignores the causal-informational distinction, because I do not always agree with the classification (e.g., Deaux & Farris 1977). Further, in at least one study (Deaux & Farris 1977), reverse-scoring should have been used to determine ability attributions in failure conditions and was not, making it appear as if men were more likely than women to blame their failure on lack of ability when the reverse was the case. Swim and Sanna (1996) also found it difficult to differentiate between cause and information in several of the experiments reviewed.

The overall differences Whitley et al. report are small, leading them to conclude that men and women are attributionally more alike than different. I agree with that conclusion, but I think the results are somewhat misleading, because of the problems discussed in note 4, and because they did not distinguish between tasks at which men would be expected to do better and those at which women would be expected to do better (Swim & Sanna 1996). The attributional differences in certain areas may be greater than it appears from the studies available.

7. Increasingly, African-American men and Latinos who succeed are portrayed as owing their success to affirmative action procedures. The benefits white men accrue from success are thereby denied to minority men. Under some conditions, race overrides gender.

For minority men, masculinity is not straightforwardly reinforced by success. Actions that might otherwise seem mysterious—such as proposals by some successful minority men that affirmative action programs (intended to counter the negative effects of racism and sexism) should be abolished—can be explained in the light of the interaction of race and gender schemas. Some successful minority men feel robbed of the benefits white men obtain from their successes and stigmatized by affirmative action. In criticizing such programs, minority men express their belief that they could have been successful on the basis of merit alone. The only flaw in their reasoning is the false presupposition that white men have been successful on the basis of merit alone.

Chapter 10

1. Ethnic minorities are extremely underrepresented in the professions. There are few data separately tracking the progress of nonmajority ethnic groups in upper management positions. (See Sokoloff 1992 for data on and an analysis of race and sex.)

2. Eighteen percent of all female lawyers in the study were admitted to the bar between 1970 and 1974; 82 percent were admitted between 1975 and 1979 (calculated from Curran et al. 1985, table 1.3.3). The comparable figures for male lawyers are 41 percent and 59 percent.

3. My computations used the following data from Curran et al. (1985). From Table 1.3.3 I calculated that between 1971 and 1974 6,230 women and 80,678 men were admitted to the bar, and that between 1975 and 1979 27,703 women and 114,542 men were admitted. For that decade, then, 18 percent of the women and 41 percent of the men in the study were admitted in the years 1971 to 1974. From Table 1.7.14 I calculated that in 1980 there were 13,505 women associates and 1,081 women partners, compared to 67,592 men associates and 23,516 men partners. I then made two simplifying assumptions: (1) that roughly 18 percent of the total women and 41 percent of the total men were admitted between 1971 and 1974; (2) that no men or women from the 1975–1979 cohort were partners in 1980. (Both assumptions are oversimplifications but should not affect the validity of the conclusion.) Thus, 2,625 of the decade's women in law firms were admitted between 1971 and 1974, and 37,354 of the decade's men were admitted between 1971 and 1974. Those figures provided the denominators, and the number of female and male partners provided the numerators: 1,081 of the 2,625 women from the 1971–1974 cohort, or 41 percent, were partners in 1980; 23,516 of the 37,354, or 63 percent, were partners.

4. Date of birth data were available only for 633, or 29 percent, of the total sample of 2,182 lawyers. I am assuming that the data are representative. Epstein et al. (1995) also note that lateral hires (hires from other firms) appear to be more common for female than male attorneys, who are more likely to be promoted from within. Billable hours were measured only for a subset of the sample; among full-time workers there were no sex differences.

5. Weiss and Lillard (1982), cited by Spurr (1990), argue that women academics' lower productivity accounts for their slower promotion rate. They used the same stochastic model for academics that Spurr used for lawyers and found that women were required to reach a lower standard than men. Spurr points out certain features of their analysis that might account for the differences between their findings for academics and his findings for lawyers. First, Weiss and Lillard assumed that all institutions use the same standard for promotion; in fact, Spurr made a similar assumption himself, but, because his sample was much more homogeneous, it was more justified. Second, they included people after they left an institution, whereas Spurr restricted his analysis to success within a given institution. As a result, Weiss and Lillard counted someone who, within 5 years, left a state university for a job at a community college and became an associate professor there as more productive than someone who, within 6 years, became an associate professor at an elite university.

6. Resnick's (1990) report is based on a survey conducted by Altman and Weil; full data are not available to the scholarly community except by purchase at a substantial price. Franklin's (1992) articles summarize results of a study by Ernst and Young conducted for the Association of the Bar of the City of New York and the American Corporate Counsel Association. Again, full data are not available to the scholarly community except by purchase at a substantial price. France's (1994) data summarize a study conducted by Price Waterhouse.

7. I used the same procedures detailed in note 3 to control for the varying admission rates of women throughout the 1970s. The simplifying assumptions, however, probably oversimplify more drastically for the judiciary than they do for private law firms: some admittees from the 1975 to 1979 cohort are likely to have become judges. Further, judges are more likely to be chosen from outside the judiciary than law partners are likely to be chosen from outside that firm's associates. In any event, the assumption that all judges came from the 1971–1974 admission cohort still yields a sex disparity: 73 percent of males compared to 44 percent of females were judges.

Chapter 11

1. Because northeastern and mid-Atlantic schools pay better than those in other regions, I restrict the institutions sampled, for the most part, to those areas. In the case of the elite public universities, however, this was not possible, because there are none in the northeast.

2. The median is the score above which 50 percent of the scores lie and below which the other 50 percent lie. It is thus less affected by extreme values than is the arithmetic mean, in which all scores are added and divided by the total. Using median scores makes it unlikely that males who earn very high salaries will exaggerate male-female income disparities.

3. There are various differences in the ways the data for humanists and for scientists and engineers were tabulated; exact quantitative comparisons are thus not possible, although more general comparisons, such as those made in the text, are justified.

4. The variation may therefore simply reflect regression to the mean.

5. Why young female and male biologists fare equally well is not known. One possible explanation comes from a study in which senior biologists rated a small group of junior biologists on a four-point scale (Sonnert 1995). Although not asked to do so, the senior biologists implicitly took quality, as well as quantity, of publications into account. Their ratings of women were slightly higher than those of the men, a difference that disappeared when citation rate was adjusted for. Taken together, the data suggest that biologists' assessments are more sensitive than those of other scientists to quality and that that difference helps women achieve parity.

6. The AAUP figures are from institutions reporting tenure information. Some institutions do not have a tenure system. Because women are likely to be overrepresented at such institutions, the disparity between the percentage of men who are tenured and the percentage of tenured women is larger than the figures in the text indicate.

7. Although the study is dated, more recent data from the National Science Foundation confirm the pattern Rosenfeld found, in less detail. Unfortunately, the American Psychological Association figures cited earlier do not include cohort or matching information and thus do not address the questions Rosenfeld asks.

Chapter 12

1. Although VMI claimed that the institution would change fundamentally if women were admitted, when it lost its appeal and prepared to admit women it decided not to change its procedures (Allen 1996). The decision was apparently made in the expectation that women would be unable to tolerate VMI's adversative methods and would drop out. What VMI was unable to win in the courts it would try to win through strict application of its methods.

After the Supreme Court decision, VMI's alumni association tried to raise $100 million to buy the school from the state of Virginia. If the school were private, the government could not force it to accept women. The school's superintendent claimed that he could raise the money "with 10 phone calls" (Allen 1996), but he was not an accurate prophet: the $100 million did not materialize. The alumni association did spend more than $10 million in court-related costs in their rear-guard attempt to keep women out. The Citadel, a military school in South Carolina, spent $7 million fighting the same battle (Allen 1996).

2. My discussion of the variables and theory related to human capital is very limited. In particular, it leaves out factors such as the role of an expanding or contracting economy, the relative diminution of manufacturing jobs compared to service jobs, corporate downsizing, the change in the duties of jobholders in certain categories, and the effects of sex segregation in jobs. For a fuller picture, see Blau and Ferber (1992), Goldin (1990), Madden (1985), O'Neill (1991), and Reskin and Roos (1990).

3. Men's advantage above and beyond their greater human capital is often termed discrimination. Some applications of *residualism*—that is, taking the residual unexplained disparity in regression equations as evidence of discrimination—have been criticized as incorrectly assuming that all relevant factors have been measured, and that the single variable of discrimination accounts for any remaining unexplained differences (S. Cole & Fiorentine 1991). What appears to be discrimination may be the effect of male-female differences the investigators have not taken into account.

The opposite claim has also been made, that some economic studies have, if anything, erred by including variables that may themselves be consequences of discrimination (Madden 1985). Lesser work skills, for example, may result from unequal access to opportunities to acquire skills, as the text suggests. While both dangers exist, the studies to date appear not to systematically underestimate or overestimate discrimination (Blau & Ferber 1992), nor to overlook major factors. The studies by Sonnert and Holton (1996a, 1996b) are particularly searching in their attempt to account for possible human-capital variables but continue to find that women suffer because of their gender.

4. Long and his colleagues have examined sex differences in scientific careers extensively (Long 1978, 1987, 1990, 1992; Long, Allison, & McGinnis 1993; Long & McGinnis 1981). Their data come primarily from biochemists who received their degrees before 1970. Because my focus is on the current publishing patterns of people whose degrees were obtained after 1970, I make only limited use of their data.

5. A similar study of academics from a range of disciplines in Norway found that women with children were more productive than women without children (Kyvik 1990). However, unlike those in the Fox and Faver (1985) study, women whose children were under ten years old were less productive than those with older children. Even women with children under ten, however, had the same levels of productivity as women with no children.

6. The lowest promotion rate was for single women with children, of whom only 33 percent had been promoted. Because there were probably relatively few women in that category in 1979, the data are less reliable.

7. Single men with children had the highest rate of promotion—80 percent. As there were probably almost no men in that category in 1979, I consider that datum extremely unreliable.

Chapter 13

1. Other work has shown that private litigation under Title VII of the 1964 Civil Rights Act increased the percentage of African Americans in management (Leonard 1984).

2. The finding about costs may not apply to all types of organizations. A study estimating the impact of affirmative action procedures on a variety of firms reported that following affirmative action guidelines entailed extra costs averaging 6.5 percent (Griffin 1992). That would suggest that, all other things being equal, firms complying with affirmative action would be less profitable. Since the study did not present data separately for type of firm, type of position, or type of employee, it is difficult to draw firm conclusions about the costs of affirmative action, or to determine whether they are compensated for by other advantages.

3. Other work has concluded that, in industries with high proportions of African Americans, the firms are more productive than those with small proportions (Galle, Wiswell, & Burr 1985; Tomaskovic-Devey 1988).

4. Not all underrepresented groups respond to affirmative action in the same way. African-American students, for example, do not show a psychological cost for race-related affirmative action procedures (Doverspike & Arthur 1995).

5. If performance could be quantified, one would say that an individual's performance should be within a standard deviation of the lower side of the mean.

Chapter 14

1. There are a number of theories explaining how information and expectations based on gender schemas interact with information and expectations based on people's individual characteristics (e.g., Brewer 1988; Fiske & Neuberg 1990; Kunda & Thagard 1996). In a review of several studies, Kunda and Thagard suggest that while schemas appear to require less effortful processing, the processing of individual pieces of information has typically not been varied experimentally and thus is of unknown difficulty. They also point out that schemas do not influence evaluations if judges have absolutely unambiguous information that is at odds with the schema but do influence them if information is ambiguous. In the professional world, absolutely unambiguous information is seldom available.

References

Preface

Fidell, L. S. 1975. Empirical verification of sex discrimination in hiring practices in psychology. In *Woman: dependent or independent variable?*, R. K. Unger & F. L. Denmark, eds., pp. 774–82. New York: Psychological Dimensions, Inc.

Geis, F. L., Carter, M. R., & Butler, D. J. 1982. Research on seeing and evaluating people. Unpublished manuscript, Newark, Del.: Office of Women's Affairs, University of Delaware.

Haslett, B., Geis, F. L., & Carter, M. R. 1992. *The organizational woman: Power and paradox.* Norwood, N.J.: Ablex.

Tavris, C. 1992. *The mismeasure of woman.* New York: Simon and Schuster.

A Note on Method and Scope

Cole, E. R., & Stewart, A. J. 1996. Meanings of political participation among Black and White women: Political identity and social responsibility. *Journal of Personality and Social Psychology* 71:130–40.

Crocker, J., & Major, B. 1989. Social stigma and self-esteem: The self-protective properties of stigma. *Psychological Review* 100:19–28.

Filardo, E. K. 1996. Gender patterns in African American and white adolescents' social interactions in same-race, mixed-gender groups. *Journal of Personality and Social Psychology* 71:71–82.

Landrine, H. 1995. *Bringing cultural diversity to feminist psychology: Theory, research, and practice.* Washington, D.C.: American Psychological Association.

Malveaux, J. 1990. Gender difference and beyond: An economic perspective on diversity and commonality among women. In *Theoretical perspectives on sexual difference,* D. L. Rhode, ed. New Haven: Yale University Press.

Chapter 1

Armstrong, S. L., Gleitman, L. R., & Gleitman, H. 1983. What some concepts might not be. *Cognition* 13:263–308.

Bakan, D. 1966. *The duality of human existence.* Chicago: Rand McNally.

Biernat, M., Manis, M., & Nelson, T. 1991. Stereotypes and standards of judgment. *Journal of Personality and Social Psychology* 60:5–20.

Bem, S. 1993. *The lenses of gender: Transforming the debate on sexual inequality.* New Haven: Yale University Press.

Cole, J., & Singer, B. 1991. A theory of limited differences: Explaining the productivity puzzle in science. In *The outer circle: Women in the scientific community,* H. Zuckerman, J. R. Cole, & J. T. Bruer, eds., pp. 277–310. New York: W. W. Norton.

Collaer, M. L., & Hines, M. 1995. Human behavioral sex differences: A role for gonadal hormones during early development? *Psychological Bulletin* 118: 55–107.

Deaux, K. 1985. Sex and gender. *Annual Review of Psychology* 36:49–81.

Eagly, A. H. 1987. *Sex differences in social behavior: A social-role interpretation.* Hillsdale, N.J.: Erlbaum.

Fierman, J. 1990. Why women still don't hit the top. *Fortune,* 30 July, pp. 40–66.

Fiske, S. T., Bersoff, D. N., Borgida, E., Deaux, K., & Heilman, M. 1991. Social science research on trial: Use of sex stereotyping research in *Price Waterhouse v. Hopkins. American Psychologist* 46:1049–60.

Fiske, S. T., & Taylor, S. E. 1991. *Social cognition,* 2nd ed. New York: McGraw-Hill.

Fox, M. F. 1981. Sex, salary and achievement: Reward-dualism in academia. *Sociology of Education* 54:71–84.

Fox, M. F. 1985. Publication, performance, and reward in science and scholarship. In *Higher education: Handbook of theory and research,* J. Smart, ed., pp. 255–82. New York: Agathon.

Greene, K., & Greene, R. 1996. The 20 top-paid women in corporate America. *Working Woman,* February, pp. 40–44.

Gutek, B. A. 1993. Changing the status of women in management. *Applied Psychology: An International Review* 42:301–11.

Haslett, B., Geis, F. L., & Carter, M. R. 1992. *The organizational woman: Power and paradox.* Norwood, N.J.: Ablex.

Hoffman, C., & Hurst, N. 1990. Gender stereotypes: Perception or rationalization? *Journal of Personality and Social Psychology* 58:197–208.

Long, J. S. 1990. The origins of sex differences in science. *Social Forces* 68: 1297–1315.

Martell, R. F., Lane, D. M., & Emrich, C. 1996. Male-female differences: A computer simulation. *American Psychologist* 51:157–58.

Merton, R. K. 1948. The self-fulfilling prophecy. *Antioch Review* 8:193–210.

Merton, R. K. 1968. The Matthew Effect in science. *Science* 159:56–63.

Rohter, L. 1993. Tough "front-line warrior": Janet Reno. *New York Times,* 12 February, pp. 1, 22.

Rosenthal, R. & Jacobson, L. 1968. *Pygmalion in the classroom.* New York: Holt, Rinehart & Winston.

Spence, J. T., & Helmreich, R. L. 1978. *Masculinity and femininity: Their psychological dimensions, correlates, and antecedents.* Austin: University of Texas Press.

Spence, J. T., & Sawin, L. L. 1985. Images of masculinity and femininity: A reconceptualization. In *Women, gender, and social psychology,* V. E. O'Leary, R. K. Unger, & B. S. Wallston, eds., pp. 35–66. Hillsdale, N.J.: Erlbaum.

Truell, P. 1996. Success and sharp elbows: One woman's path to lofty heights on Wall Street. *New York Times,* 2 July, pp. D1 and D4.

Unger, R. K. 1990. Imperfect reflections of reality: Psychology constructs gender. In *Making a difference: Psychology and the construction of gender,* R. T. Hare-Mustin & J. Marecek, eds., pp. 102–49. New Haven: Yale University Press.

Chapter 2

Biernat, M., & Wortman, C. B. 1991. Sharing of home responsibilities between professionally employed women and their husbands. *Journal of Personality and Social Psychology* 60:844–60.

Blair, S. L., & Lichter, D. T. 1991. Measuring the division of household labor: Gender segregation of housework among American couples. *Journal of Family Issues* 12:91–113.

Bridges, J. S. 1993. Pink or blue: Gender-stereotypic perceptions of infants as conveyed by birth congratulations cards. *Psychology of Women Quarterly* 17:193–205.

Burnham, D. K., & Harris, M. B. 1992. Effects of real gender and labeled gender on adults' perceptions of infants. *Journal of Genetic Psychology* 153:165–83.

Carter, B. (with J. K. Peters). 1996. *Love, honor, and negotiate: Making your marriage work.* New York: Pocket Books.

Condry, J., & Condry, S. 1976. Sex differences: A study of the eye of the beholder. *Child Development* 47:812–19.

Eagly, A. H. 1987. *Sex differences in social behavior: A social-role interpretation.* Hillsdale, N.J.: Erlbaum.

Eccles, J. S., & Blumenfeld, P. 1985. Classroom experiences and student gender: Are there differences and do they matter? In L. C. Wilkinson & C. B. Marrett, eds., *Gender influences in classroom interaction,* pp. 79–114. Orlando, Fla.: Academic Press.

Fagot, B. I. 1985. Changes in thinking about early sex role development. *Developmental Review* 5:83–98.

Ferree, M. M. 1991. The gender division of labor in two-earner marriages: Dimensions of variability and change. *Journal of Family Issues* 12:158–180.

Gleason, J. B., & Greif, E. B. 1983. Men's speech to young children. In B. Thorne, C. Kramarae, & N. Henley, eds., *Language, gender, and society,* pp. 140–50. Rowley, Mass.: Newbury House.

Goodnow, J. J. 1988. Children's household work: Its nature and functions. *Psychological Bulletin* 103:5–26.

Grusec, J. E., Goodnow, J. J., & Cohen, L. 1996. Household work and the development of concern for others. *Developmental Psychology* 32:999–1007.

Hochschild, A. (with A. Machung). 1989. *The second shift.* New York: Avon Books.

Hoffman, C., & Hurst, N. 1990. Gender stereotypes: Perception or rationalization? *Journal of Personality and Social Psychology* 58:197–208.

Langlois, J. H., & Downs, A. C. 1980. Mothers, fathers, and peers as socialization agents of sex-typed play behaviors in young children. *Child Development* 51:1217–47.

Lennon, M. C., & Rosenfield, S. 1994. Relative fairness and the division of housework: The importance of options. *American Journal of Sociology* 100:506–31.

Lewis, C., Scully, D., & Condor, S. 1992. Sex stereotyping of infants: A reexamination. *Journal of Reproductive and Infant Psychology* 10:53–61.

Lytton, H., & Romney, D. M. 1991. Parents' differential socialization of boys and girls: A meta-analysis. *Psychological Bulletin* 109:267–96.

Maccoby, E. E., & Jacklin, C. N. 1980. 1974. *The psychology of sex differences.* Stanford: Stanford University Press.

Mahony, R. 1995. *Kidding ourselves: Breadwinning, babies, and bargaining power.* New York: BasicBooks.

Major, B. 1993. Gender, entitlement, and the distribution of family labor. *Journal of Social Issues* 49:141–59.

Prentice, D. A., & Crosby, F. 1987. The importance of context for assessing deservingness. In *Social comparison, social justice, and relative deprivation: Theoretical, empirical, and policy perspectives,* J. C. Masters & W. P. Smith, eds., pp. 165–82. Hillsdale, N.J.: Erlbaum.

Robinson, J. P. 1988. Who's doing the housework? *American Demographics* 10 (December): 24–28, 63.

Rubin, J., Provenzano, F., & Luria, Z. 1974. The eye of the beholder: Parents' views on sex of newborns. *American Journal of Orthopsychiatry* 44:512–19.

Sanchez, L. 1994. Gender, labor allocations, and the psychology of entitlement within the home. *Social Forces* 73:533–53.

Snow, M. E., Jacklin, C. N., & Maccoby, E. E. 1983. Sex-of-child differences in father-child interaction at one year of age. *Child Development* 54:227–32.

South, S. J., & Spitze, G. 1994. Housework in marital and nonmarital households. *American Sociological Review* 59:327–47.

Starrels, M. E. 1994. Husbands' involvement in female gender-typed household chores. *Sex Roles* 31:473–91.

Stern, M., & Karraker, K. H. 1989. Sex stereotyping of infants: A review of gender labeling studies. *Sex Roles* 20:501–22.

Thompson, L. 1991. Family work: Women's sense of fairness. *Journal of Family Issues* 12:181–96.

Vogel, D. A., Lake, M. A., Evans, S., & Karraker, K. H. 1991. Children's and adults' sex-stereotyped perceptions of infants. *Sex Roles* 24:605–16.

Weiner, T. S., & Wilson-Mitchell, J. E. 1990. Nonconventional family life-styles and sex typing in six-year-olds. *Child Development* 61:1915–33.

White, L. K., & Brinkerhoff, D. B. 1981. The sexual division of labor: Evidence from childhood. *Social Forces* 60:170–81.

Chapter 3

Archer, J. 1992. Childhood gender roles: Social context and organisation. In *Childhood social development: Contemporary perspectives,* H. McGurk, ed., pp. 31–61. Hillsdale, N.J.: Erlbaum.

Becker, J. 1981. Differential teacher treatment of males and females in mathematics classes. *Journal of Research in Mathematics Education* 12:40–53.

Brophy, J. 1985. Interactions of male and female students with male and female teachers. In *Gender influences in classroom interaction,* L. C. Wilkinson & C. B. Marrett, eds., pp. 115–42. Orlando, Fla.: Academic Press.

Cornelius, R. R., Gray, J. M., & Constantinople, A. P. 1990. Student-faculty interaction in the college classroom. *Journal of Research and Development in Education* 23:189–97.

Dweck, C., Davidson, W., Nelson, S., & Enna, B. 1978. Sex differences in learned helplessness: II. The contingencies of evaluative feedback in the classroom; III. An experimental analysis. *Developmental Psychology* 14:268–76.

Eccles, J. S., & Blumenfeld, P. 1985. Classroom experiences and student gender: Are there differences and do they matter? In *Gender influences in classroom interaction,* L. C. Wilkinson & C. B. Marrett, eds., pp. 79–114. Orlando, Fla.: Academic Press.

Fagot, B. I. 1985. Changes in thinking about early sex role development. *Developmental Review* 5:83–98.

Fagot, B. I., & Hagan, R. 1985. Aggression in toddlers: Responses to the assertive acts of boys and girls. *Sex Roles* 12:341–51.

Fagot, B. I., Hagan, R., Leinbach, M. D., & Kronsberg, S. 1985. Differential reactions to assertive and communicative acts of toddler boys and girls. *Child Development* 56:1499–1505.

Fagot, B. I., & Leinbach, M. D. 1989. The young child's gender schema: Environmental input, internal organization. *Child Development* 60:663–72.

Fagot, B. I., & Leinbach, M. D. 1993. Gender-role development in young children: From discrimination to labeling. *Developmental Review* 13:205–24.

Fagot, B. I., Leinbach, M. D., & Hagan, R. 1986. Gender labeling and the adoption of sex-typed behaviors. *Developmental Psychology* 22:440–43.

Frey, K. S., & Ruble, D. N. 1992. Gender constancy and the "cost" of sex-typed behavior: A test of the conflict hypothesis. *Developmental Psychology* 28:714–21.

Huston, A. C. 1983. Sex-typing. In *Handbook of child psychology,* P. H. Mussen, ed., 4th ed., vol. 4: 387–467. New York: Wiley.

Jacklin, C. N., & Maccoby, E. E. 1978. Social behavior at 33 months in same-sex and mixed-sex dyads. *Child Development* 49:557–69.

Jacobs, J. E., & Eccles, J. S. 1992. The impact of mothers' gender-role stereotypic beliefs on mothers' and children's ability perceptions. *Journal of Personality and Social Psychology* 63:932–44.

Jussim, L., & Eccles, J. S. 1992. Teacher expectations II: Construction and reflection of student achievement. *Journal of Personality and Social Psychology* 63:947–61.

Karkau, K. 1976. Sexism in the fourth grade. In *Undoing sex stereotypes: Research and resources for educators,* M. Guttentag & H. Bray, eds., pp. 64–80. New York: McGraw-Hill.

Langlois, J. H., & Downs, A. C. 1980. Mothers, fathers, and peers as socialization agents of sex-typed play behaviors in young children. *Child Development* 51:1217–47.

Lockheed, M. E. 1985. Sex and social influence: A meta-analysis guided by theory. In *Status, rewards and influence,* J. Berger & M. Zelditch, eds., pp. 406–29. San Francisco: Jossey-Bass.

Lummis, M., & Stevenson, H. W. 1990. Gender differences in beliefs and achievement: A cross-cultural study. *Developmental Psychology* 26:254–63.

Lytton, H., & Romney, D. M. 1991. Parents' differential socialization of boys and girls: A meta-analysis. *Psychological Bulletin* 109:267–96.

Maccoby, E. E. 1988. Gender as a social category. *Developmental Psychology* 24:755–65.

Maccoby, E. E., & Jacklin, C. N. 1987. Gender segregation in childhood. In *Advances in Child Development,* vol. 20, E. H. Reese, ed., pp. 239–287.

Martell, R. F., Lane, D. M., & Emrich, C. 1996. Male-female differences: A computer simulation. *American Psychologist* 51:157–58.

Martin, C. L. 1990. Attitudes and expectations about children with nontraditional and traditional gender roles. *Sex Roles* 22:151–65.

Merrett, F., & Wheldall, K. 1992. Teachers' use of praise and reprimands to boys and girls. *Educational Review* 44:73–79.

Powlishta, K. K., & Maccoby, E. E. 1990. Resource utilization in mixed-sex dyads: The influence of adult presence and task type. *Sex Roles* 23:223–40.

Ryckman, D., & Peckham, P. 1987. Gender differences in attributions for success and failure. *Journal of Early Adolescence* 7:47–63.

Sadker, M., & Sadker, D. (1994). *Failing at fairness: How America's schools cheat girls*. New York: Macmillan.

Serbin, L. A., Powlishta, K. K., & Gulko, J. 1993. The development of sex typing in middle childhood. *Monographs of the Society for Research in Child Development* 58, no. 2, serial no. 232:1–85.

Slaby, R. G., & Frey, K. S. 1975. Development of gender constancy and selective attention to same-sex models. *Child Development* 46:849–56.

Smetana, J. G. 1986. Preschool children's conceptions of sex-role transgressions. *Child Development* 57:862–71.

Steinkamp, M. W., Harnisch, D. L., Walberg, H. J., & Tsai, S-L. 1985. Cross-national gender differences in mathematics attitude and achievement among 13-year-olds. *The Journal of Mathematical Behavior* 4:259–77.

Stipek, D. J. 1984. Sex differences in children's attributions for success and failure on math and spelling tests. *Sex Roles* 11:969–81.

Stipek, D. J., & Gralinski, J. H. 1991. Gender differences in children's achievement-related beliefs and emotional responses to success and failure in mathematics. *Journal of Educational Psychology* 83:361–71.

Thorne, B. 1993. *Gender play: Girls and boys in school*. New Brunswick, N.J.: Rutgers University Press.

Weiner, T. S., & Wilson-Mitchell, J. E. 1990. Nonconventional family life-styles and sex typing in six-year-olds. *Child Development* 61:1915–33.

Chapter 4

Berenbaum, S. A., & Hines, M. 1992. Early androgens are related to childhood sex-typed toy preferences. *Psychological Science* 3:203–06.

Berenbaum, S. A., & Snyder, D. 1995. Early hormonal influences on childhood sex-typed activity and playmate preferences: Implications for the development of sexual orientation. *Developmental Psychology* 31:31–42.

Berk, L. E. 1994. *Child development*, 3rd ed. Boston, Mass.: Allyn and Bacon.

Bettencourt, B. A., & Miller, N. 1996. Gender differences in aggression as a function of provocation: A meta-analysis. *Psychological Bulletin* 119:422–447.

Buchanan, C. M., Eccles, J. S., & Becker, J. B. 1992. Are adolescents the victims of raging hormones: Evidence for activational effects of hormones on moods and behavior at adolescence. *Psychological Bulletin* 111:62–107.

Cohen, D., Nisbett, R. E., Bowdle, B. F., & Schwarz, N. 1996. Insult, aggression, and the southern culture of honor: An "experimental ethnography." *Journal of Personality and Social Psychology* 70:945–60.

Collaer, M. L., & Hines, M. 1995. Human behavioral sex differences: A role for gonadal hormones during early development? *Psychological Bulletin* 118: 55–107.

Cossette, L., Malcuit, G., & Pomerleau, A. 1991. Sex differences in motor activity during early infancy. *Infant Behavior and Development* 14:175–86.

Eagly, A. H., & Steffen, V. J. 1986. Gender and aggressive behavior: A meta-analytic review of the social psychological literature. *Psychological Bulletin* 100:309–30.

Eaton, W. O., & Enns, L. R. 1986. Sex differences in human motor activity level. *Psychological Bulletin* 100:19–28.

Gouchie, C., & Kimura, D. 1991. The relationship between testosterone levels and cognitive ability patterns. *Psychoneuroendocrinology* 16:323–34.

Hall, J. A. Y., & Kimura, D. 1995. Sexual orientation and performance on sexually dimorphic motor tasks. *Archives of Sexual Behavior* 24:395–407.

Hampson, E. 1990a. Variations in sex-related cognitive abilities across the menstrual cycle. *Brain and Cognition* 14:26–43.

Hampson, E. 1990b. Estrogen-related variations in human spatial and articulatory-motor skills. *Psychoneuroendocrinology* 15:97–111.

Kimura, D. 1996. Sex, sexual orientation and sex hormones influence human cognitive function. *Current Opinion in Neurobiology* 6:259–63.

Kimura, D., & Hampson, E. 1994. Cognitive pattern in men and women is influenced by fluctuations in sex hormones. *Current Directions in Psychological Science* 3:57–61.

Knight, G. P., Fabes, R. A., & Higgins, D. A. 1996. Concerns about drawing causal inferences from meta-analyses: An example in the study of gender differences in aggression. *Psychological Bulletin* 119:410–21.

Maccoby, E. E., & Jacklin, C. N. 1980. Sex differences in aggression: A rejoinder and reprise. *Child Development* 51:964–80.

McConnell-Ginet, S. 1983. Intonation in a man's world. In *Language, gender, and society*, B. Thorne, C. Kramarae, & N. Henley, eds., pp. 69–88. Rowley, Mass.: Newbury House.

Mead, M. 1935. *Sex and temperament in three primitive societies*. New York: William Morrow.

Moore, C. L. 1985. Another psychobiological view of sexual differentiation. *Developmental Review* 5:18–55.

Neisser, U., Boodoo, G., Bouchard, T. J., Jr., Boykin, A. W., Brody, N., Ceci, S. J., Halpern, D. F., Loehlin, J. C., Perloff, R., Sternberg, R. J., & Urbina, S. 1996. Intelligence: Knowns and unknowns. (Report of a task force established by the American Psychological Association.) *American Psychologist* 51:77–101.

Parsons, J. E. 1982. Biology, experience, and sex-dimorphic behaviors. In *The fundamental connection between nature and nurture*, W. R. Grove & G. R. Carpenter, eds., pp. 137–70. Lexington, Mass.: Lexington Books.

Tieger, T. 1980. On the biological basis of sex differences in aggression. *Child Development* 51:943–63.

Udry, J. R., & Talbert, L. M. 1988. Sex hormone effects on personality at puberty. *Journal of Personality and Social Psychology* 54:291–95.

Chapter 5

Battista, M. T. 1990. Spatial visualization and gender differences in high school geometry. *Journal for Research in Mathematics Education* 21:47–60.

Belenky, M. F., Clinchy, B. M., Goldberger, N. R., & Tarule, J. M. 1986. *Women's ways of knowing: Development of self, voice, and mind.* New York: Basic Books.

Bem, S. 1993. *The lenses of gender: Transforming the debate on sexual inequality.* New Haven: Yale University Press.

Benbow, C. P. 1992. Academic achievement in mathematics and science of students between ages 13 and 23: Are there differences among students in the top one percent of mathematical ability? *Journal of Educational Psychology* 84:51–61.

Ben-Chaim, D., Lappan, G., & Houang, R. T. 1988. The effect of instruction on spatial visualization skills of middle school boys and girls. *American Educational Research Journal* 25:51–71.

Block, J. H. 1983. Differential premises arising from differential socialization of the sexes: Some conjectures. *Child Development* 54:1335–54.

Bridgeman, B., & Wendler, C. 1991. Gender differences in predictors of college mathematics performance and in college mathematics course grades. *Journal of Educational Psychology* 83:275–84.

Byrnes, J. P., & Takahira, S. 1993. Explaining gender differences on SAT-math items. *Developmental Psychology* 29:805–10.

Casey, M. B., Nuttall, R., Pezaris, E., & Benbow, C. P. 1995. The influence of spatial ability on gender differences in mathematics college entrance test scores across diverse samples. *Developmental Psychology* 31:697–705.

Casey, M. B., Pezaris, E., & Nuttall, R. L. 1992. Spatial ability as a predictor of math achievement: The importance of sex and handedness patterns. *Neuropsychologia* 30:35–45.

Collaer, M. L., & Hines, M. 1995. Human behavioral sex differences: A role for gonadal hormones during early development? *Psychological Bulletin* 118: 55–107.

Delgado, A. R., & Prieto, G. 1996. Sex differences in visuospatial ability: Do performance factors play such an important role? *Memory & Cognition* 24:504–10.

Fausto-Sterling, A. 1985. *Myths of gender: Biological theories about women and men.* New York: Basic Books.

Favreau, O. E., & Everett, J. C. 1996. A tale of two tails. *American Psychologist* 51:268–69.

Feingold, A. 1988. Cognitive gender differences are disappearing. *American Psychologist* 43:95–103.

Feingold, A. 1992. Sex differences in variability in intellectual abilities: A new look at an old controversy. *Review of Educational Research* 62:61–84.

Feingold, A. 1994. Gender differences in variability in intellectual abilities: A cross-cultural perspective. *Sex Roles* 30:81–92.

Fennema, E., & Tartre, L. A. 1985. The use of spatial visualization in mathematics by girls and boys. *Journal for Research in Mathematics Education* 16:184–206.

Fenson, L., Dale, P. S., Reznick, J. S., Bates, E., Thal, D. J., & Pethick, S. J. 1994. Variability in early communicative development. *Monographs of the Society for Research in Child Development* 59 (5, serial no. 242):v–173.

Friedman, L. 1995. The space factor in mathematics: Gender differences. *Review of Educational Research* 65:22–50.

Gallagher, A. M., & De Lisi, R. 1994. Gender differences in Scholastic Aptitude Test-Mathematics problem solving among high-ability students. *Journal of Educational Psychology* 86:204–11.

Gallagher, S. A. 1989. Predictors of SAT Mathematics scores of gifted male and gifted female adolescents. *Psychology of Women Quarterly* 13:191–203.

Gallagher, S. A., & Johnson, E. S. 1992. The effect of time limits on performance of mental rotations by gifted adolescents. *Gifted Child Quarterly* 36:19–22.

Geary, D. C. 1996. Sexual selection and sex differences in mathematical abilities. *Behavioral and Brain Sciences* 19:229–84.

Grice, P. 1989. *Studies in the way of words.* Cambridge: Harvard University Press.

Halpern, D. F. 1989. The disappearance of cognitive gender differences: What you see depends on where you look. *American Psychologist* 44:1156–58.

Hedges, L. V., & Nowell, A. 1995. Sex differences in mental test scores, variability, and numbers of high-scoring individuals. *Science* 269:41–45.

Hyde, J. S., Fennema, E., & Lamon, S. J. 1990. Gender differences in mathematics performance: A meta-analysis. *Psychological Bulletin* 107:139–55.

Hyde, J. S., & Linn, M. C. 1988. Gender differences in verbal ability: A meta-analysis. *Psychological Bulletin* 104:53–69.

Kail, R., Carter, P., & Pellegrino, J. 1979. The locus of sex differences in spatial ability. *Perception & Psychophysics* 26:182–86.

Law, D. J., Pellegrino, J. W., & Hunt, E. B. 1993. Comparing the tortoise and the hare: Gender differences and experience in dynamic spatial reasoning tasks. *Psychological Science* 4:35–40.

Linn, M. C., & Petersen, A. C. 1985. Emergence and characterization of sex differences in spatial ability: A meta-analysis. *Child Development* 56:1479–98.

Low, R., & Over, R. 1989. Detection of missing and irrelevant information within algebraic story problems. *British Journal of Educational Psychology* 59:296–305.

Low, R., & Over, R. 1990. Text editing of algebraic word problems. *Australian Journal of Psychology* 42:63–73.

Low, R., & Over, R. 1993. Gender differences in solution of algebraic word problems containing irrelevant information. *Journal of Educational Psychology* 85:331–39.

Lubinski, D., & Benbow, C. P. 1992. Gender differences in abilities and preferences among the gifted: Implications for the math-science pipeline. *Current Directions in Psychological Science* 1:61–66.

Lummis, M., & Stevenson, H. W. 1990. Gender differences in beliefs and achievement: A cross-cultural study. *Developmental Psychology* 26:254–63.

Masters, M. S., & Sanders, B. 1993. Is the gender difference in mental rotation disappearing? *Behavior Genetics* 23:337–41.

Mills, C. J., Ablard, K. E., & Stumpf, H. 1993. Gender differences in academically talented young students' mathematical reasoning: Patterns across age and subskills. *Journal of Educational Psychology* 85:340–46.

Okagaki, L., & Frensch, P. A. 1994. Effects of video game playing on measures of spatial performance: Gender effects in late adolescence. *Journal of Applied Developmental Psychology* 15:33–58.

Pattison, P., & Grieve, N. 1984. Do spatial skills contribute to sex differences in different types of mathematical problems? *Journal of Educational Psychology* 76:676–89.

Sharps, M. J., Price, J. L., & Williams, J. K. 1994. Spatial cognition and gender: Instructional and stimulus influences on mental image rotation performance. *Psychology of Women Quarterly* 18:413–25.

Sharps, M. J., Welton, A. L., & Price, J. L. 1993. Gender and task in the determination of spatial cognitive performance. *Psychology of Women Quarterly* 17:71–83.

Sheldon, A. 1992. Conflict talk: Sociolinguistic challenges to self-assertion and how young girls meet them. *Merrill-Palmer Quarterly* 38:95–117.

Sheldon, A. 1996. You can be the baby brother but you aren't born yet: Preschool girls' negotiation for power and access in pretend play. *Research on Language and Social Interaction* 29:57–80.

Steinkamp, M. W., Harnisch, D. L., Walberg, H. J., & Tsai, S-L. 1985. Cross-national gender differences in mathematics attitude and achievement among 13-year-olds. *The Journal of Mathematical Behavior* 4:259–77.

Voyer, D., Voyer, S., & Bryden, M. P. 1995. Magnitude of sex differences in spatial abilities: A meta-analysis and consideration of critical variables. *Psychological Bulletin* 117:250–70.

Wainer, H., & Steinberg, L. S. 1992. Sex differences in performance on the Mathematics section of the Scholastic Aptitude Test: A bidirectional validity study. *Harvard Educational Review* 62:323–36.

Wilson, D. & Sperber, D. 1986. *Relevance: Communication and cognition.* Cambridge: Harvard University Press.

Chapter 6

Barnett, R. C., Marshall, N. L., Raudenbush, S. W., & Brennan, R. T. 1993. Gender and the relationship between job experiences and psychological distress: A study of dual-earner couples. *Journal of Personality and Social Psychology* 64:794–806.

Baker, L. C. 1996. Differences in earnings between male and female physicians. *New England Journal of Medicine* 334:960–64.

Beal, C. R. 1994. *Boys and girls: The development of gender roles.* New York: McGraw-Hill.

Bonner, T. N. 1992. *To the ends of the earth: Women's search for education in medicine.* Cambridge: Harvard University Press.

Chodorow, N. 1978. *The reproduction of mothering: Psychoanalysis and the sociology of gender.* Berkeley: University of California Press.

Conway, M., Pizzamiglio, M. T., & Mount, L. 1996. Status, communality, and agency: Implications for stereotypes of gender and other groups. *Journal of Personality and Social Psychology* 71:25–38.

Deaux, K. 1987. Psychological constructions of masculinity and femininity. In *Masculinity/femininity: Basic perspectives,* J. M. Reinisch, L. A. Rosenblum, & S. A. Sanders, eds. New York: Oxford University Press.

Deaux, K., & Lewis, L. L. 1984. The structure of gender stereotypes: Interrelationships among components and gender label. *Journal of Personality and Social Psychology* 46:991–1004.

Dinnerstein, D. 1976. *The mermaid and the minotaur.* New York: Harper & Row.

Eagly, A. H. 1987. *Sex differences in social behavior: A social-role interpretation.* Hillsdale, N.J.: Erlbaum.

Feingold, A. 1994. Gender differences in personality: A meta-analysis. *Psychological Bulletin* 116:429–56.

Fiske, S. T., & Taylor, S. E. 1991. *Social cognition,* 2nd ed. New York: McGraw-Hill.

Gilligan, C. 1982. *In a different voice.* Cambridge, Mass.: Harvard University Press.

Herek, G. M. 1993. Sexual orientation and military service: A social science perspective. *American Psychologist* 48:538–49.

Hoffman, C., & Hurst, N. 1990. Gender stereotypes. *Journal of Personality and Social Psychology* 58:197–208.

Judd, C. M., & Park, B. 1993. Definition and assessment of accuracy in social stereotypes. *Psychological Review* 100:109–28.

Kimmel, M. 1995. *Manhood in America: A cultural history.* New York: Free Press.

Kuhn, T. S. 1962. *The structure of scientific revolutions.* Chicago: University of Chicago Press.

Loveday, L. 1981. Pitch, politeness and sexual role: An exploratory investigation into the pitch correlates of English and Japanese politeness formulae. *Language and Speech* 24:71–89.

McConnell-Ginet, S. 1983. Intonation in a man's world. In *Language, gender, and society,* B. Thorne, C. Kramarae, & N. Henley, eds., pp. 69–88. Rowley, Mass.: Newbury House.

Miller, D. T., Taylor, B., & Buck, M. L. 1991. Gender gaps: Who needs to be explained? *Journal of Personality and Social Psychology* 61:5–12.

Mitchell, J. 1984. *Women: The longest revolution.* New York: Pantheon.

Nisbett, R., & Ross, L. 1980. *Human inference: Strategies and shortcomings of social judgment,* pp. 167–92. Englewood Cliffs, N.J.: Prentice-Hall.

Ortner, S. B. 1974. Is female to male as nature is to culture? In *Woman, culture, and society,* M. Z. Rosaldo & L. Lamphere, eds., pp. 67–87. Stanford: Stanford University Press.

Parsons, T., & Bales, R., eds. 1955. *Family, socialization, and interaction process.* New York: Free Press.

Reskin, B. B., & Roos, P. A. 1990. *Job queues, gender queues: Explaining women's inroads into male occupations.* Philadelphia: Temple University Press.

Rosaldo, M. Z. 1974. Woman, culture, and society: A theoretical overview. In *Woman, culture, and society,* M. Z. Rosaldo & L. Lamphere, eds., pp. 17–42. Stanford: Stanford University Press.

Ross, L., Lepper, M. R., & Hubbard, M. 1975. Perseverance in self-perception and social perception: Biased attributional processes in the debriefing paradigm. *Journal of Personality and Social Psychology* 32:880–92.

Sachs, J., Lieberman, P., & Erikson, D. 1973. Anatomical and cultural determinants of male and female speech. In *Language attitudes: Current trends and prospects,* R. W. Shuy & R. W. Fasold, eds. Washington, D.C.: School of Languages and Linguistics, Georgetown University.

Spence, J. T., Deaux, K., & Helmreich, R. L. 1985. Sex roles in contemporary American society. In *Handbook of social psychology,* vol. 2, G. Lindzey & E. Aronson, eds. New York: Random House.

Spence, J. T., & Helmreich, R. L. 1978. *Masculinity and femininity: Their psychological dimensions, correlates, and antecedents.* Austin: University of Texas Press.

Spence, J. T., & Sawin, L. L. 1985. Images of masculinity and femininity: A reconceptualization. In *Women, gender, and social psychology,* V. E. O'Leary, R. K. Unger, & B. S. Wallston, eds., pp. 35–66. Hillsdale, N.J.: Erlbaum.

Tavris, C. 1992. *The mismeasure of woman.* New York: Simon and Schuster.

Wark, G. R., & Krebs, D. L. 1996. Gender and dilemma differences in real-life moral judgment. *Developmental Psychology* 32:220–30.

Wason, P. 1960. On the failure to eliminate hypotheses in a conceptual task. *Quarterly Journal of Experimental Psychology* 12:129–40.

Chapter 7

Brown, V., & Geis, F. L. 1984. Turning lead into gold: Leadership by men and women and the alchemy of social consensus. *Journal of Personality and Social Psychology* 46:811–24.

Butler, D., & Geis, F. L. 1990. Nonverbal affect responses to male and female leaders: Implications for leadership evaluation. *Journal of Personality and Social Psychology* 58:48–59.

Carli, L. L., LaFleur, S. J., & Loeber, C. C. 1995. Nonverbal behavior, gender, and influence. *Journal of Personality and Social Psychology* 68:1030–41.

Chused, R. H. 1988. The hiring and retention of minorities and women on American law school faculties. *University of Pennsylvania Law Review* 137:537–69.

Cole, J. R. 1979. *Fair science: Women in the scientific community.* New York: Free Press.

Drogosz, L. M., & Levy, P. E. 1996. Another look at the effects of appearance, gender, and job type on performance-based decisions. *Psychology of Women Quarterly* 20:437–45.

Eagly, A. H., Karau, S. J., & Makhijani, M. G. 1995. Gender and the effectiveness of leaders: A meta-analysis. *Journal of Personality and Social Psychology* 117:125–45.

Eagly, A. H., Makhijani, M. G., & Klonsky, B. G. 1992. Gender and the evaluation of leaders: A meta-analysis. *Psychological Bulletin* 111:3–22.

Fidell, L. S. 1975. Empirical verification of sex discrimination in hiring practices in psychology. In *Woman: Dependent or independent variable?*, R. K. Unger & F. L. Denmark, eds., pp. 774–82. New York: Psychological Dimensions.

Fiske, S. T., Bersoff, D. N., Borgida, E., Deaux, K., & Heilman, M. 1991. Social science research on trial: Use of sex stereotyping research in *Price Waterhouse v. Hopkins*. *American Psychologist* 46:1049–60.

Gillen, B. 1981. Physical attractiveness: A determinant of two types of goodness. *Personality and Social Psychology Bulletin* 7:277–81.

Greenhaus, J. H., & Parasuraman, S. 1993. Job performance attributions and career advancement prospects: An examination of gender and race effects. *Organizational Behavior and Human Decision Processes* 55:273–97.

Heilman, M. E. 1980. The impact of situational factors on personnel decisions concerning women: Varying the sex composition of the applicant pool. *Organizational Behavior and Human Performance* 26:386–95.

Heilman, M. E., Block, C. J., Martell, R. F., & Simon, M. C. 1989. Has anything changed? Current characterizations of men, women, and managers. *Journal of Applied Psychology* 74:935–42.

Heilman, M. E., & Stopeck, M. H. 1985. Attractiveness and corporate success: Different causal attributions for males and females. *Journal of Applied Psychology* 70:379–88.

Kemper, S. 1984. When to speak like a lady. *Sex Roles* 10:435–43.

Lerner, M. J. 1975. The justice motive in social behavior: An introduction. *Journal of Social Issues* 31:1–19.

Lytton, H., & Romney, D. M. 1991. Parents' differential socialization of boys and girls: A meta-analysis. *Psychological Bulletin* 109:267–96.

Morrow, P. C., McElroy, J. C., Stamper, B. G., & Wilson, M. A. 1990. The effects of physical attractiveness and other demographic characteristics on promotion decisions. *Journal of Management* 16:723–36.

Ochs, E. 1992. Indexing gender. In *Rethinking context: Language as an interactive phenomenon*. A. Duranti & C. Goodwin, eds. Cambridge: Cambridge University Press.

Olian, J. D., Schwab, D. P., & Haberfeld, Y. 1988. The impact of applicant gender compared to qualifications on hiring recommendations: A meta-analysis of experimental studies. *Organizational Behavior and Human Decision Processes* 41:180–95.

Porter, N., & Geis, F. L. 1981. Women and nonverbal leadership cues: When seeing is not believing. In *Gender and nonverbal behavior*. C. Mayo & N. Henley, eds. New York: Springer Verlag.

Ragins, B. R. 1991. Gender effects in subordinate evaluations of leaders: Real or artifact? *Journal of Organizational Behavior* 12:259–68.

Rosen, B., Jerdee, T. H., & Prestwich, T. L. 1975. Dual-career marital adjustment: Potential effects of discriminatory managerial attitudes. *Journal of Marriage and the Family* 37:565–72.

Sackett, P. R., DuBois, C. L. Z., & Noe, A. W. 1991. Tokenism in performance evaluation: The effects of work group representation on male-female and white-black differences in performance ratings. *Journal of Applied Psychology* 76: 263–67.

Schein, V. E. 1973. The relationship between sex role stereotypes and requisite management characteristics. *Journal of Applied Psychology* 57:95–100.

Spencer, B. A., & Taylor, G. S. 1988. Effects of facial attractiveness and gender on causal attributions of managerial performance. *Sex Roles* 19:273–85.

Swim, J., Borgida, E., Maruyama, G., & Myers, D. G. 1989. Joan McKay versus John McKay: Do gender stereotypes bias evaluations? *Psychological Bulletin* 105:409–29.

Chapter 8

Bailey, S. 1991. Some women faulting demand for equal pay; Graf says there's no need to make more. *Washington Post,* 2 June, p. B9.

Butler, D., & Geis, F. L. 1990. Nonverbal affect responses to male and female leaders: Implications for leadership evaluation. *Journal of Personality and Social Psychology* 58:48–59.

Clayton, S. D., & Crosby, F. J. 1992. *Justice, gender, and affirmative action.* Ann Arbor: University of Michigan Press.

Cole, J. R., & Singer, B. 1991. A theory of limited differences: Explaining the productivity puzzle in science. In *The outer circle: Women in the scientific community.* H. Zuckerman, J. R. Cole, & J. T. Bruer, eds., pp. 277–310, 319–23, 338–40. New York: W. W. Norton.

Crocker, J., & Major, B. 1989. Social stigma and self-esteem: The self-protective properties of stigma. *Psychological Review* 96:608–30.

Crosby, F. J. 1982. *Relative deprivation and working women.* New York: Oxford University Press.

Dovidio, J. F., Ellyson, S. L., Keating, C. F., Heltman, K., & Brown, C. E. 1988. The relationship of social power to visual displays of dominance between men and women. *Journal of Personality and Social Psychology* 54:233–42.

Eccles, J. S. 1987. Gender roles and achievement patterns: An expectancy value perspective. In *Masculinity/Femininity: Basic perspectives.* J. M. Reinisch, L. A. Rosenblum, & S. A. Sanders, eds. Oxford: Oxford University Press.

Fiorentine, R. 1988. Sex differences in success expectancies and causal attributions: Is this why fewer women become physicians? *Social Psychology Quarterly* 51:236–49.

Gallo, B. 1996. A Grand Slam against women. *Denver Westword,* 31 January, p. 47.

Heilman, M. E. 1980. The impact of situational factors on personnel decisions concerning women: Varying the sex composition of the applicant pool. *Organizational Behavior and Human Performance* 26:386–95.

Josephs, R. A., Markus, H. R., & Tafarodi, R. W. 1992. Gender and self-esteem. *Journal of Personality and Social Psychology* 63:391–402.

Kahn, A., O'Leary, V., Krulewitz, J. E., & Lamm, H. 1980. Equity and equality: Male and female means to a just end. *Basic and Applied Social Psychology* 1:173–97.

Major, B. 1987. Gender, justice, and the psychology of entitlement. In *Sex and gender. Review of personality and social psychology,* vol. 7. P. Shaver & C. Hendrick, eds., pp. 124–48. Newbury Park, Calif.: Sage.

Reskin, B. F., & Roos, P. A., eds. 1990. *Job queues, gender queues.* Philadelphia: Temple University Press.

Rosa, E., & Mazur, A. 1979. Incipient status in small groups. *Social Forces* 58:18–37.

Sharps, M. J., Price, J. L., & Williams, J. K. 1994. Spatial cognition and gender: Instructional and stimulus influences on mental image rotation performance. *Psychology of Women Quarterly* 18:413–25.

Skrypnek, B. J. & Snyder, M. 1982. On the self-perpetuating nature of stereotypes about women and men. *Journal of Experimental Social Psychology* 18: 277–91.

Smith, J. 1989. *Misogynies: Reflections on myths and malice,* pp. 120–21. New York: Fawcett Columbine.

Snyder, M., Tanke, E. D., & Berscheid, E. 1977. Social perception and interpersonal behavior: On the self-fulfilling nature of social stereotypes. *Journal of Personality and Social Psychology* 35:656–66.

Spencer, S. J., & Steele, C. M. 1992. The effect of stereotype vulnerability on women's math performance. Paper presented at the 100th Annual Convention of the American Psychological Association. Washington, D.C.

Wilden, A. 1972. *System and structure: Essays in communication and exchange.* London: Tavistock.

Chapter 9

Ashcraft, M. H. 1994. *Human memory and cognition,* 2nd ed. New York: Harper Collins.

Aube, J., & Koestner, R. 1992. Gender characteristics and adjustment: A longitudinal study. *Journal of Personality and Social Psychology* 63:485–93.

Bar-Tal, D., & Frieze, I. H. 1977. Achievement motivation for males and females as a determinant of attributions for success and failure. *Sex Roles* 3:301–14.

Deaux, K. 1976. Sex: A perspective on the attribution process. In *New directions in attribution research,* vol. 1. J. H. Harvey, W. J. Ickes, and R. F. Kidd, eds., pp. 335–52. Hillsdale, N.J.: Erlbaum.

Deaux, K. 1984. From individual differences to social categories: Analysis of a decade's research on gender. *American Psychologist* 39:105–16.

Deaux, K., & Emswiller, T. 1974. Explanations of successful performance on sex-linked tasks: What is skill for the male is luck for the female. *Journal of Personality and Social Psychology* 29:80–85.

Deaux, K., & Farris, E. 1977. Attributing causes for one's own performance: The effects of sex, norms, and outcome. *Journal of Research in Personality* 11:59–72.

Fiorentine, R. 1988. Sex differences in success expectancies and causal attributions: Is this why fewer women become physicians? *Social Psychology Quarterly* 51:236–49.

Greenhaus, J. H., & Parasuraman, S. 1993. Job performance attributions and career advancement prospects: An examination of gender and race effects. *Organizational Behavior and Human Decision Processes* 55:273–97.

Kiesler, S. B. 1975. Actuarial prejudice toward women and its implications. *Journal of Applied Social Psychology* 5:201–16.

Locksley, A., Borgida, E., Brekke, N., & Hepburn. 1980. Sex stereotypes and social judgment. *Journal of Personality and Social Psychology* 39:821–31.

McGill, A. L. 1993. Selection of a causal background: Role of expectation versus feature mutability. *Journal of Personality and Social Psychology* 64:701–07.

O'Heron, C. A., & Orlofsky, J. L. 1990. Stereotypic and nonstereotypic sex role trait and behavior orientations, gender identity, and psychological adjustment. *Journal of Personality and Social Psychology* 58:134–43.

Potter, M. C. 1990. Remembering. In *Thinking,* D. N. Osherson & E. E. Smith, eds., pp. 3–32. Cambridge: MIT Press.

Robinson, J. G., & McIlwee, J. S. 1989. Women in engineering: A promise unfulfilled? *Social Problems* 36:455–72.

Rosenthal, P., Guest, D., & Peccei, R. 1996. Gender differences in managers' causal explanations for their work performance: A study in two organizations. *Journal of Occupational and Organizational Psychology* 69:145–51.

Russo, N. F., Kelly, R. M., & Deacon, M. 1991. Gender and success-related attributions: Beyond individualistic conceptions of achievement. *Sex Roles* 25: 331–50.

Sokoloff, N. J. 1992. *Black women and white women in the professions.* New York: Routledge.

Sonnert, G., & Holton, G. 1996. Career patterns of women and men in the sciences. *American Scientist* 84:63–71.

Spence, J. T., & Sawin, L. L. 1985. Images of masculinity and femininity: A reconceptualization. In *Women, gender, and social psychology.* V. E. O'Leary, R. K. Unger, & B. S. Wallston, eds., pp. 35–66. Hillsdale, N.J.: Erlbaum.

Sweeney, P. D., Moreland, R. L., & Gruber, K. L. 1982. Gender differences in performance attributions: Students' explanations for personal success or failure. *Sex Roles* 8:359–73.

Swim, J. K., & Sanna, L. J. 1996. He's skilled, she's lucky: A meta-analysis of observers' attributions for women's and men's successes and failures. *Personality and Social Psychology Bulletin* 22:507–19.

Travis, C. B., Burnett-Doering, J., & Reid, P. T. 1982. The impact of sex, achievement domain, and conceptual orientation on causal attributions. *Sex Roles* 8: 443–54.

Weiner, B. 1983. Some methodological pitfalls in attributional research. *Journal of Educational Psychology* 75:530–43.

Weiner, B., Frieze, I., Kukla, A., Reed, L., Rest, S. & Rosenbaum, R. M. 1971. *Perceiving the causes of success and failure.* Morristown, N.J.: General Learning Press.

Whitley, B. E., Jr., McHugh, M. C., Frieze, I. H. 1986. Assessing the theoretical models for sex differences in causal attributions of success and failure. In *The psychology of gender: Advances through meta-analysis.* J. S. Hyde & M. C. Linn eds., pp. 102–35. Baltimore: Johns Hopkins University Press.

Chapter 10

Acosta, R. V., & Carpenter, L. J. 1992. Women in intercollegiate sport: A longitudinal study—fifteen year update, 1977–1992. Brooklyn College. CUNY: Unpubl. MS.

American Bar Association Commission on Women in the Profession. December 1995a. *Basic facts from women in the law: A look at the numbers.* Chicago: American Bar Association.

Baker, L. C. 1996. Differences in earnings between male and female physicians. *New England Journal of Medicine* 334:960–64.

Becker, G. 1957. *The economics of discrimination.* Chicago: University of Chicago Press.

Blau, F. D., & Ferber, M. A. 1992. *The economics of women, men, and work,* 2nd ed. Englewood Cliffs, N.J.: Prentice-Hall.

Brooks, N. R., & Groves, M. 1996. Woman to run house that Barbie built. *Los Angeles Times,* 23 August, p. A1.

Cart, J. 1995. Women consider Australian Open boycott over prizes. *Los Angeles Times,* 12 November, p. C12.

Cox, T. H., & Harquail, C. V. 1991. Career paths and career success in the early career stages of male and female MBAs. *Journal of Vocational Behavior* 39:54–75.

Curran, B. A., with Rosich, K. J., Carson, C. N., & Puccetti, M. C. 1985. *The lawyer statistical report: A statistical profile of the U.S. legal profession in the 1980s.* Chicago: American Bar Foundation.

Curran, B. A., & Carson, C. N. 1991. *Supplement to the lawyer statistical report: The U.S. legal profession in 1988.* Chicago: American Bar Foundation.

Davis, A. 1995. Women's networking spreads work around. *National Law Journal,* 9 October, p. A1.

Dixon, J. & Seron, C. 1995. Stratification in the legal profession: Sex, sector, and salary. *Law & Society Review* 29:381–412.

Egan, M. L., & Bendick, M., Jr. 1994. International business careers in the United States: Salaries, advancement and male-female differences. *International Journal of Human Resource Management* 5:33–50.

Elmore, C. 1996. French Open disputes claims that men attract more viewers. *Palm Beach Post,* 2 June, p. 3C.

Epstein, C. F. 1993. *Women in law,* 2nd ed. Urbana: University of Illinois Press.

Epstein, C. F., Saute, R., Oglensky, B., & Gever, M. 1995. Glass ceilings and open doors: Women's advancement in the legal profession. *Fordham Law Review,* 64:306–449.

Ferretti, F. 1980. 6 shares and lots of cheek. *New York Times,* 30 April, pp. C1, C10.

Fierman, J. 1990. Why women still don't hit the top. *Fortune* 122 (30 July): 40–66.

Foster, S. E. 1995. Comment: The glass ceiling in the legal profession: Why do law firms still have so few female partners? *UCLA Law Review* 42:1631–89.

France, M. 1994. In-house counsel pay shows gender gap. *National Law Journal,* 28 November, p. A6.

Franklin, B. D. 1992a. Survey shows women earn less in-house than men. *National Law Journal,* 29 October, p. 1.

Franklin, B. D. 1992b. Women get lower pay in law departments. *National Law Journal,* 9 November, p. 17.

Fuller, R., & Schoenberger, R. 1991. The gender salary gap: Do academic achievement, internship experience, and college major make a difference? *Social Science Quarterly* 72:715–26.

Gerhart, B. 1990. Gender differences in current and starting salaries: The role of performance, college major, and job title. *Industrial and Labor Relations Review* 43:418–33.

Goldin, C. 1990. *Understanding the gender gap: An economic history of American women.* New York: Oxford University Press.

Greene, K., & Greene, R. 1996. The 20 top-paid women in corporate America. *Working Woman*, February, pp. 40–44.

Jacobs, J. J. 1992. Women's entry into management: Trends in earnings, authority, and values among salaried managers. *Administrative Science Quarterly* 37: 282–301.

Kahn, L. 1991. Discrimination in professional sports: A survey of the literature. *Industrial and Labor Relations Review* 44:395–418.

Kay, F. M., & Hagan, J. 1995. The persistent glass ceiling: Gendered inequalities in the earnings of lawyers. *British Journal of Sociology* 46:279–310.

Knoppers, A., Bedker Meyer, B., Ewing, M., & Forrest, L. 1989. Gender and the salaries of coaches. *Sociology of Sport Journal* 6:348–61.

National Law Journal. 1993. 1992 Law firm associate income. 15, no. 36 (10 May): 511.

Olson, J. E., & Frieze, I. H. 1987. Income determinants for women in business. In *Women and work: an annual review*, vol. 2, A. H. Stromberg, L. Larwood, & B. A. Gutek, eds., pp. 173–206. Newbury Park, Calif.: Sage.

O'Neill, J. 1991. Women and wages: Gender pay ratios. *Current* 331:10–16.

Paglin, M., & Rufolo, A. M. 1990. Heterogeneous human capital, occupational choice, and male-female earnings differences. *Journal of Labor Economics* 8:123–44.

Powell, G. N. 1988. *Women and men in management*. Newbury Park, Calif.: Sage.

Resnick, R. 1990. Fiscal rewards of the practice. *National Law Journal*, 26 March, p. S12.

Robinson, J. G., & McIlwee, J. S. 1989. Women in engineering: A promise unfulfilled? *Social Problems* 36:455–72.

Scott, J. N. 1987. A woman's chance for a law partnership. *Sociology and Social Research* 71:119–22.

Sokoloff, N. J. 1992. *Black women and white women in the professions*. New York: Routledge.

Spurr, S. J. 1990. Sex discrimination in the legal profession: A study of promotion. *Industrial and Labor Relations Review* 43:406–17.

Stangl, J. M., & Kane, M. J. 1991. Structural variables that offer explanatory power for the underrepresentation of women coaches since Title IX: The case of homologous reproduction. *Sociology of Sport Journal* 8:47–60.

Stroh, L. K., Brett, J. M., & Reilly, A. H. 1992. All the right stuff: A comparison of female and male managers' career progression. *Journal of Applied Psychology* 77:251–60.

Truell, P. 1996. Success and sharp elbows: One woman's path to lofty heights on Wall Street. *New York Times*, 2 July, pp. D1, D4.

Vecsey, G. 1996. Women's soccer: 76,481 fans, 1 U.S. gold. *New York Times,* 2 August, B9.

Weiner, T. 1994. Women, citing bias, may sue the C.I.A. *New York Times,* 28 March, p. A10.

Weiss, Y., & Lillard, L. 1982. Output variability, academic labor contracts, and waiting times for promotion. In *Research in labor economics,* vol. 5, R. G. Ehrenberg, ed., pp. 157–88. Greenwich, Conn.: JAI Press.

Women's Sports Foundation. 1992. Participation, information, and statistics. Participation information packet. New York.

Chapter 11

American Association of University Professors (AAUP). 1981. Annual report on the economic status of the profession, 1980–1981. *Academe* 67, no. 2 (March–April): 1–75.

American Association of University Professors. 1996. The annual report on the economic status of the profession, 1995–96. *Academe* 82, no. 2 (March–April).

American Association of University Professors. 1997. The annual report on the economic status of the profession, 1996–1997. *Academe* 83, no. 2 (March–April).

American Psychological Association. 1995. *Report of the task force on the changing gender composition of psychology.* Washington, D.C.: American Psychological Association.

Finklestein, M. 1984. The status of academic women: An assessment of five competing explanations. *Review of Higher Education* 7:223–46.

Ingram, L., & Brown, P. 1997. *Humanities doctorates in the United States: 1995 profile.* Washington, D.C.: National Academy Press.

National Center for Education Statistics. 1992. *Digest of education statistics,* p. 236, Table 224. Washington, D.C.

National Center for Education Statistics. 1996. *Digest of education statistics,* p. 249, Table 235. Washington, D.C.

National Research Council, Office of Scientific and Engineering Personnel. 1991. *Humanities doctorates in the United States: 1989 profile.* Washington, D.C.: National Academy Press.

National Science Foundation. 1996. *Characteristics of doctoral scientists and engineers in the United States: 1993.* Arlington, Va.: National Science Foundation.

Pion, G. M., Mednick, M. T., Astin, H. S., Hall, C. C. I., Kenkel, M. B., Keita, G. P., Kohout, J. L., & Kelleher, J. C. 1996. The shifting gender composition of psychology: Trends and implications for the discipline. *American Psychologist* 51:509–28.

Reskin, B. F. 1978. Scientific productivity, sex, and location in the institution of science. *American Journal of Sociology* 83:1235–43.

Reskin, B. F., & Hargens, L. L. 1979. Scientific advancement of male and female chemists. In *Discrimination in organizations,* R. Alvarez & K. G. Lutterman, eds., pp. 100–22. San Francisco: Jossey-Bass.

Ries, P., & Thurgood, D. H. 1993. *Summary report 1991: Doctorate recipients from United States universities.* Washington, D.C.: National Academy Press.

Rosenfeld, R. A. 1984. Academic career mobility for women and men psychologists. In *Women in scientific and engineering professions,* V. B. Haas & C. C. Perrucci, eds., pp. 89–127. Ann Arbor: University of Michigan Press.

Simmons, R. O., & Thurgood, D. H. 1995. *Summary report 1994: Doctorate recipients from United States universities.* Washington, D.C.: National Academy Press.

Sonnert, G., & Holton, G. 1996a. *Gender differences in science careers: The Project Access study.* New Brunswick, N.J.: Rutgers University Press.

Sonnert, G., & Holton, G. 1996b. *Who succeeds in science? The gender dimension.* New Brunswick, N.J.: Rutgers University Press.

Wennerås, C. & Wold, A. 1997. Nepotism and sexism in peer-review. *Nature* 387:341–43.

Chapter 12

Ahern, N. F., & Scott, E. L. 1981. *Career outcomes in a matched sample of men and women Ph.D.s: An analytical report.* Washington, D.C.: National Academy Press.

Aisenberg, N., & Harrington, M. 1988. *Women of academe: Outsiders in the sacred grove.* Amherst, Mass.: University of Massachusetts Press.

Allen, M. 1996. Defiant V.M.I. to admit women, but will not ease rules for them. *New York Times,* 22 September, pp. A1, A36.

Bailey, S. 1991. Some women faulting demand for equal pay; Graf says there's no need to make more. *Washington Post,* 3 June, p. B9.

Barnett, R. C., Marshall, N. L., Raudenbush, S. W., & Brennan, R. T. 1993. Gender and the relationship between job experiences and psychological distress: A study of dual-earner couples. *Journal of Personality and Social Psychology* 64:794–806.

Becker, G. S. 1993. *Human capital: A theoretical and empirical analysis, with special reference to education,* 3rd ed. Chicago: University of Chicago.

Blau, F. D., & Ferber, M. A. 1991. Career plans and expectations of young women and men: The earnings gap and labor force participation. *Journal of Human Resources* 26:581–607.

Blau, F. D. & Ferber, M. A. 1992. *The economics of women, men, and work,* 2nd ed. Englewood Cliffs, N.J.: Prentice-Hall.

Chambers, D. L. 1989. Accommodation and satisfaction: Women and men lawyers and the balance of work and family. *Law and Social Inquiry* 14:251–87.

Cole, J. R. 1979. *Fair science: Women in the scientific community.* New York: Free Press.

Cole, J. R., & Singer, B. 1991. A theory of limited differences: Explaining the productivity puzzle in science. In *The outer circle: women in the scientific community,* H. Zuckerman, J. R. Cole, & J. T. Bruer, eds., pp. 277–310, 319–23, 338–40. New York: W. W. Norton.

Cole, J. R., & Zuckerman, H. 1984. The productivity puzzle: Persistence and change in patterns of publication of men and women scientists. In *Advances in motivation and achievement,* P. Maehr & M. W. Steinkamp, eds., pp. 217–56. Greenwich, Conn.: JAI Press.

Cole, S., & Fiorentine, R. 1991. Discrimination against women in science: The confusion of outcome with process. In *The outer circle: Women in the scientific community,* H. Zuckerman, J. R. Cole, & J. T. Bruer, eds., pp. 205–26, 314–16, 334–5. New York: W. W. Norton.

De Vaus, D., & McAllister, I. 1991. Gender and work orientation: Values and satisfaction in Western Europe. *Work and Occupations* 18:72–93.

Dipboye, R. L. 1987. Problems and progress of women in management. In *Working women: Past, present, future,* K. S. Koziara, M. H. Moskow, & L. D. Tanner, eds. Washington, D.C.: Bureau of National Affairs.

Eccles, J. S. 1994. Understanding women's educational and occupational choices: Applying the Eccles et al. model of achievement-related choices. *Psychology of Women Quarterly* 18:585–609.

England, P. & McCreary, L. 1987. Integrating sociology and economics to study gender and work. In *Women and work: An annual review,* vol. 2, A. H. Stromberg, L. Larwood, & B. A. Gutek, eds., pp. 143–72. Newbury Park, Calif.: Sage Publications.

Epstein, C. F., Saute, R., Oglensky, B., & Gever, M. 1995. Glass ceilings and open doors: Women's advancement in the legal profession. *Fordham Law Review* 64:306–449.

Etzkowitz, H., Kemelgor, C., Neuschatz, M., & Uzzi, B. 1992. Athena unbound: Barriers to women in academic science and engineering. *Science and Public Policy* 19:157–79.

Finklestein, M. 1984. The status of academic women: An assessment of five competing explanations. *Review of Higher Education* 7:223–46.

Fiorentine, R. 1988. Sex differences in success expectancies and causal attributions: Is this why fewer women become physicians? *Social Psychology Quarterly* 51:236–49.

Fox, M. F. 1985. Publication, performance, and reward in science and scholarship. In *Higher education: Handbook of theory and research,* J. Smart, ed., pp. 255–82. New York: Agathon.

Fox, M. F., & Faver, C. A. 1985. Men, women, and publication productivity: Patterns among social work academics. *Sociological Quarterly* 26:537–49.

Goldin, C. 1990. *Understanding the gender gap: An economic history of American women.* New York: Oxford University Press.

Greenhouse, L. 1996. Justices appear skeptical of V.M.I.'s proposal for women. *New York Times,* 18 January, p. A18.

Harrington, M. 1993. *Women lawyers: Rewriting the rules.* New York: Plume.

Helmreich, R., Spence, J., Beane, W., Lucker, G. W., & Matthews, K. 1980. Making it in academic psychology: Demographic and personality correlates of attainment. *Journal of Personality and Social Psychology* 39:896–908.

Jacobs, J. J. 1992. Women's entry into management: Trends in earnings, authority, and values among salaried managers. *Administrative Science Quarterly* 37: 282–301.

Kolpin, V. W., & Singell, L. D., Jr. 1996. The gender composition and scholarly performance of economics departments: A test for employment discrimination. *Industrial and Labor Relations Review* 49:408–23.

Kyvik, S. 1990. Motherhood and scientific productivity. *Social Studies of Science* 20:149–60.

Long, J. S. 1978. Productivity and academic position in the scientific career. *American Sociological Review* 43:889–908.

Long, J. S. 1987. Problems and prospects for research on sex differences in the scientific career. In *Women: Their underrepresentation and career differentials in science and engineering,* L. S. Dixon, ed., pp. 157–69. Washington, D.C.: National Technical Information Service.

Long, J. S. 1990. The origins of sex differences in science. *Social Forces* 68:1297–1315.

Long, J. S. 1992. Measures of sex differences in scientific productivity. *Social Forces* 71:159–78.

Long, J. S., Allison, P. D., & McGinnis, R. 1993. *American Sociological Review* 58:703–22.

Long, J. S., & McGinnis, R. 1981. Organizational context and scientific productivity. *American Sociological Review* 46:422–42.

Madden, J. F. 1985. The persistence of pay differentials: The economics of sex discrimination. In *Women and work: An annual review,* vol. 1, L. Larwood, A. H. Stromberg, & B. A. Gutek, eds., pp. 76–114. Newbury Park, Calif.: Sage Publications.

Major, B., McFarlin, D. B., & Gagnon, D. 1984. Overworked and underpaid: On the nature of gender differences in personal entitlement. *Journal of Personality and Social Psychology* 47:1399–1412.

Major, B., Vanderslice, V., & McFarlin, D. B. 1984. Effects of pay expected on pay received: The confirmatory nature of initial expectations. *Journal of Applied Social Psychology* 14:399–412.

Martell, R. F. 1991. Sex bias at work: The effects of attentional and memory demands on performance ratings of men and women. *Journal of Applied Social Psychology* 21:1939–60.

McFarlin, D. B., Frone, M. R., Major, B., & Konar, E. 1989. Predicting career-entry pay expectations: The role of gender-based comparisons. *Journal of Business and Psychology* 3:331–40.

Okin, S. M. 1989. *Justice, gender, and the family.* New York: Basic Books.

Olson, J. E., & Frieze, I. H. 1987. Income determinants for women in business. In *Women and work: An annual review,* vol. 2, A. H. Stromberg, L. Larwood, & B. A. Gutek, eds., pp. 173–206. Newbury Park, Calif.: Sage Publications.

O'Neill, J. 1991. Women and wages: Gender pay ratios. *Current* 331:10–16.

Reskin, B. F., & Roos, P. A. 1990. *Job queues, gender queues: Explaining women's inroads into male occupations.* Philadelphia: Temple University Press.

Rosenfeld, R. A. 1984. Academic career mobility for women and men psychologists. In *Women in scientific and engineering professions,* V. B. Haas & C. C. Perrucci, eds., pp. 89–127. Ann Arbor: University of Michigan Press.

Rubin, A., & Powell, D. M. 1987. Gender and publication rates: A reassessment with population data. *Social Work* 32:317–20.

Sidanius, J., & Crane, M. 1989. Job evaluation and gender: The case of university faculty. *Journal of Applied Social Psychology* 19:174–97.

Sonnert, G. 1995. What makes a good scientist? Determinants of peer evaluation among biologists. *Social Studies of Science* 25:35–55.

Sonnert, G., & Holton, G. 1996a. *Gender differences in science careers: The Project Access study.* New Brunswick, N.J.: Rutgers University Press.

Sonnert, G., & Holton, G. 1996b. *Who succeeds in science? The gender dimension.* New Brunswick, N.J.: Rutgers University Press.

Stack, S. 1994. The effects of gender on publishing: The case of sociology. *Sociological Focus* 27:81–83.

Zuckerman, H. 1987. Persistence and change in the careers of men and women scientists and engineers: A review of current research. In *Women: Their underrepresentation and career differentials in science and engineering,* L. S. Dixon, ed., pp. 123–56. Washington, D.C.: National Technical Information Service.

Zuckerman, H. 1991. The careers of men and women scientists: A review of current research. In *The outer circle: Women in the scientific community,* H. Zuckerman, J. R. Cole, & J. T. Bruer, eds., pp. 27–56, 312–13, 325–28.

Chapter 13

Allen, M. 1996. Defiant V.M.I. to admit women, but will not ease rules for them. *New York Times,* 22 September, pp. 1, 36.

American Psychological Association. 1991. In the Supreme Court of the United States: *Price Waterhouse v. Ann B. Hopkins:* Amicus curiae brief for the American Psychological Association. *American Psychologist* 46:1061–70.

Applebome, P. 1995. Appeals court opens way for female cadet at The Citadel. *New York Times,* 14 April, p. 10.

Arthur, W., Doverspike, D., & Fuentes, R. 1992. Recipients' affective responses to affirmative action interventions: A cross-cultural perspective. *Behavioral Sciences and the Law* 10:229–43.

Bergmann, B. R. 1996. *In defense of affirmative action.* New York: New Republic Book/Basic Books.

Binion, G. 1987. Affirmative action reconsidered: Justifications, objections, myths and misconceptions. *Women and Politics* 7:43–62.

Bolick C. 1996. *The affirmative action fraud: Can we restore the American civil rights vision?* Washington, D.C.: Cato Institute.

Butler, D., & Geis, F. L. 1990. Nonverbal affect responses to male and female leaders: Implications for leadership evaluations. *Journal of Personality and Social Psychology* 58:48–59.

Clayton, S. D., & Crosby, F. J. 1992. *Justice, gender, and affirmative action.* Ann Arbor: University of Michigan Press.

Doverspike, D., & Winfred, A. 1995. Race and sex differences in reactions to a simulated selection decision involving race-based affirmative action. *Journal of Black Psychology* 21:181–200.

Eastland, T. 1996. *Ending affirmative action: The case for colorblind justice.* New York: Basic Books.

Fiske, S. T., Bersoff, D. N., Borgida, E., Deaux, K., & Heilman, M. 1991. Social science research on trial: Use of sex stereotyping research in *Price Waterhouse v. Hopkins. American Psychologist* 46:1049–60.

Galle, O. R., Wiswell, C. H., & Burr, J. A. 1985. Racial mix and industrial productivity. *American Sociological Review* 501:20–23.

Griffin, P. 1992. The impact of affirmative action on labor demand: A test of some implications of the Le Chatelier principle. *Review of Economics and Statistics,* 74:251–60.

Heilman, M. E., Block, C. J., Martell, R. F., & Simon, M. C. 1989. Has anything changed? Current characterizations of men, women, and managers. *Journal of Applied Psychology* 74:935–42.

Heilman, M. E., Lucas, J. A., & Kaplow, S. R. 1990. Self-derogating consequences of sex-based preferential selection: The moderating role of initial self-confidence. *Organizational Behavior and Human Decision Processes* 46:202–16.

Heilman, M. E., Rivero, J. C., & Brett, J. F. 1991. Skirting the competence issue: Effects of sex-based preferential selection on task choices of women and men. *Journal of Applied Psychology* 76:99–105.

Heilman, M. E., Simon, M., & Repper, D. 1987. Intentionally favored, unintentionally harmed? The impact of sex-based preferential selection on self-perceptions and self-evaluations. *Journal of Applied Psychology* 72:62–68.

Holmes, S. A. 1994. Some employees lose right to sue for bias at work. *New York Times,* 18 March, pp. A1, B6.

Jackson-Leslie, L. 1995. Race, sex, and meritocracy. *Black Scholar* 25:24–29.

Kanter, R. 1983. *The change masters: Innovation in the American corporation.* New York: Simon & Schuster.

Kellough, J. E. 1990. Federal agencies and affirmative action for blacks and women. *Social Science Quarterly* 71:83–92.

Kravitz, D. A., & Platania, J. 1993. Attitudes and beliefs about affirmative action: Effects of target and of respondent sex and ethnicity. *Journal of Applied Psychology* 78:928–38.

Leonard, J. S. 1984. Antidiscrimination or reverse discrimination: The impact of changing demographics, Title VII, and affirmative action on productivity. *Journal of Human Resources* 19:145–74.

Leonard, J. S. 1989. Women and affirmative action. *Journal of Economic Perspectives* 3:61–75.

Lerner, M. J. 1980. *The belief in a just world.* New York: Plenum.

McIlwee, J. S., & Robinson, J. G. 1992. *Women in engineering: Gender, power and the workplace.* Albany: State University of New York Press.

Nossiter, A. 1997. A cadet is dismissed and 9 are disciplined for Citadel harassment. *New York Times,* 11 March, p. A15.

Pettigrew, T. F., & Martin, J. 1987. Shaping the organizational context for black American inclusion. *Journal of Social Issues* 43:41–78.

Rimer, S. 1995. Women are "no big deal" at an old military college. *New York Times,* 6 September, p. A16.

Schmitt, E. 1994. Pentagon must reinstate nurse who declared she is a lesbian. *New York Times,* 2 June, pp. A1, A17.

Sellers, P. 1996. Women, sex and power. *Fortune* 134 (5 August): 42–46.

Selvin, P. 1993. Jenny Harrison finally gets tenure in math at Berkeley. *Science* 261:287.

Skrentny, J. D. 1996. *The ironies of affirmative action: Politics, culture, and justice in America.* Chicago: University of Chicago Press.

Sowell, T. 1990. *Preferential policies: An international perspective.* New York: Morrow.

Steel, B. S., & Lovrich, Jr., N. P. 1987. Equality and efficiency tradeoffs in affirmative action—real or imagined? The case of women in policing. *Social Science Journal* 24: 53–70.

Steele, S. 1990. *The content of our character: A new vision of race in America.* New York: St. Martin's Press.

Tomaskovic-Devey, D. 1988. Labor force composition, market concentration, structural power, and industrial productivity. In *Industries, firms, and jobs: Sociological and economic approaches,* G. Farkas & P. England, eds., pp. 66–97. New York: Plenum.

Tomaskovic-Devey, D. 1993. *Gender and racial inequality at work: The sources and consequences of job segregation.* Ithaca, N.Y.: ILR Press.

Tversky, A., & Kahneman, D. 1973. Availability: A heuristic for judging frequency and probability. *Cognitive Psychology* 5:207–32.

Weiner, T. 1994. Women, citing bias, may sue the C. I. A. *New York Times,* 28 March, p. A10.

Chapter 14

Aisenberg, N., & Harrington, M. 1988. *Women of academe: Outsiders in the sacred grove.* Amherst: University of Massachusetts Press.

Arenson, K. W. 1997. A: One, from Romania; Q: How many women have won the top math contest? *New York Times,* 1 May, pp. B1, B4.

Arthur, J. B. 1994. Effects of human resource systems on manufacturing performance and turnover. *Academy of Management Journal* 37:670–87.

Blair, I. V., & Banaji, M. R. 1996. Automatic and controlled processes in stereotype priming. *Journal of Personality and Social Psychology* 70:1142–63.

Brewer, M. B. 1988. A dual process model of impression formation. In *Advances in social cognition,* T. K. Srull & R. S. Wyer, eds., pp. 1–36. Hillsdale, N.J.: Erlbaum.

Brown, V., & Geis, F. L. 1984. Turning lead into gold: Leadership by men and women and the alchemy of social consensus. *Journal of Personality and Social Psychology* 46:811–24.

Butler, D., & Geis, F. L. 1990. Nonverbal affect responses to male and female leaders: Implications for leadership evaluations. *Journal of Personality and Social Psychology* 58:48–59.

Carter, B., with J. K. Peters. 1996. *Love, honor, and negotiate: Making your marriage work.* New York: Pocket Books.

Chang, D. 1997. Woods as policy guide? *New York Times,* 18 April, p. A32.

Chused, R. H. 1988. The hiring and retention of minorities and women on American law school faculties. *University of Pennsylvania Law Review* 137:537–69.

Dovidio, J. F., Ellyson, S. L., Keating, C. F., Heltman, K., & Brown, C. E. 1988. The relationship of social power to visual displays of dominance between men and women. *Journal of Personality and Social Psychology* 54:233–42.

Dweck, C. S. 1986. Motivational processes affecting learning. *American Psychologist* 41:1040–48.

Fiske, S. T., & Neuberg, S. L. 1990. A continuum of impression formation, from category-based to individuating processes: Influences of information and motivation on attention and interpretation. In *Advances in experimental social psychology,* M. Zanna, ed., pp. 1–74. San Diego: Academic Press.

Fiske, S. T., & Taylor, S. E. 1991. *Social cognition,* 2nd ed. New York: McGraw-Hill.

Fried, L. P., Francomano, C. A., MacDonald, S. M., Wagner, E. M., Stokes, E. J., Carbone, K. M., Bias, W. B., Newman, M. M., & Stobo, J. D. 1996. Career development for women in academic medicine: Multiple interventions in a department of medicine. *Journal of the American Medical Association* 276:898–905.

Geis, F. L., Boston, M. B., & Hoffman, N. 1985. Sex of authority role models and achievement by men and women: Leadership performance and recognition. *Journal of Personality and Social Psychology* 49:636–53.

Geis, F. L., Brown, V., & Wolfe, C. 1990. Legitimizing the leader: Endorsement by male versus female authority figures. *Journal of Applied Social Psychology* 20:943–70.

Geis, F. L., Carter, M. R., & Butler, D. J. 1982. Research on seeing and evaluating people. Unpubl. MS. Newark, Del.: Office of Women's Affairs, University of Delaware.

Grover, S. L., & Crooker, K. J. 1995. Who appreciates family-responsive human resource policies: The impact of family-friendly policies on the organizational attachment of parents and non-parents. *Personnel Psychology* 48:271–88.

Hall, D. T., & Parker, V. A. 1993. The role of workplace flexibility in managing diversity. *Organizational Dynamics* 22:5–18.

Hamilton, D. L., & Gifford, R. K. 1976. Illusory correlation in interpersonal perception: A cognitive basis of stereotypic judgments. *Journal of Experimental Social Psychology* 12:392–407.

Heilman, M. E. 1980. The impact of situational factors on personnel decisions concerning women: Varying the sex composition of the applicant pool. *Organizational Behavior and Human Performance* 26:386–95.

Heilman, M. E., & Stopeck, M. H. 1985. Attractiveness and corporate success: Different causal attributions for males and females. *Journal of Applied Psychology* 70:379–88.

Hellmuth, C. T. 1997. Tiger Woods didn't need affirmative action. *New York Times,* 17 April, p. A22.

Hoffman, C., & Hurst, N. 1990. Gender stereotypes. *Journal of Personality and Social Psychology* 58:197–208.

Hyde, J. S. 1984. Children's understanding of sexist language. *Developmental Psychology* 20:697–706.

Kanter, R. M. 1979. Differential access to opportunity and power. In *Discrimination in organizations,* R. Alvarez & K. G. Lutterman, eds., pp. 52–68. San Francisco: Jossey-Bass.

Kinicki, A. J., Carson, K. P., & Bohlander, G. W. 1992. Relationship between an organization's actual human resource efforts and employee attitudes. *Group and Organization Management* 17:135–52.

Koys, D. J. 1991. Fairness, legal compliance, and organizational commitment. *Employee Responsibilities and Rights Journal* 4:283–91.

Kunda, Z., & Thagard, P. 1996. Forming impressions from stereotypes, traits, and behaviors: A parallel-constraint-satisfaction theory. *Psychological Review* 103:284–308.

Martell, R. F. 1991. Sex bias at work: The effects of attentional and memory demands on performance ratings of men and women. *Journal of Applied Social Psychology* 21:1939–60.

Nelson, T. E., Biernat, M. R., & Manis, M. 1990. Everyday base rates (sex stereotypes): Potent and resilient. *Journal of Personality and Social Psychology* 59: 664–75.

Pion, G. M., Mednick, M. T., Astin, H. S., Hall, C. C. I., Kenkel, M. B., Keita, G. P., Kohout, J. L., & Kelleher, J. C. 1996. The shifting gender composition of psychology: Trends and implications for the discipline. *American Psychologist* 51:509–28.

Ragins, B. R., & Sundstrom, E. 1989. Gender and power in organizations: A longitudinal perspective. *Psychological Bulletin* 105:51–88.

Ragins, B. R., & Sundstrom, E. 1990. Gender and perceived power in manager-subordinate relations. *Journal of Occupational Psychology* 63:273–87.

Ridgeway, C. L. 1982. Status in groups: The importance of motivation. *American Sociological Review* 47:76–88.

Rynes, S. & Rosen, B. 1995. A field survey of factors affecting the adoption and perceived success of diversity training. *Personnel Psychology* 48:247–70.

Sanbonmatsu, D. M., Akimoto, S. A., & Gibson, B. D. 1994. Stereotype-based blocking in social explanation. *Personality and Social Psychology Bulletin* 20:71–81.

Schaller, M. 1992. In-group favoritism and statistical reasoning in social inference: Implications for formation and maintenance of group stereotypes. *Journal of Personality and Social Psychology* 63:61–74.

Schaller, M., Asp, C. H., Rosell, M. C., & Heim, S. J. 1996. Training in statistical reasoning inhibits the formation of erroneous group stereotypes. *Personality and Social Psychology Bulletin* 22:829–44.

Valian, V. 1977. Learning to work. In *Working it out,* S. Ruddick & P. Daniels, eds., pp. 163–78. New York: Pantheon.

Weiner, T. S., & Wilson-Mitchell, J. E. 1990. Nonconventional family life-styles and sex typing in six-year-olds. *Child Development* 61:1915–33.

Author Index

Subject Index

for partnership, 291–293
for school admission, 299–301
for tenure, 297–299
Lawyers, 188, 198, 199, 267, 347n2,
347n3, 348n4, 348n5
in-house, 204–206, 214
Leadership, 125–127
ability, 126
perception of, 127, 255, 282, 324
covariation of, with rank, 310
and expert knowledge, 326
and gender schemas, 284, 291, 310–
311, 324
legitimization of, 316–317
military, 252
style, 129, 133–134, 323
Legal ability, 258, 260
Luck, 21, 137, 170, 182

Male-dominated professions, 138,
186
Marriage. *See* Household responsibilities; Child care
Masculine gender schema, 11, 13–14,
70, 110–112, 133, 177–178, 182,
197, 256, 284, 346n5
and success and failure, 20–21
Math skills, 61, 66, 81, 153. *See also*
Mental Rotation
application of, 84–85
cultural differences in, 85
gendered explanations of success and
failure, 62
influence of teachers' expectations
(*see* Teachers)
jobs requiring, 192
problem solving, 84–85, 339n4
and professional success, 60
SAT-Math, 63, 90, 93, 156, 192,
338n2
self-rating, 61, 337n5
sex differences in, 62, 83, 153, 156–
157, 339n5
underestimation of girls' math abilities, 64

variability, 93
word problems, 84–85, 86, 87, 88
and conversational principles,
88–89
MBA's, 193–195, 203, 214
Median score (definition) 349n2
Medicine, 187, 208–210, 319. *See
also* Professions
Memory process, 168–169
Mental rotation, 70, 157, 339n9. *See
also* Hormones
and math, 84, 94–96, 339n6
Mentors, 320, 325
Meta-analysis
activity level, 75, 338n6
aggression, 77–78
attributions, 170–172, 178, 182–
183, 346n6
evaluation bias, 341n3
influence and leadership, 56,
133–134
mathematics, 83
mental rotation, 94–95
parental behavior, 27–28, 59, 335n2,
336n1
personality, 110
Military character, 252
and cohesion, 122
and sexual orientation, 122–123,
294, 317, 340n6 (*see also*
Homosexuals)
training methods for building,
252–253
and women, 121
Military schema, 121
Minority. *See also* African American
minorities, 179–180277, 287, 315,
347n1
men, 347n7
Mixed-motives defense, 292, 295–
296, 298
Money, 217
Motherhood, 115, 269–270
and part-time work in law
and productivity in academia